FIFTY KEY FIGURES IN SCIENCE FICTION

Fifty Key Figures in Science Fiction is a collection of engaging essays on some of the most significant figures who have shaped and defined the genre. Diverse groups within the science fiction community are represented, from novelists and filmmakers to comic-book and television writers. Important and influential names discussed include:

- Octavia E. Butler
- George Lucas
- Robert A. Heinlein
- Gene Roddenberry
- Stan Lee
- Ursula K. Le Guin
- H.G. Wells.

This outstanding reference guide charts the rich and varied landscape of science fiction and includes helpful and up-to-date lists of further reading at the end of each entry. Available in an easy to use A–Z format, *Fifty Key Figures in Science Fiction* will be of interest to students of Literature, Film Studies, and Cultural Studies.

Mark Bould is Reader in Film and Literature at the University of the West of England, UK. He is the author of *Film Noir: from Berlin to Sin City* and *The Cinema of John Sayles*.

Andrew M. Butler is Senior Lecturer in Media and Cultural Studies at Canterbury Christ Church University, UK. He is the author of Pocket Essential volumes on *Cyberpunk*, *Film Studies*, *Postmodernism*, and *Philip K. Dick*.

Adam Roberts is Professor of Nineteenth-Century Literature at Royal Holloway, University of London, UK. He is the author of many science fiction novels and has published widely on nineteenth-century literature and science fiction studies.

Sherryl Vint is Assist iversity, Canada. She is the aut

ALSO AVAILABLE FROM ROUTLEDGE

Fifty Key British Films
Edited by Sarah Barrow and John White
978-0-415-43330-3

Communication, Cultural and Media Studies: The Key Concepts (third edition)
John Hartley
978-0-415-26889-9

Cinema Studies: The Key Concepts (third edition)
Susan Hayward
978-0-415-36782-0

Cultural Theory: The Key Concepts (second edition)
Edited by Andrew Edgar and Peter Sedgwick
978-0-415-28426-4

Television Studies: The Key Concepts (second edition)
Neil Casey, Bernadette Casey, Justin Lewis, Ben Calvert, and Liam French
978-0-415-17237-0

Fifty Contemporary Filmmakers
Edited by Yvonne Tasker
978-0-415-18974-3

The Routledge Companion to Gothic
Edited by Catherine Spooner and Emma McEvoy
978-0-415-39843-5

The Routledge Companion to Postmodernism (second edition)
Edited by Stuart Sim
978-0-415-33359-7

The Routledge Companion to Critical Theory
Edited by Simon Malpas and Paul Wake
978-0-415-33296-5

FIFTY KEY FIGURES IN SCIENCE FICTION

Edited by
Mark Bould, Andrew M. Butler, Adam Roberts, and Sherryl Vint

LONDON AND NEW YORK

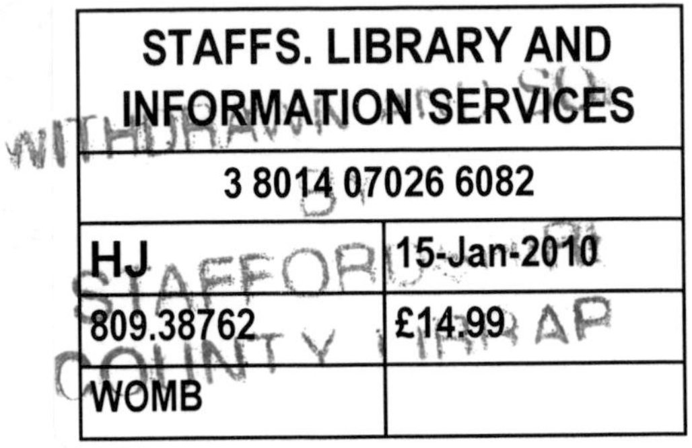

First published 2010
by Routledge
2 Park Square, Milton Park, Abingdon, Oxon, OX14 4RN

Simultaneously published in the USA and Canada
by Routledge
270 Madison Avenue, New York, NY 10016

Routledge is an imprint of the Taylor & Francis Group, an informa business

Typeset in Bembo by
Taylor & Francis Books
Printed and bound in Great Britain by
TJ International Ltd, Padstow, Cornwall

British Library Cataloguing in Publication Data
A catalogue record for this book is available from the British Library

Library of Congress Cataloging in Publication Data
Fifty key figures in science fiction / edited by Mark Bould [… et al.].
p. cm.
1. Science fiction – Bio-bibliography. 2. Fantasy fiction – Bio-bibliography. I. Bould, Mark.
PN3433.4.F54 2009
809.3'876203 – dc22
[B]
2009002032

ISBN10: 0-415-43949-3 (hbk)
ISBN 10: 0-415-43950-7 (pbk)
ISBN 10: 0-203-87470-6 (ebk)
ISBN 13: 978-0-415-43949-7 (hbk)
ISBN 13: 978-0-415-43950-3 (pbk)
ISBN 13: 978-0-203-87470-7 (ebk)

CONTENTS

ALPHABETICAL LIST OF CONTENTS

CHRONOLOGICAL LIST OF CONTENTS

CONTRIBUTORS

Stacey Abbott is Senior Lecturer in Film and Television Studies at Roehampton University and the author of *Celluloid Vampires* (2007). She is currently researching contemporary developments in cult television.

Brian Attebery is editor of the *Journal of the Fantastic in the Arts*. His most recent book is *Decoding Gender in Science Fiction* (2002). He has also written books and articles on fantasy, children's literature, folklore, and the theories that underlie the field of American studies. *The Norton Book of Science Fiction* (1994), which he edited with Ursula K. Le Guin and Karen Joy Fowler and for which he also wrote a teacher's guide, has had a significant (and some would say pernicious) influence on the teaching of science fiction in the US.

Douglas Barbour, poet, critic, and Professor Emeritus of English at the University of Alberta, has published many books of criticism and poetry, including *Fragmenting Body etc.* (2000), *Lyric/Anti-lyric: essays on contemporary poetry* (2001), *Breath Takes* (2002), *A Flame on the Spanish Stairs* (2003), *Continuations*, with Sheila E. Murphy (2006), and most recently *Wednesdays'* (2008). He has taught sf and published widely in the field. He was inaugurated into the City of Edmonton Cultural Hall of Fame in 2003.

Mark Bould is Reader in Film and Literature at the University of the West of England, UK. He is the author of *Film Noir: from Berlin to Sin City* (2005) and *The Cinema of John Sayles: lone star* (2008), and co-editor of *Parietal Games: critical writings by and on M. John Harrison* (2005), *Neo-noir* (2009), and *Red Planets: Marxism and science fiction* (2009). He co edits *Science Fiction Film and Television* and is an advisory editor for *Extrapolation*, *Historical Materialism*, *Paradoxa*, and *Science Fiction Studies*.

Mark Broughton is Lecturer in Film Studies at the University of Reading. In 2008 he completed his Ph.D. on landscape gardens and storytelling in post-Second World War British film and television. He is currently writing a monograph on Nigel Kneale.

William J. Burling, Professor of English at Missouri State University, was the editor of *Kim Stanley Robinson Maps the Unimaginable: critical essays* (forthcoming 2009) and the author of articles on the ideology of time travel in sf, Kim Stanley Robinson, China Miéville, and Ursula K. Le Guin. He passed away on March 7 2009 and will be missed by the sf community.

Andrew M. Butler is editor of *An Unofficial Companion to the Novels of Terry Pratchett* (2007) and *Christopher Priest: the interaction* (2005). He has also written Pocket Essentials on *Philip K. Dick* (2000, 2007), *Cyberpunk* (2000), *Terry Pratchett* (2001), *Film Studies* (2002, 2005, 2008), and *Postmodernism* (2003). He co-edits *Extrapolation* and is Senior Lecturer in Media and Cultural Studies at Canterbury Christ Church University.

Jim Casey is Assistant Professor at High Point University, North Carolina. Primarily a Shakespearean scholar, he has also published on textual theory, performance theory, Chaucer, *Battlestar Galactica*, and comics artist David Mack.

Istvan Csicsery-Ronay Jr is Professor of English and World Literature at DePauw University, Indiana. He is the author of *The Seven Beauties of Science Fiction* (2008) and co-editor of *Robot Ghosts and Wired Dreams: Japanese science fiction from origins to anime* (2007). He is also co-editor of *Science Fiction Studies* and managing editor of *Humanimalia*.

Nicholas J. Cull is Professor of Public Diplomacy at the University of Southern California in Los Angeles and President of the International Association for Media and History. He trained at Leeds University and, before USC, held the chair in American Studies at the University of Leicester. He has published widely on media and history, including sf. His latest work is *Projecting Empire: imperialism and popular cinema* (2009), co-written with James Chapman.

Neil Easterbrook is Associate Professor of Critical Theory and American Poetry at Texas Christian University. A consulting editor for *Science Fiction Studies* and *Extrapolation*, he has published on Søren Kierkegaard, William Carlos Williams, William Gibson, ancient Assyrian friezework, lexicography, and bad jokes.

Arthur B. Evans is Professor of French at DePauw University, Indiana. The managing editor of *Science Fiction Studies*, he has published widely on Jules Verne and early French science fiction, including the award-winning *Jules Verne Rediscovered* (1988). He is general editor of Wesleyan University Press's "Early Classics of Science Fiction" book series.

Carl Freedman, Professor of English and Director of English Graduate Studies at Louisiana State University, is the author of three books – *George Orwell: a study in ideology and literary form* (1988), *Critical Theory and Science Fiction* (2000), and *The Incomplete Projects: Marxism, modernity, and the politics of culture* (2002) – and the editor of *Conversations with Isaac Asimov* (2005), *Conversations with Ursula K. Le Guin* (2008), and *Conversations with Samuel R. Delany* (2009).

Joan Gordon is Professor of English at Nassau Community College, New York, and Fulbright Distinguished Visiting Chair at the Maria Curie-Skłodowska University. A past president of the Science Fiction Research Association, she is the co-editor of *Blood Read: the vampire as metaphor in contemporary culture* (1997), *Edging into the Future: science fiction and contemporary cultural transformation* (2002), and *Queer Universes: sexualities in science fiction* (2008). She is currently working on a book triangulating among sociobiology, animal studies, and sf. She co-edits *Science Fiction Studies*.

Gwyneth Jones is a writer and critic of sf and fantasy, who also writes for teenagers as Ann Halam. She lives in Brighton, keeps a blog at <http://blog.boldaslove.co.uk/> and a homepage at <http://homepage.ntlworld.com/gwynethann>. Her latest works are *Spirit* (2009) and, as Ann Halam, *Snakehead* (2007), and a collection of short stories, *Grazing the Long Acre* (2009).

Abraham Kawa teaches Cultural Studies at the University of the Aegean. A novelist and scriptwriter, he has also published articles on comics and popular culture.

Victoria Lamont is Associate Professor of English Literature at the University of Waterloo, Canada. She has been collaborating with Dianne Newell on the study of mid-twentieth-century women's sf since 2004, and they have published a series of articles on frontier themes in women's sf in the journals *Science Fiction Studies* and *Foundation*. Victoria Lamont brings to this collaboration her interest in women's writing of the American frontier in the nineteenth and early twentieth century. She is the author of several essays on topics including popular westerns by women and the culture of woman's suffrage.

Rob Latham is Associate Professor of English at the University of California at Riverside. The author of *Consuming Youth: vampires, cyborgs, and the culture of consumption* (2002), he is currently working on a book on New Wave sf. He co-edits *Science Fiction Studies.*

Michael Levy is Professor of English and Chair of the English and Philosophy Department at the University of Wisconsin-Stout. A past president of both the Science Fiction Research Association and the International Association for the Fantastic in the Arts, he co-edits *Extrapolation.*

Roger Luckhurst is Professor of Modern Literature at Birkbeck College, University of London. He is the author of *"The Angle between Two Walls": the fiction of J.G. Ballard* (1997), *The Invention of Telepathy* (2002), *Science Fiction* (2005), and *Trauma Culture* (2008).

Graham J. Murphy teaches with Trent University's Cultural Studies Program and Department of English Literature and at Seneca College of Applied Arts and Technology, Toronto. He is the co-author of *Ursula K. Le Guin: a critical companion* (2006) and is currently working on the intersections between utopian/speculative fiction, post/humanism, and insect discourse.

Susan Napier was born and raised in Cambridge, Massachusetts, and received her undergraduate and graduate degrees from Harvard University. She taught for twenty years at the University of Texas and is currently Professor of Japanese Studies at Tufts University. She is the author of four books: *Escape from the Wasteland: romanticism and realism in the works of Mishima Yukio and Oe Kenzaburo* (1991), *The Fantastic in Modern Japanese Literature* (1995), *Anime: from Akira to Howl's Moving Castle* (2006), and, most recently, *From Impressionism to Anime: Japan as fantasy and fan cult in the mind of the West* (2007).

Dianne Newell is Professor of History and Director of the Peter Wall Institute for Advanced Studies at the University of British Columbia. She has developed an interest in early women's sf through her expertise in the socioeconomic history of technology, publishing book chapters and essays in journals such as *Biography, Life Writing, European Journal of American Culture*, and, with Victoria Lamont, *Science Fiction Studies* and *Foundation.*

Patrick Parrinder, whose books include *Science Fiction: its criticism and teaching* (1980), *James Joyce* (1984), *Shadows of the Future* (1995), and *Nation and Novel* (2006), is a Vice-President of the H.G. Wells Society and has edited ten of Wells's sf titles for Penguin Classics, including *The Country of the Blind and Other Selected Stories* (2007). Recently retired from a professorship of English at the University of Reading, he is General Editor of the forthcoming multi-volume *Oxford History of the Novel in English.*

Wendy Gay Pearson is Assistant Professor in Film Studies at the University of Western Ontario. She has published widely on discourses of sexuality, race, citizenship, and belonging in both sf and contemporary Canadian film and literature. She is a co-editor of *Queer Universes: sexualities in science fiction* (2008).

Michelle Reid is Research Officer for the LearnHigher CETL and a study adviser at the University of Reading, UK. The assistant editor of *Foundation: the international review of science fiction*, she co-edited *Parietal Games: critical writings by and on M. John Harrison* (2005) and has published articles on Damien Broderick, Nalo Hopkinson, and Charles de Lint.

John Rieder is Professor of English at the University of Hawai'i at Mānoa. The author of *Colonialism and the Emergence of Science Fiction* (2008) and editor of *Biography*'s special issue on "Life Writing and Science Fiction" (2007), he has also published on British Romanticism, children's literature, horror cinema, and Marxist theory.

Adam Roberts is Professor of Nineteenth-Century Literature at Royal Holloway, University of London, and the author of *Science Fiction* (2000) and *The History of Science Fiction* (2006). His most recent sf novels are *Gradisil* (2006), *Land of the Headless* (2007), *Splinter* (2007), and *Swiftly* (2008).

Robin Roberts is Associate Dean and Professor of English and Women's and Gender Studies at Louisiana State University. She is the author of five books on gender and popular culture, including *Star Trek: The Next Generation and gender* (1999), and, most recently, *Anne McCaffrey: a life with dragons* (2007).

Andy Sawyer is the librarian of the Science Fiction Foundation Collection at the University of Liverpool Library, and Director of their MA in Science Fiction Studies. He is reviews editor of *Foundation: the international review of science fiction*. Recent publications include essays on Gwyneth Jones, Ramsey Campbell,

Ursula K. Le Guin, and Terry Pratchett, and notes for new Penguin Classics editions of several of H.G. Wells's novels.

Sherryl Vint is Assistant Professor of English at Brock University, Canada. She is the author of *Bodies of Tomorrow* (2007) and has recently completed *Animal Alterity: science fiction and the question of the animal*. She co-edits *Extrapolation*, *Science Fiction Film and Television*, and *Humanimalia*.

Phillip E. Wegner teaches at the University of Florida and is the author of *Life between Two Deaths, 1989–2001: US culture in the long nineties* (2009) and *Imaginary Communities: utopia, the nation, and the spatial histories of modernity* (2002). His essays on sf and utopia have appeared in *Diacritics*, *New Literary History*, *LiberArte*, *Rethinking Marxism*, and *Utopian Studies*, as well as in a variety of edited collections. He is currently completing a book entitled *Periodizing Jameson: the adventures of theory in post-contemporary times*, and a second manuscript on sf and globalization.

Gary Westfahl, who teaches at the University of California, Riverside, is the author, editor, or co-editor of over 20 books about science fiction and fantasy, including the Hugo Award-nominated *Science Fiction Quotations* (2005), *The Greenwood Encyclopedia of Science Fiction and Fantasy* (2005), and *Hugo Gernsback and the Century of Science Fiction* (2007); he also writes commentaries and film reviews for the Locus Online website. In 2003 he received the Science Fiction Research Association's Pilgrim Award for lifetime contributions to science fiction and fantasy scholarship.

Jennifer Woodward is Lecturer in Film Studies at Edge Hill University, UK, where she teaches Japanese cinema, film adaptation, and sf/horror film. A graduate of the University of Liverpool's MA in Science Fiction Studies, where her dissertation focused on mythic patterns in *Babylon 5*, she is currently writing her Ph.D. on "British Disaster Fiction 1898–1945." She has published reviews in *Foundation* and the *Times Higher Education Supplement* and is a contributor to *The Critical Companion to Science Fiction Film Adaptations* (2010).

Peter Wright is Reader in English Literature and Film Studies at Edge Hill University, UK. He is the author of *Attending Daedalus: Gene Wolfe, artifice and the reader* (2003), co-editor of *British Television Science Fiction* (2005), and editor of *Shadows of the New Sun: Gene Wolfe on readers, writers and writing* (2007). He is currently co-editing *The Critical Companion to Science Fiction Film Adaptations* (2010).

Lisa Yaszek is Associate Professor in Literature, Communication, and Culture at the Georgia Institute of Technology, and curator of the Bud Foote Science Fiction Collection. President of the Science Fiction Research Association, she is the author of *The Self Wired: technology and subjectivity in contemporary American narrative* (2002) and *Galactic Suburbia: recovering women's science fiction* (2008).

INTRODUCTION

While many people have a fairly clear idea about what they think science fiction (sf) is, typically no two of them agree precisely. Some have called it a literature of ideas, emphasizing works that imagine new and better ways to organize human society or that explore the implications of genetics or astrophysics. Some will insist that sf is not merely a "literature," "paraliterature," or "popular literature," but has long existed in other media, and others will point to quite how ridiculous many of sf's ideas actually are (what would it be like if there were a species of cat women on the moon?). Some consider sf to be a visionary genre, imagining the environment at the heart of a star or encounters with god-like beings. Others will point to the banality of much sf, in which aliens all speak English and spaceships are driven like cars or behave like fighter planes (and sound like them, too, despite being in a vacuum). Sometimes sf offers thought-experiments in which an idea is entertained for the pleasure of rigorously pursuing it to its conclusion or charting the ethical and political issues that arise from it: what would happen if half a mind was replaced with a computer? How could this be done? How would it affect notions about and the experience of subjectivity? At other times, sf throws open the galaxy as a playground in which to have adventures, or brings the world crashing to a halt so we can see what happens afterwards. And amid this wild variety, different people and institutions will judge some texts and practices central to the genre and others marginal, shaping understandings of sf in complex and contradictory ways.

Consequently, in selecting just fifty figures, we inevitably faced some tough decisions. Rather than endorse a particular view of sf, we have included figures that point to a number of these competing understandings of the genre. Initially, each editor came up with a list of 50 names, which gave us a core of around 100 figures. From then on there were arguments, debates, horse-trading, cajoling, and the occasional sulk. The publisher's readers all suggested names we had missed – with little overlap – and then the final choices were made.

Naturally we regret omissions such as David Bowie (1947–), Lois McMaster Bujold (1949–), Pat Cadigan (1953–), John W. Campbell (1910–71), John Carnell (1912–72), George Clinton (1941–), Charlotte Perkins Gilman (1860–1936), Cele Goldsmith Lalli (1933–2002), Judith Merril (1923–97), Lise Meitner (1878–1968), Nishikado Tomohiro (1944–), Orlan (1947–), Alex Raymond (1909–56), Pamela Sargent (1948–), Bruce Sterling (1954–), Tezuka Osamu (1926–89), Alvin Toffler (1928–), Douglas Trumbull (1842–), Wernher von Braun (1912–77), and Sigourney Weaver (1949–) (to name but 20), let alone Copernicus (1473–1543) or Dolly the Sheep (1996–2003). We do not pretend that our choices are the fifty *greatest* sf figures, whatever that would mean, but we would argue that each of them is key to sf and that sf is key to each of them.

Sf comes from many places, and it has many definitions and disputed origins. Darko Suvin traces a sense of estrangement back to writers such as Lucian of Samosata (c. 125–80 AD) and Thomas More (1478–1535) (Suvin 1979). The claim that Mary Shelley should be regarded as the form's mother has been advanced by Brian W. Aldiss (1973) and Edgar Allan Poe (1809–49) as its father by Thomas M. Disch (1998). Roger Luckhurst argues that sf developed as a response to nineteenth-century industrial modernity (2005), while James Gunn contends that Jules Verne "jump-started the genre" (2005: 172) and Edward James begins his account of the form with H.G. Wells (1994). Gary Westfahl champions US pulp magazine publisher Hugo Gernsback as the originator of sf as a *genre* in the late 1920s, in part as a defense against criticisms of the editor by commentators such as Aldiss. Other candidates have been and will be suggested – in this volume the roles of Shelley, Verne, Wells, and Gernsback are all examined, and we do not arbitrate among them. Nor is there space here to do justice to the many competing definitions of sf. (The first section of the present editors' *Routledge Companion to Science Fiction* offers a series of histories of sf from the sixteenth century to the present day across a variety of media; on definitions, see Clute and Nicholls (1993: 311–14) and Wolfe (1986: 108–11).)

Such *literary* histories focus on writers (and to a lesser extent editors), but may not be as useful when it comes to sf in other media. Film's origins lie in the equipment devised by Auguste Lumière (1862–1954) and Louis Lumière (1864–1948), among others (and their first public screening in 1895 coincidentally makes a neat parallel with the publication of Wells's *The Time Machine* (1895), which itself deploys imagery suggestive of pre-cinematic visual technologies). The existence of other, earlier, film pioneers such as Louis Le Prince (1842–90?), Wordsworth Donisthorpe (1847–1913), Thomas Edison (1847–1931), and William Friese-Greene (1855–1921) can perhaps be seen to parallel Wells's earlier attempts at the novel from 1887. Brooks Landon describes early film itself as a form of special effect (1992) – and note how the photographic records of movement taken by Eadweard Muybridge (1830–1904) offer a distant precursor to the bullet time of *The Matrix* (Wachowski brothers 1999). From *The Mechanical Butcher* (Lumière brothers 1895) and *A Trip to the Moon* (Méliès 1902) to *Metropolis* (Lang 1927), there are a number of important sf films, with the director – as controlled by producers and an emerging studio system – being key to the medium's meaning. Early television put more trust in writers, in conjunction with directors, but always at the beck and call of producers; with the growing industrialization of culture, high concept television is a product of creator-writer-executive producer hyphenates, working in conjunction with a small team of trusted writer-director-producers, but still at the mercy of the networks. Comics require a serial or simultaneous collaboration between writer and artist (although in this volume we have focused on writers).

We have included figures from television, films, comics, theater, books, magazines, and critical theory in our selection. There is a numerical bias towards Anglo-American prose fiction, reflecting initial fan reception and, from the late 1960s on, the academic study of sf. This is where the canon has formed or is developing – although of course many more people will have seen *Star Trek* in any of its various incarnations than will have read even the most popular of the pulp magazines. The definition of what is "central" to the field is contingent, in flux, and constantly struggled over by the various overlapping groups – including writers, critics, scholars, and fans – who make up the sf community. We have tried to represent the diversity of the field, with a broad and inclusive sense of what constitutes sf.

We have included the high literary sf tradition (Karel Čapek, H.G. Wells) and highly regarded filmmakers (Stanley Kubrick, Fritz Lang) alongside pulp writers (Leigh Brackett, Hugo Gernsback) and filmmakers who are generally more popularly than critically acclaimed (George Lucas, Steven Spielberg). We have included anglophone writers from outside the US and UK (the Australian Greg Egan, the Caribbean-Canadian Nalo Hopkinson) and non-anglophone writers (the Polish Stanisław Lem, the French Jules Verne) and filmmakers (the German Fritz Lang, the Japanese Oshii Mamoru). Our coverage of other media is signaled not merely by the selection of film directors, but also by entries on comic-book writers (Stan Lee, Alan Moore) and television writers and producers (Gerry Anderson, Nigel Kneale, Gene Roddenberry, J. Michael Straczynski). We have added essays on theorists of sf (Jean Baudrillard, Donna Haraway, Darko Suvin) who have had a major influence on how the genre has been conceptualized and taught, and one fictional character (The Doctor) whose appearances in and development across various media demonstrate the ways in which sf creations can exist as complex, cross-media intertexts. We were not able to find space for noted critics, fans, games designers, poets, special effects technicians, musicians, artists, and so on.

The result is a mosaic depiction of the landscape of sf, and 50 of its most significant voices. Inevitably our choices will cause arguments – why on earth did you include him?/exclude her? – but that only goes to demonstrate the richness of sf, and is of course half the fun. Our notion of sf means that we note that many figures are responding to each other in their work – and many essays act as one exemplar of several potential ones to represent movements or subgenres. Iain M. Banks, Leigh Brackett, George Lucas, C.L. Moore, and Gene Roddenberry have all worked within the area of space opera, and could have been matched by entries on, say, Flash Gordon, Buck Rogers, or Dan Simmons (1948–). Authors such as Asimov, Heinlein, and Hubbard represent the influential editorship of John W. Campbell, as well as their own contributions to the genre, while the New Wave is represented by J.G. Ballard and Michael Moorcock, with Moorcock serving double duty as a significant (probably the most important) British editor. William Gibson and Neal Stephenson between them illustrate the history of cyberpunk, even as both of them have developed beyond it in distinct ways. In each case, other possible figures were unfortunately squeezed out.

Our selection made, we approached some of the leading critical writers within sf studies and gave each the task of outlining the significance of a figure. The variety of the 50 figures' contributions to the genre is reflected in the different approaches the essays take. Some entries analyze key works, while others are more biographical than critical, placing the figure in his or her context or in relation to a specific movement. Taken together, the 50 figures discussed in this volume demonstrate something of the richness of sf.

Bibliography

Aldiss, B. (1973) *Billion Year Spree: the history of science fiction*, Garden City, NY: Doubleday.

Clute, J. and Nicholls, P. (eds.) (1993) *The Encyclopedia of Science Fiction*, London: Orbit.

Disch, T.M. (1998) *The Dreams Our Stuff Is Made of: how science fiction conquered the world*, New York: The Free Press.

Gunn, J. (2005) Contribution to "Jules Verne Roundtable," *Science Fiction Studies*, 32(1): 172.

James, E. (1994) *Science Fiction in the 20th Century*, Oxford: Opus.

Landon, B. (1992) *The Aesthetics of Ambivalence: rethinking science fiction film in the age of electronic (re)production*, Westport, CT: Greenwood Press.

Luckhurst, R. (2005) *Science Fiction*, Cambridge: Polity.

Suvin, D. (1979) *Metamorphoses of Science Fiction: on the poetics and history of a literary genre*, New Haven, CT: Yale University Press.

Westfahl, G. (1998) *The Mechanics of Wonder: the creation of the idea of science fiction*, Liverpool: Liverpool University Press.

Wolfe, G.K. (1986) *Critical Terms for Science Fiction and Fantasy: a glossary and guide to scholarship*, Westport, CT: Greenwood Press.

ANDREW M. BULTER, MARK BOULD, ADAM ROBERTS AND SHERRYL VINT

FIFTY KEY FIGURES IN SCIENCE FICTION

GERRY ANDERSON (1929–)

British television producer of sf series, including *Thunderbirds* (1964–66).

Gerry Anderson found fame working with puppets and then moved on to live-action drama and more recently computer-generated animation. While his work was widely seen outside Britain, he has a unique place in British popular culture. His major series, developed with his second wife, Sylvia, were *Supercar* (1960–62), *Fireball XL5* (1962–63), *Stingray* (1964–65), *Thunderbirds* (including two spin-off films, *Thunderbirds Are GO* (Lane 1966) and *Thunderbird 6* (Lane 1968)), *Captain Scarlet and the Mysterons* (1967–68), *Joe 90* (1968–69), *UFO* (1970–73), and *Space: 1999* (1975–78). Anderson continues to work, collaborating on the Japanese anime series *Firestorm* (2000–2003) and most recently creating *Gerry Anderson's New Captain Scarlet* (2005), a CGI reboot of his original show. In 1981 his work inspired the founding of the fan organization Fanderson (www.fanderson.org.uk), and in 2001 Anderson received the Order of the British Empire for services to British television.

Born in 1929 in north London, Anderson left school at 15, planning a career in architecture, only to discover that he was allergic to the plaster used to make model buildings. He found alternative employment as a trainee film editor, working first at the Colonial Film Unit and then at Gainsborough Studios. Following national service in the RAF as an air traffic controller, he formed AP Films to make commercials, hoping to graduate to large-scale entertainment. When commissions proved elusive, he reluctantly began making puppet films for children's television, beginning with *The Adventures of Twizzle* (1957–58) and *Torchy the Battery Boy* (1958–59). Anderson recognized that the puppet format had the potential to allow him to develop in miniature themes and ideas he would have liked to see on the big screen. He embraced the medium with a series devised by his own team, a fantasy western called *Four Feather Falls* (1960).

While Anderson had a personal fascination with aviation and the space race, and caught the spirit of the age of Sputnik, the initial reason for his move into sf was more pragmatic. He soon realized that the one thing puppets do really badly is walk, and that his shows would work better if built around a dramatic device that would allow them to have adventures sitting down. The obvious answer was to develop series around fantastic machines and aircraft, such as the flying car in *Supercar*, the spacecraft in *Fireball XL5*, and the super-submarine in *Stingray*. Technology remained prominent in Anderson's programs, with the fantastic rescue craft of *Thunderbirds*, the space interceptors and submarine-launched jet fighter in *UFO*, and the Eagle transporters in *Space: 1999*. The vehicles were presented as weathered and "lived-in," adding a new sense of realism to this sort of show. Anderson got round the other major defect of puppets – their immobile hands – by cutting in close-ups of live actors, while an electronic device allowed the puppets' mouths to be synchronized with actors' voices. Anderson named this entire puppet process "Supermarionation."

Anderson's Supermarionation programs were championed by self-styled British television mogul Lew Grade, who ran the Independent Television Corporation (ITC) and eventually purchased AP Films as a subsidiary. Grade's budgets permitted exceptionally high production values, most immediately evident in the color film stock used for all programs from 1964 onward. These values were necessary to crack Grade's target market – the United States – but also aided the longevity of Anderson's shows beyond that of their contemporaries. When *Thunderbirds* failed to secure US distribution, Grade commissioned *Captain Scarlet and the Mysterons*, a series about a future battle of nerves between Spectrum, a human military organization, and invisible Martians able to replicate the dead. The hero, Captain Scarlet, was a human agent who had accidentally become indestructible. The show had a complexity and a darkness of tone that belied the youth of its purported target audience. *Captain Scarlet* broke with Anderson's earlier work in other ways. From this point on, the puppet heads were in proportion to their bodies and carved with more naturalistic features. Anderson's next series, *Joe 90*, had a lighter tone. It followed the adventures of a boy who, thanks to a device invented by his father which could copy brainwaves, is able to operate as a secret agent equipped with skills borrowed from adult brains. Anderson's run of success ended in 1969 with *The Secret Service*, a series which featured a puppet version of British comedian Stanley Unwin as a priest/spy. Unwin was famous for a routine in which he lapsed into a gobbledygook language called "Unwinese," and his character did the same. Grade hated the show, and as soon as he saw samples of the first season he canceled it.

In 1960 Anderson had produced and directed a live-action thriller called *Crossroads to Crime*. It was not well received, but by the late 1960s Anderson's success was such that he was able to return to feature film, producing *Doppelgänger* (aka *Journey to the Far Side of the Sun* (Robert Parrish 1969)), in which astronauts travel to a newly discovered planet only to find that it is an exact mirror image of Earth. The live-action sf series *UFO* and *Space: 1999* followed, along with the non-sf *The Protectors* (1972–74). *UFO* dealt with near-future resistance to alien incursions onto Earth to harvest organs from humanity. It played well at home and abroad, attracting a particular following in Italy. The American office of ITC complained about the darker and more character-based episodes of the series – they especially disliked an episode called "A Question of Priorities" (1970), in which the lead character's son died and his marriage fell apart – but they liked the material set on the moon. Anderson appeased them by basing his next project *Space: 1999* exclusively on the moon after a nuclear explosion wrenches it out of the Earth's orbit and sends it careening off into deep space. The show unfolded rather like a British *Star Trek*, with an ensemble cast on a voyage of discovery. It acquired one of the *Star Trek* (1966–69) production team, Fred Freiberger, as a producer in its final, second season in place of Sylvia Anderson, from whom Anderson had acrimoniously split.

In the 1980s Anderson made a modest comeback with a space-defense themed puppet show called *Terrahawks* (1983–86), a fantasy animation called *Dick Spanner PI* (1987), and a number of visually inventive commercials. In 1991 the BBC began a nationwide re-screening of *Thunderbirds*, and the show attracted an entirely new audience. Christmas 1992 brought brawls in toy shops over the remaining supplies of *Thunderbirds* toys. Anderson built on this resurgence of public interest with the live-action series *Space Precinct* (1994–95) and a stop-motion animated series, *Lavender Castle* (produced 1996–98, broadcast 1999–2000), but these shows failed to match the achievement or capture the public interest of his classic work.

Part of the secret of Anderson's success was the stability of the AP Films team. His classic series were produced with essentially the same group of writers, designers, and film crew. At the heart of his output was his own work with Sylvia, with whom he devised the format and characters, and wrote the pilot episode. Sylvia Anderson had joined AP Films as a production assistant and married Anderson in 1960. She also designed costumes and voiced characters, most famously *Thunderbirds*' Lady Penelope.

Whether live-action or Supermarionation, Anderson's programs had a distinctive style – a mix of technology and the character play necessary to bring the drama to life with all the tricks of suspense filmmaking to keep the audience engaged. The whole package was bound together by the music of Barry Gray. Along the way, Anderson created a distinctive future architecture, though the limits of the medium required that the streets and cities depicted were decidedly underpopulated. Anderson's heroes frequently operated from elaborate secret bases concealed under innocuous buildings. This was, in part, to avoid the necessity of creating a suitable exterior set.

Anderson's vision of the future was every bit as humanist as that of *Star Trek* creator **Gene Roddenberry**. He strove to bring ethnic and gender diversity to his stories and to avoid obvious stereotyping of his villains. While ahead of the competition, Anderson's shows remain "of their time" and tend to place female characters in a subordinate role. In *Stingray*, Marina, the female lead, is a mute mermaid, and the presentation of female characters in the live-action *UFO* was notoriously demeaning. Anderson's picture of the future routinely included numerous cooperative organizations aligned with a world government: a line projected forward from the postwar creation of the UN in 1945 to a better tomorrow. There is a World Aquanaut Sea Patrol in *Stingray*, a world president in *Captain Scarlet*, and a World Intelligence Network in *Joe 90*. "Survival" (1971), an episode of the near-future *UFO*, even implied that racism had finally died out on Earth back in the 1970s.

It is possible to identify Cold War concerns in Anderson's stories, including enemies within, heroic agents, and nuclear weapons, but perhaps his most enduring theme was the necessity of the human component of the machine. This was especially obvious in *Thunderbirds*, a series built around the adventures of an international rescue organization operated in secret by a multimillionaire ex-astronaut and manned by his five sons, in which the action was typically driven by missions to rescue people from technology which had overreached itself. The courage of the Thunderbirds team rather than the technology saved the day.

Never a great businessman, Anderson sold his rights to *Thunderbirds* and most other Supermarionation shows in the mid-1970s and was powerless to prevent attempts to update or edit his work. In the 1980s *Thunderbirds* inspired a Japanese anime version, *Thunderbirds 2086* (1982), and the 1990s saw both a heavily edited version in the USA with new music and dialogue and *Turbocharged Thunderbirds* (1994–95), in which live-action teenagers interacted with the puppets. More recently, Universal released a live-action film of *Thunderbirds* (Frakes 2004). Anderson had no role in the project and the film did not do well. Meanwhile, Anderson worked on the new version of *Captain Scarlet*, which pleased fans, maintained interest in the original series, and justified a second season, despite an unhelpful Saturday morning slot.

The impact of Anderson's sf is difficult to quantify. Veterans of his productions brought their know-how to a string of Hollywood sf films: Derek Meddings worked on special effects for four Bond movies, *Superman* (Donner 1978) and its first two sequels, and *Batman* (Burton 1989); and Brian Johnson similarly contributed to *Alien* (Scott 1979), *Star Wars: Episode V – The Empire Strikes Back* (Kershner 1980) and *Aliens* (Cameron 1986). For his viewers, Anderson was the gateway to the world of sf. His stories were not merely experienced on television but had their associated ranges of toys, candy, books, records, comics, clothing, and dressing-up costumes. They remain a reference point for comedians, advertisers, and other filmmakers. Homages to *Thunderbirds* can be found in Nick Park's Wallace and Gromit film *A Close Shave* (1995); the cult sitcom *Spaced* (1999–2001); and *Team America: World Police* (Parker 2004). A toy Thunderbird 2 rests in a case in London's Science Museum as an icon of life in the 1960s. This imaginary vehicle was also used as an image of Britishness in the montages at the Millennium Dome, Greenwich, in 2000, and in the foyer of the British Council, Britain's cultural diplomacy agency, from 2002 to 2004.

See also: **The Doctor, Nigel Kneale, Gene Roddenberry, and J. Michael Straczynski**

Bibliography

Archer, S. and Hearn, M. (2002) *What Made Thunderbirds Go! the authorized biography of Gerry Anderson*, London: BBC Books.

Cull, N.J. (2005) "The Man Who Made Thunderbirds: an interview with Gerry Anderson," in J.R. Cook and P. Wright (eds.) *British Science Fiction Television: a hitchhiker's guide*, London: I.B. Tauris.

——(2006) "Was Captain Black Really Red? the tv science fiction of Gerry Anderson in its cold war context," *Media History*, 12(2): 193–207.

NICHOLAS J. CULL

ISAAC ASIMOV [BORN ISAAK JUDAH OZIMOV] (1920–92)

US sf and science writer.

Born in Russia, Isaac Asimov emigrated with his parents to New York City in 1923, where – apart from two decades in Boston – he spent nearly all the rest of his life. Asimov wrote at a furious pace that made him one of the most prolific authors of his time. He himself counted almost 500 volumes in his *oeuvre*, though bibliographic research has demonstrated that the number of actually distinct books he produced is much closer to 200 (still a stupendous figure, of course). Unlike most extremely prolific authors, Asimov wrote in a fairly wide variety of fictional and nonfictional genres, but two literary modes account for the great majority of his output and for nearly all of his enduring fame: sf and popular science writing.

It was sf in which Asimov began writing and in which he attained his first renown. An avid consumer of pulp sf magazines in the 1930s, Asimov was the kind of fan whose special intensity (and talent) made him determined to become a writer as well as a reader of the genre, and his first professionally published stories appeared in 1939. He soon joined the legendary cohort of writers nurtured by John W. Campbell, the trail-blazing editor who in 1937 had taken over *Astounding Science-Fiction* with a determination to raise pulp sf from its then abysmal literary and scientific standards. No author became more important to Campbell's project than Asimov (nor was any more fiercely loyal to Campbell personally). By the end of the 1940s, Asimov's work for Campbell and other pulp editors had established him as one of the so-called "Big Three" of science fiction (along with **Robert A. Heinlein** and A.E. van Vogt, and, as van Vogt's productivity and popularity waned, then with Heinlein and **Arthur C. Clarke**). Most of Asimov's best sf books (and many of his best stories) were published in the following decade, the 1950s – his "gold decade," as he once termed it. By the 1960s he was writing much less sf, largely because science writing and other forms of nonfiction came to occupy most of his energy. Though the radical innovations that sf underwent in the 1960s and 1970s at the hands of writers like **Philip K. Dick**, **Ursula K. Le Guin**, and **Samuel R. Delany** soon made Asimov's work in the genre look rather old-fashioned – as he acknowledged more than once – his popularity with fans (like that of Heinlein and Clarke) never faded, and his work remains a major landmark for anyone wishing to appreciate the history of American sf.

Asimov's stature and influence in sf depend mainly on two large achievements: the series of robot stories and novels (1948–57, 1983–85), and the *Foundation* sequence (first trilogy, in magazine form, 1942–51, as books 1951–53; later volumes 1982–93). Both originate in the stories Asimov published in pulp magazines in the 1940s, though neither attained book form until the 1950s. In his robot fiction Asimov created the most consequential image of artificially fabricated intelligent life since **Mary Shelley**'s *Frankenstein, or the modern Prometheus* (1818), whose attitude toward science he self-consciously set out to refute. In contrast to Shelley's implicit fear and mistrust of scientific discovery, Asimov's robot fiction is based on his conviction that scientific and technological progress, while not without hazards, is a fundamentally beneficent force. The famous Three Laws of Robotics (which Asimov credited Campbell with formulating for him) help to assure that robots remain safe and useful to humanity; and, despite mistakes and accidents, Asimov's robots ultimately turn out to be capable of nothing less than the social salvation of humanity. During the past half century there has hardly been an important representation of robots in prose fiction, film, or television that has failed to evince Asimov's influence.

The most significant single volume of Asimov's robot fiction is *I, Robot* (1950), his second book. Working in the rich American genre of the story cycle (as typified by Sherwood Anderson's *Winesburg, Ohio* (1919), Ernest Hemingway's *In Our Time* (1925), and William Faulkner's *Go Down, Moses* (1942)), Asimov synthesized some of the stories published in the 1940s into a well-shaped book that, while not exactly a conventional novel, possesses an overarching narrative line as well as a variety of individual tales. *I, Robot* is given a sense of unity by the increasing technical sophistication and social importance of the robots and through the dominant character of Dr Susan Calvin, the founder of the imaginary science of "robopsychology" (i.e., robot psychology). She is Asimov's most memorable single character and, as he once claimed, probably the first major female character in American sf. In addition to *I, Robot*, mention should be made of Asimov's sf detective stories and novels, many of which involve robots, most notably *The Naked Sun* (1957), which is considered by some to be Asimov's best novel of the 1950s, and which features the Holmes-and-Watson pairing of the detective Elijah Baley and his robot sidekick R. Daneel Olivaw.

The *Foundation* sequence is perhaps an even more considerable achievement than the robot fiction. The trilogy *Foundation* (1951), *Foundation and Empire* (1952), and *Second Foundation* (1953) was not the first work of sf to represent a galactic civilization, but it set a new standard in this regard; Asimov's galaxy of many inhabited worlds has probably been even more widely influential than his robots. Its impact can be seen in such huge productions of mass culture as the *Star Trek* (1966–) and *Star Wars* (1977–) franchises, but also, for instance, in a work of high Joycean modernism like Delany's *Stars in My Pocket Like Grains of Sand* (1984). Tremendously ambitious in its time scale as well as its spatial setting, the *Foundation* trilogy spans many centuries to tell the saga of the rise and decline of entire planetary societies, with previously dominant worlds becoming marginalized and new ones rising to wealth and power. The structure of the trilogy ingeniously combines, on the one hand, the sort of fictional (and future) history pioneered by **Olaf Stapledon** in *Last and First Men* (1930) – with its multisecular temporality and its stress on broad social trends – and, on the other hand, a wide range of relatively self-contained narratives along the way (the latter largely adapted from Asimov's work in the pulps). As the robot fiction prominently features the invented sciences of robotics and robopsychology, the *Foundation* sequence invents the science of psychohistory (based essentially on a synthesis of the highly simplified American versions of psychoanalysis and historical materialism to be found in the New York intellectual air Asimov breathed during the 1930s and 1940s). Hari Seldon, the founder of psychohistory, is (along with his posthumous adversary, the Mule) the most memorable character in the *Foundation* saga, but it is really the "Seldon Plan" – Hari's scheme to shape the course of the galaxy for centuries to come – which is closest to being a protagonist for the series.

In the 1980s Asimov began writing new novels that extended the *Foundation* sequence and that also returned to his concern with robots. Though popular with his many avid fans, these later volumes seem unlikely to enhance Asimov's reputation in the long run. But the original three volumes may well constitute the most important trilogy in all of sf, a genre in which trilogies have flourished.

At least two other works of Asimov's sf deserve to be mentioned even in this brief survey. One is *The End of Eternity* (1955). Somewhat atypical among Asimov's fiction, and perhaps therefore underdiscussed, it is independent of both the *Foundation* and the robot material, and it displays relatively little of either the humor or the didacticism so prominent (and popular) in Asimov's work generally. But it is one of the author's most tightly constructed fictions, and its austere, haunting quality has an appeal of its own; a significant minority of Asimov's readers have long considered it his best work. Concerned with the Eternals, a caste of technicians who roam through the centuries, monitoring and adjusting the causal relationships that stretch across time, *The End of Eternity* is one of the more ingenious novels about time travel and its paradoxes since **H.G. Wells**'s *The Time Machine* (1895) placed the subject permanently on sf's agenda.

The Gods Themselves (1972) was Asimov's first new sf novel since *The Naked Sun* (not counting the minor *Fantastic Voyage* (1966), a film novelization), and it responded memorably to many of the changes that had taken place in sf and in American society during the intervening years. For the first time Asimov represents sexual experience – between humans and also among an alien race that is divided into three sexes (who have sexual "intercourse" by merging their amorphous bodies). The novel also deals with issues of energy supply and of possible environmental catastrophe in ways that seem even more pertinent today than when it first appeared. Evidence that Asimov was capable, in at least this instance, of being influenced by younger writers like Le Guin and Delany, *The Gods Themselves* is almost certainly his most artfully constructed work of fiction. He once identified it as his own favorite.

Some discussion is in order of Asimov's work as a science writer: not only because it forms the bulk of his output, nor only because sf and science writing are related genres whose combination in individual careers forms an important motif in the history of sf, from Wells, through Asimov and Clarke, to Gregory Benford today, but also because Asimov's work in popular science helps to illuminate his sf. As a science writer – as the greatest *explainer* of his age (in Carl Sagan's admiring description) – Asimov served as an advocate not only for science itself but for the whole *Weltanschauung* of liberal rationalism. When we turn from his (mostly later) science writing back to his (mostly earlier) sf, it becomes quite clear that this same advocacy animates the fiction too. Though Asimov is well aware that people may wrongheadedly resist the beneficence of liberal reason – *The Gods Themselves* takes its title from Schiller's maxim "The gods themselves struggle in vain against stupidity" – he is supremely confident, in nonfiction and fiction alike, that there are few problems liberal reason is incapable of solving if only it is allowed to do so. For Asimov, there are many puzzles but no ultimate mysteries and few real villains, many difficulties but no irreconcilable differences of material interest.

Thus, for instance, Asimov's demolition, in his robot fiction, of what he called the "Frankenstein complex" reaches its culmination in the vision of a world ruled benignly by intelligent machines driven purely by rationality and beyond any conceivable partisanship. In the *Foundation* trilogy, Hari Seldon's elaborate scheme saves humanity from centuries of ignorance and misery; the implication seems clear that we should submit to the rational social planning of those who know best. Admittedly, a minority of readers have felt that the Mule, who nearly succeeds in overthrowing the Seldon Plan, is the secret hero of the trilogy; but, if so, the secret remains hidden from the author and from the "official" ideology of the text. With perfect liberal balance and reasonableness, however, *The End of Eternity* warns that even rational social planning can be taken too far. Asimov's extraordinarily *pure* commitment to liberal reason has always been a minority stance, and has been emulated by few writers after him in any genre. But the distinctiveness and imaginative power with which he embodied this viewpoint in works of sf remains unsurpassed.

See also: **Greg Bear, Alfred Bester, Leigh Brackett, Octavia Butler, Arthur C. Clarke, Samuel R. Delany, Philip K. Dick, William Gibson, Donna J. Haraway, Robert A. Heinlein, Frank Herbert, L. Ron Hubbard, Ursula K. Le Guin, Stanisław Lem, C.L. Moore, Kim Stanley Robinson, Joanna Russ, Olaf Stapledon, Neal Stephenson, Sheri S. Tepper, James Tiptree Jr, H.G. Wells, and Gene Wolfe**

Bibliography

Freedman, C. (ed.) (2005) *Conversations with Isaac Asimov*, Jackson: University Press of Mississippi.

Gunn, J. (1982) *Isaac Asimov: the foundations of science fiction*, Oxford: Oxford University Press.

Olander, J. and Greenberg, M.H. (eds.) (1977) *Isaac Asimov*, New York: Taplinger.

Patrouch, J. (1974) *The Science Fiction of Isaac Asimov*, Garden City, NY: Doubleday.

CARL FREEDMAN

J[AMES] G[RAHAM] BALLARD (1930–2009)

British novelist, short-story writer, and essayist.

J.G. Ballard was born in Shanghai into a wealthy British expatriate family. Interned in a Japanese prisoner-of-war camp during the Second World War, he traveled to England for the first time in 1946. These early experiences were the basis of his fictionalized autobiographies *Empire of the Sun* (1984) and *The Kindness of Women* (1991), events retold in his memoir *Miracles of Life* (2008). These extreme exposures to casual cruelty, colonial violence, privation, and death no doubt contributed to Ballard's total detachment from conceptions of English identity, cultural respectability, and the tradition of the mainstream novel. Precisely because of his subversion of the indigenous realist novel, many critics now regard Ballard as one of the most important post-Second World War writers, regardless of generic markers. This recognition was slow in coming, largely because he was identified as an sf writer for the first half of his career. One of his major achievements was to help transform perceptions of the genre, which he did by fusing the low cultural energies of magazine sf with the avant-garde in the 1960s, using it to produce an extraordinary vision of alienated, science-fictionalized existence in the technologically saturated, advanced-capitalist West. The adjective "Ballardian" is rapidly entering the English-speaking lexicon as the shorthand for this alienated-yet-ecstatic state induced by shopping malls, business parks, and the non-places of airports, motorway systems, and distribution centers.

Ballard began publishing short stories in English and American sf magazines in 1956. From the start, he wrote in a highly stylized way about vividly realized landscapes, emphasizing hallucinatory description of environments over human agency. Early stories were collected as *Vermilion Sands* (1971), in which a desert resort is the backdrop for the psychological games of profoundly traumatized people. *Vermilion Sands* showed Ballard's interest in exteriorizing psychic states in extreme physical settings. The clearest and most sustained influence on his work in this regard has been surrealist painting, particularly the work of Paul Delvaux and Salvador Dalí. The stories also introduced Ballard's interest in repetition and modulation: he tells the same story over and over, obsessively teasing out different resonances from the same scenario. His work came in clusters as he pursues a particular idea until its potential was exhausted. This was evident in his first four novels, *The Wind from Nowhere* (1961), *The Drowned World* (1962), *The Drought* (1965), and *The Crystal World* (1966), known collectively as the "disaster quartet." Each explores a global disaster and the perverse reactions of the dwindling survivors. Unlike the heroic tradition in which a band of scientists or engineers reverse the disaster and save humanity, Ballard's enervated figures seek ways of actively embracing the postdisaster world, often finally choosing physical death. *The Drowned World*, in which London is submerged by floods, openly carried debts to surrealism and the holistic psychology of Carl Jung. *The Drought* explored the postcatastrophic existential world of a desertified Earth, this time referencing the painter Yves Tanguy and the "absurdist" philosophy of Albert Camus. These books secured the attention of mainstream literary commentators, while the passivity appalled many in the American sf world. Some accused him of embracing a death-wish; Ballard delightfully agreed, thus ensuring he would remain resolutely marginal to American sf readerships.

Ballard's main genre association in England was with the sf magazine *New Worlds*. The editor John ("Ted") Carnell was the first to publish Ballard in the 1950s, but in 1964 the editorship of *New Worlds* passed to the young turk **Michael Moorcock**. With Ballard and others, Moorcock planned to revolutionize the magazine in the hope of making sf an aesthetic and political avant-garde. Moorcock proved to be in complete synchronicity with the times: between 1962 and 1970 *New Worlds* became a leading London avant-garde journal and the home of New Wave sf. Ballard and Moorcock encouraged cross-fertilizations between countercultural literary, film, and art-worlds, and the magazine even gained an Arts Council grant to become a glossy, heavily illustrated journal. At this time, Ballard associated with Pop artists and avant-garde writers such as Eduardo Paolozzi, Richard Hamilton, and William S. Burroughs more than those in the sf world. Even so, he was declared "the Voice" of New Wave sf by Moorcock.

Ballard's manifesto, "Which Way to Inner Space?" (1962), published in *New Worlds*, demanded an sf that abandoned outer space for the kinds of psychological climates and emotional territories his own work had been exploring. Ballard then embarked on a series of extreme experiments in "condensed novels" that attempted to find a new form to address violent times. Eventually collected as *The Atrocity Exhibition* (1970), these difficult and confrontational works explore the assassination of John F. Kennedy and the psychic impacts of televised wars like Vietnam and Biafra, and detail the cultural obsession with celebrity and violent death. The texts largely abolish any notion of consistent character or realized context. The central figure is loosened even from a fixed name (he is known variously as Tallis, Traven, Talbot, etc.) and eventually disappears entirely as the chapters are replaced by experiments in found texts or disturbingly altered scientific reports. Notoriously, texts such as "Plan for the Assassination of Jacqueline Kennedy" (1966) and "Why I Want to Fuck Ronald Reagan" (1968) resulted in protests in the House of Commons and successful prosecutions for obscenity in England. The American edition of *The Atrocity Exhibition* was withdrawn and destroyed by Ballard's American publishers, Doubleday. It was eventually published by Grove Press, home of subversive modernist texts by Burroughs and Georges Bataille. *The Atrocity Exhibition* survives as an exemplary record of the 1960s counterculture, mixing the cultural theory of Marshall McLuhan and Guy Debord with the stylized Pop Art of Andy Warhol and the collages of Robert Rauschenberg, and the anti-psychiatry of R.D. Laing, who was busy idealizing schizophrenia as a form of modern shamanism. All of these elements were fused into Ballard's icy, theoretical prose, presented in short paragraphs that read like deranged curatorial annotations to unseen pictures. They are

Ballard's most important but also most uncomfortable works; they seethe with the unresolved psychic damage of the era.

After 1970, when the New Wave largely disintegrated, Ballard wrote fewer short stories and concentrated on the novel. He wrote a trilogy of books about the transformation of the London landscape (*Crash* (1973), *Concrete Island* (1974), *High-Rise* (1975)), which explored the psychopathology of new technologies and their environments. *Crash* secured Ballard's career as a provocateur, detailing the new sexual possibilities of car crashes in the newly Americanized landscapes of the flyovers and gyratory traffic systems to the west of London. He collapsed any chance of determining the irony of this new techno-sexual hypothesis by naming the central character "James Ballard" and always discussing the book extra-textually with an entirely straight face. After his own accident, "Ballard" is drawn into a circle of experimentalists fusing sex, death, and technology on the exit ramps and hard shoulders of motorway systems. The ecstatic combinations of genitals and instrument binnacles prompted one reader of the manuscript to declare that the author was "beyond psychiatric help," a judgment Ballard embraced. The controversy was reignited in 1996 with **David Cronenberg**'s (necessarily) sanitized film adaptation. It was denounced by the conservative English press as the "most depraved film ever made" and prompted a weakened Conservative government to push for a ban, which was only patchily enforced. Ballard's program to bait the English establishment was successful once again.

After the concrete trilogy, Ballard wrote an atypically lush fantasy, *The Unlimited Dream Company* (1979), which unquestionably exposed a Romantic strand of sublime longing for transcendence that has always run alongside Ballard's dark visions. In this novel, a pilot called Blake crashes and drowns in the Thames at Shepperton only to be resurrected as a local god, whose sacrifice transforms the anonymous suburb into a paradisiacal island outside of ordinary space and time. The painterly references here are to the tropical fantasies of Paul Gauguin and the weirdly English terrains of Stanley Spencer's work, in which Christian eschatology is played out in small towns along the Thames. Ballard's ecstatic transformation of Shepperton (his adopted home town) is described in overheated, almost embarrassing prose. The reader is forced to occupy a remorselessly visionary (or possibly just insane) apprehension of the world in an intoxicating (or possibly just suffocating) way. Pilots are typical Ballardian heroes, acting as emblems of potential escape and transformation. They also embody a death-drive exposed by the technological saturation of the postwar world. In a series of stories that includes the brilliant "Myths of the

Near Future" (1982), astronauts become symbolic figures of a post-catastrophic universe. The attempt to push beyond the bounds of Earth only unleashes inertia, fugue, and the triumph of the unconscious. Ballard's erasure of outer by inner space was never clearer.

Ballard's shift of genre to the war novel in *Empire of the Sun* (1984) resulted in shortlisting for the Booker Prize, the most prominent annual literary prize in England (he lost to the unadventurous miserabilist Anita Brookner). Ballard was repositioned as a "serious" mainstream novelist, a process furthered by **Steven Spielberg**'s film adaptation (1987). Ballard subsequently became a tireless reviewer, commentator, and vox pop provocateur in the English press, a beaming old man usually politely advocating more violence and pornography on television. In *Running Wild* (1988), Ballard made the last generic shift of his career, beginning a series of sly rewritings of detective fiction. In *Running Wild,* all the benign, middle-class parents of a new gated community on the wealthy outskirts of London are brutally murdered and the children are kidnapped. The leaden detective eventually arrives at the conclusion that is glaringly obvious to the reader from the start: the children have rebelled against their completely surveilled, technocratically managed lives, and have carefully planned the murders before effecting their escape. They return as international terrorists, targeting systems that embody the "iron cage" of instrumental reason. The novella is a neat satirical use of the detective tradition, as the detective slowly uncovers an utterly perverse yet entirely logical outcome of modern social control. Ballard rehearses the same plot with very little modulation in *Cocaine Nights* (1996), *Super-Cannes* (2000), and *Millennium People* (2003). In each, a slow-witted figure takes on the role of the detective in an alluring closed community of vast privilege and wealth. This postnational, postindustrial elite live in protected estates in Spain or France or London. Each community hides a secret: they are so cocooned from actual experience that they have to engineer criminal activity to re-engage with life. This escalates into acts of murder, at which point our detective arrives to reveal gradually this hidden world of violent impulse. Ballard hammers home the same thesis: perfected manufactured environments where risk is completely managed cannot erase and indeed actively foster irruptions of unconscious violence and desire. By the time Ballard repeated this plot again in *Kingdom Come* (2006), centered on a shopping mall, the satire feels heavy-handed and the thesis exhausted.

Ballard is undoubtedly a significant literary figure who has engineered a lasting vision of the post-1945 world. His relations to sf remain ambiguous. Like Kurt Vonnegut, another writer with extraordinary Second World War experience, Ballard was largely uninterested in the history and culture of sf. While Ballard influenced many mainstream writers, from Martin Amis to Will Self, his genre influence tended to be on those, like **William Gibson**, who want to push at and beyond its boundaries. Instead, sf provided Ballard with the devices and tropes to develop a haunting and evocative imaginary of our postcatastrophic world. All too often, the world feels like it is becoming ever more Ballardian. There can be no higher praise for a writer than that, whatever the genre.

See also: **Iain M. Banks, Jean Baudrillard, Arthur C. Clarke, David Cronenberg, William Gibson, Gwyneth Jones, China Miéville, Michael Moorcock, Steven Spielberg, Olaf Stapledon, and H.G. Wells**

Bibliography

Delville, M. (1998) *J.G. Ballard*, London: Northcote House in association with the British Council.

Gasiorek, A. (2005) *J.G. Ballard*, Manchester: Manchester University Press.

Luckhurst, R. (1997) *"The Angle between Two Walls": the fiction of J.G. Ballard*, Liverpool: Liverpool University Press.

ROGER LUCKHURST

IAIN M[ENZIES] BANKS (1954–)

Scottish novelist and short-story writer.

Born in Dunfermline in 1954, Iain Banks studied English, Philosophy, and Psychology at Stirling University (1972–75). Before finding success with *The Wasp Factory* (1984), he wrote a number of sf novels which would finally be published, in revised form, under the name Iain M. Banks. *The Wasp Factory* was linked in some reviews to the then current moral panic about video nasties, and he – like fellow Scots Alasdair Gray, James Kelman, Alan Warner, and Irvine Welsh – rapidly attracted a cult audience who rejected the suburban supposed realism of the comic social novel. Its shocked reception obscured what is in fact a subtle Gothic tale which explores issues of gender. *Walking on Glass* (1985) features three distinct narratives – one realistic, one fantastical, and one science-fictional – woven together at the end. His next novel, *The Bridge* (1985), built up the fantasy element, paying homage to Franz Kafka and Mervyn Peake while interconnecting the narratives of three parts of the psyche of a car-crash victim on the Forth Road Bridge.

In 1984 Banks had moved south to England, settling in Faversham, Kent, and become a lawyer, but the success of his early novels allowed him to become a professional writer. From 1985 he alternated between books written under the names Iain Banks and Iain M. Banks – although some of the books of the former still contained fantastical elements, the latter's work is purely sf. In 1988 Banks moved back to Scotland, settling in North Queensferry.

Banks's sf novels combine manipulated humans, wise-cracking AIs, high technology, medieval societies, and improbably named spaceships. They marked the re-emergence of the once-derided subgenre of space opera – melodramatic narratives set against improbably galactic backgrounds. The form was developed in the 1930s US sf pulp magazines by writers such as **Leigh Brackett**, John W. Campbell, Edmond Hamilton, E.E. "Doc" Smith, and Jack Williamson, and in 1930s comic strips and movie serials featuring characters such as Buck Rogers and Flash Gordon. It had recently re-emerged in the cinema – with films such as the first *Star Wars* trilogy (1977–83) – and on television – with series such as *Battlestar Galactica* (1978–79) and *Buck Rogers in the Twenty-Fifth Century* (1979–81). With rare exceptions, such as *Flash Gordon* (Hodges 1980), these revived space operas used nostalgia and pastiche to disguise essentially conservative ideologies. However, Banks, as a Scot, was writing within a (problematically) postimperial world and was well aware of the politics of sexism and racism. His writing still had literary aspirations in terms of narrative structure, characterization, and theme, as well as demonstrating a strong sense of irony.

Banks describes himself as being politically to the left of center. The main conceit of most of his sf is the Culture, a seemingly utopian galactic empire in an era of postscarcity, which can afford to embrace socialism and anarchy – "socialism within, anarchy without" (Banks 1994). All the real work is done by machines, freeing sentient beings to play games if they so choose. In a setting in which all necessary resources are plentiful, the notion of money and exchange value (and thus capitalism) might seem to be obsolete, although a number of the early Culture novels involve the purchase of labor by the Culture. Like a capitalist economy which requires expansion to maintain the circulation of capital, part of the Culture is always looking outward to new civilizations: "The Culture trades culture for peace and hegemony … What the Culture gets from Contacted species is an injection of fresh variety, which Contact itself destroys as it imposes utopia" (Mendlesohn 2005: 118; see also Vint 2007). The Culture in fact assimilates and consumes – as many an empire has before it; the books need to be read with an awareness of such ambiguities.

The first Iain M. Banks novel was *Consider Phlebas* (1987). Its protagonist, Bora Horza Gobuchul, is a mercenary working for the highly religious Idiran empire, which is locked into war with the Culture. The ending of the novel downplays the significance of the events it has described in terms of the wider galaxy, and appendices cast them in a new light. In what may be an ongoing homage to **Ursula K. Le Guin**'s *Hainish* novels, *The Player of Games* (1988) is likewise structured around an encounter between the Culture and another society. As part of its diplomatic mission, the Culture recruit Jernau Morat Gurgeh to join a games tournament on the planet Azad. While he finds games easy to master, it becomes increasingly clear that he is a pawn in the Culture's game, and that the A.I. Minds that govern the Culture may not be as benign as they initially seem. *Use of Weapons* (1990) adapts the complex structures of novels such as *The Bridge* to space opera: the story of Cheradenine Zakalwe being re-recruited into the Culture as a dirty tricks specialist alternates with a backward-told account of his earlier career. A twist at the violent climax reveals that the reader has been carefully misled throughout the novel.

The next Culture novel was *Excession* (1996), a shaggy dog narrative about first contact with an extra-terrestrial artifact. In the interim, Iain M. Banks had published *Against a Dark Background* (1992), featuring a pilot and thief who must be killed to allow the birth of a messiah, and *Feersum Endjinn* (1994), four interwoven accounts of the search for the titular artifact (one of which, like the title, is told in phonetic prose). *Inversions* (1998) may or may not be a Culture novel, depending on the interpretation of the word "Culture" in the preface to some editions. In a quasi-medieval society, Oelph relates the story of Dr Vosill's attempts to remold the outlook of Quience, an absolute leader. Meanwhile, on the other side of a mountain range, De War, a bodyguard to a protector, General UrLeyn, fears an assassination attempt and tells stories of two lovers in distant Lavishia, who may in fact be Vosill and himself. The novel presents itself as a manuscript from the past, but might be an account of a Contacted society being drawn into the Culture. Just as *Consider Phlebas* took its title from Eliot's *The Waste Land* (1922), so too does *Look to Windward* (2000), in which Major Quilan, a survivor of a civil war sparked by a failed intervention by the Culture, seeks revenge. He travels to Masaq, a Culture orbital space station, so as to – apparently – persuade the composer Mahrai Ziller to return to Chel; but the Culture suspect a more sinister motive. Once more Banks moves from the intimate to the distant, finishing the narrative from the perspective of millions of years later.

Banks took another break from the Culture with *The Algebraist* (2004), which features an interstellar empire held together by wormholes. When the Beyonders destroy one of the portals, leaving a system cut off from the rest of civilization, a human, Fassin Taak, is ordered to track down the advanced technology possessed by the posthuman Dwellers who live in the atmosphere of gas giant planets. This MacGuffin narrative enables Banks to describe his imagined society in detail, demonstrating his ongoing interest in the working practices – in fact, the leisure practices – of the people within his imagined system, and the superstructure which arises from a particular economic base. Furthermore, following Nick Bostrom's simulation hypothesis, in which our apparently real universe is just a virtual world, he also suggests that any of the events in the novel may be a computer simulation.

Matter (2008) is set on the shellworld Sursamen, a series of nested spheres occupied by species of varying levels of complexity. Each layer is guarded and mentored by another, more advanced, species. Djan Seriy Anaplian, a daughter of King Hausk who ruled the eighth level of Sursamen, returns home from the Culture to pay respects to her dead father. There is a conspiracy at work to seize power, which may lead to the destruction of Sursamen. The narrative is apparently resolved, but this is a false ending undercut by the appendices and an epilog. Once more Banks uses narrative sleight of hand to mislead his readers.

In October 2004 Banks was one of the signatories of the Declaration of Calton Hill, calling for Scottish independence. He destroyed his British passport in protest against the Iraq invasion and was part of a campaign to have British prime minister Tony Blair impeached. These concerns have shown up in his non-sf, Iain Banks novels, notably *Dead Air* (2002), which is set at the time of the 11 September 2001 attacks on the World Trade Center and the Pentagon, and in the portrayal of American capitalists in *The Steep Approach to Garbadale* (2007). While some have complained that the characters in Iain Banks's novels sound too much like the author, his political arguments are more subtle and nuanced within the sf frameworks of Iain M. Banks's novels.

Banks is not the only contemporary British sf writer to explore space opera from a leftist position. Colin Greenland won popular and critical acclaim with the self-reflexive romp of *Take back Plenty* (1990) and the ironic steampunk of *Harm's Way* (1993), both of which feature female protagonists. Banks's friend Ken MacLeod produced the *Fall Revolution* quartet (1995–99), which featured Trotskyist and libertarian characters and politics, and the *Engines of Light* trilogy (2000–2002). Perhaps most ambitious – but not left of center – is Peter F. Hamilton's *Night's Dawn* trilogy (1996–99): set in a twenty-seventh-century empire of over 900 worlds, and explored from the viewpoints of many different characters, its convoluted narrative covers more than 3,000 pages.

Sf writers in Britain have enjoyed much success since the mid-1990s. A new British sf magazine, *Interzone* (1982–), was initially perceived as being a revamped *New Worlds* (1946–76, 1978–9) – indeed it published such major British New Wave writers as Brian Aldiss, **J.G. Ballard**, M. John Harrison, **Michael Moorcock**, and John Sladek. However, among many other new writers, *Interzone* boosted the careers of Stephen Baxter, Kim Newman, Alastair Reynolds, and Charles Stross, and published Banks's "A Gift from the Culture" (1987). John Jarrold, Banks's initial sf editor at Orbit before he moved to Legend, Earthlight, and then went freelance, was one of a number of dedicated figures supporting the British sf industry. But it is important not to overlook the role of Banks himself; he proved it was still possible to write sf on a grand scale and be outward-looking, while maintaining a rich moral and political complexity.

See also: **J.G. Ballard, Leigh Brackett, Arthur C. Clarke, Gwyneth Jones, Ursula K. Le Guin, China Miéville, Michael Moorcock, and H. G. Wells**

Bibliography

Banks, I.M. (1994) "A Few Notes on the Culture." Online. Available: <http://www.cs.bris.ac.uk/~stefan/culture.html> (accessed 1 January 2009).

Butler, A.M. (1999) "Strange Case of Mr Banks: doubles and *The Wasp Factory*," *Foundation*, 76: 17–27.

Guerrier, S. (1999) "Culture Theory: Iain M. Banks's 'Culture' as utopia," *Foundation*, 76: 28–38.

Hardesty, W.H. (1999) "Mercenaries and Special Circumstances: Iain M. Banks's counter-narrative of utopia, *Use of Weapons*," *Foundation*, 76: 39–47.

MacLeod, K. (2003) "Phlebas Reconsidered," in A.M. Butler and F. Mendlesohn (eds.) *The True Knowledge of Ken MacLeod*, Reading: Science Fiction Foundation.

Mendlesohn, F. (2005) "The Dialectic of Decadence and Utopia in Iain M. Banks's Culture Novels," *Foundation*, 93: 116–24.
Middleton, T. (1999) "The Works of Iain M. Banks: a critical introduction," *Foundation*, 76: 5–16.
Nairn, T. (1993) "Iain Banks and the Fiction Factory," in G. Wallace and R. Stevenson (eds.) *The Scottish Novel since the Seventies*, Edinburgh: Edinburgh University Press.
Palmer, C. (1999) "Galactic Empires and the Contemporary Extravaganza: Dan Simmons and Iain M. Banks," *Science Fiction Studies*, 26(1): 73–90.
Vint, S. (2007) "Cultural Imperialism and the Ends of Empire: Iain M. Banks' *Look to Windward*," *Journal of the Fantastic in the Arts*, 18(1): 85–98.

ANDREW M. BUTLER

JEAN BAUDRILLARD (1929–2007)

French theorist, photographer, and poet, associated with postmodernism (although he almost never used the term himself).

In *The Gulf War Did Not Take Place* (1995), Jean Baudrillard writes: "A simple calculation shows that, of the 500,000 American soldiers involved during the seven months of operations in the Gulf, three times as many would have died from road accidents alone had they stayed in civilian life" (Baudrillard 1995: 69). He does not provide the exact figures, nor does he give any sources for them. This is typical of a certain strand of continental philosophy in which the argument lies in the performance of the rhetoric rather than verifiable fact, and which perhaps is easier to comprehend as ironic or satiric.

Baudrillard's work reads like the peculiar blend of estrangement and cognition associated with sf – and he has engaged with the writings of **Philip K. Dick** (e.g., Baudrillard 1983, 1991b) and **J.G. Ballard** (Baudrillard 1991a). Yet even sf is not radical enough to describe the contemporary world: "the 'good old' SF imagination is dead, and … something else is beginning to emerge (and not only in fiction, but also in theory). Both traditional SF and theory are destined to the same fate: flux and imprecision are putting an end to them as specific genres" (Baudrillard 1991b: 309). His theorizing around simulation and the simulacra – copies with no originals – was of particular interest to sf critics working on cyberpunk and notions of the virtual, although a 1991 forum on his work in *Science Fiction Studies* was largely hostile. He is situated among a cluster of intellectuals who can be described as postmodern – alongside Jean-François Lyotard and Fredric Jameson (the latter also a major figure in sf theory and criticism) – but it is perhaps better to situate Baudrillard as part of a tradition of French intellectuals who take popular culture seriously.

Roland Barthes, for example, wrote a series of magazine articles (collected in *Mythologies* (1957)) examining such topics as Einstein's brain, steak and chips, and soap advertisements. Reversing the order of analysis from Saussurean structuralism, Barthes argued that the first level of the sign is produced when a signifier (a means of representation, such as a word, a sound, a photograph, a road sign) and a signified (a concept such as "cat," "warning: left turn ahead") come together on the level of denotation. In Barthes's own example, a photograph of a black soldier is a representation of that soldier. But there is a second level, in which that sign becomes another signifier with a further, more political, level of signification – connotation. The black soldier becomes symbolic of French colonial policy, assimilation, and the upholding of the status quo. The first stage of the sign is language, the second is myth and is associated with the ideological justification of the state of the contingent world as natural and inevitable. This notion of myth is very suggestive of the way Baudrillard looks at images and simulacra.

Jacques Derrida also built on and modified structuralism, noting how one signifier (e.g., "cat") represents many signifieds (e.g., "feline," "domestic animal," "whip," "catalytic converter," and so on) but communication and criticism tend to reduce this to a one-to-one relationship. A deconstructive reading is open to the multiplicity of meanings and the other signifier–signified relationships that have been ignored or suppressed. He notes that when Plato's *Phaedrus* describes writing as a *pharmakon*, the word means both "poison" and "cure," although previous commentary mainly focused on "poison." It is not that Derrida reverses the standard interpretation, but that the dominant reading of a text has a shadow interpretation which may be seen to be at odds with the author's (possibly assumed) intention; the meaning of the terms is modified by this multiple reading. Derrida's work is also part of an attempt to break with the Western metaphysical tradition that began with Plato and that opposes the categories of being to nonbeing, presence to nonpresence (or absence), truth to falsehood. These (non-)oppositions become central to Baudrillard's work.

Having studied the German language at the Sorbonne, Baudrillard became a German teacher at a school from 1958 to 1966. His doctorate, at Université de Paris-X Nanterre under the French philosopher Henri Lefebvre, was in sociology. Baudrillard was to teach the subject at Nanterre, which was then a new, radical university and played a part in the student uprising of May 1968. The uprising failed because the unions and the communists failed to rally round, and this sense of betrayal became a watershed moment in French intellectual circles; thereafter some apparently turned their back on Marxist ideas, whereas others – such as Jean-Luc Godard – became more radicalized. Baudrillard felt that Marxism did not go far enough in its attack on capitalism; the Marxist Frankfurt School noted how the operations of capitalism meant that people were increasingly controlled by commodities, but this was not as apocalyptic as Baudrillard's worldview.

Baudrillard argues that capitalism is "the limitless rule of exchange value" (Baudrillard 2001b: 94). Socialism, Marxism, and communism emphasize use value – the utility of things – over exchange value, but this ideology is not enough to destroy capitalism. Capitalism's machinations are hidden by mythology, most obviously in the "*evil genius of advertising*" (Baudrillard 2001a: 134) which intervenes in the gap between signifier and signified. The contemporary state of the media is such that a new epoch has begun: "Western rationality has always been based, as regards discourse, upon the criteria of truth and falsehood" (Baudrillard 2001d: 71). It is not that everything is false – although Baudrillard suggests that everything in politics is faked – but that the staging has become so widespread that truth no longer has any meaning.

For Baudrillard, the history of representation has gone through four stages. The good appearance, in which a signifier is a reflection of reality, was followed by the bad appearance, which masks reality, for example in faking an event. Third, an element of sorcery enters representation, in that the images mask an absence of reality; Baudrillard suggests that iconoclasts overturn imagery of (absent) gods who may not exist. Finally, there is the simulacrum, the hyperreal, which bears no relation to any reality: the copy with no original, the model, the opinion poll, the virtual, the fear of crime, and the theme park. Baudrillard argues that "Disneyland is there to conceal the fact that it is the 'real' country, all of 'real' America, which is Disneyland … Disneyland is presented as imaginary in order to make us believe that the rest is real, when in fact all of Los Angeles and the America surrounding it are no longer real, but of the order of the hyperreal and of simulation" (Baudrillard 1983: 25). He goes on to describe a fly-on-the-wall documentary about a family and the breakdown of the central couple's marriage. The presence of cameras must have changed events, but it was filmed as if the crew were not there, offering "an aesthetics of the hyperreal, a thrill of vertiginous and phony exactitude, a thrill of alienation and of magnification" (Baudrillard 1983: 50). Meanwhile the family do not watch television, television watches them. It is not a spectacle: the spectacular has been abolished in favor of the banal.

In the age of the simulacra, in which there is no longer a coherent, convincing justificatory worldview to trust (what Lyotard calls a "metanarrative"), the exchanges of capitalism dominate everything and the "human race has dropped out of history" (Baudrillard 2001c: 122). Events no longer have causes or consequences. There is no room here for desire – in fact Baudrillard argues that the sexual liberation of the 1960s has accomplished more repression than did "puritanical repression" (Baudrillard 2001e: 65). There is only the banality of consumption and exchange. The subject has disintegrated under the impact of the media onslaught – and Baudrillard uses Richard Kongrosian, a character in Philip K. Dick's *The Simulacra* (1964), to exemplify this (Baudrillard 1988).

In the age of the suicide bomber, aggressor and victim, hostage and terrorist become interchangeable. In the 1991 Gulf War – which Baudrillard discussed in three articles in *Libération* (Baudrillard 1995) – the imbalance between the combatants was so great that it could not be called a war. The Americans never quite came face to face with the Iraqis, whilst they had so many bombs to use that they ran out of targets. Saddam Hussein's palace guard disappeared, as it were, in a puff of smoke, while US generals gathered their intelligence from CNN news coverage. The dictator who was to remain in power for a further decade, CNN, and the weapons manufacturers all profited from war. (Of course, anyone who had direct experience of combat, rather than as mediated events, would likely have a rather different view of them.)

In contrast to the banal nonevent of the Gulf War, for Baudrillard the attacks on the World Trade Center and Pentagon of 11 September 2001 were an absolute event. With the targets being signifiers for globalization and capitalism, and the perception of Islam as offering a force of resistance (as socialism and Marxism had meant to offer), there is space to read 9/11 as a blow *for* freedom *against* capitalism and symbolic exchange. But it can also be read as "*the delusion of a visible confrontation*" (Baudrillard 2002: 11) in which the towers collapse under their own symbolism, and in which globalization attacks itself. In the meantime, the people themselves seem to virtualize events, without the need for media intervention.

Istvan Csicsery-Ronay Jr argues that Baudrillard (and **Donna Haraway**, another science-fictional theorist) "seduc[e] us to shift our gaze and see our place in a world we have made but have not yet recognized" (Csicsery-Ronay 1991: 401). Baudrillard is open to charges of denying reality and embracing irrationalism, of writing obscure prose, and of not being serious enough as a philosopher. Equally, following his rejection of socialism – in part occasioned by May 1968 and subsequent elections in Europe through the 1970s – it is hard to see what the solution to the crisis he describes might be. More recently, Baudrillard has gained a new cachet of cool through the appearance of his book *Simulacra and Simulation* (1981) in *The Matrix* (Wachowski brothers 1999), a film which Baudrillard himself has denounced as misrepresenting his thought (although see Constable 2009).

See also: **J.G. Ballard, Samuel R. Delany, Philip K. Dick, Donna J. Haraway, and Darko Suvin**

Bibliography

Barthes, R. (1973) *Mythologies*, trans. A. Lavers, London: Paladin.

Baudrillard, J. (1983) *Simulations*, trans. P. Patton, P. Foss, and P. Beitchman, New York: Semiotext(e).

——(1988) *The Ecstasy of Communication*, trans. B. and C. Schutze, ed. S. Lotringer, New York: Semiotext(e).

——(1991a) "Ballard's *Crash*," *Science Fiction Studies*, 18(3): 313–20.

——(1991b) "Simulacra and Science Fiction," *Science Fiction Studies*, 18(3): 309–13.

——(1995) *The Gulf War Did Not Take Place*, trans. and ed. P. Patton, Sydney: Power.

——(2001a) "Barbara Kruger," in G. Genosko (ed.) *The Uncollected Baudrillard*, London and Thousand Oaks, CA: Sage.

——(2001b) "The Divine Left," in G. Genosko (ed.) *The Uncollected Baudrillard*, London and Thousand Oaks, CA: Sage.

——(2001c) "Dropping out of History: an interview with Sylvere Lotringer," in G. Genosko (ed.) *The Uncollected Baudrillard*, London and Thousand Oaks, CA: Sage.

——(2001d) "Mass (Sociology of)," in G. Genosko (ed.) *The Uncollected Baudrillard*, London and Thousand Oaks, CA: Sage.

——(2001e) "Power and Play," in G. Genosko (ed.) *The Uncollected Baudrillard*, London and Thousand Oaks, CA: Sage.

——(2002) *The Spirit of Terrorism: and requiem for the twin towers*, trans. C. Turner, London: Verso.

Constable, C. (2009) *Philosophy as Adaptation: Jean Baudrillard and the Matrix trilogy*, Manchester: Manchester University Press.

Csicsery-Ronay Jr, I. (1991) "The SF of Theory: Baudrillard and Haraway," *Science Fiction Studies*, 18(3): 387–404.

Derrida, J. (1981) "Plato's Pharmacy," in *Disseminations*, Chicago: University of Chicago Press.

ANDREW M. BUTLER

GREG[ORY DALE] BEAR (1951–)

US fiction writer.

Greg Bear has published over 20 novels and collections, garnered multiple awards, and been judged one of the field's dominant writers, and yet his work has been difficult to place. For example, "Petra" (1982) was included in Bruce Sterling's *Mirrorshades* (1986) anthology, and *Blood Music* (1985) helped invent the language and conceptual terrain for nanotechnology, so both were considered cyberpunk texts. Cyberpunk was anarchistic, libertarian, and self-consciously literary. At the same time, however, Bear was associated with a group of Californian hard sf writers, including Jerry Pournelle, Larry Niven, and Gregory Benford, who were typically situated on the right. Pournelle formed the Citizen Advisory Panel on National Space Policy, which delivered a report, *Mutual Assured Survival* (1984), to President Reagan that argued for the imperative to militarize space and pursue Project High Frontier (soon to be known as "Star Wars"). Bear signed this report and added an appendix entitled "Conversion," in which he offered himself as typical of many modern liberals who had realized that the militarization of space offered much promise.

Bear's fiction can be linked together by one persistent concern: catastrophe. His novels repeatedly stage end times or the catastrophic transformation of humanity into new conditions of being. Early in his career the catastrophe was predominantly nuclear. Bear's second novel, *Psychlone* (1979), opens with an apparently unmotivated epigraph that simply reads "8.16 a.m., August 6th, 1945." This date of the atomic explosion over Hiroshima prefaces all versions of Bear's catastrophism. *Psychlone* uses the Gothic register to figure the legacy of Hiroshima. Frenzied fatal attacks erupt in small-town American locales, one incident wiping out an entire town in gruesome forms of torture and death. These transpire to be murderous hauntings, visitations from a psychic residue of American soldiers imprisoned in Hiroshima in August 1945. Within the folkloric logic of hauntings, vengeance is visited upon those who have actively suppressed history. In an escalation that will become familiar in Bear's fiction, the attacks intensify in rage. It is left to a group of misfit parapsychologists to express the greater horror at the new secret weapon that annihilates the last residues of these tortured souls but which also inaugurates a weapon that can erase all natural and supernatural traces of the human. There is a chilly closure in *Psychlone*: a worse catastrophe awaits.

In *Eon* (1985), the record of a nuclear war that annihilates 2.5 billion people is one of the shocking revelations hidden inside The Stone, an anomalous object that appears in orbit around the Earth, having arrived from a possible human future. The library includes a volume called *Brief History of the Death*, composed in 2135, detailing a history that the first emissaries to The Stone realize is weeks away from beginning. The cool objectivity of the historical account of the Death contrasts with the sublime subjective experience of nuclear annihilation at the climax of *The Forge of God* (1987), in which the last two characters on Earth await death in Yosemite Park as chains of hydrogen bombs are triggered along Earth's tectonic plates. While the Earth recovers in *Eon*, *The Forge of God* annihilates it completely. The Second World War's nuclear apocalypse still dominates an intergalactic twenty-fourth century in *Beyond Heaven's River* (1980), in which the human test subject used to decide whether the species is appropriate for the next stage of evolutionary development is a Japanese military pilot, plucked from 1942.

The second form of catastrophe explored by Bear is the notion of the technological Singularity. This is the moment when technological advance reaches a point of transformation beyond any hope of human control, typically envisaged in terms of machines reaching a level of intelligence sufficient to produce other machines. The Singularity is promissory, designed not so much to predict the future as to accelerate the pace of contemporary investments or anxieties. Bear rehearses numerous catastrophic Singularities in his fiction, but his best-known work is *Blood Music* because it occupied the interval between fact and fiction in nascent biotechnological engineering in the early 1980s to such dramatic effect. It starts in the high-tech private research companies of Silicon Valley, in a company exploring Medically Applicable Biochips at the nano-level where technological and biological engineering converge. A dysfunctional lab researcher, Vergil I. Ulam (an anagram of "I am Gulliver"), manufactures human cells with the ability to program and reprogram segments of their DNA. His ethical breach discovered, Ulam injects the cells into his body to smuggle them out of the lab. His transformation begins as the new cells reproduce, cluster, and develop a group intelligence, subtly rebuilding their host before reaching the threshold of consciousness and exploding the human form. Ulam is killed before this proceeds very far, but nanotechnological emissaries beyond his body ensure viral transmission and rapid multiplication across America. The tour de force of the book is a description of New York dis-articulated and re-composed as a single bio-mass, witnessed by a lone survivor from the heights of the World Trade Center.

Bear pursues the double meaning of "apocalypse." Often taken as a synonym for "disaster" or "catastrophe," its original meaning was "revelation" or "disclosure," an unveiling of a secret, and in the Christian tradition an ecstatic vision of last things that promises a new epoch: kingdom come. *Blood Music* engineers a further stage of nano-evolution, in which the concentrations of consciousness in the "noösphere" reach a second Singularity and vanish from the material world to be distributed into the informational flows of the universe itself. Individuals can be reconstructed at will in this sphere, yet the last survivors of the individualized point of view in the novel experience an ecstatic subsumption into the immortal race-memory of DNA codings (the blood music of the title), and willingly embrace the posthuman. *Blood Music* is quintessential sf in its final vision of the transcendence of human biological limits that arrives at a numinous language precisely *through* its adherence to hard science. Its catastrophism pulls utopia from the dystopian disaster by recalibrating perception away from the human scale.

The third catastrophe explored by Bear is Darwinian. Recent evolutionary theory can be crudely divided between gradualism and catastrophism. Gradualism is the strictly Darwinian stance, regarding evolution as a blind process unfolding through a lengthy series of accidental variations. In the 1970s, however, a new scientific account of catastrophism emerged, mainly associated with Stephen Jay Gould's theory of "punctuated equilibrium." Using biological and geological evidence, Gould proposed that the eons of relatively stable development might be interrupted by sudden catastrophic periods of evolutionary change, perhaps from massive environmental shifts. *Darwin's Radio* (1999) is set in a near future that experiences the onset of the catastrophic beginnings of a human species change. Pregnant women appear to contract a virus that causes them to abort. Within thirty days, they are spontaneously pregnant again, only this time with deformed fetuses. In the sequel, *Darwin's Children* (2003), a new generation of beings emerges. The outbreak is initially understood as a disease, but a diverse group of scientists begin to explore the notion that this is speciation produced by retroviral elements incorporated into human DNA that have lain dormant for millennia. This "code-key" has responded to the stress on human biology and caused a sudden adaptation of the genome. These biological changes are therefore either a kind of maladaptive stress response or else a properly adaptive response to the new conditions of late modernity, "not a disease, but an upgrade" (Bear 1999: 201).

Even while Bear wants to educate his readers with extrapolations from the advanced fronts of current work on molecular strategies of biological evolution or the transmission of human endogenous retroviruses, *Darwin's Radio* and *Darwin's Children* are impressive novels because they are fully realized portraits of the social embeddedness of scientific practice. His catastrophism is not worked out in isolated laboratories, but offers a complex social portrait of species change. This story is overdetermined by weaving together government security agencies, Senate hearings, journalistic scoops, scientific conferences, anthropologists in difficult disputes over artifacts in Native American territories, private drug companies competing for patents, disease control agencies, and the pressure of the evangelical Christian right. This is a matrix in which we encounter the social, scientific, and cultural consequences of catastrophism as all of a piece.

Since September 2001, America has not needed to resort to the imagination of disaster to grasp the risks of modernity. Bear's recent work carries its own marks of this catastrophe too. *Vitals* (2002) starts from the premise that humans could be considered a large, motile colony of bacteria. The book undergoes a kind of generic catastrophism, changing from sf premises to a slick international thriller undergirded by a conspiracy theory plot that rewrites twentieth-century history. A Soviet scientist, under Stalin's sanction in the 1930s, developed the means to "tag" individuals with bacteria, allowing them to be controlled by government agents. The manufactured bacteria are spread through modified *E. coli* globally by 1945, so that theoretically anyone can now be "switched on" and controlled. This is not a partisan Cold War thriller, since the scientist transfers his experiments to the heart of Manhattan in the 1950s with American sanction, and the security state now runs a biologically "tagged" President.

Vitals is an anxious and paranoid vision of the American polity, revealing an ongoing political catastrophe engineered by scientists who are portrayed almost universally as lunatics. This is a hybrid novel for the catastrophic ambiguities of a post-9/11 America – not just of the attack itself, but the traumas of so-called "homeland security" measures. *Quantico* (2005) is more squarely behind the agencies of the security state, generating a fiction of future attacks not from the model of the World Trade Center but from the enigmatic cases of anthrax poisoning that convulsed America in October and November 2001. Bear envisages a bio-terrorism that has catastrophic global consequences, unleashing uncontainable bacterial agents to multiply in the atmosphere. The book seems to concur with security state measures.

Dead Lines (2004) might also be read as a 9/11 fiction. Here, a new generation of mobile phones uses a previously unknown source of bandwidth. This is also the zone where the dead reside, and the handsets become portals for their ghostly return. This invasion accelerates to catastrophic levels. The book is also an impressive account of a man haunted by traumatic loss and given the ambiguous prospect of recovering his dead daughter. As the ripples of this technological catastrophe move out from the valley homes of Los Angeles, the book evokes a nation confronting malignant spectral forms.

One final way of traversing Bear's catastrophe fiction is to reflect on its possible relationships to Christian eschatology, the way of reading catastrophes as signs of the onset of the "Tribulations." In this discourse, the breakdown of law and order can be regarded as the beginning of the rule of Satan or as the first indications that the righteous are soon to be lifted from the Earth in the Rapture. As a hard sf writer, one would expect Bear to be a strong advocate of rationalist science. The provocatively titled *The Forge of God* is excoriating about the President's passive, apocalyptic interpretation of the message from the aliens that the world is to end: his delusion leaves him sidelined with his spiritual advisor whilst his rational underlings attempt resolution. Yet Bear often reaches for a transcendence that inheres in catastrophe, and religious elements do appear in Bear's disasters. The idea of the Rapture, the few thousand of the truly Saved, hovers about those who survive nuclear annihilation in both *Eon* and *The Forge of God*. In *Blood Music*, the scientist doomed to experiment on his own transformed body parallels his contact with the noösphere to that of an initiate inspired by God. From *Psychlone* to *Dead Lines* the living are haunted by tortured souls in fictions that openly acknowledge a spiritual realm that subtends the material world. In this regard too, then, Bear is a remarkable echo box for contemporary American catastrophism.

See also: **Isaac Asimov, Alfred Bester, Leigh Brackett, Octavia Butler, Samuel R. Delany, William Gibson, Robert A. Heinlein, Frank Herbert, Ursula K. Le Guin, C.L. Moore, Kim Stanley Robinson, Joanna Russ, Neal Stephenson, Sheri S. Tepper, James Tiptree Jr, and Gene Wolfe**

Bibliography

Bear, G. (1999) *Darwin's Radio*, London: HarperCollins UK.
Hatfield, L. (1990) "The Galaxy within: paradox and synecdoche as heuristic tropes in Greg Bear's science fiction," *Extrapolation*, 31(3): 240–57.
Palmer, C. (2006) "Big Dumb Objects in Science Fiction: subliminity, banality and modernity," *Extrapolation*, 47(1): 95–111.
Vorda, A. (1990) "The Forging of Science Fiction: an interview with Greg Bear," *Extrapolation*, 31(3): 197–215.

ROGER LUCKHURST

ALFRED BESTER (1913–87)

US writer, comic-book writer, and editor.

Alfred Bester had a sporadic but important relationship with sf in a career that included writing comic books (*Superman*, *Green Lantern*), radio plays (*Charlie Chan*, *The Shadow*, *Nero Wolfe*), and for *Holiday* magazine, where he served as senior editor from 1963 to 1971. It was within sf, however, that he both began and ended his wide-ranging writing career; although his participation in the genre is moderate measured in page numbers, his innovative use of genre tropes and his attention to wordplay has had a lasting influence. In 1988 the Science Fiction Writers of America recognized his contribution with a Grand Master Award.

From the beginning, Bester's participation in the field was charmed. His first published short story, "The Broken Axiom," appeared in *Thrilling Wonder Stories* (April 1939) after winning an amateur story competition. His first novel, *The Demolished Man* (magazine serialization 1952, in book form 1953), won the first Hugo for Best Novel. Much of Bester's reputation is based on this and another novel, *The Stars My Destination* (magazine serialization 1956–57, as *Tiger! Tiger!*, 1956, also in book form as *The Stars My Destination* 1957).

The Demolished Man is one-part sf and one-part detective story, seasoned heavily with Freudian theory and garnished with playful semiotics, especially the graphic representation of word sounds. Recounting the saga of Ben Reich's obsession with his business rival D'Courtney, the novel explores the complications of planning a murder in a world populated by telepaths. Reich believes he must murder D'Courtney or risk financial ruin, but the alert reader will notice from the opening chapter that the answer received to the offer to merge – WWHG – is the code for "accept merger"; yet Reich insists the merger was refused and launches the plot – and his own inevitable demolition (the erasure of his psyche and reprogramming as a new individual). The novel is ultimately more interested in the psychopathology of the individual – Reich's nightmares of The Man With No Face, his insistence on reading the material world through this pathology – than it is with solving the murder mystery. It demonstrates Bester's talent for meticulously working through his imagined worlds and for pushing the boundaries of what sf might do. The conversations among telepaths, for example, are presented as a sort of concrete poetry, visually straining the limits of text to show overlapping and intersecting oral and mental exchanges, anticipating later postmodern experiments such as Mark Danielewski's *House of Leaves* (2000). The management of telepaths of various levels via early training and a eugenics program seems to have inspired the creation by **J. Michael Straczynski** of the Psi Corps in *Babylon 5* (1994–98), and of course Walter Koenig's villainous character Al Bester pays direct homage to this novel and its creator.

The Stars My Destination, which introduced into our vocabulary the term "jaunting" for teleportation, is a reworking of Alexandre Dumas' *The Count of Monte Cristo* (1844–45) and was adapted as a graphic novel by Howard Chaykin in 1979. Space merchant marine Gully Foyle is judged the "stereotype Common Man" by his personnel evaluation, a man of "physical strength and intellectual potential stunted by lack of ambition" (Bester 1991: 18). This changes when he is marooned in his ship, *Nomad*. The pivotal moment for Gully is not his experience of surviving this period of isolation but rather of being wrongly abandoned by the ally ship, *Vorga-T 1339*, which sees him but chooses to leave him there. Gully transforms himself into a single-minded agent of revenge, who in short order rescues himself, finds a way to attack the *Vorga* (later recognizing that his true target should be the captain who made the decision, and even later focusing his attack on the owner who commanded the captain), escapes from prison, appropriates the *Nomad*'s secret cargo of PyrE (a substance able to release energy catalyzed by thought), attains great riches, and finally confronts the heir to the Presteign fortune, Olivia, who owned the ship and gave the order to leave him. Like *The Demolished Man*, this novel is driven more by character than by plot, focusing on Gully's distorted personality. He is described as a "remorseless, lecherous, treacherous, kindless villain" (Bester 1991: 119) by one of those he ruins in his quest for revenge, a line taken from *Hamlet* (c. 1601); yet Hamlet speaks this line when berating himself for procrastinating, while Gully is defined by his leap into vengeance. The allusion encourages us to think complexly about the relationship between character and action. For all its emphasis on character *The Stars My Destination* is also a frantically paced and action-packed caper. The novel is ambivalent about obsession: Gully repents, says the tiger in him is now gone, and insists upon releasing the secret of PyrE despite the potential danger, defending the rights of Common Men to make their own choices and decisions. Yet we cannot help but admire all that Gully achieves through his obsession. Bester experiments with narrative form in a sequence in which Gully experiences synaesthesia, using typographic wordplay to convey sound and sensation as vision.

The best of Bester's short fiction demonstrates playfulness with conventional sf motifs and plots. "Disappearing Act" (1953) investigates the mystery of soldiers who disappear from a hospital ward and reappear in various historical settings. Anachronisms alert the reader to the fact that this is not conventional time travel, and it is eventually revealed they travel to a past of their own imagining, a dream made material reality. War propaganda insists: "We are not fighting for ourselves, but for our Dreams; for the Better Things in Life which must not disappear from the face of the earth" (Bester 1997b: 7). The story concludes when the general sends for the last in a number of narrowly trained experts to solve the crisis: a poet. He finds none exist in this America, "a tool chest of hardened and sharpened specialists" (Bester 1997b: 21).

"Fondly Fahrenheit" (1954) plays with **Isaac Asimov**'s Three Laws of Robotics. An android and his master flee various locations, leaving bodies and murder investigations behind. The master laments owning a valuable yet homicidal android, but the android sometimes announces its directives prevent it from harming human life. The rather prosaic answer to the murder mystery is that the android malfunctions above a certain temperature; yet Bester does something more complex with the story. It is a tale not just of technological malfunction but also of psychotic projection. The android commits the murders, but the desire may originate with the owner. The conflation of psyches is conveyed by shifting use of pronouns, moving in and out of a first person that is sometimes android and sometimes man, producing intriguing sentences such as "He wept and counted his money and I beat the android again" (Bester 1997c: 98). Bester adapted this story for television as "Murder and the Android," which aired on *Sunday Showcase* on 18 October 1959 and was nominated for the 1960 Hugo for Best Dramatic Presentation.

Although most of Bester's work is written in an upbeat tone, it is also ironic and at times dark. The endings are generally optimistic, but often the future the characters desire is different from the one they experience. Nowhere is this more apparent than in "Adam and No Eve" (1941), which begins with the conventional plot of a scientist designing a prototype rocket that promises grand discoveries but portends disaster: it will destroy all life on Earth if just one drop of its fuel falls back to Earth. The technocratic hero insists that his design is failsafe, but in Bester's work technology is not infallible. Crashed on Earth after a malfunction, the injured scientist crawls toward the ocean, desperately trying to stay ahead of the fire encircling the globe as he reflects on the end of his life. The conclusion remains upbeat, however, as he realizes that although he will not survive, life on the planet in the form of amoeba and bacteria will flourish on his dying flesh and life will begin anew. Similarly, "The Devil's Invention" (1950, also published as "Oddy and Id"), the story of a good-luck prone boy, insists it is a story about a monster; the reality his luck materializes reflects the selfish desires of his id, not the more altruistic ones he espouses. "The Roller Coaster" (1953) begins uncomfortably with "I knifed her a little" (Bester 2000: 238), the voice of a time-traveling protagonist who journeys to the past to experience the thrill of brute emotions and violence, not "to explore or study or any of that science fiction crap. Our time's an amusement park to them, that's all. Like the roller coaster" (Bester 2000: 247).

Bester's work is flawed by misogyny – Gully rapes the first woman who threatens his plans and is "redeemed" when he meets a woman like himself and is horrified by the tiger in her; Barbara D'Courtney is put through a process of infantilization which ends with her marrying the police captain who stood in for her father; and Gretchen, the warrior princess heroine of *Golem*^{100} (1980), indulges in a sexual frenzy as part of a ritual to choose a new "queen bee" that ends with her killing her final lover when she rips his penis off with her vulva. Bester is at his most conventional when dealing with gender and at his best when defying conventions and pushing sf toward greater maturity.

His story "5,271,009" (1954, also published as "The Star Comber") might be read as an analogy for his relationship to sf. The mysteriously powered Mr Aquila must purge artist Jeffrey Halsyon of his childish regression so that he may become a great artist. Aquila accomplishes this by allowing Halsyon to live out fantasies that are stereotypical of the worst sf: he is the last fertile man on Earth required to service 5,271,009 virgins; he is the one man with the secret knowledge (that two comes before three, not *after*) required to save Earth from the evil Grssh; he is returned to his childhood body with the knowledge of an adult; and he is the last man on Earth compelled to restart civilization with the last woman, the beautiful daughter of the well-meaning but careless scientist who ended human life in the first place. In each case, the material reality proves far less appealing than the fantasy, culminating in Halsyon shooting himself in the head in front of the beautiful daughter as she is not a dentist and he suffers from a toothache. When such fantasies no longer compel Halsyon, Aquila asserts that Halsyon is ready to be an artist because "A man cannot start making adult decisions until he has purged himself of the dreams of childhood" (Bester 1997a: 87), insisting: "It is you, the artists, who must lead them out as I have led you. I purge you; now you purge them" (Bester 1997a: 88). The title refers to the number of decisions a man makes in his life – childish or otherwise – as well as the number of virgins in the fantasy.

Bester's best work strives to purge us of our childish fantasies and to create sf as an adult genre; sadly, his later works – *The Computer Connection* (serialized as *The Indian Giver* 1974–75, book 1975, also published as *Extro*), *Golem^{100}*, and *The Deceivers* (1981) are examples of childish fantasy and stereotypical pulp writing, although even in these inferior works he continues to push the boundaries of text as a medium, incorporating musical lyrics, pictures, and other graphical elements. His lasting influence can be seen in the difference between the Golden Age sf that was dominant when he began his career and the more literary and inner-worlds oriented sf of the New Wave and beyond. Although his work has received little critical attention, Bester must be recognized as one of the pioneers who early saw the potential for sf to be an innovative genre in terms of both form and content.

See also: **Isaac Asimov, Greg Bear, Leigh Brackett, Octavia Butler, Samuel R. Delany, Philip K. Dick, William Gibson, Robert A. Heinlein, Frank Herbert, L. Ron Hubbard, Ursula K. Le Guin, C.L. Moore, Kim Stanley Robinson, Joanna Russ, Neal Stephenson, J. Michael Straczynski, Sheri S. Tepper, James Tiptree Jr, and Gene Wolfe**

Bibliography

Bester, A. (1991) *Tiger! Tiger!* [1956], London: Mandarin.

——(1997a) "5,271,009," in *Virtual Unrealities: the short fiction of Alfred Bester* [1954], New York: Vintage.

——(1997b) "Disappearing Act," in *Virtual Unrealities: the short fiction of Alfred Bester* [1954], New York: Vintage.

——(1997c) "Fondly Fahrenheit," in *Virtual Unrealities: the short fiction of Alfred Bester* [1954], New York: Vintage.

——(2000) "The Roller Coaster," in *Redemolished* [1953], New York: ibooks, inc.
Blackmore, T. (1990) "The Bester/Chaykin Connection: an examination of substance assisted by style," *Extrapolation*, 31(2): 101–24.
McCarthy, P.A. (1983) "Science Fiction as Creative Revisionism: the example of Alfred Bester's *The Stars My Destination*," *Science Fiction Studies*, 10(1): 58–69.

SHERRYL VINT

LEIGH [DOUGLASS] BRACKETT (1915–78)

US novelist, short-story writer, and scriptwriter.

Leigh Brackett was one of a handful of women associated with early American sf. She is one of the only ones remembered for writing space opera, which she began doing for the pulp magazines in the early 1940s, when it was popular but looked down upon by many writers and editors. The tenacity and volume of her writing in this subgenre led to her being given the title the "Queen" of space opera. A consummate science-fantasist, she is remembered for her very visual picture of Mars and Venus and for Eric John Stark, the maverick, part-native hero she created to wander the solar system. Through the repackaging of her classic science fantasy, especially her Stark stories of the 1950s, Brackett contributed to the new traditions in, and revival of, space opera in the 1970s, though she was at odds with emerging feminist approaches to sf.

Brackett grew up in California. Her diverse and prolific career spanned from the 1940s, her period of greatest activity in the sf magazines, until her death. Her first story, the realistic "Martian Quest" (1940), was written for *Astounding Science-Fiction*, but she moved on to writing space opera for the pulp magazines *Planet Stories*, *Startling Stories*, and *Thrilling Wonder Stories*, scripts for Hollywood thrillers and westerns (notably for Howard Hawks), hard-boiled detective stories and novels, television scripts, and updating her Stark stories for 1970s audiences. At the time of her death, she had drafted the screenplay for *Star Wars: Episode V – The Empire Strikes Back* (Kershner 1980), for which she posthumously received a Hugo in 1981. She is often (perhaps overly) discussed in the context of her marriage to Edmond Hamilton, a popular author of classic space opera.

Brackett's rendering of Mars was inspired by Edgar Rice Burroughs's Mars stories, of which she was a voracious reader, and to a lesser extent by Rudyard Kipling, H. Rider Haggard, and A. Merritt. Like Burroughs, Brackett drew from American frontier mythology to represent Mars as a far more ancient planet than Earth, a planet whose "civilized" period had long since passed. First appearing in *Planet Stories* in 1949, Brackett's Stark is a forerunner to the morally ambivalent frontier heroes of westerns in the 1960s. Whereas Burroughs's John Carter embodies unambiguously American cultural superiority over the declining civilization of Barsoom (Mars), Stark is introduced as a mercenary with ambiguous allegiances. A human raised by the indigenes of Mercury in a semi-savage state, Stark is captured while still a child by human colonists who display him in a cage like a zoo animal, before he is rescued and civilized by Simon Ashton, who works for an agency implicated in the administration of Earth's interplanetary empire. With his allegiances thus divided between his savage adopted tribe and his civilizing foster-father, Stark is as likely to take the side of the indigenous inhabitants of Mars and Venus as that of the colonizers. For example, in "Queen of the Martian Catacombs" (1949), Stark exposes the plot of a Martian chieftain to install himself in a puppet government propped up by colonial "outlanders." In "The Enchantress of Venus" (1949), Stark searches for a friend who has disappeared and finds himself entangled in the attempts of the declining ruling class to maintain their tyrannical hold over the people of Shuruun. In both cases, Stark is offered the opportunity to rule at the side of a conniving princess if he will only prop up her rule, and he refuses.

Stark is a complex character, haunted by his primitive upbringing and suffering from frequent flashbacks to his childhood, when, as N'Chaka, he lived in a state of constant vigilance. Civilization has not completely supplanted the primitive part of his character, which surfaces during moments of threat. Stark frequently feels fear, a sensation linked to his primitivity – but one which gives him an advantage by enabling him to respond to threats with the instinctive speed of an agile, wild animal. Brackett further figures Stark as racially mixed, his skin burnt "dark" by the hot sun of his home planet Mercury.

Martian romantic exotica also flourished in Brackett's "Black Amazon of Mars" (1951), "The Last Days of Shandakor" (1952), and "The Arc of Mars" (1953), at a time when most sf visions of Mars moved away from romance to take on new, realistic overtones as a result of scientific investigations. Brackett's sf and her hero Stark had already expanded into other worlds – mainly Venus, notably in "Lorelei of the Red Mist" (1946, with Ray Bradbury), "The Moon that Vanished" (1948), and "Enchantress of Venus."

Contrary to the common view that she moved away from the genre after the 1950s, Brackett continued to publish and reprint sf and science fantasy for the rest of her life. She always claimed that she wrote what she loved to read. Sf alone, she said, allowed a "soaring freedom of the imagination," but for money, she added, she wrote in other fields (Mallardi and Bowers 1969: 19–20).

In the 1940s and 1950s the reception of Brackett's space opera was mixed; it was praised for its rich settings and imaginative fantasy, but also found derivative and simplistic. Anxious to legitimize a disreputable pulp genre, sf critics have long deployed space opera and science fantasy as the "other" of sf, constructing a canon purportedly based on scientific accuracy. By these standards, the big winner for Brackett was her postapocalyptic, non-space-opera "legitimate" sf epic *The Long Tomorrow* (1955), which received rave reviews – for its realism, serious subject matter, and literary quality – from major critics such as Damon Knight and Anthony Boucher, and more recently John Clute and Brian Stableford. It also garnered Brackett a Hugo nomination. Set a couple of generations after a nuclear apocalypse, it depicts a future America under the sway of Mennonite principles. The Mennonites, a Christian sect that eschews technological development, find themselves in a position of power when technological civilization has been all but destroyed. Blamed for the nuclear apocalypse, advanced technology of all kinds is forbidden. A complex and subtle exploration of the relationship between the technological and the social, *The Long Tomorrow* enabled Brackett to explore issues that the short, sensational pulp format could not comfortably accommodate. It would be a mistake, however, to characterize Brackett as a "serious" writer trapped in the pulps, for she was a lifelong avid fan and defender of the popular.

Brackett revived her Stark series in the 1970s – this time in interstellar space, with *The Ginger Star* (1974), *The Hounds of Skaith* (1974), and *The Reavers of Skaith* (1976) – to good reviews. Paul A. Carter described Skaith as a prime example of the dying planet archetype, and Frederick Patten compared Skaith to J.R.R. Tolkien's Middle-earth. Whereas the earliest Stark tales depicted the Earth-led galactic empire as exploitative of the worlds in its path, the *Skaith* trilogy shifted away from the critique of empire, casting the Galactic Union as liberators. This mirrors the cultural climate in which Brackett was writing, which was in transition from the counterculturalism of the 1960s and polarized by US involvement in Vietnam.

The praise of male editors and critics of the 1970s notwithstanding, Brackett's sf understandably came under the scrutiny of feminist sf critics and anthologists of that decade. In interviews, Brackett spoke warmly about the sf community and denied that gender was an obstacle for her. Tellingly, she once remarked that if she was going to include a woman in one of her stories, she has to be *doing* something, suggesting that Brackett was critical of conventions of female passivity in space opera. If so, she did not confront these conventions, but chose to focus on male-centered adventure stories and maverick heroes such as Stark, in which the most prominent female characters tend to be exotic alien queens or princesses. Not easily fitting the mold of the emerging feminist sf of the 1970s, Brackett (and space opera) were criticized by the likes of **Joanna Russ** and excluded from Pamela Sargent's groundbreaking *Women of Wonder* (1975) anthology. Although Brackett's work made it into Sargent's *More Women of Wonder* (1976), her masculine style and aggressive heroes were emphasized as characteristic of her sf, and the fact that it did not seem to matter to readers that she was a woman was noted (Sargent 1976: xix). In later decades, however, Brackett was reconsidered by feminist critics such as Sargent, who praised her strong female characters.

Despite Brackett's intentionally hard-boiled approach in her sf writing, she capitalizes upon the classic identification between the categories of the alien, the primitive, and the land, which in Western culture have a long tradition of identification with the feminine, to create alien beings and landscapes that function as less obvious, yet potent, sites of identity subversion. For example, "The Woman from Altair" (1951) is told by a man but centered around an alien woman who appears, but turns out to be far from, frail. Similarly, feminine psychic power – the ability to empathize with and assimilate foreign subjects, whether human or alien – is a futuristic manifestation of traditional feminine influence. Psychic or empathetic female characters appear in Brackett's "Mars Minus Bisha" (1954) and *Alpha Centauri – or Die!* (1963). In *Alpha Centauri*, Brackett also describes the chaotic atmosphere aboard a ship, focusing in particular on domesticity in outer space and depicting a woman-led mutiny against the ship's captain.

Yet, despite her impressive accomplishments, Brackett's long, media-spanning career garnered her no sf awards in her lifetime (though she did win the 1957 **Jules Verne** Fantasy Award and the 1963 Western Writers of America Golden Spur Award). Perhaps she was not in the end appreciated in sf circles; no critical studies of her work exist and only one anthology of her sf stories not edited by herself was published during her lifetime: Edmond Hamilton's *The Best of Leigh Brackett* (1977). There are, however, signs that Brackett's reputation is undergoing a revival. **Michael Moorcock** in an anthology of her early stories listed a "who's who" of male sf authors who would count her as an important influence, including himself (Moorcock 2002: xi–xvi). In 2005 she was awarded the Cordwainer Smith Foundation Rediscovery Award. In their 2006 examination of the space opera "renaissance," David Hartwell and Kathryn Cramer remind us that Brackett's contribution to the *Star Wars* franchise established a link between space opera and commercial success. Brackett is also beginning to receive attention as a pioneer of women's sf. It is clear that Leigh Brackett was a prolific, versatile, and thoughtful writer whose space opera and science fantasy stories and books continue to lend themselves to reinterpretation.

See also: **Isaac Asimov, Greg Bear, Alfred Bester, Octavia Butler, Samuel R. Delany, Philip K. Dick, William Gibson, Robert A. Heinlein, Frank Herbert, Nalo Hopkinson, L. Ron Hubbard, Gwyneth Jones, Ursula K. Le Guin, George Lucas, Michael Moorcock, C.L. Moore, Kim Stanley Robinson, Joanna Russ, Mary Shelley, Neal Stephenson, Sheri S. Tepper, James Tiptree Jr, Jules Verne, and Gene Wolfe**

Bibliography

Anon. (1942) "Ps's Feature Flash: Leigh Brackett" *Planet Stories*, 11(1): 39.

Arbur, R. (1982a) *Leigh Brackett, Marion Zimmer Bradley, and Anne McCaffrey: a primary and secondary bibliography*, Boston, MA: G.K. Hall.

——(1982b) "Leigh Brackett: No 'Long Goodbye' Is Good Enough," in T. Staicar (ed.) *The Feminine Eye: science fiction and the women who write it*, New York: Frederick Ungar.

Benson Jr, G. (1986) *Leigh Brackett and Edmond Hamilton: the enchantress and the world wrecker, a working bibliography*, 2nd revised edition, Albuquerque, NM: Galactic Central Bibliographies for the Avid Reader.

Brackett, L. (1975) "Beyond Our Narrow Skies," in L. Brackett (ed.) *The Best of Planet Stories No. 1*, New York: Ballantine.

Carr, J.L. (1982) *Leigh Brackett: American writer*, Polka City, IA: Chris Drumm.

Carter, P.A. (1977) "The Bright Illusion: the feminine mystique in science fiction," in *The Creation of Tomorrow: fifty years of magazine science fiction*, New York: Columbia University Press.

Hamilton, E. (ed.) (1977) *The Best of Leigh Brackett*, New York: Ballantine.

Hartwell, D.G. and Cramer, K. (eds.) (2006) *The Space Opera Renaissance*, New York: Tor.

Mallardi, B. and Bowers, B. (eds.) (1969) "Comment," in *The Double Bill Symposium*, Akron, OH: Double Bill Press.

Moorcock, M. (2002) "Queen of the Martian Mysteries: an appreciation of Leigh Brackett," in L. Brackett, *Martian Quest: the early Brackett*, Royal Oak, MI: Haffner.

Patten, F. (1977) "Review," *Delap's SF Review*, 3(5): 21.
Sargent, P. (ed.) (1976) *More Women of Wonder: science fiction novelettes by women about women*, New York: Vintage.
Schweitzer, D. (1978) "The Amazing Interview: Edmond Hamilton and Leigh Brackett," *Amazing*, 51(2): 116–21, 123.
Stableford, B. (1978) "The Best of Hamilton and Brackett," *Vector: the critical journal of the British Science Fiction Association*, 90: 21–8.

DIANNE NEWELL AND VICTORIA LAMONT

OCTAVIA E[STELLE] BUTLER (1947–2006)

The first significant female African-American sf author.

Never prolific, Octavia E. Butler published 12 novels and one short-story collection over a 35 year career, but many of these are considered classics. She received a Hugo for "Speech Sounds" (1983) and both the Hugo and the Nebula for "Bloodchild" (1984), Nebula nominations for "The Evening and the Morning and the Night" (1987) and *Parable of the Sower* (1993), and a Nebula for *Parable of the Talents* (1998), but her most prestigious recognition came from outside of sf: a MacArthur Foundation "Genius" Grant in 1995 and a PEN West lifetime achievement award in 2000. Butler has been a strong influence on the careers of other black writers, such as **Nalo Hopkinson**, Steven Barnes, and Tananarive Due.

Butler's first short story, "Crossover," was published in 1971, but she came to wider attention with her *Patternist* novels, *Patternmaster* (1976), *Mind of My Mind* (1977), *Survivor* (1978), *Wild Seed* (1980), and *Clay's Ark* (1984). *Patternmaster* is set in a future America where Patternists, humans with psychic powers – including the ability to control weaker Patternists and normal humans – battle Clayarks, the alien descendants of people infected by a virus brought back by humanity's first interstellar expedition. It lacks the strong female and African-American characters who were to become Butler's trademark, but introduces one of her all-consuming themes, power and the difficulty of maintaining self-respect in the face of it. *Mind of My Mind*, set in a near-future America, describes the struggle between Doro – an immortal African telepath who can jump from body to body – and Mary – the final product of Doro's ongoing breeding program – who revolts against her master, establishing her own vision of the future, the Patternists. *Survivor* describes a human space colony, founded by white, fundamentalist Christians who have fled the Patternist/Clayark war on Earth, and the problems of a black child adopted by one of the colonists. *Wild Seed* – the first Patternist novel in terms of internal chronology – details the struggle between Doro, the selfish, body-hopping slaver of *Mind of My Mind*, and Anyanwu, an immortal shapechanger with a superhuman talent for healing. Beginning in eighteenth-century Africa, moving to pre-Civil War Louisiana, and ending in nineteenth-century California, the novel delineates a complex love–hate relationship as Doro learns that he can control Anyanwu but not entirely dominate her. Their relationship bears similarities to that between Rufus and Dana in Butler's pre-Civil War time-travel tale *Kindred* (1979), and Anyanwu is an obvious precursor of the protagonists of *Dawn* (1987), the *Parable* series, and *Fledgling* (2005). All of these characters struggle against oppression, often in the form of powerful individuals who refuse to see them as fully human, sometimes, but not always, because of racial differences, in order to create stable communities. *Clay's Ark* describes the lives of the first humans taken over by the Clayark virus, the first generation of Clayarks, and the futile attempt to prevent the virus from escaping into society. The *Patternist* novels (except *Survivor*) were collected as *Seed to Harvest* (2007).

While Butler was working on *Wild Seed*, she was also writing what is widely considered to be her most important novel, *Kindred*. This is the book which deals most directly with white racism and which is primarily responsible for the respect Butler achieved outside of sf as an explicitly African-American writer. It tells the story of a modern black American, Dana, who finds herself repeatedly thrust back into the antebellum South to save the life of Rufus, the son of a brutal white plantation owner. Heavily influenced, like *Wild Seed*, by the autobiographical narratives of Frederick Douglass and other former slaves, Butler's novel strips away the veneer of romanticism that imbues such popular books about the old South as *Gone with the Wind* (1936), portraying plantation life as brutal and ugly. What ties *Kindred* to Butler's other work is the irony inherent in Dana's relationship with Rufus. Although she despises slavery and the subservient status she must endure even as a free Negro, she soon realizes that she has to help Rufus because he is her direct ancestor. If he dies, she may well cease to exist. Further, in a manner reminiscent of Anyanwu's relationship with Doro, although Dana recognizes that Rufus is a monster, she cannot help sympathizing with his genuine pain and feeling some affection for him. Put into an intolerable situation, she is forced to become a collaborator in order to survive.

The necessity for collaboration with the enemy was much on Butler's mind in the 1980s. The characters in *Clay's Ark* know that the virus with which they have been infected "wants" to spread, but they resist it because they realize that doing so could doom humanity. They are, however, already raising a generation of Clayark children, whom they love. Published in the same year, "Bloodchild" is set on a world where humanity lives in symbiosis with the Tlic, an insectoid species who provide them with extended life and great pleasure; the Tlic truly seem to love their humans. The aliens, however, require that some people allow them to lay eggs in their bodies, an enormously painful and sometimes fatal experience. Although "Bloodchild" has often been interpreted as being about slavery, Butler denied this, insisting that it is a love story.

In 1987 Butler published *Dawn*, the first volume in her *Xenogenesis* trilogy, followed by *Adulthood Rites* (1988) and *Imago* (1989); all three were collected as *Lilith's Brood* (2000). In *Dawn*, Lilith Iyapo, an African-American from our near future, having survived a nuclear war, awakens on a gigantic, living starship. Her alien hosts, the Oankali, tell her that years have passed since the war and that she and other human survivors have been kept in suspended animation while the Oankali repaired the world. Now she is asked to help awaken and train the other survivors in preparation for their return to Earth. There is, however, an enormous catch. The Oankali are gene traders who interbreed with other sentient species, whether their "partners" like it or not. Lilith and the others have been genetically altered to have sex with the aliens and give birth to children, called "constructs," who are half-human and half-Oankali. Needless to say, many people, Lilith included, are distraught about this, but the Oankali, who combine benevolence with an insufferable sense of the rightness of their actions, are adamant. Humans who refuse to interbreed can return to Earth, if they behave, but will be sterile. *Dawn*'s sequels center on Lilith's construct children, and reveal another part of the Oankali plan, the eventual destruction of Earth to create the next generation of living starships. In *Lilith's Brood*, Butler again explores the complex love–hate relationships that evolve in the face of enormous power differentials, this time making implicit use of slave narratives. The Oankali, although more sympathetic and well meaning than either Doro or Rufus, control their human captives more efficiently than any slave owner. Similarities between *Lilith's Brood* and "Bloodchild" are even more obvious. In later years Butler returned to the theme of human–alien sexual collaboration with "Amnesty" (2003) and *Fledgling*.

Butler, who once described herself as "a pessimist if I'm not careful" (Butler 2004), had a long-standing interest in stories about the collapse of civilization. Fear of a possible viral apocalypse hangs over *Clay's Ark*, and nuclear war is the starting point for *Dawn*. The near-future California of "Speech Sounds" is on the verge of collapse because people have lost the ability to understand language. In *Parable of the Sower*, Butler introduces Lauren Olamina, an African-American teenager living in an America tottering on the brink of environmental, moral, and economic disaster. Lauren suffers from hyperempathy syndrome, a crippling capacity to feel the pain of others. Recognizing that her world is out of control, she responds by creating a new religion, Earthseed, which deifies Change itself. Fleeing the destruction of her southern California home, she takes to the very dangerous road, creating her own community and drawing strength from the belief that, although she cannot control Change, she can shape it. Eventually, she founds Acorn, a multiracial utopian community based on the principles of Earthseed. However, in *Parable of the Talents*, much of which is narrated by Lauren's embittered daughter, Larkin, Butler relates the destruction of Acorn by the forces of Christian America, an implicitly racist organization founded by a fundamentalist US president who may, in part, have been modeled on the politically ambitious televangelist Pat Robertson. Combining Larkin's narrative with chapters written from Lauren's viewpoint, and those of her much older husband and her estranged brother, himself, ironically enough, a Christian America minister, Butler fleshes out our view of both her dystopian future and Lauren herself. The result is a masterpiece of didactic speculative fiction.

Seven years later Butler published *Fledgling*, a vampire novel. Following in the tradition of Richard Matheson's *I Am Legend* (1954), she eschews the supernatural, preferring science-fictional explanations for her monsters. Butler's vampires are simply a different species – nocturnal, incredibly tough and long-lived, but mortal – who require human blood to survive. Like the Patternists, they can control human beings and weaker vampires, though they use pheromones to do so. Shori – a human–vampire crossbreed, black-skinned in contrast to the pale white vampires – is the result of a genetic experiment to develop viable offspring who can stay awake during the day and tolerate sunlight. Unfortunately, her mere existence is an affront to some vampire clans, who take it upon themselves to wipe out Shori's family and those who support her. It soon becomes the young vampire's mission simply to stay alive while bringing together enough human beings to support her need for blood, and, finally, proving her worth to the extended vampire community, some of whom see her as an abomination. *Fledgling* features several themes that have been central to

Butler's fiction from the beginning, including the importance of community, the evil of racism, and the difficulty of making a place for oneself when power relationships are unequal. Shori must deal with an enemy who is much older and stronger than she is, and her humans must come to terms with the fact that they, like the protagonists of so many Butler works, are not free agents but are under the control of a more powerful being. *Fledgling* also shares with *Kindred* and *Lilith's Brood* the theme of forced – or at least not entirely consensual – sexual encounters, and with the *Parable* books the idea of a near-child or apparent child (since Shori looks 11 but is actually over 50) having sexual relations with an older man.

Butler's fiction seems very much of a piece. The author shares with sf writers such as **Sheri S. Tepper** and Judith Moffett a deep and abiding skepticism concerning humanity's ability to overcome its hereditary needs to form environmentally destructive hierarchies, define those who are different as inferior, and create master–slave relationships. Though there are limited happy endings in Butler's work, particularly when communities can be formed, she is perhaps more of a pessimist than she might wish to admit. Her fiction has generated a significant amount of critical attention; the essays recommended below represent no more than a sampling of the scholarship available.

See also: **Isaac Asimov, Greg Bear, Alfred Bester, Leigh Brackett, Samuel R. Delany, Philip K. Dick, William Gibson, Donna J. Haraway, Robert A. Heinlein, Frank Herbert, Nalo Hopkinson, L. Ron Hubbard, Gwyneth Jones, Ursula K. Le Guin, C.L. Moore, Kim Stanley Robinson, Joanna Russ, Mary Shelley, Neal Stephenson, Sheri S. Tepper, James Tiptree Jr, and Gene Wolfe**

Bibliography

Bedore, P. (2002) "Slavery and Symbiosis in Octavia Butler's *Kindred*," *Foundation*, 84: 73–81.

Butler, O.E. (2004) "A Brief Conversation with Octavia E. Butler." Online. Available: <http://www.sfwa.org/members/butler/autobiography.html> (accessed 1 January 2009).

Callaloo (2009), special Octavia E. Butler issue.

Foundation, 72 (1998), special Octavia E. Butler issue.

Jesser, N. (2002) "Blood, Genes and Gender in Octavia Butler's *Kindred* and *Dawn*," *Extrapolation*, 43(1): 36–61.

Luckhurst, R. (1996) "'Horror and Beauty in Rare Combination': the miscegenation fiction of Octavia Butler," *Women: A Cultural Review*, 7(1): 28–38.

Vint, S. (2007) "'Only by Experience': embodiment and the limitations of realism in neo-slave narratives," *Science Fiction Studies*, 34(3): 452–72.
Zaki, H.M. (1990) "Utopia, Dystopia, and Ideology in the SF of Octavia Butler," *Science Fiction Studies*, 17(2): 239–51.

MICHAEL LEVY

KAREL ČAPEK (1890–1938)

Czech novelist, short-story writer, dramatist, essayist, and journalist.

Karel Čapek's international reputation as an sf writer rests on the play *RUR* (*Rossum's Universal Robots*, 1920; translated into English 1923) and the novels *The Absolute at Large* (1922), *Krakatit* (1924), and *War with the Newts* (1936), but his stature as the greatest Czech writer of his generation rests on a far larger and more varied body of work, highlighted by the allegorical drama *From the Life of the Insects* (1921), the trilogy of philosophical novels *Hordubal* (1933), *Meteor* (1934), and *An Ordinary Life* (1934), the stunning detective fiction collected in *Tales from Two Pockets* (1929), the biographical essay *President Masaryk Tells His Story* (1934), and an extensive, as yet uncollected and largely untranslated, body of short journalistic essays or feuilletons (some excellent examples, along with superior translations of *RUR* and the second act of *From the Life of the Insects*, can be found in Kussi 1990).

Despite this large, varied, and distinguished body of writing, Čapek probably remains best known in the English-speaking world as the man who coined the word "robot" in the title and body of his play *RUR*. But most of the word's associations have little to do with Čapek's play. The word derives from the Czech word for worker, and Čapek is, indeed, far less interested in mechanical men than in dehumanized workers, not only in *RUR* but throughout his career from "System" (1908) to his sf masterpiece *War with the Newts*. In "System," a cigar-smoking bourgeois boasts that he has solved the problem of workers' rebellions by choosing his workers from the poorest, the worst educated, the mentally incompetent – in short, the most abject members of society – and then systematically depriving them of any stimulation in order to render them free of ideas and desires, making them, as he puts it, as reliable as machines. The depiction of the robots in *RUR* emphasizes that the Rossum corporation's products have been rendered more efficient and tractable than human laborers by depriving them of emotions and souls rather than by virtue of their artificially constructed bodies. And although the workers of *War with the Newts* are a species of intelligent salamander, they clearly stand for racialized natives at the beginning of the narrative and, by its end, for an international proletariat that has been systematically denied access to the society that lives upon its labor. These are stories about class division rather than about artificial humans. In all three cases the story's resolution has the dehumanized workers turning against their erstwhile masters and – in strikingly different ways – grasping the consciousness and dignity earlier denied them.

As opposed to the simple association of Čapek with the term "robot," the main thrust of the critical response to Čapek's work has emphasized his political commitment to liberal democracy, his distrust of contemporary communism, and his opposition to fascism (Bradbrook 1998; Harkins 1962; Klima 2002). Čapek's close ties with Tomáš Masaryk, president of the first Czech republic, and the banning of his works in Czechoslovakia – following the Nazi invasion of 1938 and again under Soviet rule – have lent strong support to this emphasis. The correlative reading of the philosophical, and especially epistemological, themes in Čapek's work has focused on his skepticism, his liberal humanist distrust of doctrinaire positions and party organizations, and his interest in pragmatism, the subject of his dissertation (he received his Doctorate of Philosophy from Charles University in Prague in 1915). However, sf critics, in striking contrast to those writing about Čapek's entire corpus, have depicted a more radical writer, one more concerned with the vicissitudes of class struggle than with the epistemological problem of self-knowledge that dominates Čapek's trilogy or the bemused skepticism that predominates in many of the *Tales from Two Pockets*. *RUR*, *The Absolute at Large*, and *War with the Newts* are all exercises in imagining apocalypse, and in each case the apocalypse involves the dialectical, self-destructive unfolding of the logic of capitalism and capitalist industrialism. Some readers of Čapek's sf have emphasized the workings of the Hegelian-Marxist dialectic of mastery and slavery in these works (Kinyon 1999; Rieder 2005), while others have emphasized the dialectical tension between utopia and dystopia (Suvin 1979). Nonetheless, critics of Čapek's sf have generally found it more consistently and strongly engaged with the Hegelian and Marxist elements of his philosophical training than with American pragmatism, and with a collective and apocalyptically oriented vision than with the individualism and everyday life of his detective fiction or the bulk of his feuilletons.

Whether one focuses on Čapek's sf or on his entire career, it was definitely *RUR* that gave rise to his international reputation. After its first production in January 1921, at Prague's National Theater, the play was quickly translated into several languages and became a hit in New York in 1922 and London in 1923, where G.K. Chesterton and George Bernard Shaw took part in a public debate over its significance. Čapek himself remarked that the debaters seemed obsessed with the robots at the expense of the people in the play. The play's reputation and success depended heavily upon the spectacle of the expressionless, uniformed robots, numbers blazoned on their chests, marching in step onto the stage to announce, at the end of the second act, the end of the age of man and the beginning of the age of machines, as if to epitomize the traumatic transformation of modern society by the First World War and the Fordist assembly line. The appeal of the idea of the robots perhaps overshadowed the actual drama, or at least the apocalypse of the middle acts tended to overshadow the comic tone of the opening, in which the five directors of the Rossum Corporation simultaneously fall in love with a lovely visitor to the factory, Helena Glory, and the sentimentalism of the finale, where the last man alive witnesses two robots awakening to the emotion of love.

Čapek's second major piece of sf, *The Absolute at Large* (or *Factory of the Absolute*), appeared in serial form in the newspaper *Lidové noviny* from September 1921, the same venue in which *War with the Newts* would appear in 1936. It is not so much a novel as a sequence of strung-together feuilletons. Its fragmented and extravagant structure (or lack of one) produces many brilliant moments, but Čapek manages the overall coherence less successfully than in *War with the Newts*. The premise is a 100 percent efficient atomic motor that nonetheless releases as waste "the Absolute," which is initially identified as the divine that was imprisoned in the matter that the engine has used up. The Absolute manifests itself in two ways. First, it floods those in the vicinity of the engine with feelings of ecstatic communion with the godhead, allowing them to perform miracles, levitate, and so on. Second, it takes over the production process itself, producing torrents and mountains of products – nails, cloth, money – in such enormous quantities as to render them worthless. Čapek pointedly compares this prolific and senseless production to the order of the physical universe itself in its vastness and its absurdity. On the one hand, the Absolute, seemingly the technological boon that solves mankind's wants forever, ends up subverting any rational economy of goods and production, and, on the other, its quasi-religious effects lead to sectarian warfare of an order and ferocity never before attained. Much of the last half of the book recounts civilization's descent into universal warfare based on the elevated fanaticism that the Absolute inspires in its miracle-working, ecstatic subjects. One of Čapek's satirical targets is belief in "Absolutes" of any sort, and a wide variety of them come up for ridicule. An equally important joke is that the manufacturers of the Absolute persist in distributing their product well after its disastrous effects have begun to manifest themselves. Here, as in *RUR* and *War with the Newts*, the human race cannot hold back from destroying itself for short-term gain despite its awareness of the long-term consequences.

War with the Newts combines the capitalism run amok of *The Absolute at Large* with the apocalyptic workers' revolt of *RUR*. It also employs the journalistic form used in *The Absolute at Large* with the same extravagance and brilliance as formerly, but now combined with an overriding coherence provided by Čapek's precise, hilarious, and devastating articulation of what one might call the fantasy-logic of capitalism – the fantasy of an endlessly growing economy providing ever more commodities for ever more consumers – combined with that of colonialism – the fantasy of invisible natives hospitably providing empty lands and free labor for the expanding needs of their masters. Both of these fantasies are abundantly realized in *War with the Newts*, but in their realization they dialectically reverse themselves into nightmarish catastrophes. Along the way from the discovery of the Newts to their inundation of the world and destruction of human civilization, Čapek scatters a great deal of topical material, including an antifascist parody of Oswald Spengler and pointed allusions to Hitler's demands for *Lebensraum*. However, the fundamental target of the satire, the systematic logic of capitalism itself, is the same in the 1936 fable as it was in 1921, and remains just as pertinent today as it was at the moment of its composition.

Čapek's other major sf piece is the novel *Krakatit*. It is strikingly different both in form and in tone from the other three works discussed here. The story concerns a scientist who invents an atomic explosive substance – the "krakatit" of the title – and is pursued by corporate and government agents, some of them seductive and some diabolical, all seeking possession of his secret. But the scientist is feverish and hallucinatory through significant portions of the narrative, so much so that some critics have suggested the entire novel is to be taken as a dream, while others have found in it an unsuccessful attempt to blend realism and allegory. The scientist's erotic encounters and his fascination with and pursuit of a mysterious veiled woman with whom he never catches up have been interpreted autobiographically, connected to the novel's having an underlying fairy-tale structure, and praised as one of the great sexual love poems in Czech literature. In the face of all this, one can say with certainty that *Krakatit* also comprises a significant and complex reworking of the sf motifs of the marvelous invention and the mad scientist.

Other pieces by Čapek that border upon sf include the surreal drama *From the Life of the Insects*, which contributed as much to his international reputation in the 1920s and 1930s as *RUR*, and *The Makropulos Secret* (1922), a play about a woman who possesses a formula that grants not-quite-eternal youth. Much of Čapek's important work has been newly translated and republished by Catbird Press in the last two decades, hopefully paving the way for more widespread appreciation by English-speaking audiences of its range and complexity as well as its place in the history of sf.

See also: **Isaac Asimov, Philip K. Dick, Fritz Lang, Stanisław Lem, Oshii Mamoru, Olaf Stapledon, and H.G. Wells**

Bibliography

Bradbrook, B.R. (1998) *Karel Čapek: in pursuit of truth, tolerance, and trust*, Brighton: Sussex Academic Press.
Harkins, W.E. (1962) *Karel Čapek*, New York: Columbia University Press.
Kinyon, K. (1999) "The Phenomenology of Robots: confrontations with death in Karel Čapek's *RUR*," *Science Fiction Studies*, 26(3): 379–400.
Klima, I. (2002) *Karel Čapek: life and work*, trans. N. Comrada, North Haven, CT: Catbird Press.
Kussi, P. (ed.) (1990) *Toward the Radical Center*, North Haven, CT: Catbird Press.
Maslen, E. (1987) "Proper Words in Proper Places: the challenge of Čapek's *War with the Newts*," *Science Fiction Studies*, 14(1): 82–92.
Matuska, A. (1964) *Karel Čapek: an essay*, London: George Allen & Unwin.
Rieder, J. (2005) "Science Fiction, Colonialism, and the Plot of Invasion," *Extrapolation*, 46(3): 373–94.
Suvin, D. (1979) *Metamorphoses of Science Fiction: on the poetics and history of a literary genre*, New Haven, CT: Yale University Press.

JOHN RIEDER

SIR ARTHUR C[HARLES] CLARKE (1917–2008)

British author and science writer, knighted in 1998.

Probably best known for his script for and novel of *2001: A Space Odyssey* (Kubrick 1968) and his role as a communicator on science and scientific progress, Arthur C. Clarke's importance to sf is more fundamental. Clarke's propaganda for space travel was based upon a thorough understanding of the necessary science and technology, even as he argued, in what was to become known as Clarke's Second Law, that the only way to discover the limits of the possible was to venture into the impossible. In fiction, however, his vision embraced humanity's future in space as both symbol and actuality of the kind of secular mysticism he encountered as a schoolboy in **Olaf Stapledon**'s *Last and First Men* (1930).

Born in Minehead, Somerset, Clarke developed two childhood passions: science and sf. His brother, Fred Clarke, recalls experiments with rockets, the wireless, and photography, and in *Astounding Days* (1989) Arthur C. Clarke recounts how acquiring his first sf magazine irrevocably changed his life. By the time he left Huish Grammar School in 1936 for London and the Civil Service, he had contacted both sf fandom and the British Interplanetary Society, founded in 1933 by Philip E. Cleator (Clarke served as its chairman in the late 1940s and early 1950s). Like much of his early writing, his first published story, "Travel by Wire" (1937), an amusing account of matter-transportation, appeared in a fanzine. After working on radar during the Second World War, he published, in *Wireless World* in 1945, the first theoretical article on positioning communications satellites in geosynchronous orbit. His first professional fiction sales, "Rescue Party" and "Loophole," appeared in *Astounding* in 1946.

Building on his nonfiction *Interplanetary Flight* (1950), Clarke's first novel, *Prelude to Space* (1951), is told by an American historian, Dirk Alexson, recording the background to the first moon landing in 1978. While *Prometheus*'s lift-off to the tones of Big Ben affirmed Clarke's advocacy of a continuing British presence in the Space Race, *national* rivalries are absent from the novel, which apart from a vague reference to the "unsettled 1950s" overlooks the Cold War. Rather, Interplanetary, the (British-dominated) international body putting its arguments for space travel into practice, derives from the pre-Second World War "Interplanetary Societies" of enthusiasts, hobbyists, and visionaries. For Clarke, the project is a single step in the long voyage of *understanding* the universe. In the epilog, set thirty years later, Alexson, one of thousands of people with heart conditions whose lives have been saved by the moon's low gravity, reflects on the isolation of the moon, his interior monolog segueing into the narrator's "And now at last, after all these ages, its loneliness was coming to an end" (Clarke 1951: 132). Clarke is not arguing that humanity *will* move into space but persuading his readers that it *should*, even as the project's Director-General reflects upon the inevitability of "eternal night" and poses the question: by understanding its place in the universe, can humanity stand against the unavoidable end? Clarke's stoic utopianism is hardly geared to give a cozy answer.

Gibson, the observer-protagonist of *The Sands of Mars* (1951), is an sf writer who chooses to remain on Mars when his task of writing about the new colony is over. A rather awkward subplot – the youngest member of the *Ares* crew turns out to be Gibson's son by a failed relationship – explores personal rather than cosmic loneliness, but the revelation of a terraforming project pushes the novel to the verge of what C.S. Lewis would call "eschatological fiction." This concern with "cosmic" goals shapes Clarke's masterpiece *Childhood's End* (1953) and *Against the Fall of Night* (1948; revised as *The City and the Stars* (1956)), as well as *2001*. Like Stapledon, Clarke's grand sweeps of vision eschew comfort and accept the possibility of unease. *Fall/City* thus considers the concept of utopia, one which *Prelude*'s "bright Renaissance" might imply is a necessary consequence of technological progress, but which is threatening precisely through its assumption of fulfillment and stasis. The alternative utopias, Diaspar and Lys, are each, despite their marvelous developments, limited. There are wonders – and dangers – in the universe which transcend them. Even the utopia which *Childhood's End*'s alien Overlords force upon humanity is a false paradise, a step toward the sublimation of humankind into a new trans-species identity. Poignantly, the Overlords, who assist Humanity's transition into the Overmind, are unable to make that transition themselves, suggesting that knowledge about our own place in the universe will not necessarily be comforting.

A number of Clarke's short stories are masterpieces in this mode. In the enigmatic and haunting "The Sentinel" (1951), an alien artifact discovered on the moon is programmed to broadcast a signal if disturbed. The narrator contemplates the result: a welcome or a threat? "The Nine Billion Names of God" (1953) demonstrates Clarke's gift for a simple arresting image. Tibetan monks, whose self-appointed task is to list all the possible names of God (and thus fulfill the purpose of the universe), have installed a computer system to speed up the process. The technicians, nervous about the monks' reaction when the list is complete and nothing happens, leave. One of them looks up to the sky: "Overhead, without any fuss, the stars were going out" (Clarke 2001: 422). It is that "without any fuss" that lifts Clarke's prose from the effective to the occasionally startling. (Perhaps the most famous example of this quiet technique is the final sentence of *2001*. The astronaut Bowman, transformed into the godlike "Star Child," hovers over the face of the earth, unsure of what to do next: "But he would think of something" (Clarke 1968: 256).)

More than almost anyone, Clarke evokes the numinous in sf's "sense of wonder," as "The Star" (1955) demonstrates: a Jesuit priest and scientist, returning from a world whose civilization was destroyed by a supernova, has to come to terms with the fact that this occurred (if his religious beliefs are true) so that the Star would shine above the stable in Bethlehem. This interest in religion is continued, more critically, in later fiction. In *The Songs of Distant Earth* (1986), a spaceship from a destroyed Earth, en route to terraform a new world, visits a utopian colony. The Thalassans, selected for physical traits, have been given only a carefully edited version of Earth's culture. "With tears in their eyes, the selection panels had thrown away the Veda, the Bible, the Tripitaka, the Qu'ran, and all the immense body of literature – fiction and nonfiction – that was based upon them … they could not be allowed to reinfect virgin planets with the ancient poisons of religious hatreds, belief in the supernatural, and … pious gibberish" (Clarke 1986: 83). The crew must decide whether to continue their voyage or to stay and risk disrupting utopia. The melancholy in this novel moves from a sense of love between individuals knowing that they may be separated by time and space to the fact that even highly technological, advanced civilizations know loss.

Other important Clarke books are *Profiles of the Future*, a much-revised collection of speculative essays first published in 1962, *Rendezvous with Rama* (1973), *Imperial Earth* (1976), and *The Fountains of Paradise* (1979). *2001*, which made Clarke for a time the best-known sf writer in the world, was less a director–scriptwriter teaming than a collaboration between two talented men with strong, sometimes opposing, opinions about the nature of the enterprise. Based upon several sources in Clarke, it shows Stanley Kubrick's obsessive attention to detail and Clarke's visionary realism at work. Various sequences – the match-cut from the bone hurtled into the air to an orbiting spaceship; the dance of the space-station and the docking spacecraft, accompanied by Johann Strauss II's *Blue Danube Waltz* (1867); the chilly rebellion of the HAL 9000 computer which jeopardizes the Jupiter mission – are among the most unforgettable in all cinema.

After 1956 Clarke lived in Sri Lanka, the setting for *The Fountains of Paradise*, where he was Chancellor of the University of Moratuwa. His awards, both in literary and scientific fields, were numerous. A Patron of the Science Fiction Foundation, President of the British Science Fiction Association, Chancellor of the International Space University, holder of the UNESCO Kalinga Prize and the NASA Distinguished Public Service Medal, he was also awarded several honorary degrees, one of which (from the University of Liverpool) was fittingly conferred by satellite link. He was one of the few genuinely bestselling sf writers, and one of the most indefatigable. He announced his "retirement" several times, and for many years illness kept him in a wheelchair; but he continued to write. Many later novels were collaborations, including three sequels (1989–93) to *Rendezvous with Rama* with Gentry Lee; *The Light of Other Days* (2000) and the *Time Odyssey* trilogy (2003–2007) with Stephen Baxter; and his final novel, *The Last Theorem* (2008), with Frederik Pohl.

Although Clarke's enthusiasm for scientific progress sometimes caught him out (the 1999 edition of *Profiles of the Future* wryly notes his wrong or overoptimistic predictions), his novels and stories are among the finest in the genre, distinguished by two interwoven voices. First, he is the poet of the 1950s vision of space travel as, particularly, articulated through the postwar British sensibility which saw rebuilding the country, and the world, after the horrors of the Second World War as a challenge willingly to be met. If other British sf writers such as John Wyndham and John Christopher showed the anxiety of the 1950s, Clarke's early novels – and stories such as the six linked vignettes published in a 1956 newspaper as "Venture to the Moon" – showed the dream: that history does not have to be the way it is, and that humanity can take control of its destiny. It is a dream built upon its own anxieties and the tension between its conservatism and its dramatic vision. That Britain would play a major role in the forthcoming space age remained a simple fantasy, but at the time it offered many a possible shape for a new post-Empire Britain.

Second, and perhaps of greater importance, there is a more universal sense of futurity. Clarke's reputation will remain attached to a vision of the future which *assumed*, years before it happened, that space travel was both possible and desirable. Much of his fiction can be seen as documents of the space age by someone who was trying to make it happen. He was, however, more than a propagandist. In the penultimate chapter of *Prelude to Space*, Alexson recalls the "image of the lonely island lost on a boundless and untraveled sea" (Clarke 1951: 156). The chapter's final words suggest a tentatively hopeful resolution as the "first frail ship" embarks upon the great project of knowing the universe.

See also: **Isaac Asimov, J.G. Ballard, Iain M. Banks, Gwyneth Jones, Stanley Kubrick, China Miéville, Michael Moorcock, Mary Shelley, Olaf Stapledon, and H.G. Wells**

Bibliography

Blackford, R. (2001) "Technological Meliorism and the Posthuman Vision," *New York Review of Science Fiction*, 159: 1, 10–20.
Clarke, A.C. (1951) *Prelude to Space*, New York: World Editions.
——(1968) *2001: a space odyssey*, London: Hutchinson.
——(1986) *The Songs of Distant Earth*, London: Gollancz.
——(1989) *Astounding Days: a science fictional autobiography*, London: Gollancz.
——(2001) *The Collected Stories*, London: Gollancz.
Clarke, F. (1987) "Arthur C. Clarke: the early days," *Foundation*, 41: 9–14.
James, E. (1987) "The Future Viewed from Mid-Century Britain: Clarke, Hampson and the Festival of Britain," *Foundation*, 41: 42–51.
——(2005) "Arthur C. Clarke," in D. Seed (ed.) *A Companion to Science Fiction*, London: Blackwell.
Kilgore, D.W.D. (2003) "Will There Always Be an England? Arthur C. Clarke's new Eden," in *Astrofuturism: science, race, and visions of utopia in space*, Pennsylvania: University of Pennsylvania Press.
Lewis, C.S. (1966) "On Science Fiction," in *Of Other Worlds: essays and stories* [1955], London: Geoffrey Bles.
McAleer, N. (1992) *Odyssey: the authorised biography of Arthur C. Clarke*, London: Gollancz.

ANDY SAWYER

DAVID [PAUL] CRONENBERG (1943–)

Canadian film director, scriptwriter, and actor.

David Cronenberg's films demonstrate a synergy between his two main academic influences, science and English Literature, and the creative expression he found in the filmmaking medium. This unique confluence of interests makes him one of the most literary of sf film directors. Able to straddle the line between mainstream and art cinema through his engagement with both the spectacular and the intimate, his films convey a coherent vision, focused upon issues of physical, social, and sexual transgression.

Generally considered a master of horror, his filmmaking career began with two rather abstract avant-garde sf films which undermine conventional narrative structure by creating meaning through the juxtaposition of sound and image. *Stereo* (1969) tells the story of the Canadian Institute for Erotic Inquiry, a foundation analyzing the human capacity for telepathy by experimenting upon the bodies of its patients. In *Crimes of the Future* (1970), the female population has died out due to a virus found in cosmetics, forcing scientists to explore alternative methods of reproduction and evolution. These films established Cronenberg's fascination with the impact of science upon the body as well as his preoccupation, for which he has received much criticism, with the relationships among the body, disease, and sexuality. Both films share a coldly clinical aesthetic characterized by a modernist *mise-en-scène*, slow and deliberate camera movements, and a nonsynchronized soundtrack. This visual and aural approach constructs an alienating vision of the world that consistently reappears in his films from *Shivers* (1975) to *Crash* (1996, adapted from **J.G. Ballard**'s 1973 novel). Moreover, these films established Cronenberg as an intensely cerebral filmmaker – like *Videodrome*, the sadomasochistic television program that features in his film of the same name (1983), he can be described as "having a philosophy."

After his early experimental films, Cronenberg moved to the more commercially oriented horror genre, a choice causing some to argue that his work is not sf at all. Yet what he brought from the earlier films was his preoccupation with scientists, scientific and technological institutions, and the impact of science and technology upon human physiognomy and sexuality, elements which he carefully infused into the conventions of horror. Films such as *Shivers*, *Rabid* (1977), and *The Brood* (1979), with their narratives of sexual violence, vampiric bloodlust, and murderous rage alongside their graphic depictions of the monstrous body, may aim to shock and at times horrify, but they have sf at their core. They explore the horrific results of unchecked science in the form of the ambitions of his scientist protagonists, Dr Hobbes, Dr Keloid, and Dr Raglan, respectively. In each case, it is the practical reality of their theoretical philosophies or scientific experimentation that creates the horror. For instance, Hobbes's belief that humanity has lost touch with its natural self causes him to create a virus that is part aphrodisiac, part venereal disease. The spread of this disease transforms a rather banal and antiseptic apartment complex into a den of orgiastic excess. Similarly, Keloid's desire to be more than the "Colonel Sanders" of plastic surgery encourages him to operate upon a victim of a motorcycle accident and use untested skin grafts to heal her internal injuries. He saves her life, but the grafts cause her to develop a vampiric appendage through which she must feed on blood. Finally, it is Raglan's theories of "psychoplasmics" – a process of psychically projecting rage onto the body – that leads to violence and multiple murders. The severely traumatized Nola Carveth manifests her rage in the form of deformed, murderous children, born from an external birthing sac. The image of Nola biting into the sac in order to remove a child and then licking it clean is one of abject body-horror, but it is the scientist Raglan who, like Frankenstein, creates the monster. The contagion narratives of *Shivers* and *Rabid* capture anxieties about the spread of a scientifically developed disease across society, while *The Fly* (1986) reflects upon the horror of disease spreading through and across the individual body.

While it is common for sf to use the figure of the scientist to critique the dangers of ambition and to challenge the notion of "progress," Cronenberg's films are notable for their ambivalent presentation of scientists. While many of his films, from *Stereo* to *Dead Ringers* (1988), feature scientist protagonists who are the driving force behind the narrative, in *The Fly* and *Dead Ringers* the scientists have themselves become the monsters: Seth Brundle accidentally fuses his body with that of a house fly in a teleportation experiment, sparking the horrific transformation of his body and mind, while gynecologists Beverly and Elliot Mantle are presented as human monsters whose monstrosity emerges from the combination of their physiognomy (they are twins) and their scientific and emotional detachment from society. In Cronenberg's world, however, scientists are ambiguously presented as neither purely evil nor entirely good. For instance, Brundle's invention of teleportation does not emerge from ambition, although he does talk about it being the invention that will change society as we know it, but from his regular experience of motion sickness – a condition that reinforces his childlike persona. Furthermore, it is his emotional naiveté and jealousy, rather than arrogance, that causes him to test the equipment on himself while drunk and without proper supervision. His transformation into a fly is, therefore, equally presented as horrific and tragic. While the Mantle twins are presented as far more alien and unknowable than Brundle, their struggle with identity – Beverly looks for some form of independence, while Elliot fights against separation – is decidedly human. Their gradual physical and psychological deterioration is therefore both disturbing and moving. Even the earlier films present scientists as simply putting their philosophies and beliefs into practice, leaving the audience to judge the merits and/or horrors of their work. This ambivalence seems connected to the fact that Cronenberg has often said that he personally empathizes with his scientists and sees them as representing his own persona. This image of Cronenberg is reinforced by his regular casting as a doctor or scientist (he plays the gynecologist in *The Fly*'s dream sequence, as well as Dr Decker in *Nightbreed* (Barker 1990), Dr Wimmer in *Jason X* (Isaac 2001), and Dr Brezzel in the television series *Alias* (2001–06)). For Cronenberg, the scientist represents each person's struggle to understand their purpose in life and maintain a balance between healthy ambition and ethical restraint, a balance that is usually disturbed in his films with severe penalties. In presenting them in this manner, Cronenberg's scientists are inherently human rather than evil.

Another key component of Cronenberg's work is his resistance to generic categorization. Walking a slippery line between horror and sf, his hybrid films offer an approach to both genres that is best described as Cronenbergian. The Cronenbergian film, replete with hallucinatory imagery, literary allusions, and graphic corporeal special effects, challenges our understanding of sf cinema. Rather than looking outward to space, or presenting fantastic spectacles of glossy special effects, Cronenberg turned his sf eye inward at the body, which is usually considered as falling within the purview of the horror genre. Seeing the body as the essence of the self, Cronenberg uses his films to explore his preoccupation with the Cartesian split between mind and body, which all of his films take great pains to challenge. Like Raglan's "psychoplasmics," Cronenberg's films portray the mind and body as indelibly linked. Both *Videodrome* and *Naked Lunch* (1991, adapted from William S. Burroughs's 1959 novel) present hallucinatory states as physical experiences in which the imagery focuses upon transgressing the boundaries and taboos of the body. In *Videodrome*, television producer Max Renn imagines his stomach splitting into a vaginal opening into which a videotape is inserted as a form of mental programming. In *Naked Lunch*, writer Bill Lee's drug-induced visions are replete with polymorphously perverse bodily encounters with talking bugs and anthropomorphized typewriters turned insects, constructed through physical special effects. In *Scanners* (1981), Cronenberg reimagines telepathy as a physical process described by Dr Ruth, a professed expert on "scanning," as "the direct linking of two nervous systems separated by space." This physicality is illustrated during a demonstration of scanning abilities for a group of military and corporate representatives. Before beginning, the presenter warns that it can be a painful process, "sometimes resulting in nosebleeds, earaches, stomach cramps, nausea," and of course the conclusion to this sequence is the infamous moment when the scanner is himself scanned to the point of his head exploding. The film's climactic battle between protagonist Cameron Vale and his demented, power-hungry brother, Daryl Revok, equally presents this "battle of wills" as physical when the men's attempts to absorb each other's mental energy causes their bodies to ripple, rupture, bleed, and finally burst into flames. Even the more horror-oriented film *The Dead Zone* (1983, adapted from Stephen King's 1979 novel) shares this mind–body equation when Dr Weizak informs psychic Johnny Smith that as his mental power develops, his physical body deteriorates (a point reinforced by Christopher Walken's increasingly distorted, misshapen performance).

Cronenberg's vision further explores the mind–body duality by addressing their extensions through technology. *Videodrome* and *eXistenz* (1999) both focus upon entertainment technologies in the form of television and video games to consider the impact of our media-saturated culture upon the body and soul. In both cases, Cronenberg presents an ambiguous image of our increasing dependence upon media-stimulation. *Crash*, on the other hand, presents a disturbingly alienated view of modern society in which technology in the form of automobiles and car crashes is necessary both to arouse otherwise muted and unfulfilling sex drives and to remind the characters, through near-death experiences, that they are indeed alive. In each of these cases, technology is represented as a physical extension of the human body, whether that be the fusion of Max Renn's hand with a gun as he chants "long live the new flesh" (*Videodrome*); the bioports at the base of the spine into which a game is plugged directly into the central nervous system (*eXistenZ*); or the image of Gabrielle's scarred leg entwined in its metallic leg brace as she enticingly leans over the side of a black convertible (*Crash*). This last image fully embodies the psycho-sexual eroticism of the New Flesh of the Cronenbergian film – in which mind, body, and technology are fused and through which a new type of sexuality is born. Cronenberg does not judge the New Flesh but rather simply offers a knowing look at its existence. His ambivalence has left him open to criticism; he is often described as right wing, misogynist, and misanthropic. These criticisms, however, miss the point of the Cronenbergian vision. He presents, and invites the audience to consider, an image of evolving humanity. This can often create uncomfortable viewing and provoke thought.

See also: **Gerry Anderson, J.G. Ballard, Jean Baudrillard, Philip K. Dick, Nalo Hopkinson, Stanley Kubrick, Fritz Lang, George Lucas, and Steven Spielberg**

Bibliography

Beard, W. (2006) *The Artist as Monster: the cinema of David Cronenberg*, Toronto: University of Toronto Press.

Browning, M. (2007) *David Cronenberg: author or film-maker?*, Bristol: Intellect.
Grant, M. (ed.) (2000) *The Modern Fantastic: the films of David Cronenberg*, Trowbridge: Flicks.
Grunberg, S. (2006) *David Cronenberg*, London: Plexus.
Handling, P. (1983) *The Shape of Rage: the films of David Cronenberg*, Toronto: General Publishing Group.
Porton, R. (1999) "The Film Director as Philosopher: an interview with David Cronenberg," *Cineaste*, 24(4): 4–94.
Rodley, C. (ed.) (1992) *Cronenberg on Cronenberg*, London: Faber and Faber.

STACEY ABBOTT

SAMUEL R[AY] DELANY (1942–)

US novelist and critic.

Born in Harlem, New York City, Samuel R. Delany is one of the most influential innovators in modern sf. He has to date published over 40 books, roughly two thirds of them works of fiction and a third nonfiction. Though he has made notable contributions to several fields, his most important and renowned achievements have been in sf and sf criticism. Among formal honors in the field, he has received four Nebula awards, two Hugos, the Pilgrim Award for lifetime achievement in sf criticism and scholarship, and induction into the Science Fiction Hall of Fame.

Delany established himself as a major sf author with a series of nine novels published between 1962 and 1968, beginning with *The Jewels of Aptor* (which he completed in manuscript while still in his teens) and concluding with the most acclaimed works of his early period, *Babel-17* (1966), *The Einstein Intersection* (1967), and *Nova* (1968). Though innovative in important ways, these nine novels are also rooted in the pulp sf tradition. Unlike the contemporary New Wave sf authors of the 1960s, who sought to break with the pulp tradition and from whom Delany has often dissociated himself, Delany loved pulp fiction, especially space opera; and his first nine novels show that during this period his project was to rejuvenate the received forms and motifs of pulp sf rather than to leave them behind. The main narrative elements that characterize Delany's early work were the common property of his pulp predecessors: mighty battles in outer space, with heroic spaceship captains and awful superweapons; post-apocalyptic settings, with civilization struggling to recover from catastrophe; interplanetary political intrigues; the long, difficult quest journey; contact between human beings and alien intelligences; and conventional heterosexual love interest. Indeed, for pure space opera, perhaps no finer or more exciting narratives than *Babel-17* and *Nova* have ever been composed.

Yet Delany was a talent of noteworthy originality from the beginning. Even in his five earliest novels – *The Jewels of Aptor*, the three volumes collectively known as *The Fall of the Towers* (1963–65), and *The Ballad of Beta-2* (1965) – there are signs of the major innovator Delany would become. In these books we find a sophisticated interest in language and in the process of literary composition that, at the time, was quite rare in sf; there is also an unusually rigorous understanding of politics, one that goes beyond mere intrigue or adventure to encompass economics and complex social conflict. We also find, though more tentatively, the first signs of the problematization of hegemonic racial and gender roles for which Delany would become famous.

A new standard of innovation and craftsmanship is attained in Delany's next four novels. *Empire Star* (1966) combines exciting space-opera adventure with ontological puzzles and with a searing parable of race and slavery. *Babel-17* offers well-told space battles but also a complex engagement with ideas related to the Sapir–Whorf hypothesis about the function of language in the construction of reality. *The Einstein Intersection* displays perhaps the most original post-holocaust environment yet represented in American sf, combined with an intricate examination of race and gender; it also represents Delany's first major use of the formal techniques of literary modernism in sf. *Nova* (whose protagonist is casually revealed to be black – at the time a deeply shocking move in American sf) features space opera of considerable excitement and also constitutes a sustained meditation on the political and emotional consequences of economic scarcity. With these four novels, Delany became generally recognized as one of the main talents of the field.

Pulp elements are absent from Delany's next sf novel, *Dhalgren* (1975), the first major work of his full maturity and for many readers still his masterpiece. *Dhalgren* was hugely popular from the start, making more money in its first year than any sf novel had done before; and the critical reaction was also overwhelmingly favorable (e.g., Theodore Sturgeon proclaimed *Dhalgren* to be the very best book that sf had ever produced). Set, evidently, in the 1960s and in the fictional Bellona – a large industrial city in the Midwestern US – *Dhalgren* is a major fictional exploration of urban America. Because of some bizarre cosmic catastrophe, Bellona has been largely (but not completely) cut off from the outside world: most of its inhabitants have fled (while a few adventurous immigrants have arrived), and inherited social structures are deteriorating. *Dhalgren* explores the social and personal changes experienced in this environment by the unnamed protagonist (called the Kid) and by an immense cast of supporting characters – and in so doing undertakes by far Delany's most ambitious consideration to that point of race and gender. Racial conflict (including interracial rape) is a major plot concern; so is the closely related matter of class conflict. Sexual arrangements are experimental, and the book features the first overt representations of homosexual experience in Delany's sf. With *Dhalgren*, Delany also went further than probably any other author (except **J.G. Ballard**) in incorporating the techniques of Joycean modernism into sf. It ought to be added, though, that much of the novel is straightforwardly realistic in presentation (the same is true of *Ulysses* (1922) itself).

Delany's next novel, *Triton: an ambiguous heterotopia* (1976) – later republished as *Trouble on Triton* – superficially seems to recall Delany's earlier sf: it is set on a moon of Neptune and has subordinate elements of space opera. But it surpasses even the best of Delany's early work. It features the author's most sustained examination of sex and gender roles so far, and interestingly inverts the structure of *Dhalgren*: whereas the earlier novel had presented a sexually emancipated protagonist in the ruins of a conformist society, *Triton* features the sexually conservative Bron Helstrom and his unhappy attempts to function within a liberated, nonsexist world. *Triton* is also one of the best comedies of manners in sf: the elaborate scene describing Bron's dinner date with an ardently desired female companion is reminiscent of Jane Austen. Another innovation is that the book displays Delany's increasing sophistication as a scholar of modern critical theory; with *Triton*, Delany emerges as a master of the novel of ideas.

He consolidated that position with the four volumes of the *Nevèrÿon* series (1979–87). Here ideas are everywhere, derived from Delany's reading in the texts of modern thinkers such as G.W.F. Hegel, Karl Marx, Friedrich Nietzsche, Sigmund Freud, Ferdinand de Saussure, Ludwig Wittgenstein, György Lukács, Theodor W. Adorno, Ernst Bloch, Claude Lévi-Strauss, Frantz Fanon, Jacques Lacan, Michel Foucault, Jacques Derrida, and Fredric Jameson. The series also contains many of the most exciting stories and compellingly developed characters in the entire Delany *oeuvre* – and, stylistically, some of the finest writing. Though it can be debated whether the *Nevèrÿon* sequence should be classified as sf, it fits easily into the category of sword-and-sorcery, which Delany himself has often regarded as a subgenre of sf; and, despite the frequent "feel" of fantasy, hardly anything actually fantastic happens. Like most sf, the *Nevèrÿon* books are materialist in viewpoint.

The sequence is certainly Delany's most ambitious published fiction. It contains innumerable characters and subplots, but is also unified by the presiding narrative of the dark-skinned Gorgik's successful struggle to abolish slavery in the ancient empire of Nevèrÿon. Once again, slavery and race are central to Delany's concerns. Gorgik is also Delany's first protagonist of primarily homosexual orientation, and with these books gay themes become increasingly prominent in Delany's writing. Sexuality is explored with a psychoanalytic shrewdness unprecedented in sf, and with a frankness equally unprecedented. The series also expresses Delany's long-standing interest in the economic basis of society, and is one of the more important works in American fiction written under the direct inspiration of Marxist theory. There is also much in the *Nevèrÿon* books that relates to Delany's interest in language and theories of representation.

Stars in My Pocket Like Grains of Sand (1984), Delany's most recent novel of indisputably science-fictional character, appeared during the production of the *Nevèrÿon* sequence (since which Delany has published no work that is even arguably sf). The text represents an invented lifeworld in which there are over 6,000 planets inhabited by sentient species, each one, evidently, as amply stocked with biological and cultural diversity as the Earth. The total amount of variety is thus unthinkably huge. The protagonist, Mark Dyeth, is an "industrial diplomat," someone whose occupation is to make sense of this staggering heterogeneity and to interpret different cultures and species to one another. In this way, *Stars in My Pocket* is one of the most serious and convincing efforts yet made in sf to convey what life in a galactic federation might actually feel like. The book's exploration of the extremely difficult interpretive problems such life would entail is a culmination of the concern with language, with artistic construction, and with models and representations that Delany's work had displayed from the beginning. The text's attempt to comprehend literally unimaginable degrees of diversity, and its wrestling with species and planetary difference, constitute perhaps the most total effort Delany has yet made to understand human differences of race, of class, of power, of gender, and of sexual orientation – and a total effort made in full Derridean awareness that achieved totalization is unattainable. A novel of ideas, *Stars in My Pocket* also features the most passionate love story in the Delany *oeuvre*. In a masterstroke of structural composition, the story of the love affair between Mark

Dyeth and his very different lover, Rat Korga, is beautifully fused with the overall theme of social, cultural, and biological difference.

It remains to comment on Delany's sf criticism, by far the most important body of critical work produced by any sf novelist. With the lone exception of **Darko Suvin**, no other critic has done as much as Delany to professionalize the study of sf, to make it as intellectually rigorous and as theoretically deft and resourceful as any other area of literary criticism. Probably the most influential of Delany's critical books is his first, *The Jewel-Hinged Jaw: notes on the language of science fiction* (1977). As the title implies, Delany's concern is not to define sf (a project he regards as fruitless), nor, for the most part, to examine (like Suvin) sf themes and structure, but instead to focus on sentence production itself, to study sf as a distinctive linguistic and stylistic practice. Whereas earlier sf critics had often been limited by not being widely read outside of sf itself, Delany draws on an extensive knowledge of the poetry, fiction, and literary theory of the nineteenth and twentieth centuries. In addition to important general theorizing, Delany's criticism is distinguished by close readings of particular texts, most notably **Ursula K. Le Guin**'s *The Dispossessed* (1974) and Thomas Disch's "Angouleme" (1971).

See also: **Isaac Asimov, J.G. Ballard, Greg Bear, Alfred Bester, Leigh Brackett, Octavia Butler, Philip K. Dick, William Gibson, Donna J. Haraway, Robert A. Heinlein, Frank Herbert, L. Ron Hubbard, Ursula K. Le Guin, Michael Moorcock, C.L. Moore, Kim Stanley Robinson, Joanna Russ, Neal Stephenson, Darko Suvin, Sheri S. Tepper, James Tiptree Jr, and Gene Wolfe**

Bibliography

Barbour, D. (1979) *Worlds Out of Words: the sf novels of Samuel R. Delany*, Frome, Somerset: Bran's Head Books.

Broderick, D. (1995) *Reading by Starlight: postmodern science fiction*, London and New York: Routledge.

Delany, S.R. (1977) *The Jewel-Hinged Jaw: notes on the language of science fiction*, Elizabethtown, NY: Dragon Press.

Fox, R.E. (1987) *Conscientious Sorcerers: the black postmodernist fiction of LeRoi Jones/Amiri Baraka, Ishmael Reed and Samuel Delany*, Westport, CT: Greenwood Press.

Freedman, C. (2000) *Critical Theory and Science Fiction*, Hanover and London: University Press of New England/Wesleyan University Press.

——(ed.) (2009) *Conversations with Samuel R. Delany*, Jackson: University Press of Mississippi.

McEvoy, S. (1984) *Samuel R. Delany*, New York: Frederick Ungar.

Sallis, J. (ed.) (1996) *Ash of Stars: on the writing of Samuel R. Delany*, Jackson: University Press of Mississippi.
Slusser, G.E. (1977) *The Delany Intersection: Samuel R. Delany considered as a writer of semi-precious words*, San Bernadino, CA: Borgo Press.
Tucker, J.A. (2004) *A Sense of Wonder: Samuel R. Delany, race, identity and difference*, Middletown, CT: Wesleyan University Press.
Weedman, J.B. (1982) *Samuel R. Delany*, Washington, D.C.: Starmont House.

CARL FREEDMAN

PHILIP K[INDRED] DICK (1928–82)

US novelist and short-story writer.

Philip K. Dick began his career after sf had coalesced into a self-conscious genre in which authors, to a greater or lesser extent, sought to persuade readers that their imagined worlds were real within the framework of their fiction. Dick, however, was more interested in entropy and destruction than world-building: "I like to build universes that *do* fall apart … I like to see how the characters in the novels cope with the problem" (Dick 1995: 262). His writing not only exposed the sheer arbitrariness of such fictional environments, but also questioned the reality of the "real" world. His stories asked "What is real?" and went on to explore the ethics of the individual's behavior in an environment where nothing is definitely real.

Dick had a difficult childhood: born in Chicago, he was the survivor of a pair of twins, and his parents soon divorced. His mother raised him in Berkeley, California, then a hotbed of radical activity. Writing fiction and poetry from an early age, Dick's first short stories were published in the sf pulps in 1951. He was initially prolific in this format – four of the five volumes of his *Collected Stories* (1987) feature materials dating from the 1950s – but Dick soon realized better money was to be made by writing novels, beginning with *Solar Lottery* (1955). He continued to write stories, but they were often dry runs for novels. He found his distinctive voice with *Eye in the Sky* (1957), in which tourists, caught in an explosion, wake up in an alternate world, and then pass through a series of such pocket-universes, until they think they have returned to what they take to be reality.

The ambiguous ending is typical of Dick's work. Sometimes the characters begin in "reality" and then hallucinate, as in *Flow My Tears, the Policeman Said* (1974), with no certainty that the delusion is escapable. Sometimes, as in *Time out of Joint* (1959) and the Hugo-Award-winning *The Man in the High Castle* (1962), the protagonist realizes he is in a constructed reality and escapes into what is assumed to be an authentic realm – although there is no evidence to confirm this. Ultimately, the difference between real and not real is impossible to determine; this is especially true of *The Three Stigmata of Palmer Eldritch* (1964) and *Ubik* (1969). Sequences in *Lies, Inc.* (1984) might be hallucinations, delusions, LSD trips, psychotic fugues, alternate histories, or even data projected from a satellite in orbit around the Earth – or then again, they might be authentic reality.

Just because the world is not necessarily real does not mean that the protagonist is free to act as he – and it is usually he – sees fit. Rather he finds himself ethically and morally committed to those around him. Rick Deckard, in *Do Androids Dream of Electric Sheep?* (1968), undergoes ethical challenges in his job as bounty hunter tracking down escaped androids. Due to technological advances, humans are only distinguishable from androids by the degree of empathy they possess – empathy requiring others to be treated as subjects rather than as usable objects. To perform his job, Deckard must repress his empathy for androids who themselves may be empathic. The point is to demonstrate compassion for the other, irrespective of their empathy. For example, in *Now Wait for Last Year* (1966), Eric Sweetscent elects to go back to his addicted wife because he is committed to her.

Dick's representation of the working man's alienation by corporations within a capitalist framework led to him being labeled a Marxist writer. Dick's suspicion of the Cold War (for example, in "The Defenders" (1953) and *The Penultimate Truth* (1964) populations are told that a long-concluded war still continues), his depiction of corrupt corporations, his demonstration of ideological systems, his recognition of the dangers of the culture industries and the perils of commodification and consumerism (especially in *Ubik*), and his digs at Richard Nixon, ensured his work appealed to the counterculture of the 1960s and beyond. In *Eye in the Sky*, which attacks McCarthyism, Dick lists a set of left-liberal causes for which he himself had sympathy. But in his celebration of the little man there is perhaps a nostalgia-tinged valorization of the petty bourgeois who gains limited ownership of his means of production, rather than reaching for a wider social transformation. All that is solid melts, but it is the small group that coalesces in response. Whereas novels by **Alfred Bester** and Robert Sheckley from the period shared Dick's metaphysical sleights of hand, they lack his *appearance* of a social agenda.

The position of women within this is particularly problematic. Whilst the central male protagonist often battles an ambivalent patriarchal figure, such as bad fathers or bosses, women occur in two basic types: either an ill-tempered, hen-pecking, castrating wife, such as *Now Wait for Last Year*'s Kathy Sweetscent, who might betray the protagonist, or a young, seductive, dark-haired creature, usually little more than a girl, such as the same novel's Phyllis Ackerman, who constitutes a wish-fulfillment fantasy, oscillating between unlikely desire for the middle-aged protagonist and for the elderly boss. Given Dick's awkward relationship with his parents, his dead twin, and his five marriages, it is tempting to give these types an autobiographical spin. There are, however, exceptions to this pattern – the independent Marsha Hamilton in *Eye in the Sky*, the trapped housewives in *Martian Time-Slip* (1964), Angel Archer in *The Transmigration of Timothy Archer* (1982) – and Dick was hardly more sexist than most other male writers of the period.

After publishing 20 novels in the 1960s, Dick's personal life underwent major upheavals. His fourth marriage collapsed and, after a November 1971 break-in, Dick felt under attack. He fled to Canada, then moved to Fullerton, California, in 1973, close to the university where he had deposited his manuscripts. As the delayed *Flow My Tears* was published, Dick had a series of experiences which were to obsess him for the rest of his life. These included surreal hallucinations (possibly brought on by an overdose of vitamin C), a voice telling him his son had a hernia, visions of first-century Rome, and a radio abusing him. Dick speculated on these events in what he called his Exegesis, in turns thinking the voices were a message from God, the Prophet Elijah, the spirit of wisdom Sophia, his twin, the late James Pike (the Bishop of California), aliens, or scientists in Leningrad – or they might have been (he thought) brought on by drugs or a nervous breakdown.

The first public fruit of all this was the scramble suit in *A Scanner Darkly* (1977). Bob Arctor is the undercover identity of S.A. Fred, a narcotics agent who takes drugs so as to convince the people he has under surveillance that he is a legitimate part of their world. Not even his superiors know his identity. He cracks under the pressure of spying on himself and taking Substance D. By the end of the novel, it becomes apparent that this drug was developed by the government.

Dick created another divided protagonist in a fictionalization of the 1974 events, *VALISystem A* (completed 1976, published as *Radio Free Albemuth* 1987). Author Phil Dick has a friend – Nicholas – who has a series of visions which seem destined to bring down the Nixon-like President Ferris F. Fremont. Phil shares the visions, and is told by the secret police that they will write his novels if he does not cooperate. Dick's editor wanted some rewrites, but Dick produced a new novel, *VALIS* (1981). Horselover Fat (Philip = lover of horses in Greek, Dick = Fat in German) becomes Dick's alter ego, but there is the sense that he is also displaced onto the cynical Kevin and the Catholic David – characters who are also versions of Orange County writers K. W. Jeter and Tim Powers. The novel becomes an account of an extraterrestrial invasion by a child of a divine being, and includes a pocket-sized version of Dick's Exegesis.

Some critics saw this as showing that Dick had finally gone mad – a conclusion Dick would sometimes share – whereas others embraced the apparent lunacy. In *The Divine Invasion* (1981), the story is told in more science-fictional terms, as the son of God appears in a dystopian future run by a Catholic–Communist alliance. The absurdities are less troubling in a nonrealist setting. *The Transmigration of Timothy Archer* rounds off what is perceived to be a thematic trilogy (although Dick planned a further related volume, *The Owl in Daylight*). Narrator Angel mourns the death of her husband, her husband's father, and her husband's father's mistress in a *roman à clef* about James Pike, who had supposedly been contacted by his dead son, and who died in the Israeli desert, looking for evidence that the Gospels were covers for a mushroom cult. In the novel Pike/Archer might be reincarnated, but the ultra-rational Angel rejects this.

Dick died in March 1982, just before the release of the *Do Androids Dream* adaptation *Blade Runner* (Scott 1982). Despite its initial box office failure, a number of adaptations have followed, most of them substituting action for metaphysics (although see Ellis 1995 on *Total Recall* (Verhoeven 1990)). *A Scanner Darkly* (Linklater 2006) has come closest so far to capturing the spirit of the source, and original works such as *Dark City* (Proyas 1998) and *eXistenZ* (Cronenberg 1999) feel more Dickian than some of the official adaptations. The posthumous *Transmigration* was the first of a number of unpublished novels to appear. It was joined by two versions of the complete "The Unteleported Man" (1964, 1984; as *Lies, Inc.* 1985), *Radio Free Albemuth*, and a children's sf novel, *Nick and the Glimmung* (1988). Dick's various realist novels, deemed unpublishable in the 1950s and early 1960s (aside from *Confessions of a Crap Artist* (written 1959, published 1975)), also finally saw print in the 1980s, the earliest of them, *Voices from the Street*, eventually appearing in 2007; together, they document low-key infidelities and tragedies in television shops, radio stations, car dealerships, and jazz clubs in small-town America – a kind of Beat *Death of a Salesman*. Dick had reused elements of these novels, notably

Voices in *Dr Bloodmoney* (1965) and *Humpty Dumpty in Oakland* (1986), in *The Penultimate Truth* and *The Simulacra* (1964).

The 1980s also saw Dick embraced by academia – although *Science Fiction Studies* had devoted a special issue to his work as early as 1975 (and Dick had denounced the editors to the FBI; he also denounced **Stanisław Lem**, despite/because of the latter's championing of him). Before **William Gibson**, he and **Ursula K. Le Guin** were the most discussed sf authors, and he was particularly beloved by postmodernists such as Fredric Jameson and **Jean Baudrillard**. *Blade Runner* slowly became a cult hit and academic darling, its *mise-en-scène* widely copied but rarely bettered. In 1992 a supposed *Director's Cut* removed the voiceover narration, added some footage, and trimmed the ending; in 2007 *The Final Cut* tidied some errors and cleaned up the picture and sound. Today Philip K. Dick is becoming a commodity – a tool to gain tenure in academia, a means to sell popcorn in the cinema – and although there have not yet been any Philip K. Dick™ novels, K.W. Jeter has written three authorized sequels to *Blade Runner.* Describing the world as "being like a Philip K. Dick novel" has passed into general currency, and his many devotees continue to celebrate his fiction as the real thing.

See also: **Isaac Asimov, Jean Baudrillard, Greg Bear, Alfred Bester, Leigh Brackett, Octavia Butler, Samuel R. Delany, William Gibson, Robert A. Heinlein, Frank Herbert, L. Ron Hubbard, Gwyneth Jones, Ursula K. Le Guin, Stanisław Lem, Michael Moorcock, C.L. Moore, Kim Stanley Robinson, Joanna Russ, Steven Spielberg, Neal Stephenson, Darko Suvin, Sheri S. Tepper, James Tiptree Jr, and Gene Wolfe**

Bibliography

Butler, A.M. (2007) *Philip K. Dick*, Harpenden: Pocket Essentials.

Dick, P.K. (1995) "How to Build a Universe that Doesn't Fall Apart Two Days Later," in L. Sutin (ed.) *The Shifting Realities of Philip K. Dick: selected literary and philosophical writings*, New York: Pantheon.

Ellis, R.J. (1995) "'Are You a Fucking Mutant?' *Total Recall*'s fantastic hesitations," *Foundation*, 65: 81–97.

Freedman, C. (1984) "Towards a Theory of Paranoia: the science-fiction of Philip K. Dick," *Science Fiction Studies*, 11(1): 15–24.

Robinson, K.S. (1987) "Afterword," in P.K. Dick, *VALIS*, Worcester Park, Surrey: Kerosina.

Sutin, L. (1989) *Divine Invasions: a life of Philip K. Dick*, New York: Harmony Books.

ANDREW M. BUTLER

THE DOCTOR (1963–)

Fictional character, sometimes renegade Time Lord, and protagonist of the BBC's popular episodic sf adventure serial *Doctor Who* (1963–).

The most prominent character in British sf, and a significant figure in popular culture, the Doctor has featured in a range of ancillary narratives including over 400 novels and novelizations, over 160 audio dramas, many comic strips, and the noncanonical films *Doctor Who and the Daleks* (Flemyng 1965) and *Daleks – Invasion Earth 2150 A.D.* (Flemyng 1966). Conceived by Sidney Newman (Head of Drama Group), Donald Wilson (Head of Serials), writer C.E. Webber, and staff writers Donald Bull and Alice Frick, *Doctor Who* originally reflected the BBC's mission to both educate and entertain (see Cull 2001: 95–98; Chapman 2006: 12–20). The Doctor was thus initially characterized as a mysterious old man adventuring in time and space, imparting incidental lessons in history and science. He was later revealed to be a renegade Time Lord fleeing his tedious homeworld, Gallifrey. With various companions, he undertakes a self-imposed moral crusade against (often synonymous) authority and tyranny. As a Time Lord, he can "regenerate" to overcome trauma or decrepitude; to date he has regenerated nine times, enabling ten actors to play perhaps the most popular role on British television.

As Tulloch and Alvarado suggest, *Doctor Who* is "something of an institution in British cultural life" (1983: 1). His stolen TARDIS, a faulty chameleonic space–time vessel configured as a Police Box, emblematizes his character. It connotes his Britishness and "the persistence of mid-twentieth century British-ness within the series" (Cull 2001: 99). This derives, in part, from his literary ancestry. He is a distillation of H.G. Wells's Time Traveller, Arthur Conan Doyle's Sherlock Holmes and Professor Challenger, and the English "boffin." Equally, he descends from the savior–scientist personified by **Nigel Kneale**'s Quatermass and by John Fleming, the hero of *A for Andromeda* (1961) and *The Andromeda Breakthrough* (1963). He embodies "the conceptions of British-ness [that] consistently stress values of fair-play, law, order and 'decency'" (Cull 2001: 99–100), and occasionally expresses both Quatermass's paternalistic benevolence and the anger of Fleming's humanist scientist when faced with egotistical political and military authority.

Emerging from BBC Director General Hugh Carleton Greene's "liberal era," the Doctor quickly occupied a neutral middle ground from where he criticized contemporary mores. His liberalism did not manifest immediately, however. In early serials, William Hartnell's

First Doctor (1963–66) is selfish and detached, his characteristic curiosity unmitigated by consideration for others. Any positive effect he has in the universe is the byproduct of pragmatic meddling to satisfy his own agenda (most notably in "The Daleks" (1963–64)). Only through "The Sensorites" (1964), "Planet of Giants" (1964), "The Dalek Invasion of Earth" (1964), and "The Ark" (1966) did his potential for social and political commentary emerge.

This critical role was consolidated with the development of the series' Manichean view of the universe during Patrick Troughton's period as the more paternal Second Doctor (1966–69). As the historical stories were displaced by more popular futuristic encounters with "evil" alien races, tyrants, and dictators, the Doctor's opposition to such extremes became clear. His pedagogic function shifted away from science and history toward morality and integrity. In addition to the reappearance of genocidal, totalitarian, or assimilative species like the Daleks, the Cybermen, and the Ice Warriors, further "take-over" narratives marked the Doctor as an advocate of ethical interventionism opposed to oppression ("The Dominators" (1968)), megalomania ("The Invasion" (1968)), and imperialism ("The Krotons" (1968–69)).

The Doctor's anti-authority position was complicated following his exile to Earth. Recruited as scientific advisor to the United Nations Intelligence Taskforce (UNIT), a military force combating alien threats, Jon Pertwee's Third Doctor (1970–74) was absorbed into, but not fully contained by, the Establishment; he was both its agent and its critic. He defends a Britain besieged by Cold War-inspired alien invaders and by a literal national self-doubt. Fading as an imperial power, sidelined in the space race, and experiencing increasing cultural hybridity, Britain required popular reassurance and a reinvigorated conscience. To this end, Pertwee's Doctor is the most ideologically inflected incarnation, his adventures forming a series of political allegories of Britain's entry into the Common Market ("The Curse of Peladon" (1972)), decolonization ("The Mutants" (1972)), and problematic industrial relations ("The Monster of Peladon" (1974)). He reassured viewers that Britain remained central to world events while "consistently adopt[ing] the liberal populist role in criticising 'sectionalist' forces of 'Left' and 'Right', and in rebuking the 'official' and powerful in big business, the military, government and militant unions" (Tulloch and Alvarado 1983: 54). Here, the program drew on the soft science of its Wellsian model to investigate alternative cultures and advocate "a responsible cultural perspectivism" (Tulloch and Alvarado 1983: 41). Through the Third Doctor, the series promoted "a liberal discourse of 'tolerance' and 'balance' against the militaristic tendencies of the Bug Eye Monster (BEM) syndrome" (Tulloch and Alvarado 1983: 41–42). His failure at the climax of "Doctor Who and the Silurians" (1970), in which UNIT entombs a revived antediluvian species, is both an indictment of imperialist oppression and a plea for racial tolerance.

Pertwee's aristocratic aspect informed Tom Baker's Fourth Doctor (1974–81), a bohemian adventurer in whom Pertwee's patriarchal posturing and moral authority were supplanted by a more contemplative character who nevertheless underwent considerable revisions during Baker's tenure. The end of his exile on Earth not only removed obvious narrative constraints but also indicated a loss of faith in an effective Establishment, possibly reflecting disillusionment with Edward Heath's troubled government and Harold Wilson's fragile, unimaginative administration. His pantomimic cavorting in the 1977–79 seasons now seem a despairing attempt to alleviate the cultural gloom surrounding the Winter of Discontent. Similarly, his final, somber season was informed by the social and political strife of 1980–81.

However, his continued moralism restated a liberal "Britishness." Less allegorical than Pertwee's period, the Fourth Doctor era remained concerned with power relationships, with defending the individual against totalitarianism, and with animating acquiescent populations against their oppressors (see the anti-capitalist satire "The Sunmakers" (1977)). This pitting of the individual against the state epitomizes frustration at the 1970s' sense of decline, and reveals that the Doctor is reactive; lacking "a systematic political project … [his] reactive politics are linked to his lack of attachment to politics" (McKee 2004: 208) and his strong moral sensibility. This observation accounts for the narrative structure of his travels. His departure at the conclusion of each story not only satisfies the requirements of serial television but also identifies him as a moral rather than a political activist. He leaves because he is itinerant and because he does not subscribe to any particular form of socioeconomic organization beyond a vague yet enlightened society wherein everyone is treated justly.

Significantly, the activities of the "lordly" Third and Fourth Doctors suggest that they were "the last dilettante farewell of a ruling class culture" (Tulloch and Alvarado 1983: 35), the meddling of gentleman-amateurs abstracted from consequence. In later regenerations, this aristocratic resonance was muted. Attired in Edwardian cricketing clothes, Peter Davison's gentle, vulnerable Fifth Doctor (1982–84) suggested an upper class figure, but he lacked the necessary confidence and assurance. Indeed, his portrayal connoted a deposed masculine authority in keeping with the consequences of Thatcherite economic reforms, while anticipating the emergent "new man" of the early 1990s.

Margaret Thatcher's reforms exerted a literal influence over Colin Baker's brief period as the waspish Sixth Doctor (1984–86) (see Chapman 2006: 154–55). Poor production values, a frozen license fee, foreshortened seasons, and an eighteen-month suspension in production all damaged the program's viability. In hindsight, the peevishness of the Sixth Doctor implied Baker's cantankerousness at his treatment by the BBC as much as it recaptured the irritability of the First. His unpopular self-importance often overwhelmed weak stories, and only the satiric treatment of video nasties in "Vengeance on Varos" (1985) recaptured the Doctor's moral function.

Subsequently revised as a Machiavellian games-player, Sylvester McCoy's Seventh Doctor (1987–89) is a more ambiguous character. In several stories (notably "The Curse of Fenric" (1989)), the series' conventional conflicts appear alongside mythic contests between the Doctor and alien intelligences he has manipulated throughout history. This mythopoeic characterization and plotting implies dissatisfaction with material struggles and a growing ambivalence regarding the Doctor's hitherto unproblematized relationship to humans. Indeed, he is reworked to indicate that humanity is not simply the subject *of* his activities but is, in fact, subject *to* his actions. This change is unsurprising given the contemporary discontent with, and skepticism toward, authority figures that followed the stock market crash of 1987 and eight years of Thatcher government.

After the series' cancellation in 1989, the Doctor returned in the Anglo-American *Doctor Who: The Movie* (Sax 1996). Following his regeneration, the Eighth Doctor (Paul McGann) is framed visually as Christ. Although this may imply a continuation of the mythic arc begun by the Seventh Doctor, it was in fact visual shorthand designed to assist American audiences in understanding an unfamiliar character. Additionally, the Doctor was clawed back from his location as an asexual alien outsider to a position of socio-centrality where he was a half-human, heterosexual, political conservative with an uncharacteristic faith in technology. This attempt to move the Doctor toward an assumed universally appealing centrality leached the character of his idiosyncrasy. Intellectually numbing, politically complicit, and culturally stagnant, the film failed in the US and the Doctor was again consigned to history.

When *Doctor Who* returned in 2005, writer-producer and fan Russell T. Davies substantially revised both series and character. Although retaining its critical tone, critiquing human indifference, capitalism, dehumanization, and media and political manipulation, it was reconfigured as an emotionally based action-adventure. Much of its effect originated from the Ninth Doctor, who attained a previously unrealized depth of character. Played with Christopher Eccleston's customary intensity, the Doctor is the survivor of a "time war" in which the Daleks destroyed the Time Lords. His emotional and psychological trauma, which provokes bipolar swings between intense melancholy and manic activity, suggested the immediate post-9/11 Western zeitgeist. Indeed, the threats posed to various New Yorks throughout the series confirmed the program's contemporary cultural landscape, as did the emergence of the Daleks as religious fundamentalists.

The Ninth Doctor teeters on the brink of the Nietzschean abyss, struggling to resist adopting the Daleks' genocidal impulses. In his final encounter with the Daleks, he attains a new mythicism as a deity who is both savior and destroyer ("The Parting of the Ways" (2005)). Following his regeneration, the Tenth Doctor (David Tennant) is frequently described or visualized in religious terms. In "New Earth" (2006), he even describes himself as the only "higher authority." Nevertheless, he is an ambiguous savior figure, becoming, as the series unfolds, a vengeful character who not only defeats his enemies but also metes out terrible retribution ("The Family of Blood" (2007)). His actions position the audience in an ambivalent relationship with the character. As a merciless, conflicted hero, he requires the audience to question the nature of other self-professed defenders of human liberty and autonomy, to doubt and test the veracity of authority figures and their actions. In this way, he completes the trajectory begun by the Seventh Doctor.

Beneath a veneer of sexual ambivalence and doomed romanticism, the Ninth and Tenth Doctors form a metonymic expression of the division in British attitudes toward acts of intervention, manifestations of heroism, and the motivations behind undertaking punitive action that followed the 2003 invasion of Iraq. By interrogating the assumptions informing the series' original ideology of productive intervention, *Doctor Who* has acquired a new cultural significance. The character is now deconstructing itself to challenge the acceptance of self-styled messianic figures. Davies's retirement as writer-producer and the subsequent resignation of Tennant leave the character's future trajectory uncertain in the hands of experienced writer-producer Steven Moffat and relatively unknown actor Matt Smith.

See also: **Gerry Anderson, Nigel Kneale, Gene Roddenberry, J. Michael Straczynski, and H.G. Wells**

Bibliography

Butler, D. (ed.) (2007) *Time and Relative Dissertations in Space: critical perspectives on Doctor Who*, Manchester: Manchester University Press.

Chapman, J. (2006) *Inside the Tardis: the worlds of Doctor Who*, London: I.B. Tauris.

Cull, N. (2001) "'Bigger on the inside': *Doctor Who* as British Cultural History," in G. Roberts and P.M. Taylor (eds.) *The Historian, Television and Television History*, Luton: University of Luton Press.

McKee, A. (2004) "Is Doctor Who Political?," *European Journal of Cultural Studies*, 7(2): 201–17.

Tulloch, J. and Alvarado, M. (1983) *Doctor Who: the unfolding text*, London: Macmillan.

PETER WRIGHT

GREG[ORY MARK] EGAN (1961–)

Australian author.

Greg Egan has published eight novels and over 50 short stories, many collected in *Axiomatic* (1995), *Our Lady of Chernobyl* (1995), *Luminous* (1998), and *Dark Integers and Other Stories* (2008). He holds a B.S. in Mathematics (University of Western Australia) and has been a full-time writer since 1992. He won the John W. Campbell Memorial Award for *Permutation City* (1994) and the Hugo, *Locus*, and *Asimov's* Readers Awards for "Oceanic" (1998). Widely considered one of the preeminent figures of post-cyberpunk sf, he has been described as possibly "the best new hard-science writer to enter the field since **Greg Bear**" (Dozois 2007: 457).

Egan's fictions are replete with hard-sf devices, including computer simulations (*Permutation City*, "A Kidnapping" (1995)), genetic hybridity ("The Caress" (1990)), biology ("Yeyuka" (1997)), neurobiology ("Reasons to Be Cheerful" (1997)), evolution (*Teranesia* (1999)), nanotechnology ("Axiomatic" (1990)), (post)organic bodies ("The Cutie" (1989), *Diaspora* (1997), "Riding the Crocodile" (2006), *Incandescence* (2008)), and quantum mechanics ("The Planck Dive" (1998), *Schild's Ladder* (2002)). Egan has no qualms about deploying hard sf to service his metaphysical thought experiments: "What happens in my novels is that the border between science and metaphysics shifts … I'm writing about extending science into territory that was once believed to be metaphysical, not about abandoning or 'transcending' science at all" (Pavón 1998).

Diverse posthuman universes provide Egan with a hard-sf canvas on which to address such concerns as being, desire, ethics/morality, simulation, identity, and the very fabric of reality. "Learning to Be Me" (1990) and "Closer" (1992) feature the Ndoli Device, a neural computer that perfectly imitates the organic brain, thus enabling escape from corporeal limitations; in these stories, posthumans routinely swap bodies. In "Closer," both Michael and Sian test their relationship and the subjective *experience* of reality by switching bodies in various configurations before temporarily synchronizing their Ndoli Devices to experience the *same* reality *simultaneously*. Beyond exploring the limitations and scope of experiential reality, "Closer" is queerly provocative: malleable bodies can readily adopt male or female physiology, thereby prompting questions regarding the straight mind of heteronormativity. "The Cutie" also provokes reconsiderations of gender, biology, and parenting. Frank, unable to convince his girlfriend Diane to bear his child, opts to become pregnant with his own genetically tailored offspring. The Taiwanese "Cutie kit" allows him to carry a baby to term and experience fatherhood, even if that baby is not technically human. In "Axiomatic," Mark Carver also takes matters into his own hands when he circumvents his own moral code by snorting an off-the-shelf nanotechnological behavior modifier (an axiomatic) so that he can fulfill his desire to kill his wife's murderer.

As these stories demonstrate, a major theme in Egan's work is the use of science and technology to surmount biological limitations and open new vistas of experience. For example, "Riding the Crocodile" opens with the matter-of-fact statement that "In the ten thousand, three hundred and ninth year of marriage, Leila and Jasim began contemplating death" (Egan 2007b: 458), and *Incandescence*'s Rakesh is "affronted" when asked, "Are you a child of DNA?" (Egan 2008: 1). Egan's posthuman universes, in which distributed or networked consciousness is the norm, sound the "death knell for the unified self" (Farnell 2000: 74). The posthumanity in *Diaspora*'s far-future is even organized into at-times rival posthuman polises. In the Konishi polis, citizens are "grown from a mind seed, a string of instruction codes like a digital genome" in the re-creation of "neuroembryology in software" (Egan 1997: 5). Anachronistic fleshers still have their organic bodies, while Gleisner robots house human minds in robot chassis. *Diaspora* includes a universe-spanning quest for scientific knowledge conducted by thousands of copies of Carter-Zimmerman, a polis that, atypically, has not become solipsistic and still values materiality, even if "it's as arbitrary as any other choice of values"

(Egan 1997: 217). Similarly, the *Subjective Ontology* cycle – *Quarantine*, *Permutation City*, *Distress* (1995) – envisions "the human/computer connection not as a question of technology … but as an ontological inquiry into the relation of humans to the universe … each of the novels speculates that there are deep connections between human consciousness and the computational processes that generate the universe" (Hayles 2005: 218).

Egan also sounds the death knell for mortality. Denizens of his futures are generally laissez faire about their immortality – they "switch" via Ndoli Devices, upload themselves into virtual domains ("A Kidnapping"), or clone bodies ("The Caress") – but the consequences of this attitude are problematic, often driving the plots. Egan's style is instructive: a "dedicated ambivalence" (Farnell 2000: 85) permeates his work. In *Permutation City*, Paul Durham, the Copy, fails in his suicide attempt shortly after his digital resurrection. The novel also reveals that millions preferred suicide as a viable alternative to the boredom of digital immortality in the virtual world of Elysium. In "Riding the Crocodile," Leila and Jasim decide they have accomplished their life's goals and plan one more "grand and audacious" (Egan 2007b: 458) project before choosing to die, while in "Closer" Michael and Sian's relationship dies under the weight of *too much* intimacy. Rakesh, hopelessly bored by his posthuman existence in *Incandescence*, likens it to a "stupefying dream that had gone on so long he's stopped believing that it could ever end" (Egan 2008: 3). When Frank's Cutie begins to exceed its programming, impossibly exhibiting verbal skills, he must consider whether this biological simulacrum is any less deserving of his anguish when its lifespan eventually terminates than a "real" child would have been. Similarly, in "A Kidnapping" David reasons that the kidnapped *simulation* of his wife Loraine is as worthy of saving as the "real" Loraine, and he therefore agrees to pay the interminable yearly ransom.

Egan is as likely to leave his characters on a metaphysical precipice as on a peak. In "Axiomatic," Mark's newfound axiomatic-induced unshakeable certainty that death "simply didn't matter, any more than the death of a fly or an amoeba" (Egan 1995: 135), leads him to become unexpectedly dependent on the axiomatic: "having tasted the freedom of certainty I find I can't live without it" (Egan 1995: 135). The protagonist of "Reasons to be Cheerful" uses his neural prosthesis to control his entire emotional spectrum and is left "walking the convoluted border between meaningless happiness and meaningless despair" (Egan 1998: 227). The mathematical principles structuring the universe in "Luminous" and "Dark Integers" (2007) are posited not as timeless equations contained in a "universal book of truths" (Egan 2007a: 28) but as malleable, nonuniversal, localized principles. Karpal, a Gleisner robot of *Diaspora*, reveals to Paolo Venetti the existence of a pocket-universe running on a 25,000 ton biological computer, but Paolo reels at the metaphysical conundrum: "if nature had evolved 'organisms' as divorced from reality as the inhabitants of the most inward-looking polis, where was the privileged status of the physical universe, the clear distinction between reality and illusion?" (Egan 1997: 236). Finally, *Quarantine* presupposes that human observation – the pathologically limited scope of human faculties – is responsible for an increasingly limited or stunted universe. Humanity's quarantine in the Bubble, an impenetrable shield encasing the solar system, is necessary if the universe is to grow.

Other pocket-universes appear in Egan's fiction: the central bulge of the Milky Way occupied by the Aloof of both "Riding the Crocodile" and *Incandescence*; the universe of nonstandard arithmetic that exists just beyond the "defect" in "Luminous" and "Dark Integers"; *Permutation City*'s Elysium and the Autoverse, a simulation-within-a-simulation occupied by the insectoid Lambertians. His most effective pocket-universe is the novo-vacuum of *Schild's Ladder*, the product of experimental research into loop quantum gravity and the quantum graph theory. In a universe where "humanity has become so thoroughly postbiological that most people no longer feel anxiety about losing their birth bodies" (Hayles 2005: 238), *Schild's Ladder*'s novo-vacuum is a "kind of 'other' universe that will inexorably erase and replace everything – planets, galaxies, the whole of the known universe – if it is not stopped" (Hollinger 2006: 458). Six hundred years after its accidental creation, the expanding novo-vacuum shows no sign of slowing. The Preservationists wish to stop its slow consumption of the universe; the Yielders want it preserved in the interests of scientific inquiry. The tensions between these posthuman factions are represented by Mariama and Tchicaya, whose respective philosophies affect their motivations, their love, and their shared (if not conflicted) desires. Farah Mendlesohn describes *Schild's Ladder* as an "exemplar" of sf because it embodies the genre's chief modalities: a sense of wonder; the grotesque; the thought-experiment; cognitive estrangement; subtlety; linguistic and technological metaphors; isolation and alienation; unstable gender designations; queer sexualities; and a polysemic discourse (Mendlesohn 2003: 1–11).

Egan's indebtedness to hard science extends to his website (www.gregegan.net), a cornucopia of information, including "Science Notes" (derived from his online participation on sci.physics.research), the

Foundations articles (first published in issues of *Eidolon*) on physics and science fiction, some free downloads of his shorter fiction, and java-enabled research papers. One can also find his essay on asylum claimants detained in Australia's immigration detention centers ("The Razor Wire Looking Glass" (2003)), a subject important to Egan and one that saw him take a sabbatical from writing fiction in the early years of the new millennium. Among his recent publications, both "Glory" (2007) and "Steve Fever" (2007) appeared in *The Year's Best Science Fiction: twenty-fifth annual collection* (2008). Without a doubt, Egan is "one of the most significant talents to enter the field in the last several decades," and he "is still growing in range, power, and sophistication" (Dozois 2007: 457).

See also: **Iain M. Banks, Jean Baudrillard, Greg Bear, William Gibson, Donna J. Haraway, Nalo Hopkinson, Gwyneth Jones, and China Miéville**

Bibliography

Dozois, G. (ed.) (2007) *The Year's Best Science Fiction: twenty-fourth annual collection*, New York: St. Martin's Griffin.

Egan, G. (1995) "Axiomatic," in *Axiomatic*, London: Millennium.

——(1997) *Diaspora*, London: Orion.

——(1998) "Reasons to be Cheerful," in *Luminous*, London: Millennium.

——(2007a) "Dark Integers," *Asimov's Science Fiction*, October/November: 20–51.

——(2007b) "Riding the Crocodile," in G. Dozois (ed.) *The Year's Best Science Fiction: twenty-fourth annual collection*, New York: St. Martin's Griffin.

——(2008) *Incandescence*, San Francisco: Night Shade Books.

Farnell, R. (2000) "Attempting Immortality: AI, A-life, and the posthuman in Greg Egan's *Permutation City*," *Science Fiction Studies*, 27(1): 69–91.

Hayles, N.K. (2005) *My Mother Was a Computer: digital subjects and literary texts*, Chicago: University of Chicago Press.

Hollinger, V. (2006) "Stories about the Future: from patterns of expectation to pattern recognition," *Science Fiction Studies*, 33(3): 452–72.

Kioseoglou, N. (2002) "'Wishes of Man': exploring problems of identity in times of change, as reflected in science fiction drawing upon themes of biotechnology," in D. Pastourmatzi (ed.) *Biotechnological and Medical Themes in Science Fiction*, Thessaloniki, Greece: University Studio.

Kraus, E. (2002) "Biotech Bodies, Identity and Power in Works by Rebecca Ore, Pat Cadigan, Greg Egan and Greg Bear," in D. Pastourmatzi (ed.) *Biotechnological and Medical Themes in Science Fiction*, Thessaloniki, Greece: University Studio.

Leaver, T. (2004) "Iatrogenic Permutations: from digital genesis to the artificial other," *Comparative Literature Studies*, 41(3): 424–35.

Mendlesohn, F. (2003) "Introduction: reading science fiction," in E. James and F. Mendlesohn (eds.) *The Cambridge Companion to Science Fiction*, Cambridge: Cambridge University Press.

Murphy, G.J. (2004) "Temporal Inoculation in Greg Egan's 'The Hundred-Light-Year Diary' and Robert Charles Wilson's *The Chronoliths*," *Foundation*, 91: 72–80.

Pavón, C. (1998) "The Way Things Are," *Gigamesh*, 15. Online. Available: <http://gregegan.customer.netspace.net.au/INTERVIEWS/Interviews.html#Gigamesh> (accessed 1 January 2009).

GRAHAM J. MURPHY

HUGO GERNSBACK [BORN HUGO GERNSBACHER] (1884–1967)

Luxembourg-born US inventor, publisher, editor, and writer.

Hugo Gernsback is primarily noteworthy for editing and publishing the first science-fiction magazines and establishing sf as a recognized literary genre. To be sure, many writers before Gernsback, most notably **Jules Verne** and **H.G. Wells**, had written stories which are now universally recognized as sf, but Gernsback was the first person to figure out and announce a system for recognizing, and producing, such stories. In the editorials, story introductions, and responses to readers' letters that appeared in his pioneering *Amazing Stories* and later magazines, he repeatedly announced the three characteristic features of sf, which he first named and identified in "A New Sort of Magazine," his editorial in the first issue of *Amazing Stories* (1926): an sf story was a narrative ("charming romance") that incorporated accurate scientific information ("scientific fact") and predictions logically derived from that information ("prophetic vision"). These elements provided sf with three natural audiences – general readers, bright adolescents, and working scientists and inventors – and three major purposes – to entertain, to provide a scientific education, and to offer ideas for possible scientific advances. Unlike the innumerable predictions which Gernsback kept tossing out in articles for his popular science magazines, a prediction embedded in an appealing story could reach a wide audience, including scientists and inventors who might be inspired by the story to actually construct the imagined invention or something similar to it – which made sf, by Gernsback's argument, a uniquely important form of literature. Furthermore, placing a prediction within a story could encourage writers to consider not only how an invention might be achieved, but also what effects it might have on a future society, further enhancing the value of the genre (a point recognized and proclaimed by Gernsback's most prominent successor as an sf magazine editor and commentator, John W. Campbell Jr). By vigorously promoting his ideas about sf, Gernsback was soon able to inspire and forge a growing community of enthusiasts and essentially train a new generation of writers, establishing firm foundations for the genre which have endured to the present day.

Gernsback's singular vision of sf stemmed from his lifelong devotions to practical science and writing fiction. Born in Luxembourg in 1884, he quickly immersed himself in the emerging science of electronics and as a teenager was already earning money by working in that area; however, a common story that his interest in imaginative science was first sparked by reading a German translation of a Percival Lowell book about Mars cannot be accurate, since no such translations existed during Gernsback's youth. Seeking greater opportunities to profit from one of his inventions, a new type of battery, he emigrated to America in 1904, quickly set up businesses to market innovations in electronics and radio, and began regularly publishing a catalog of electronic equipment which, in 1908, he transformed into his first magazine, *Practical Electrics*. All the while, he had also been writing for his private enjoyment, including an unpublished picaresque novel written in German, and in 1911 he seized the opportunity to combine his two interests by beginning to write a serialized novel, *Ralph 124C 41+: a romance of the year 2660* (1911–12), for his magazine.

This novel justified its appearance in a science magazine by incorporating lengthy descriptions of predicted inventions, initially as part of a leisurely paced narrative combining the genres of utopia and the travel tale, as Ralph 124C 41+ (whose numerical surname punningly translates to "one to foresee for one"), one of the world's ten greatest scientists, gives his new girlfriend Alice a guided tour of the scientific wonders of America in the year 2660. Later, though, the novel abruptly lurches into melodrama, as two rivals appear for Alice's affections, one of whom kidnaps her and flies into space, which requires Ralph to pursue them (and invent a form of radar in order to track them down); even a touch of Gothic horror emerges in the final sequence, in which Ralph must literally devise a way to bring Alice back from the dead by draining her blood and employing a special substance to revive her. Gernsback expanded and heavily revised the novel for book publication in 1925, striving to combine its disparate generic elements more smoothly and adding some touches of satire, but the work remains poorly written and clumsily executed. Still, it has been republished four times (1929, 1950, 1958, 2000), allowing the novel to exert its own limited influence on the genre (if nothing else, *Ralph 124C 41+* has been repeatedly chastised and parodied as a perfect example of the sort of sf one should avoid). The novel rewards critical attention as a compendium of potential approaches to writing sf which later authors would exploit more skillfully.

The popularity of *Ralph 124C 41+* led Gernsback to recruit other writers to produce fiction along similar lines for *Practical Electrics* and several later magazines, so he went back to devoting most of his energies to editing and publishing (which had now become his major business), though he continued to write occasional fiction, such as "The Magnetic Storm" (1918), which didactically presented his plan to end the First World War by using electromagnetism to disable all of Germany's machinery. His most prominent later works were the novels *Baron Munchhausen's New Scientific Adventures* (serialized in his magazine *Electrical Experimenter* from 1915 to 1917 and never republished in full in book form), in which the well-known eighteenth-century liar meddles in the First World War and then embarks upon an episodic journey into space that gradually loses its satiric bite and devolves into a dull utopia, and the posthumously published *Ultimate World* (1971), a fitfully intriguing tale of enigmatic alien visitors who greatly increase the intelligence of Earth's children. Nevertheless, it was as an editor of sf magazines that Gernsback would have his greatest impact on the field.

After a special "Scientific Fiction" issue of his magazine *Science and Invention* proved successful in 1923, Gernsback began planning to publish an all-sf magazine, which finally appeared as *Amazing Stories* in 1926. He initially described the fiction he was publishing as "scientifiction," a portmanteau blending of his earlier term "scientific fiction," but when he lost control of *Amazing Stories* in 1929, as a result of some controversial financial difficulties, he was obliged to devise a new term, "science fiction," for the new magazine *Science Wonder Stories*, which later combined with another new magazine, *Air Wonder Stories*, to become *Wonder Stories*. (Later research has shown that the term "science fiction" had been independently coined in 1851 by an obscure critic, William Wilson, then unknown to Gernsback and everyone else.) His early magazines saved money by featuring numerous reprinted stories by Verne, Wells, Edgar Allan Poe, and other older writers. This enabled Gernsback to effectively promulgate the first history of sf through his comments on these and other pioneering authors, although later he exclusively published original stories by living writers, including a number of prominent sf writers whose careers he launched, such as Jack Williamson, Clifford D. Simak, and Stanley G. Weinbaum. He also encouraged his readers to try their hand at writing sf by means of various story contests, one of which produced the first story written by a woman to appear in an sf magazine, Clare Winger Harris's "The Fate of the Poseidonia" (1927). Despite Gernsback's preference for stories about earthbound inventors and their extensively explained handiwork, the enormous popularity of another writer he discovered, E.E. "Doc" Smith (whose *The Skylark of Space*, co-written with Lee Hawkins Garby, first appeared in *Amazing Stories* in 1928), led in his sf magazines of the 1930s to the increasing prominence of extravagant space adventures, eventually to be sarcastically christened "space opera" by Wilson Tucker.

Among other accomplishments, Gernsback was the first to devise visual symbols for sf, including the rocketship that has become its most ubiquitous symbol, and his magazines regularly published letters from enthusiastic readers and included their addresses, enabling devotees of the genre to get in touch with each other – the first stirrings of sf fandom. To further encourage fan activity, in 1934 he set up the first formal organization of sf fans, the Science Fiction League. However, his influence over the field was diminished by his knack for alienating writers through minuscule or perpetually delayed payments for their stories: H.P. Lovecraft always described him as "Hugo the Rat," and Donald A. Wollheim joined several writers in suing Gernsback in order to receive payment for their work.

Always devoted to making money at all costs – as his detractors often observe – Gernsback temporarily abandoned the field of sf in 1936, when he sold his increasingly unprofitable magazine *Wonder Stories* (renamed *Thrilling Wonder Stories* by its new publisher) and concentrated on other publishing endeavors, most notoriously the magazine *Sexology*. But he kept writing sf for his own enjoyment, and he twice attempted to re-enter the field with short-lived publications: a comic book, *Superworld Comics* (1940), and a glossy magazine, *Science-Fiction Plus* (1953); he also began annual production of a privately published magazine (initially styled as parodies of various magazines but later entitled *Forecast*) filled with his stories and mock news articles, which he mailed to friends every year as his personal Christmas card. Although never regarded as a likable or gregarious person, Gernsback was invited to be the Guest of Honor at the 1952 World Science Fiction Convention, and fandom's most prestigious awards were named the Hugo Awards in his honor. In articles and interviews from the early 1940s, he readily embraced the epithet "father of science fiction," but he devoted more energy to celebrating himself in another way – as the world's most prolific and accurate predictor of scientific advances (the view promoted most recently in *Hugo Gernsback: a man well ahead of his time* (2007)). He continued publishing and writing, including a few essays about sf, until his death in 1967.

When sf criticism first became a serious business in the 1960s and 1970s, there was initially a tendency to dismiss Gernsback as a baleful influence on the genre because of his inept writing and insistence upon stories with extended scientific explanations – Brian W. Aldiss's *Billion Year Spree: the true history of science fiction* (1973) denounced him as "one of the worst disasters ever to hit the science fiction field" (Aldiss 1973: 209) – but more recent commentators have acknowledged his importance, and he has been the subject of several extended analyses and energetically championed by commentators like Mike Ashley and Gary Westfahl. Needless to say, Gernsback's own limited concept of the genre, as a form of literature most valuable as a forum for shoptalk among scientists and inventors considering and critiquing new scientific concepts, has endured only in the subgenre of hard sf, among writers and readers who mainly gravitate to the magazine *Analog: Science Fiction/Science Fact*; but the broader implications of his theory of sf as a genre with a unique identity and great social significance have had an impact on all of its writers and readers to this day, even those who would appear to have little in common with him.

See also: **Samuel R. Delany, Michael Moorcock, Darko Suvin, Jules Verne, and H.G. Wells**

Bibliography

Aldiss, B. (1973) *Billion Year Spree: the true history of science fiction*, Garden City, NY: Doubleday.

Ashley, M. and Lowndes, R.A.W. (2004) *The Gernsback Days: a study of the evolution of modern science fiction from 1911 to 1936*, Holicong, PA: Wildside Press.

Moskowitz, S. (1963) "Hugo Gernsback, Father of Science Fiction," in *Explorers of the Infinite: shapers of science fiction*, Cleveland, OH: World Publishing.

Stashower, D. (1990) "A Dreamer Who Made Us Fall in Love with the Future," *Smithsonian*, 21(5): 44–55.

Steckler, L. (ed.) (2007) *Hugo Gernsback: a man well ahead of his time*, Marana, AZ: Poptronix.

Westfahl, G. (1998) *The Mechanics of Wonder: the creation of the idea of science fiction*, Liverpool: Liverpool University Press.
——(2007) *Hugo Gernsback and the Century of Science Fiction*, Jefferson, NC: McFarland.

GARY WESTFAHL

WILLIAM [FORD] GIBSON (1948–)

US-born, Canadian novelist, known especially for his first novel, *Neuromancer* (1984).

Born in South Carolina and raised in Virginia, William Gibson moved to Toronto in 1968, a relocation inspired partially by the lively bohemian counterculture then developing in Toronto's Yorkville neighborhood. Married in 1972 to Deborah Thompson, he graduated from the University of British Columbia in 1977, majoring in English literature, and settled in Vancouver. He maintains dual US–Canadian citizenship.

While Gibson read sf in his youth, he did not try writing it until the professor on a UBC sf course suggested a story rather than a term paper, resulting in "Fragments of a Hologram Rose," which in 1977 was his first publication. Other stories followed: "The Gernsback Continuum" (1981) in a high-profile anthology, *Universe 11*, edited by Terry Carr; "Johnny Mnemonic" (1981), "Hinterlands" (1981), "Burning Chrome" (1982), and "New Rose Hotel" (1984) in the prestigious *Omni* magazine. These and other stories were collected as *Burning Chrome* (1986). By 1982 *Neuromancer* had been commissioned by Terry Carr as an Ace Special.

During the early 1980s Gibson befriended the writers John Shirley and Bruce Sterling, all then associated with the "punk sf" that soon became "cyberpunk," an influential if never quite coherent movement. For better or worse, cyberpunk quickly found its fellow traveler in postmodernism, especially in academic circles and among glossy promotions in mass-market magazines. By the early 1990s cyberpunk had entered senescence, but both the term and the subgenre tropes have shown remarkable resilience. Adopting "cyberpunk" from a 1983 Bruce Bethke story in *Amazing*, Gardner Dozois "defined the movement" in a *Washington Post* article "by applying the term to works set in computer-driven, high-tech near future venues inhabited by a slumming streetwise citizenry for whom the real world is an environment, not a project. In terms of traditional US sf, this was heresy" (Clute 1993: 493). Although Gibson coined the term "cyberspace" and first envisioned computer hackers called "console cowboys" in "Burning Chrome," *Neuromancer*, a book often thought to be the paradigmatic representation of cyberpunk, would be his breakthrough success.

Case, a self-destructive hacker, is recruited by the mercenary Molly to join a gang led by Armitage, who in turn is employed by the mysterious Wintermute. Others join the motley cast, which conducts two "runs": the first a heist to steal the recorded personality of the great hacker McCoy Pauley (aka The Dixie Flatline), the second a plan to penetrate the databanks of the conglomerate Tessier–Ashpool so as to enable Wintermute to merge with Neuromancer, both of which are artificial intelligences. Although the Turing Police attempt to intervene, the central impediments are the characters' own personality fragmentation, self-hatred, perversity, and despair. They do succeed, though the book ends without revealing what merged A.I.s means. Two partial sequels – *Count Zero* (magazine serial and book both 1986) and *Mona Lisa Overdrive* (1988) – explore some of the consequences. Collectively known as the *Sprawl* trilogy, since they all involve the metropolitan sprawl between Boston and Atlanta, the novels neither tell a single, sequential narrative nor offer a resolution of the plot. *Count Zero* also introduced a technique that Gibson has continued to use: multiple narrative strands in separate or alternating chapters which eventually converge or connect.

Neuromancer swept sf's major awards. The rhetoric of its reception was highly charged, with hyperbole the chief vector within both camps. Proponents praised the dark new vision of human life under global capitalism and the energetic vigor it injected into what they perceived as a moribund genre. Detractors disparaged its cynicism, nihilism, diffidence, overwrought style, and romanticization of addiction, criminality, and depravity. A high-tech hard-boiled thriller, *Neuromancer* is less notable for its exciting plot than the rich texture of its prose, its foci of attention, its engagement with mass culture, and the way it crystallizes many separate threads that would subsequently transform sf. A partial list would include: an aggressive punk-rock aesthetic; hyperbolic imagery and tropes; frank endorsements of recreational drug use; petty thieves on mean streets shadowed by the insidious, nefarious operations of the multinationals that have filled the power vacuum left by the postindustrial disarticulation of the nation-state; the transnational superimposition of the global on the local, erasing or eliding cultural and geographic borders; decentralized personal agency, often aided by prosthetic or cybernetic alterations of the human body; and particular attention to the economic and technological influence of non-Western cultures, especially Japan. Gibson's singular achievement was in synthesizing and combining such separate threads into one densely interwoven fabric.

Neuromancer represents both a radical break with sf and a profound revivification of its most cherished conventions. One example concerns body invasion and the mediation of human consciousness. The novel's treatment of prosthetic or cybernetic modification suggests a step toward a coming posthuman or cyborg amalgam of human and machine, the confrontation and conflation of which have remained a central trope in sf since its beginnings. Another example can be found in the literary style. Take the novel's justly famous first sentence: "The sky above the port was the color of television, tuned to a dead channel." Here the natural world becomes *the failure to be* a mass media technology; dead channels represent a disruptive static or cognitive dissonance, a core theme of the novel; the sentence also identifies the narrative's preference for arresting visual imagery. That this single sentence does so many things simultaneously signals something of the novel's lyric and thematic density; Gibson's richly suggestive figures are conveyed by even the smallest detail. *Neuromancer*'s tropes and ideas have so permeated sf that it is hard to replicate their initial, tactile impact. One index of that impact is the sheer amount of scholarship precipitated by the novel. In both sf studies and mainstream literary studies, more attention has centered on *Neuromancer* than on any other work of genre sf, certainly of books published since 1984.

All three *Sprawl* novels address the exotic lure of innovative technology presaging the posthuman, a new and separate species; quite possibly this change will mean transcendence, but the series remains extremely ambivalent about potential results, which are disturbingly ambiguous. The two other *Sprawl* novels are less frenetic and increasingly more controlled, the characters have greater subtlety and depth, but the stories also become more melodramatic and clichéd. They are much sadder, too, and the pathetic despair of the abject characters is less seductive than in *Neuromancer*.

Gibson's second series is usually called the *Bridge* trilogy, for two of the three titles feature characters who have transformed the San Francisco–Oakland Bay bridge into a neighborhood – tenements and businesses and bars serving the lost, the marginal, the exiled. While *Virtual Light* (1993), *Idoru* (1996), and *All Tomorrow's Parties* (1999) tell a much more tightly knit tale than the *Sprawl* books, they also are best understood as panels of a triptych – interlocking or imbricated scenes rather than a single story arc. Also telling is the modification of style: by the time of *Mona Lisa Overdrive*, the hyperbole and excess of *Neuromancer* had collapsed into a plain, by comparison almost minimalist, prose; a preference for understated, deceptively uncluttered sentences has remained Gibson's inclination. His accomplishment in these often neglected books has been undervalued; in some ways they constitute a retraction or reversal of the key motifs and representations of the *Sprawl* trilogy.

In between the *Sprawl* and *Bridge* series, Gibson co-wrote with Bruce Sterling a novel of steampunk alternate history, *The Difference Engine* (1991). Set in 1855 London amid spies and international conspiracies, it ponders what might have changed had the British mathematician Charles Babbage (with the help of Byron's daughter, Ada Lovelace) developed his early computer, an "analytic" or "difference engine." Like the two series, *The Difference Engine* is centrally interested in how burgeoning technologies reshape humanity.

The timeshifts in setting are telling, for while *The Difference Engine* occurs in our past, Gibson's work has progressively moved from the near future to the almost present. *Neuromancer*'s world is perhaps 50 years into the future, the *Bridge* triptych's not more than 20, and the most recent novels, *Pattern Recognition* (2003) and *Spook Country* (2007), are set in the nominal present. These last fictions are less overtly science-fictional than his earlier work, and Gibson has remarked that he no longer sees himself as writing sf. Nevertheless, both books still resonate within the genre, in much the same manner as new weird or steampunk writing by figures such as **China Miéville** and **Neal Stephenson**. Perhaps they may be best thought of as "slipstream" titles – mainstream books that deploy some of the tropes and topoi frequently found in sf. In *Pattern Recognition*, Cayce Pollard is a "coolhunter," someone who anticipates trends in fashion and style and sells this prescience to marketing firms. Seeking something authentic, something that is only itself rather than a brand or an attempt to make a buck, she becomes obsessed with fragments of film footage that are circulating across the internet. Funded by a nefarious advertising executive, she searches for the maker of the footage, from London to Tokyo to Moscow. The openly comic *Spook Country* finds a similar character in similar conditions. Freelance journalist Hollis Henry is writing an article for a magazine called *Node*. But *Node* does not exist – it is just another device for the nefarious ad man to yoke Hollis to search out hidden secrets, so the book also involves a code-breaker, former and current federal spies, a conspiracy to defraud the feds by stealing public cash, and a counterplot to defeat the first plot.

From "Fragments of a Hologram Rose" to *Spook Country*, certain motifs have pervaded Gibson's work. Many of the stories and all of his novels are "capers" or searches, structured around tropes of detection and interpretation. While his prose is no longer as manic or dense, the fiction's rich texture still vibrates with nuance and irony. Thematically, Gibson's work obsessively invokes a limited set of concerns. One is the cultural and economic reorganization caused by the speed and nature of the networked information technology that is transforming global culture. A second is the uneven distribution of access to and the dangerous secrecy of archived data – leading Gibson to make one of his most famous remarks, given often in interviews and widely cited: "The future is here. It's just not evenly distributed yet." A third, and perhaps the most important, is that his fiction continually returns to the liminal – the threshold moments of the collapse of one condition and the possibility of transformation, either cultural or personal.

But there has also been an acute arc that reveals significant modifications of style and attention, especially from cold, diffident surfaces toward warmer, human interiors. To use just one of many possible illustrations, in *Neuromancer* Molly cannot cry – her eyes have been walled off by prosthetic implants (the famous cyberpunk emblem of mirrorshades), so her tears are converted to spit. As a sharp contrast, *Pattern Recognition* concludes with Cayce's tears: "she was weeping for her century, though whether the one past or the one present she doesn't know" (Gibson 2003: 356). Gibson's fiction has moved from solipsistic self-enclosure to the empathetic opening to individual change. A remarkable, influential innovator, Gibson is unquestionably one of the most important figures in sf's last several decades, with one of the most distinctive voices and visions in the history of the genre.

See also: **J.G. Ballard, Jean Baudrillard, Greg Bear, Alfred Bester, Octavia Butler, David Cronenberg, Samuel R. Delany, Philip K. Dick, Donna J. Haraway, China Miéville, Michael Moorcock, Kim Stanley Robinson, Joanna Russ, Mary Shelley, and Neal Stephenson**

Bibliography

Clute, J. (1993) "William Gibson," in J. Clute and P. Nicholls (eds.) *The Encyclopedia of Science Fiction*, London: Orbit.

Csicsery-Ronay Jr, I. (1995) "Antimancer: cybernetics and art in Gibson's *Count Zero*," *Science Fiction Studies*, 22(1): 63–86.

Gibson, W. (2003) *Pattern Recognition*, New York: Putnam.

McCaffery, L. (ed.) (1991) *Storming the Reality Studio: a casebook of postmodern science fiction*, Durham, NC, and London: Duke University Press.
Myers, T. (2001) "The Postmodern Imaginary in William Gibson's *Neuromancer*," *Modern Fiction Studies*, 47(4): 887–909.
No Maps for These Territories (Mark Neale US 2001).
Rapatzikou, T.G. (2004) *Gothic Motifs in the Fiction of William Gibson*, New York: Rodopi.

NEIL EASTERBROOK

DONNA J[EANNE] HARAWAY (1944–)

US feminist scholar of science and technology who frequently uses sf in her work.

Donna Haraway's influence on the study of the genre is probably most evident in the prominence of "A Cyborg Manifesto: science, technology, and socialist-feminism in the late twentieth century." Originally published in 1985 as "Manifesto for Cyborgs: science, technology, and socialist feminism in the 1980s," it was a response to a request from *Socialist Review* to write on "what socialist-feminist priorities are in the Reagan years" (Haraway 2000: 39), comprising an analysis of the cyborg as a potent metaphor for a new subjectivity which refuses the binaries that have structured much of Western thought. Haraway's cyborg is conceived "as a fiction mapping our social and bodily reality and as an imaginative resource suggesting some very fruitful couplings" (Haraway 1991: 150). The essay's provocative claim that "the boundary between science fiction and social reality is an optical illusion" (Haraway 1991: 149) points to the interpenetration of Haraway's methodology and sf's extrapolative techniques.

Haraway is the author of five major books, all of which focus on the relationship between nature and culture: *Crystals, Fabrics and Fields* (1976), *Primate Visions* (1989), *Simians, Cyborgs and Women* (1991), *Modest_Witness@Second_Millennium.FemaleMan©Meets_OncoMouse™* (1997), and *When Species Meet* (2008). She has a Ph.D. in biology, but even in her doctoral research (which became *Crystals*) she found herself drawn to understanding "biology in a double way – as about the way the world works biologically, but also about the way the world works metaphorically" (Haraway 2000: 24). Her academic career has predominantly been spent at the innovative History of Consciousness program at the University of California, Santa Cruz, where she was hired in 1980 to the first US academic post in feminist theory. She has won the Gustavus Myers Human Rights Award (1990), the Ludwick Fleck Prize (1991) for *Modest_Witness*, the Robert K. Merton Award (1992) for *Primate Visions*, the American Book Award (1992) for *Simians*, and the J.D. Bernal Prize for lifetime achievement (2000) in the social study of science.

Haraway's mode of analysis makes her significant to the study of sf. She argues for the commonality between her concerns and those of sf authors, particularly feminists. She shares with writers such as Doris Lessing, Marge Piercy, **Joanna Russ**, **Ursula K. Le Guin**, **James Tiptree Jr**, and **Octavia E. Butler** a desire for "telling and retelling stories in the attempt to shift the webs of intertextuality and to facilitate perhaps new possibilities for the meanings of difference, reproduction, and survival for specifically located members of the primate order – on both sides of the bio-political and cultural divide between human and animal" (Haraway 1989: 377). Telling stories is central to Haraway's analyses of primatology, the biology of sex and gender, the immune system, cyborgs, genetics, the practice of science, and companion species. Moving between specific, historically located examples and the wider nexus of ideologies, histories, material practices, institutions, and lifestyles that are their context, her work insists on seeing the concrete and the discursive as facets of a single and indivisible episteme (eventually using the terms "materialsemiotic" and "natureculture" to reinforce this point). For Haraway, objects are sedimented histories of social relations, products of contingent choices, and thus open to change. Her focus includes the larger ideological frameworks her stories expose *and* the specificity of particular objects in particular times and places (generally late capitalism, which she calls "New World Order, Inc."). Haraway's work is unified by its interest in practices of naming and structures of subjectivity – "who counts as 'us'" (Haraway 1991: 155) in the discursive construction of nature and culture – and by its commitment to resisting domination and striving for better futures.

This desire to imagine the world otherwise and to think through the interpenetration of science, technology, social structures, and ideology is a quality she shares with the best sf writers. Attention to concrete examples and the practices of storytelling are a kind of intellectual work, she explains: "It's almost like my examples *are* the theories … if one were going to characterize my way of theorizing, it would be to redescribe, to redescribe something so that it becomes thicker than it first seems" (Haraway 2000: 108). Haraway insists that these thicker histories do not seek a state of innocence. Instead, she clarifies, "[y]ou have to take your implication in a fraught world as the starting point" (Olson 1995: 50) and thereby find different possibilities for action than were apparent before.

Central to this project is her work on diffraction as another way of conceptualizing knowledge as sight. In diffraction she finds a "metaphor for another kind of critical consciousness ... one committed to making a difference and not to repeating the Sacred Image of the Same" (Haraway 2000: 102). Looking at objects and entities in a diffractive manner restores to them as many contexts as possible, while maintaining a commitment to contingency and contradiction such that it is "impossible for the bottom line to be one single statement" (Haraway 2000: 105). Her most famous creation, the cyborg, is precisely an example of such diffractive attention. Although the cyborg is "the illegitimate offspring of militarism and patriarchal capitalism," she contends that "illegitimate offspring are often exceedingly unfaithful to their origins" (Haraway 1991: 151), and thus we might find in the cyborg a hopeful myth that "has no truck with bisexuality, pre-oedipal symbiosis, unalienated labor, or other seductions to organic wholeness" (Haraway 1991: 150). Her cyborg offers instead totality without totalization, fractured identities, and politics of affinity that will help us negotiate the shift from "the comfortable old hierarchical dominations to the scary new networks I have called the informatics of domination" (Haraway 1991: 161).

At the heart of the cyborg project is a commitment to contingency and irony, resistance to myths of wholeness, and a desire to find new stories, ones which diffract rather than reflect the sacred image of the same, a goal she shares with sf. She argues: "Irony is about contradictions that do not resolve into larger wholes, even dialectically, about the tension of holding incompatible things together because both or all are necessary and true" (Haraway 1991: 149). Unfortunately, cyborg theory as it has been taken up within sf studies and elsewhere has lost much of the original essay's emphasis on ambiguity and partiality, along with its commitment to radical and transformative politics. Too often such work has coalesced into more static analyses called "cyborg studies" or "cyborgology" (which Haraway is credited with inventing). In some examples of this work, the cyborg becomes a fixed object, stripped of its historical and geographical specificity. Discussing her interest in the discursive constructions of genetics, Haraway laments the way notions of the gene as object "misrepresent complexity, misrepresent process and instead fetishize, fix, reify 'complexity' into 'things'" (Haraway 2000: 21), a critique that might also be levied against some work in cyborg studies.

Haraway's own thought has moved on to other metaphors, retaining the same interest in the fusion of imaginative fiction and material reality, but at the same time acknowledging that other icons are necessary to capture more recent ideological configurations. *Primate Visions*, which argued that "western primatology is simian orientalism" (Haraway 1989: 10), was already attentive to how discourses of gender and race are joined to our conceptions of other animals; the chapter perhaps most pertinent to sf critics, "Apes in Eden, Apes in Space," begins to theorize the space program's primates as early examples of cyborgs, diffracting our understanding of the ideals of the space program through the history of primatology. Haraway's introduction to Chris Hables Gray's *The Cyborg Handbook* (1995), "Cyborgs and Symbionts: living together in the new world order," focuses on a biological rather than technocultural entity, *Mixotricha paradoxa*, a microscopic creature that lives in the hindgut of the South Australian termite and exists only in "obligatory symbiosis with five other kinds of entities" (Haraway 2000: 83). This creature, she argues, forces us to rethink our conceptions of self and other, individual and collective, as it is both one organism and also (at least) six. The central figure of *Modest_Witness* is OncoMouse™, a genetically engineered lab tool designed to get cancer, the first copyrighted biological entity, and now only one among hundreds of knock-out gene mice that regularly stock research laboratories. Haraway uses OncoMouse™ to explore notions of biology, kinship, ownership, and suffering in the biopolitical age that emerged in the late twentieth century. She puts OncoMouse™ into dialogue with Joanna Russ's Female Man, an elder sibling who also "lived at the flash point of that momentous collapse of organisms, information, and the commodity form of life" (Haraway 1997: 70).

Haraway's most recent work is organized around dogs – as exemplars of companion species, but also as fleshy and individual animals with specific histories – and draws attention to the mutual co-evolution of human and animal society and biology. In many ways, this work completes a neglected aspect of the cyborg manifesto, which argued that three important boundaries were eroding: human/animal, organism/machine, and physical/nonphysical. She sees all of the figures who serve as sites for theorizing as "creatures of imagined possibility and creatures of fierce and ordinary reality" (Haraway 2008: 4), and settles on the term "critters" to refer collectively to her menagerie of significant others and life-forms in general. Ever attentive to language, Haraway explains the term's implications: "Critters are always relationally entangled rather than taxonomically neat. I pray that all residual tones of creation have been silenced in the demotic *critter*" (Haraway 2008: 330, n.33). The increasing significance of biopolitics is explored in her second manifesto, *The Companion Species Manifesto* (2003), which finds in dogs more promise than cyborgs for informing "livable politics and ontologies in current life worlds" (Haraway 2003: 4).

Haraway's interest in the politics of affinity and her commitment to partiality and irony have led to her often being misinterpreted as a theorist interested in a radically constructionist vision of reality, where everything is a product of our discursive structures and material reality remains beyond human grasp. She frequently rejects this perspective in interviews, positioning herself outside the science wars' reductionism of "objective reality" versus "postmodern constructivism." Instead, she works to extend Sandra Harding's understanding of successor science, a science that can account for the inevitable interpenetration of the material world and human semiotics in the practice of science, arguing that this acknowledgment of the subjective and cultural will result in a better and more "real" science. Haraway argues that we need "to have *simultaneously* an account of radical historical contingency for all knowledge claims and knowing subjects, a crucial practice for recognizing our own 'semiotic technologies' for making meanings, *and* a no-nonsense commitment to faithful accounts of a 'real' world, one that can be partially shared and friendly to earth-wide projects of finite freedom, adequate material abundance, modest meaning in suffering, and limited happiness" (Haraway 1991: 187).

Her commitments to contingent knowledge, diffractive vision, and radical alterity make Haraway a difficult theorist to understand; the book-length interview *How Like a Leaf* (2000) and Joseph Schneider's introductory *Donna Haraway: live theory* (2005) offer accessible and insightful overviews. The affinity between Haraway's methods and goals and those of many sf writers establish her place in sf, both as a theorist useful to critics of the genre and as a cultural analyst who writes theory in the mode of sf.

See also: **Jean Baudrillard, Alfred Bester, Octavia Butler, David Cronenberg, Samuel R. Delany, William Gibson, Nalo Hopkinson, Gwyneth Jones, Ursula K. Le Guin, Neal Stephenson, Darko Suvin, Sheri S. Tepper, and James Tiptree Jr**

Bibliography

Haraway, D. (1989) *Primate Visions: gender, race, and nature in the world of modern science*, New York: Routledge.

——(1991) *Simians, Cyborgs, and Women: the reinvention of nature*, New York: Routledge.

——(1995) "Cyborgs and Symbionts: living together in the new world order," in C.H. Gray (ed.) *The Cyborg Handbook*, London: Routledge.

——(1997) *Modest_Witness@Second_Millennium.FemaleMan©Meets_OncoMouse™*, London and New York: Routledge.

——(2000) *How Like a Leaf: an interview with Thyrza Nichols Goodeve*, London: Routledge.

——(2003) *The Companion Species Manifesto: dogs, people, and significant otherness*, Chicago: Prickly Paradigm Press.

——(2008) *When Species Meet*, Minneapolis: University of Minnesota Press.

Harding, S. (1986) *The Science Question in Feminism*, Ithaca, NY: Cornell University Press.

Olson, G. (1995) "Writing, Literacy, and Technology: toward a cyborg writing," in G. Olson and E. Hirsch (eds.) *Women Writing Culture*, Albany: SUNY Press.

Schneider, J. (2005) *Donna Haraway: live theory*, New York: Continuum.

SHERRYL VINT

ROBERT A[NSON] HEINLEIN (1907–88)

US novelist and short-story writer.

Arguably the most important figure – because of both his pivotal popular successes and his aesthetic innovations – in the modern history of the genre, Robert A. Heinlein produced 12 collections of short fiction and 32 novels; posthumous publications have included essays, letters, unexpurgated editions of some novels, and his unpublished first novel, *For Us, the Living: a comedy of customs* (2004), written in 1939.

Heinlein was first and foremost an entertaining storyteller. Common wisdom divides his career into two, three, or perhaps even four distinct phases. Insofar as he wrote different kinds of fiction, his work divides into four overlapping stages. Although he never stopped writing short fiction, the first phase was primarily comprised of short stories, most of them following common pulp formulas and published, sometimes pseudonymously, in genre magazines, principally John W. Campbell's *Astounding Science-Fiction* (1937–71). While many were gadget tales or boys' adventures built around an engineer paradigm, most were what Heinlein called "human interest stories," especially those written after the Second World War, when he sold pieces to "slick" magazines, such as the *Saturday Evening Post* (1921–69), printed on high-quality paper and read outside genre conventions.

Many stories of this period contributed to his "Future History," an ambitious attempt to create an interlocking series that provided one unified conception of the future stages of human history.

Starting in 1947 with *Rocket Ship Galileo* and continuing through the early 1960s, Heinlein published "juveniles," adventure novels for what now are called "young adults." All were broadly optimistic concerning how science, technology, and engineering would transform human life in important, positive, even surprising ways. Like the stories, these books understood sf along the lines sketched out by **Hugo Gernsback** and Campbell: they should not only be original but also teach scientific and mathematical rigor, dramatizing these in ways that might excite a fourteen-year-old boy; their heroes reason scientifically, and their enemies illustrate the ignorant prejudices of rigid traditions rather than enlightened rationality. All present space travel in desirably realistic terms. The juveniles were modestly successful and over the past 50 years most have remained in print. While Heinlein certainly did not invent sf for young adults, he did vest it with a level of intellectual sophistication and literary intelligence that has deeply influenced writers since. In an essay drafted in 1957, Heinlein remarked that an adequate definition of sf might be "realistic speculation about possible future events, based solidly on adequate knowledge of the real world, past and present, and on a thorough understanding of the nature and significance of scientific method" (Heinlein 1959: 22). These are the most common traits of his work – at least until the final period.

Alongside his work for adults, these juveniles continued until the publisher rejected the thirteenth – the militaristic anti-communist allegory *Starship Troopers* (1959) – as too violent and too adult for young readers. Although he would publish two further juveniles, this marked the beginning of what is generally thought Heinlein's third or "mature" phase, and identifies the one major change in his aesthetic strategy (see James and Patterson 2006). Before *Starship Troopers*, Heinlein generally perfected strategies inherited from others; after, he generally invented new forms and directions. Virtually all of these books sparked controversies, since they foregrounded heterodox political and social theorizing, often amid shocking violence or violations of bourgeois taboos. *Starship Troopers* was both denounced as fascist fantasy and praised as the morally sound realization of the American tradition of duty and self-sacrifice. Except for its messianic main character, a human brought up by Martians, the satirical fantasy *Stranger in a Strange Land* (1961; unexpurgated 1990) contains no overt sf elements. Instead, its social commentary and quirky iconoclasm preach the pleasures of communal living, free love, and anarchic individualism – and precipitate a cascade of contradictions about contemporary alienation (see Franklin 1980: 136–42). Sometimes called the most controversial sf novel ever written, *Farnham's Freehold* (magazine serialization and book 1964) is a survivalist's postapocalyptic nightmare of race war, cannibalism, and the consequences, both good and bad, of "rugged individualism." The last important work of this phase is *The Moon Is a Harsh Mistress* (magazine serialization 1965–66, book 1966), a vividly entertaining re-enactment of the American revolution but an equally harsh indictment of mob democracy, bureaucratic government, and American economic policy.

A final phase began with *I Will Fear No Evil* (1970), followed by *Time Enough for Love* (1973) and *Job: a comedy of justice* (1984). These and other titles returned to the Future History but also developed several "world-as-myth" stories, with characters moving between the parallel worlds of other writers' fictional universes. With the partial exception of *Friday* (1982), these books are marked and frequently marred by the sort of "tedious sociological sermonizing" (Heinlein 1969: 37) Heinlein had earlier disparaged. They are increasingly self-indulgent, bloated by cantankerous didacta, and finally solipsistic. They "are also, paradoxically, … the largest selling segment of Heinlein's *oeuvre*" (James and Patterson 2006: 14).

The late decay of his talents, perhaps precipitated by a sharp decline in his health, is neither unprecedented nor unexpected; very few writers have continually produced valuable work across a period as long as 48 years. However, his influence and importance remain undeniable, and perhaps cannot be overstated, especially his effect on mid-twentieth-century anglophone sf. Most significantly, he is the writer *most* responsible for the *literary* forms – the underlying generic grammar – of modern sf: "Later writers and readers have internalized that grammar, that set of rules that generates a particular kind of science fiction story, which is still probably the central kind of science fiction story" (Brown *et al.* 2007: 51b).

Three features identify that aesthetic architecture. First is the "naturalness" of Heinlein's imaginative contrivances. Following another of Campbell's lessons, Heinlein excelled at constructing narrative worlds that felt "lived-in"; stylistically, this effect comes from crafting a narrative voice that achieves a comfortable intimacy with readers, who are configured as fellow travelers and participants rather than passive consumers or voyeurs. In this sense, Heinlein assumes a familiarity with the created world's subtle differences, which produces two key effects: first, he is able to avoid the expository "infodumps" that so frequently bloat sf and awkwardly subvert the narrative momentum; second, readers experience a far more uncanny sense of wonder than in fiction where they remain an outsider merely gawking from afar at the extraordinary changes. A famous example of this latter effect concerns the door that "dilates" in *Beyond this Horizon* (magazine serialization 1942, book 1948). Rather than belaboring the point that a future society's technology differs in minute and pervasive ways, Heinlein simply embeds the difference as a quotidian fact, allowing us to *experience it* and so estrange us cognitively – this is both wonderfully economical expression and the essential sense of wonder that specifically characterizes sf.

Second, instead of making characters solely the vehicles for the transmission of some scientific datum, the stories were based on the characters' feelings and thoughts as they encountered novel conditions and future changes. His commitment to the human-interest story can be seen in "On the Writing of Speculative Fiction" (1947) and in his preference for the word "speculative," which does not dismiss science so much as subordinate it to human problems (Heinlein 1964: 17). Such character-driven fiction more closely aligns with so-called "mainstream" literary fiction, but Heinlein never abandoned the genre's dedication to exploring science and technology. *Assuming a world* and *focusing on human experience* allowed Heinlein to sinuously integrate the "hard" natural sciences of physics, mathematics, and space engineering with the "soft" social sciences of political theory, sociology, and economics.

A third feature concerned literary style. Heinlein's prose was uncluttered and economical, carefully balanced and highly adept at elegant transitions between the technical vocabularies of science and the casual idioms of common American speech, both making complexities accessible and presenting them in a richer, more literary prose than had been common among genre writers. Neither **Isaac Asimov** nor **Arthur C. Clarke** was ever as stylistically proficient, neither ever wove together the natural and social sciences with the same seamless simplicity, and neither ever experimented so with generic convention.

Although justly lauded for inventing the grammar of modern sf, Heinlein's dominance is frequently lamented, even derided. Concerning that influence, **Samuel R. Delany** once echoed André Gide's quip about the poet Victor Hugo. Who is the greatest sf writer of the twentieth century? "Robert Heinlein, alas" (Delany 1977: 149). Delany neatly captures the sense of ambivalence or disappointment that sometimes seems Heinlein's legacy. With the exception of some of the final books, the brilliance of his achievement is undeniable, but the positions he took remain very controversial.

Yet discussions of Heinlein too often neatly divide into cultish hagiography or contemptuous dismissal. In my view there are as many things to disparage as to admire, but also as many to admire as to disparage. To paraphrase Thomas M. Disch, no one so engages yet enrages the liberal imagination as Heinlein. The sharp wit, bold power, and eccentric iconoclasm of his views liberate; though the didacta, delivered so often by a seemingly omniscient man, actually subordinate in subtle, powerful ways. Gender politics provide a telling example. His libertine and meritocratic views would shatter sexual double standards and professional glass ceilings, but the effect is by, through, and for men – which remains a reactionary and distinctly patriarchal position.

Almost all of the ideological interpretive controversies concern the difference between what the fictions *explicitly* say and what they *implicitly* confirm. It might appear hard to reconcile the explicit positions that many of the novels take, but implicitly the fiction is a coherent, unified whole. Explicitly, many characters and texts seem radically distinct. For example, the government in *Starship Troopers* is a sort of fascist dictatorship, one that is always right and functions flawlessly, while in *The Moon Is a Harsh Mistress* the political position advocated is "rational anarchism," an extreme form of libertarianism that postulates all governments as hopelessly inefficient and suggests that only the single self, or the nuclear family, can be trusted. In the former novel, bureaucracy is our friend, in the latter it is our enemy. So – explicitly – the two novels have no unified view.

But all of Heinlein's work seems unified by its implicit features. In addition to the aesthetic architecture mentioned above, the fiction privileges a conception of maximal individual liberty and personal freedom; meritocracy dominated by accomplished elites; a critique of complacent acceptance of the status quo, chiefly its mores and myths; a belief in human progress brought about through science, technology, and particularly space travel; a commitment to mid-century Midwestern conceptions of personal honor, civic duty, and public courtesy; but all ultimately subordinated to the authority of a single great man, a benevolent intellectual hero who is not afraid to act, violently if need be, to shape history for the good of all.

Whatever one's conclusion concerning his politics, Heinlein's prominence and importance cannot be questioned, nor should they be forgotten. His influence was immediate, authentically profound, and lasting. No one can claim to know twentieth-century sf without a close encounter with Robert A. Heinlein.

See also: **Isaac Asimov, Greg Bear, Alfred Bester, Leigh Brackett, Octavia Butler, Arthur C. Clarke, Samuel R. Delany, Philip K. Dick, William Gibson, Frank Herbert, L. Ron Hubbard, Ursula K. Le Guin, C.L. Moore, Kim Stanley Robinson, Joanna Russ, Neal Stephenson, Sheri S. Tepper, James Tiptree Jr, and Gene Wolfe**

Bibliography

Brown, C., Beamer, A., Clute, J., Sleight, G., and Wolfe, G.K. (2007) "Heinlein at 100: roundtable discussion with Charles Brown, Amelia Beamer, John Clute, Graham Sleight, and Gary K. Wolfe," *Locus*, August: 51–54.

Delany, S.R. (1977) *The Jewel-Hinged Jaw: notes on the language of science fiction*, Elizabethtown, NY: Dragon Press.

Franklin, H.B. (1980) *Robert A. Heinlein: America as science fiction*, New York: Oxford University Press.

Heinlein, R.A. (1959) "Science Fiction: its nature, faults and virtues," in B. Davenport (ed.) *The Science Fiction Novel: imagination and social criticism*, Chicago: Advent.

——(1964) "On the Writing of Speculative Fiction," in L.A. Eshbach (ed.) *Of Worlds beyond: the science of science fiction writing*, Chicago: Advent.

James, R. and Patterson Jr, W.H. (2006) "Re-visioning Robert Heinlein's Career," *Foundation*, 97: 11–27.

Panshin, A. (1968) *Heinlein in Dimension: a critical analysis*, Chicago: Advent.

Patterson Jr, W.H. (n.d.) "Robert A. Heinlein – a biography," *The Heinlein Society* webpage. Online. Available: <http://www.heinleinsociety.org/rah/biographies.html> (accessed 1 January 2009).

NEIL EASTERBROOK

FRANK [PATRICK] HERBERT (1920–86)

US novelist and short-story writer, best known for the *Dune* series.

Although Frank Herbert was the author of 23 novels and more than 40 short stories, his reputation today rests on only one work, *Dune* (1965), a book which remains one of the most celebrated and influential works of prose sf. There was little indication in Herbert's early career that such a benchmark work was coming. Throughout the 1950s and the early 1960s Herbert worked chiefly as a journalist, publishing occasional short fiction in *Astounding*, *Amazing*, and other sf magazines. His first novel, *Under Pressure* (magazine serialization 1955–56, as book *The Dragon in the Sea* 1956), is a solid but unexceptional near-future thriller set aboard a nuclear submarine. *Dune*, his second book, was serialized in *Astounding* between December 1963 and May 1965. It took him, in short order, to the forefront of the genre.

Dune is a planetary romance of unusual scope and intellectual ambition. A quasi-medieval far-future galactic empire is held together by technologies of faster-than-light travel that require pilots addicted to a pharmakon called "spice." Supplies of this drug can only be obtained on the otherwise backward desert world Arrakis, or Dune, where it is manufactured in the bodies of sandworms, enormous alien dragons living under the sands. The novel embroiders the adventures of Paul Atreides, a young man who is variously heir to the Dukedom of Arrakis (though deposed by his wicked uncle, Baron Harkonnen); the "Muad'Dib," a savior figure prophesied by Arrakis's quasi-Bedouin, aboriginal Fremen; and the "Kwisatz Haderach," the superhuman result of a generations-long breeding program by a mystic religious sisterhood called the Bene Gesserit. During the course of the novel Paul evades assassination, lives with and becomes the leader of the Fremen, and acquires an addiction to spice which gives him prophetic powers. Ultimately he overthrows Harkonnen at the head of a Fremen army, reclaims Arrakis, and seizes control of the entire empire into the bargain. The book's success, though not immediate, was considerable: it won both Nebula and Hugo awards, became an enduring bestseller, and to this day enjoys a reputation as one of the genre's best novels. It was, with J.R.R. Tolkien's *Lord of the Rings* (1954–55) and **Robert A. Heinlein**'s *Stranger in a Strange Land* (1961), a must-read novel on 1960s university campuses, and from being a countercultural success it moved into the mainstream.

Herbert continued writing sf novels (*The Green Brain* (1966), *The Eyes of Heisenberg* (1966), *The Santaroga Barrier* (1968)) but by the end of the decade the popularity of *Dune* drew him back to that imagined world. *Dune Messiah* (magazine serialization 1969, book 1970), the first of many sequels, ends with Paul being blinded by an assassin's bomb and sent into the desert to die, as is required by the rather severe code of the Fremen. In *Children of Dune* (magazine serialization and book 1976), a preternaturally aged Paul returns to rail against the corruption of his successors, like Oedipus at Colonus (Herbert deliberately worked both Aeschylean and Sophoclean elements into his *Dune* novels, evidence of his literary sophistication (or pretentiousness)). *God-Emperor of Dune* (1981) follows the prodigiously lengthened life of Paul's son, Leto, mutated into a human–sandworm hybrid, who, as planetary tyrant, acts as mouthpiece for his author's meditations on the allure and dangers of quasi-fascistic supermen.

Herbert's subsequent continuations are very dilute preparations of his original vision: in *Heretics of Dune* (1984) and *Chapterhouse Dune* (1985), set millennia later in an implausibly unaltered galactic milieu, returnees from a diasporic scattering of humanity bring a needed injection of barbaric energy to an otherwise stultified and static civilization. The significance of these books is not intrinsic, for they are not good novels. Rather they are symptoms of the way in which Herbert's *Dune* had, by the mid-1980s, metamorphosed from novel into megatext – a cultural focus for disseminated textual production and reimagining. In the case of *Dune*, Herbert's writing has been supplemented by a number of continuations by his son, Brian (and Kevin J. Anderson): two sequels (*Hunters of Dune* (2006), *Sandworms of Dune* (2007)) and no fewer than six prequels. Fans have written their own unauthorized fiction, most of it better than this, much of it available online. There have been adaptations – the big-budget but awkward film *Dune* (Lynch 1984), the more efficient made-for-television *Dune* (Harrison 2000), and *Children of Dune* (Yaitanes 2003) – as well as half a dozen video games (the best of which is *Dune II: The Battle for Arrakis* (1992)) and musical interpretations such as the moody electronica of Klaus Schulze's *Dune* (1979). The hospitality of Herbert's megatext to this sort of engagement helps explain, in part, the influence he has had on the development of sf; like **Isaac Asimov** before him, and like the creators of *Doctor Who* (1963–), *Star Trek* (1966–), and *Star Wars* (1977–), Herbert invented a world that expanded creatively as fans engaged with it. It is this, as much as the way he brought intellectual scope and range to the sf novel, that makes him a key figure.

Not that *Dune*, as a novel, is flawless. As in all his work, Herbert's style is leaden and incapable of concision (even in the apothegmatic epigraphs from various imaginary philosophical and historical works that head each chapter, and which often run to hundreds of words). His prose, mostly given over to dialog and inner monolog, lacks flavor and too often creaks under the weight of exposition – of plot or, more usually, of ideas. Moreover, Herbert's characterization is often essentialist: there is, for instance, more than a whiff of homophobia about the way Baron Harkonnen's villainy is represented as a function of his predatory, sexualized decadence.

But the book's strengths eclipse its shortcomings; it is a novel that achieves genuine grandeur. French philosopher Guy Lardreau (arguably Herbert's influence has been even greater in Europe than in the anglophone West) calls *Dune* "a major work," comparing it with "Shakespeare's great tragedies" and praising "the richness and coherence" as well as "the specificity" of its imaginative vision (Lardreau 1988: 179–82). If few anglophone critics would be quite that dithyrambic, nevertheless most would concede that, in **Gwyneth Jones**'s words, *Dune* is "the most admired of living imagined worlds" (Jones 2003: 169).

It is indeed hard to deny the power of Herbert's *mise-en-scène*: the planet Arrakis itself, its environment and alien fauna, stay powerfully with the reader. Herbert is sometimes praised for his world-building, but this is not quite right (this aspect of the novel has notable flaws, not least the absence of any means of oxygenating the planetary atmosphere). Rather, Dune's deserts function eloquently as metaphor and topographical signifier, empty enough of conventional geographical features (the frontispiece map is a blank page barely sullied by dotted lines showing occasional features) to provide an uncluttered aesthetic and imaginative space. It mediates Western perceptions of "Arabia" and Islam in an imaginatively engaging manner.

In two particular respects the book is exceptional: the scope and complexity of its representation of history, and its prescient anticipation of the sort of environmentalist concerns ("ecology" in the idiom of the 1960s) that have subsequently become culturally central. *Dune* was, indeed, the first novel with an ecological theme to have a significant impact. Herbert's Fremen live and prosper in the extreme aridity of their surroundings by hoarding their water; ultimately successful attempts to terraform Arrakis into a moister, gentler place also rob the Fremen as a people of their vigor. The whole sequence is a detailed, subtle parable of the dangers of environmental meddling, and a dramatization of the way environment in the fullest sense shapes both peoples and individuals. Appropriately, Herbert dedicated Dune to "the people whose labors go beyond ideas into the realm of 'real materials' – to the dry-land ecologists."

Herbert's representation of "history" is also well done. *Dune* was written in explicit opposition to Asimov's *Foundation* trilogy (in magazine form 1942–51, as books 1951–53), or more particularly to the old-fashioned positivism of Asimov's understanding of history as amenable to exact scientific prediction. Herbert, on the contrary, sees history on the largest scale as chaotic and finds a number of expressive metaphors for this in the novel (for example the eddies inside a sandstorm through which Paul must navigate his ornithopter). Though Paul can see the future, the future he sees is not determined; prophesy proves radically ambiguous. Herbert also conceives history as long duration, something the sheer bulk of the novels aggregates for the reader.

Overall, *Dune* details a much more fully realized political-historical canvas than sf had hitherto attempted, and achieves an impression of complexity without becoming tangled or indigestible. In a sense, Herbert's triumph in *Dune* is precisely finding simple but eloquent tropes for important but complex subjects. Simplifying the landscape of his imagined world entirely to desert enabled him more effectively to stage the difficulties and dangers of environmental niche-survival and change. His future-society is clothed in the simplified feudal lineaments of a medieval fantasy – computers are banished by religious edict, society is strictly hierarchical – but this enables him to sketch large questions of human social and political interaction, authority, mass movements, and social evolution.

That said, Herbert's desire to represent complexity in his writing did not always find such felicitous dramatic form. A number of his later novels, lacking the pared-down metaphorical clarity of *Dune*, are by comparison clogged and arid. *The Dosadi Experiment* (magazine serial and book 1977), one of a series of Herbert novels set in a future multi-alien federation called the "ConSentiency," shares form and plot similarities with *Dune*; but it lacks the central imagistic directness or metaphoricity of the earlier novel, and is much less memorable. The *Void* sequence, beginning with *Destination: Void* (1966) and continuing with several fat novels from Herbert's later career (*The Jesus Incident* (1979), *The Lazarus Effect* (1983), and *The Ascension Factor* (1988), all coauthored with Bill Ransom), has a tedious, scholastic feel: seemingly endless elaboration of quasi-theological niceties and abstract social questions all spun from the unengaging premise of a spaceship's gifted artificial intelligence that becomes a god.

Dune, in other words, is rather uncharacteristic of its author, and its continuing success gives a slightly distorted sense of Herbert's *oeuvre* as a whole. It is a *spacious* book, a novel of disclosure rather than enclosure, and it possesses, despite its various ormolu plot lines and twists, an almost minimalist feel. The book's transformation into a collective megatext is, among other things, indexical of the inviting open-endedness of its aesthetic. But this is not what we find if we turn to the rest of Herbert's work. On the contrary, his predominant aesthetic is one of *claustrophobia*. *The Dragon in the Sea* relentlessly increases the pressure on its confined, increasingly paranoid submarine crew, just as the crew in *Destination: Void* are trapped in the confines of their spaceship. Herbert returned several times to versions of human life modeled on the close-packed hive existence of insects (*The Green Brain*, *Hellstrom's Hive* (1973; serialized as *Project 40* (1972–73)), and *The Dosadi Experiment* crams 850 million individuals into 40 square kilometers. In both the *Void* and the *Dune* series, characters are repeatedly recycled: dead characters resurrected as clones, or otherwise put through their paces once again, an economy of characterization that lends a rather pinched, closed feel to the thousands of pages of verbiage. It is not that this formal embodiment of claustrophobia is not interesting, but it was not this that won Herbert his many fans. That was due to the compelling open textual space of *Dune* and its successors.

See also: **Isaac Asimov, Greg Bear, Alfred Bester, Leigh Brackett, Octavia Butler, Samuel R. Delany, Philip K. Dick, William Gibson, Robert A. Heinlein, L. Ron Hubbard, Ursula K. Le Guin, C.L. Moore, Kim Stanley Robinson, Joanna Russ, Neal Stephenson, Sheri S. Tepper, James Tiptree Jr, and Gene Wolfe**

Bibliography

Herbert, B. (2003) *Dreamer of Dune: the biography of Frank Herbert*, New York: Tor.

Jones, G. (2003) "The Icons of Science Fiction," in E. James and F. Mendlesohn (eds.) *The Cambridge Companion to Science Fiction*, Cambridge: Cambridge University Press.

Lardreau, G. (1988) *Fictions Philosophiques et Science-Fiction: récréation philosophique*, Paris: Actes Sud.

O'Reilly, T. (1980) *Frank Herbert*, New York: Frederick Ungar.

Touponce, W.F. (1988) *Frank Herbert*, New York: Twayne.

ADAM ROBERTS

NALO HOPKINSON (1960–)

Jamaica-born, Canadian-resident author and editor.

Nalo Hopkinson's writing – a collage of skin, duppies, arguing families, Granny Nanny technology, code-sliding, seals, wetsuits, transformation, gods, prostitutes, and stillborn children – is a challenging patchwork rooted in the body, sexuality, and race. It does not simply cross the boundaries of sf, fantasy, magic realism, horror, folklore, and myth; her texts are all of these things, and the identities of her writing are multiple. Hopkinson's own influences and identities are many. She grew up in Jamaica, Trinidad, and Guyana; her family emigrated to Canada when she was 16. She spent her childhood reading Greek myths, comic books, Caribbean literature, nineteenth-century novels, and discovering writers such as Harlan Ellison and **Samuel R. Delany**.

Brown Girl in the Ring (1998) won the Warner Aspect First Novel Contest, the Locus Award for Best First Novel, and the John W. Campbell Award for Best New Writer. It announced Hopkinson as an original author whose texts relocate the margins and the marginalized within the center. In this near-future novel, Toronto city center has been abandoned by the government, becoming a ghetto called the Burn. The inhabitants of the Burn use different forms of resourcefulness to survive, some creating an interdependent community, others selfishly exploiting the descent into lawlessness. Focused on communities that fall through the gaps in Canadian municipal, provincial, and federal politics, it is primarily a story of family conflict. Ti-Jeanne, a reluctant, young single mother, afraid that her spirit visions will lead to the same madness that took her mother, rejects her grandmother Gros-Jeanne's teachings, alienating herself from her Caribbean heritage. This refusal to integrate her past with her present puts her at great risk as family conflicts re-emerge. When Ti-Jeanne discovers that drug dealer Rudy is her grandfather, she realizes that she must draw on all her resources, including her spiritual power, to defeat him and free her mother's soul. Hopkinson mixes Canadian economic and environmental politics with Caribbean folklore and generational conflict to show how resourcefulness can transform from a survival strategy into a strength.

Sf and mainstream critics alike praised Hopkinson's debut as highly original because of her use of Caribbean dialect and folklore. In a departure from magic realism and in sharp contrast to the surface exoticism of **William Gibson**'s cyberspace loas in *Count Zero* (1986), Hopkinson's Voudun spirits exist alongside everyday life, fully realized and following their own rules of giving and receiving, and offering a more immediate connection to history than Western historical hierarchies. Critics highlight Hopkinson's use of Creole, which "not only challenges the dearth of ethnic voices and identities in speculative fiction, it enlarges the possibilities for genre fiction in the future" (Batty 2003: 21).

This is shown in Hopkinson's second novel, *Midnight Robber* (2000), set on the planet Toussaint, which has been colonized by an African, South American, Indian, and Euro community. The hybrid of different Creoles extrapolates how the speech of this multiethnic community might evolve, and it also expresses the community's relationship with technology. As Hopkinson (2000) explains: "So many of our stories about technology and our paradigms for it refer to Greek and Roman myth and language … I wondered what technologies a largely African diasporic culture might build, what stories its people might tell itself about technology."

One of these technologies is the A.I. network Granny Nanny, combining the names of the heroic Maroon leader Granny Nanny and the trickster spider Anansi. It is caring and protective, unlike the Western archetype Big Brother. However, the unity it provides is not without problems. It frees Toussaint inhabitants from the need to work, but it disconnects them from the reasons they left Earth. Granny Nanny also insulates Toussaint residents from the consequences of settling a "dub version" of their planet called New Half-Way Tree. Criminals and outcasts permanently exiled to New Half-Way Tree treat the native inhabitants, known as Douen, like slaves and animals, showing how a once-colonized people can themselves be blinded to the assumptions and oppressions of colonialism.

Midnight Robber tells of the exile of Tan-Tan from Toussaint and then from the human community on New Half-Way Tree. She gradually embodies the carnival figure of the Midnight Robber to help her reintegrate the dislocated parts of her identity after a disturbing, abusive relationship with her father. Parental figures in Hopkinson's work are often fiercely protective, but also overbearing and in danger of alienating their children through the power they have over them.

Midnight Robber was shortlisted for the Hugo and Nebula awards. Hopkinson's rising profile means commentators often speak of her alongside Delany and **Octavia E. Butler** as an eminent black sf writer. Although she acknowledges their influence, Hopkinson (1998) reminds us that there are many other people of color writing sf, such as Gloria Naylor and devorah major, but because their fiction is not explicitly labeled as sf, they are not reaching the genre's traditional audiences. Hopkinson encourages readers to look beyond genre boundaries and states that she has an identity as a black sf writer, but also as an sf writer, female writer, Caribbean writer, Canadian writer, and an unlabeled writer; none of these identities preclude the others.

A number of Hopkinson's short stories in *Skin Folk* (2001) explore the transformative power of technology on our bodies. In "Ganger (Ball Lightning)" (2000), Issy and Cleve engage in gender play, swapping their stimulating all-over "wetsuits." However, this swap does not mean simply wearing another gender, as Cleve still interprets the sensations in terms of his male body image; to him it is like "my dick had been /peeled/" (Hopkinson 2001: 226). The static from the suits develops a terrifying life of its own, which Issy and Cleve discharge through speaking their own sexual fears. More than an allegory about sexual communication, it asks how technology complicates gender and sexual identities. Hopkinson's fiction shows that technology does not layer new identities over old ones but gets under our skin, fusing with existing body images. Her increasingly explicit writing confronts the squeamishness about sex of much sf.

Hopkinson's third novel, *The Salt Roads* (2003), braids together stories of three women across very different times and places: Mer, a healer on a Haitian plantation; Jeanne, a cabaret performer in nineteenth-century Paris; Thais, a prostitute in fourth-century Alexandria. These women explore their desires and physicality in spaces carved out from the sexual roles imposed on them by male-dominated societies. Hopkinson connects these women through their feelings of loss, sexual pleasure, and displacement, represented by the salt roads made by their tears, sweat, and the sea which has taken them away from their homelands. Their experiences are further entwined by Ezili, a goddess of sex and love, birthed as Mer buries a stillborn child. Ezili struggles to shape her own identity, alternately inhabiting the bodies of Jeanne, Mer, and Thais. Like Toni Morrison's *Beloved* (1987), *The Salt Roads* shows how transcendence can be born from the power of grief and physical experience. However, Ezili is not a human spirit; the way Ezili moves between times and spaces is like "an alien intelligence, that scans all human suffering and joy" (Di Filippo 2003).

Hopkinson's most ambitious novel in terms of both subject matter and structure, *The Salt Roads* had a mixed reception. Its form is complex, like music riffs or dance beats, causing some to complain that it includes too many strands and does not develop all of them fully. Some critics were pleased she had "moved on," but such attempts to "save" her work from being classified as sf provoked Hopkinson to reply that she has chosen the genre because it enables her to do what she wants to do; it is not a term that is imposed on her.

The New Moon's Arms (2007) marks yet another departure in setting, environment, and mode, while revisiting some of Hopkinson's themes, such as the power of spirits alongside our everyday lives. Calamity's discovery of a web-fingered boy is interspersed with the tale of the dada-hair lady who is transported on a slave ship and summons the water goddess Uhamiri to bring her people home. The homecoming is ambiguous, as Uhamiri changes the slaves to suit a new home in the sea.

Calamity is like an older incarnation of the "hot mouthed" Ti-Jeanne, Tan-Tan, and Jeanne. Flirtatious and willful, she struggles to investigate a mystery while going through the menopause, resisting the restrictions placed on older women. Like *Brown Girl*, the story focuses on generational conflict, as Calamity comes to terms with her mother's disappearance when she was a child, and her tempestuous relationship with her own daughter, Ifeoma. The past resurfaces in the present; it is hinted that Calamity's mother left her skin behind and returned to the sea. This re-embodying of the selkie folk tale echoes the pain and freedoms of Hopkinson's other skin-shedding metamorphosis stories. However, like the complex threads of *The Salt Roads*, this subtle resolution of a major plot strand has caused some reviewers to criticize the novel's construction.

Like *Brown Girl*, the book is set in the context of local environmental and economic politics. Calamity lives on the (fictional) Caribbean archipelago of Cayaba, where small family-run salt farms are being pushed out by a multinational salt-farming corporation. The Cayaban government supports this lowering of trade restrictions as it is a condition of receiving more foreign aid. However, a courageous opposition leader highlights the problems of this neo-colonization and exploitation of local resources.

Hopkinson has also edited the anthologies *Whispers from the Cotton Tree Root: Caribbean fabulist fiction* (2000); *Mojo: conjure stories* (2003); *So Long Been Dreaming: postcolonial science fiction and fantasy* (2004), with Uppinder Mehan; and *Tesseracts 9: new Canadian speculative fiction* (2005), with Geoff Ryman. Her editorial approach is to set a challenging, open-ended concept – conjure stories, fabulist fiction, postcolonial sf and fantasy – and then invite writers to define it through their stories. This brings together authors from different literary traditions; hence the anthologies are groundbreaking from a number of perspectives: *Whispers* is the first anthology of Caribbean literature with the fantastic as its focus, but it is also the first anthology of speculative fiction that embodies a Caribbean worldview. Similarly, *So Long* is the first collection that explicitly unites postcolonial and science fictional perspectives, taking the sf memes of exploration and colonization and changing them to express the experiences of the colonized and technologically dispossessed.

Hopkinson's role as innovative editor is complemented by her dialogues about what sf can do, which occur on her blog (http://nalohopkinson.com/blogmain) and through her teaching, speaking engagements, and interviews. She often discusses the paradoxes and strengths of writing in the sf mode, which is traditionally white, Western, and male, but which also offers great subversive potential for imagining "otherness."

Hopkinson's novels are very different from each other, yet her strong themes re-emerge in each text. The challenging, sometimes deliberately awkward, structures of her novels reflect a collage of influences, voices, and worldviews grounded in the need to combine multiple identities to survive and to grow. Sf is part of the mix as it allows us to interrogate the tools we use, the societies we create, and the stories we tell ourselves about technology.

See also: **Octavia Butler, David Cronenberg, Samuel R. Delany, William Gibson, Donna J. Haraway, Gwyneth Jones, Ursula K. Le Guin, China Miéville, C.L. Moore, Joanna Russ, Mary Shelley, Neal Stephenson, Sheri S. Tepper, and James Tiptree Jr**

Bibliography

Batty, N. (2003) "Caught by a Genre: Nalo Hopkinson's dilemma," in A.L. McLeod (ed.) *The Canon of Commonwealth Literature: essays in criticism*, New Delhi: Sterling Publishers.

Clemente, B. (2004) "Tan-Tan's Exile and Odyssey in Nalo Hopkinson's *Midnight Robber*," *Foundation*, 91: 10–24.

Di Filippo, P. (2003) "Review of *The Salt Roads*," *Science Fiction Weekly*, 349. Online. Available: <http://www.scifi.com/sfw/issue349/books2.html> (accessed 1 January 2009).

Hopkinson, N. (n.d.) "Nalo's Blog." Online. Available: <http://nalohopkinson.com/blogmain> (accessed 1 January 2009).

——(1998) "Dark Ink." Online. Available: <http://nalohopkinson.com/essay_dark_ink> (accessed 1 January 2009).

——(2000) "Author Interview: Nalo Hopkinson." Online. Available: <http://www.hachettebookgroup.com/Nalo_Hopkinson_(1014237)_AuthorInterview(2).htm> (accessed 1 January 2009).

——(2001) "Ganger (Ball Lightning)," in *Skin Folk*, New York: Warner Aspect.

Johnston, N. (2001) "Nalo Hopkinson," in D. Ivison (ed.) *The Dictionary of Literary Biography Vol. 251: Canadian fantasy and science fiction writers*, Detroit, MI: The Gale Group.

Reid, M. (2005) "Crossing the Boundaries of the Burn: Canadian multiculturalism and Caribbean hybridity in Nalo Hopkinson's *Brown Girl in the Ring*," *Extrapolation*, 46(3): 297–314.

MICHELLE REID

L[AFAYETTE] RON[ALD] HUBBARD (1911–86)

US author and founder of the Church of Scientology.

As a young man, L. Ron Hubbard wrote a large quantity of pulp fiction, much of it sf; he himself claimed to have written 15 million words between 1927 and 1941, though this may be an exaggeration.

The majority of this output is justly forgotten today, although critics sometimes make the case for a few of his novels as above average examples of their sort: two in particular are *Final Blackout* (serialized in *Astounding Science-Fiction* in 1940), about a future-Europe devastated by war, and the neatly self-reflexive *Typewriter in the Sky* (published in *Unknown* in 1940), in which a character is trapped inside the novel being written by his friend, the overproductive pulp-writer Horace Hackett (a Hubbardian self-portrait). But it is not as a writer that Hubbard merits inclusion in this volume. He is much more significant for the religion he founded, a faith deeply implicated in discourses of sf.

After undistinguished service in the Second World War, Hubbard seems to have become disillusioned with the writer's life. He allegedly told a 1948 meeting of the US Eastern Science Fiction Association: "writing for a penny a word is ridiculous. If a man really wanted to make a million dollars, the best way to do it would be to start his own religion" (Sam Moskowitz, quoted in Miller 1987: 145; there are several variants of this celebrated, or infamous, quotation). Hubbard started down this path by establishing what he called "a new science of mental health" in his book *Dianetics* (1950). Effectively a self-help manual stitched together from various elements of Western and Eastern thought, and more substantively derivative of Sigmund Freud and Wilhelm Reich, excerpts first appeared in *Astounding* in 1949 (the magazine's editor, John W. Campbell Jr, became an enthusiastic advocate, although he did not similarly endorse Hubbard's later development of Scientology). *Dianetics* sold over 100,000 copies within a year, and, despite uniform hostility from the scientific and medical establishment, it attracted many followers. Hubbard established the Hubbard Dianetic Research Foundation to help – or exploit – these individuals. Building on his popular success, Hubbard enlarged Dianetics into a more systematic belief system he called "Scientology." When Hubbard declared Scientology a religion in late 1953, he was no longer writing sf, concentrating instead upon this much more lucrative occupation. In 1959 Hubbard established the world headquarters of Scientology at East Grinstead in southern England.

The religion grew through the 1960s and 1970s, and achieved greater cultural prominence through the recruitment of a number of high-profile celebrities in the 1980s and 1990s. As of 2008, the Church claimed eight million members worldwide, and although more disinterested estimates put the number much lower (probably in the high tens of thousands), it nevertheless represents a noteworthy cultural phenomenon. Like many new-minted religions, Scientology has attracted controversy and ridicule in equal measure. In part this reflects a common perception of it as a financially exploitative cult, but it also has to do with the specifically science-fictional nature of the faith, a ground of belief many consider more risible than the traditional mythic narratives of other world beliefs.

The core of Scientology is a process called "auditing" by which individuals may supposedly purge their immortal souls ("Thetans," in the Scientological idiom) of negative energy accumulated in past lives; an individual so purged is known as a "Clear." The Church runs many courses for which members pay what are often large sums in order to clear out more and more of these negative "engrams," and thereby ascend higher in the Church's hierarchical structure, a process which has proved very lucrative indeed for Scientology as a whole and the Church leaders individually. Higher-ranking Scientologists have access to key truths, most of which supposedly concern events that happened in past lives, and many of which are egregiously indebted to pulp sf. Core are a number of unmistakably sf myths. For example, Scientology teaches that the bulk of today's malaises can be traced back to a catastrophe 75 million years ago when an evil galactic dictator called Xeno, for not entirely coherent reasons, brought billions of individuals to Earth in spacecraft that exactly resembled DC-8 airplanes (but without the jet-engines), and positioned them about volcanoes into which he dropped H-bombs, thus killing them all. Scientology teaches that our souls retain the repressed memory of this trauma which continues to harm our spiritual development. But there are many other sf narratives. Reports from individual Scientologists who have been audited tell of past lives being retrieved by the process that resemble (Scientologists might argue provide the template for) pre-Second World War sf: accounts of lives spent adventuring on other planets, becoming embroiled with evil robots disguised as alluring red-headed women, tangling with flying saucers, enduring planetary attacks by clouds of radioactive gas and the like. In an earlier study of the phenomenon I found "banality and cliché" in the "sub-Pulp adventures" at the heart of Scientology's metaphysic, and reflected a little sourly that "to capture the hearts of many thousands it is not even necessary, it seems, to write poetry of the calibre of the Koran or the Gospel of St John; all one need do is plunder the traditions of second-rate Pulp SF of the sort that Hubbard himself was writing (at one cent a word) in the days before he found a more remunerative income-stream" (Roberts 2005: 340).

This manner of judgment is common among non-Church members, although naturally Church members treat this material much more respectfully, as embodying important truths. Nevertheless, popular cultural references to Scientology are much more likely to be derogatory and satirical than anything else. Two examples among many: **Greg Bear**'s novella "Heads" (1990) imagines a future religion very like Scientology that discovers unsavory truths about its long-dead, Hubbardesque founder by accessing his severed and frozen head; Frank Zappa's rock-opera *Joe's Garage* (1979) pokes fun at "L. Ron Hoover" and his church of "Appliantology," in particular its requirement that its followers have sex with household appliances.

For much of the 1970s Hubbard was domiciled aboard a large ocean-going yacht. In the 1980s he returned to the US and began once again writing sf, producing two very lengthy novels: *Battlefield Earth* (1982) and *Mission Earth* (1985–87), the latter published in ten volumes and running to some 4,000 pages. The works sold well (there are allegations that sales were inflated by Church requirements that Scientologists purchase them) but both are very bad: prolix, underpowered, unimaginative, and tedious. *Battlefield Earth*, detailing the fight back, in 3000 AD, of enslaved humanity against a vile alien occupation, was made into a film (Christian 2000) starring prominent Scientologist John Travolta. It is widely considered one of the worst sf movies ever made. *Mission Earth* aims at an encyclopedic satire of contemporary Earth, seen through the eyes of aliens from the planet Voltar, a name that perhaps flags up Hubbard's aesthetic ambition, although the result could hardly be less like Voltaire's concise and witty satirical penetration. Hubbard portrays an Earth on the verge of self-destruction: schools have been corrupted into training centers for sexual deviancy, evil corporations dominate society, rock music and drugs are used to sedate and control the population. Psychiatry, a particular bugbear of Hubbard's, is portrayed as being a crucial part of this evil global conspiracy. The novel is little more than a platform for the cranky views and eccentric hostilities of its author, and in fact reflects many of the ideological biases of Scientology as a whole.

It may seem counterintuitive to discuss a writer frankly as bad as Hubbard as a significant figure in sf. But his very badness is inextricably intertwined with the visionary brilliance Hubbard undoubtedly, if intermittently, displayed; and this fact in itself is a reflection of some importance upon the genre as a whole, which more than occasionally manifests precisely this admixture of quality. Moreover, it is hard to ignore the cultural significance of Scientology as a specifically science-fictional religion.

It is difficult to make generalizations about religion in the abstract, there being so many and such diverse examples of religion in the world. That said, it may be useful to consider the term as a twin signifier. On the one hand, a religion is almost always a body of more-or-less coherent metaphysical discourse that accounts for the cosmos (usually in supernatural terms, as the creation of a god or gods in which human beings have a special place) and provides a moral framework according to which people are supposed to live their lives. On the other hand, religions are *social* or *cultural* practices, with an emphasis upon the individual belonging to a particular community of fellow believers, a social identity many find supportive, and which bolsters a properly functioning sense of self. There are, of course, many examples of individuals who self-identify as religious despite doubting or even disregarding aspects of the metaphysical belief system associated with their faith, individuals who find solace in religious community that outweighs any reservations they have about points of doctrine. Critics of Scientology have shown themselves happy to attack the Church on both of these counts: as metaphysically risible, at best pseudoscientific, and underpinned by a farrago of ludicrous pulp sf tropes, and as a cult. On the latter point, professional sociologists of religion, for whom the distinction between religion and cult is more than a matter of rhetoric, tend to disagree. The consensus is that, functionally and socially, Scientology is a religion and not a cult (see Chagnon 1985, Kent 1990, and Ross 1988). By the same token, it is hard to find anybody outside the Church who regards the metaphysical content of the religion as anything other than absurd.

But it would be a mistake to dismiss Scientology. It is significant not least as the major example of the twentieth century's persistent fascination with the crossover between religion and sf. Religions have been invented throughout history, but twentieth-century examples of this essential human activity almost always bear the mark of sf. This is true from the smallest scale to the largest. In 1997 38 people committed suicide on the instruction of Marshall Herff Applewhite, leader of the Heaven's Gate cult, who believed that by doing so they would ascend to a UFO concealed in the tail of the Hale–Bopp comet. Nation of Islam, a predominantly American Islamic splinter religion, gives UFOs a significant place in their theology, and the Raëlian Church, an international faith that originated in France in 1974, believes humans were created by visiting extraterrestrials. Of more specific genre interest is the enormous popularity of the quasi-religious "Force," and its select warrior-priesthood, the Jedi, invented by

George Lucas for *Star Wars: Episode IV – A New Hope* (Lucas 1977). The Force, which owes a good deal to Hubbard's notions, has spilled over into real life in ways that illustrate the porous boundary between the fictional representation of sf tropes and the way people actualize their lives. In the English and Welsh census of 2001, more than 350,000 people listed their religious affiliation as "Jedi," not all of them for a joke. The point of intersection between sf and faith into which Scientology tapped is one of the mode's major nexuses of signification.

See also: **Isaac Asimov, Greg Bear, Alfred Bester, Leigh Brackett, Octavia Butler, Samuel R. Delany, Philip K. Dick, William Gibson, Robert A. Heinlein, Frank Herbert, Ursula K. Le Guin, C.L. Moore, Kim Stanley Robinson, Joanna Russ, Neal Stephenson, Sheri S. Tepper, James Tiptree Jr, and Gene Wolfe**

Bibliography

Chagnon, R. (1985) *La Scientologie: une nouvelle religion de la puissance*, Montréal: Hurtubise HMH, Collection Sociologie.

Kent, S.A. (1990) "Deviance Labelling and Normative Strategies in the Canadian 'New Religions/Counterculture' Debate," *Canadian Journal of Sociology/Cahiers canadiens de sociologie*, 15(4): 393–416.

Miller, R. (1987) *Bare-Faced Messiah: the true story of L. Ron Hubbard*, London: Cape.

Roberts, A. (2005) *The History of Science Fiction*, Basingstoke: Palgrave.

Ross, M.W. (1988) "Effects of Membership in Scientology on Personality: an exploratory study," *Journal for the Scientific Study of Religion*, 27(4): 630–36.

Wallis, R. (1977) *The Road to Total Freedom: a sociological analysis of Scientology*, New York: Columbia University Press.

ADAM ROBERTS

GWYNETH [ANN] JONES (1952–)

British novelist and sf critic.

Gwyneth Jones came to prominence with her *Aleutian* trilogy, *White Queen* (1991), *North Wind* (1994), and *Phoenix Café* (1997), and is the author of 11 other sf novels, 25 Young Adult (YA) novels (most published as Ann Halam), two short-story collections, a critical book, *Deconstructing the Starships: science, fiction, reality* (1999), and numerous essays and reviews. Jones's work has frequently been recognized by awards: the 1991 **James Tiptree Jr** Award for *White Queen*; the Children of the Night Award for Ann Halam's *The Fear Man* (1995); the 1996 World Fantasy Awards for best collection and best short fiction, for *Seven Tales and a Fable* (1995) and "The Grass Princess" (1996); the 1998 British Science Fiction Association's short-story award for "La Cenerentola" (1998); the 2002 **Arthur C. Clarke** Award for *Bold as Love* (2001); the 2004 **Philip K. Dick** Award for *Life* (2004); and the 2008 Science Fiction Research Association's Pilgrim Award for lifetime contribution to sf scholarship.

Jones's work links her speculative worlds to contemporary, real-world political struggle; innovatively uses genre tropes; frequently explores themes related to gender and power; and blurs genre boundaries between sf and fantasy. She frequently focuses on societies in transition and the overdetermination of social and political life, conscious of the complex exchanges between material reality and ideological belief.

Divine Endurance (1984) and *Flower Dust* (1993), set in far-future Malaysia, explore a mechanistic culture in decline, moving from the last gasps of the old order's remnants through the conflicted rise of a revolutionary culture. *Kairos* (1988, rev. 1995), a Greek word meaning the opportune time or place to enact change, explores a society on the edge of apocalypse and the transformative potential of a reality-altering drug. *Escape Plans* (1986) is set on the Indian subcontinent: long-abandoned by the posthuman space-faring classes, the remaining populations of biels (BLs for bonded labor) are confined to underground warrens to protect the biosphere and monitored by CHTHON, the Combined Holding Terrestrial Habitats Operational Network. The novel's focus on the dispossessed of the information age makes it an ironic counterpoint to the cyberpunk fiction published contemporaneously with it. *Escape Plans* is innovative in its use of language, inventing "acro," acronyms pronounced as words, for its dominant population, and SIND, a machine-generated language imitating an ancient subcontinental dialect, for freedom fighters that resist the economic displacement of humans into "passive" processing devices for computers. The protagonist ALIC (Aeleysi) learns to think of the biels as subjects once she abandons her privileged LECM (Local Environmental Containment Module habitat, pronounced el-ee-si-um – or Elysium) and lives among them. The novel challenges the reader to fill in the details of the larger social world and its history by struggling with the language and learning through observation, with ALIC, that material reality is often more complex and contradictory than common sense allows us to believe.

Jones's near-future novel *Life* explores this axiom from another perspective, considering the degree to which cultural beliefs shape the "reality" of scientific knowledge. Anna Senoz, a geneticist who tries to keep her science pure from life, observes a genetic shift in humans she calls "Transferred Y syndrome": X and Y chromosomes exchange genes and are becoming a matched (rather than asymmetrical) pair. Just as she wishes to separate science from daily political struggle, Anna feels she can conduct her personal life on the basis of abstract reason alone – ignoring all the messy human desires, instincts, insecurities, and fears that shape so much of what we do. In contrast, her activist friend Ramone insists that gender identity is the most important determinant of one's fate and sees in Anna's research the chance to eliminate the second-class status of women. This rich novel encompasses more than either Anna or Ramone can see. Anna's career is thwarted by institutional sexism and the psychological consequences of being raped by a fellow graduate student, yet it is her own internalized feelings of guilt and shame that limit her prospects as much as the predatory attitude of (some of) her male colleagues. She struggles rationally to place her marriage beyond the limitations of dominant gender roles, but finds nonetheless that her husband has an affair: rational beliefs and ideological commitments cannot explain all of life. Anna eventually concludes that although Transferred Y may create a situation in which biological gender difference is eliminated, this fact will not inevitably change the reality of gender roles; they have always been a convenient way to divide the world between haves and have-nots, that is, a product of economic rather than biological determinism.

This anatomy of gender roles and the problematic conflation of sex and gender develop ideas Jones investigated in her *Aleutian* trilogy, a semi-ironic exploration of the fantasies and fears that drive first contact stories. A group of aliens crash land in the Aleutian Islands on Earth. Humans call them Aleutians and later, when questioned about the name of their world, the aliens call it Aleutia. They are trying to find a way home, but decide to indulge in some trade when the opportunity presents itself. Humans, meanwhile, presume the aliens to have intentionally come to Earth and, due to misunderstandings about Aleutian physiology and social organization, also conclude they are immortal and telepathic. The consequences of colonial occupation and conquest are important themes: human social life is inevitably changed by the presence of the aliens, particularly concerning gender roles. The hermaphroditic Aleutians can only understand human gender roles indistinctly, drawing attention to the conflation of biological and social factors, not all of them concerned with sex, which form the substrate of our categories "feminine" and "masculine." The Aleutians grasp this as the division of humanity into two tribes – the "childbearers" and the "parasites" – but fail to understand how these biological roles translate into the social struggle they observe. Colloquially referred to as a war between the Women's Agenda and the Men's Agenda, this economic and political struggle sees some biological men support the "women," and vice versa; the Aleutians eventually insist that humans wear costumes with padded breasts or codpieces to indicate their allegiance.

The Aleutian influence over approximately three centuries of human history cannot be categorized as simply positive or negative: some humans establish a cult and mutilate themselves to better approximate Aleutian appearance; large-scale terraforming projects made possible by Aleutian technology mitigate some of the problems caused by climate change. A human technology that enables faster-than-light travel, the Buonarotti device, lies fallow for many years, presumed to have been made redundant by superior Aleutian science. In *Phoenix Café*, a reactionary group of humans resist the Aleutian cultural influence to recover humanity's own path, but, as always in postcolonial situations, one cannot return to the past and find a way forward uncontaminated by the reality of contact. The trilogy stresses that what we see in the alien is a reflection of our own projections, a theme explored through the motif of rape as both a metaphor for the colonial encounter and an act between individuals. The narrative structure invites readers to reflect on their own expectations derived from other sf narratives. Both Aleutians and humans understand the other within the logic of their own frames of reference, and readers, like the human characters, struggle to comprehend the alien; information is revealed gradually over the series and is only fully comprehended at its end. The Aleutians' challenging relationship to language and consensual reality, and their mode of subjectivity, which refuses to separate self from world, implicitly critique Cartesian versions of human consciousness (see Vint 2007).

The *Bold as Love* series – *Bold as Love*, *Castles Made of Sand* (2002), *Midnight Lamp* (2003), *Band of Gypsys* (2005), *Rainbow Bridge* (2006) – is a multifaceted mediation upon social transformation. Beginning with the dissolution of Great Britain into its constituent nations, the series charts the experiences of three central characters – Ax, Fiorinda, and Sage – through the governance forms that follow: a counter-cultural dictatorship established by violent coup; Ax's more enlightened dictatorship; a "Green Nazi" period dominated by Celtic extremists;

Ax's presidency after he liberates England from this regime; a period of house arrest in which the three are figurehead leaders; and finally occupation by the Chinese, who are establishing a world government. The "triumvirate" try to mitigate the worst consequences of the backlash against a dying neoliberalist order and to establish, "for the first time in history, a genuine human civilization. For everyone, not for the elite few who have always had a sweet life, any time this last however-many thousand years … [and] to give the future that could happen a chance" (Jones 2001: 82). In a concrete manifestation of what Fredric Jameson (2005) has characterized as the difference between utopia-as-program and utopia-as-impulse, they recognize that whatever solutions they enact will be "partial, fucked-up and temporary" (Jones 2001: 82), but further that "we must not be afraid of quirky small-scale initiatives, partial solutions, the piecemeal of many ideas and techniques" (Jones 2005: 119).

This series blurs the boundaries between sf and fantasy: the ability to intervene in the physical structures of the world is equally possible with technology and magic, different paths to the same ability to perceive that mind and matter are part of a single substance (an idea also explored in *Kairos*'s drug and *Phoenix Café*'s video games). The series rewrites Arthurian myth, depicting a threesome rather than allowing sexual infidelity to destroy the hope of Camelot. The novel is supported by an extensive website (http://www.boldaslove.co.uk/), which provides detailed discussion of contextual sources, insights into themes, and commentary on musical allusions, as well as some history of counter-cultural music. Jones is an extremely perceptive critic of her own work and the website is an excellent supplement to the fiction. One of the things it makes clear is genre literature's powerful potential to intervene meaningfully in the social world and the ongoing ideological struggle to enable human civilization to "develop into who knows what new forms" (Jones 2006: 240). The website points out, for example, that Fiorinda's rape during the Green Nazi regime "by the bastard who took over because I go with the territory" (Jones 2002: 277) is a continuing experience of women in war. Jones's homepage (http://homepage.ntlworld.com/gwynethann/) similarly contains a wealth of information and includes full versions of some short stories and essays.

The *Aleutian* and *Bold as Love* novels explore ecological themes, something taken up more directly in Halam's YA *Inland* series: *Daymaker* (1987), *Transformations* (1988), and *The Skybreaker* (1990). Some of the YA novels have sf premises – especially *The Hidden Ones* (1988), *Dr Franklin's Island* (2001), *Taylor Five* (2002), and *The Visitor* (2006) – but fantasy, horror, and mythology are equally prominent.

Jones characterizes her *Spirit: or the princess of Bois Dormant* (2009) as space opera. Her website suggests that this new work links together the previous two series, making the development of mind/matter tech in the *Bold as Love* series the basis for the later invention of the Buonarotti device in the *Aleutian* trilogy, which then becomes the basis for the FTL flight necessary to enable space opera plots. Just as the *Aleutian* trilogy delved into the colonial foundation of first contact stories, *Spirit* promises to transform our understanding of space opera.

See also: **J.G. Ballard, Iain M. Banks, Leigh Brackett, Octavia Butler, Arthur C. Clarke, Philip K. Dick, Donna J. Haraway, Nalo Hopkinson, Ursula K. Le Guin, China Miéville, Michael Moorcock, Alan Moore, C.L. Moore, Joanna Russ, Mary Shelley, Olaf Stapledon, Sheri S. Tepper, James Tiptree Jr, and H.G. Wells**

Bibliography

FemSpec, 5(1) (2004), special Gwyneth Jones issue.
Jameson, F. (2005) *Archaeologies of the Future: the desire called utopia and other science fictions*, London: Verso.
Jones, G. (2001) *Bold as Love: a near future fantasy*, London: Gollancz.
——(2002) *Castles Made of Sand*, London: Gollancz.
——(2005) *Band of Gypsys*, London: Gollancz.
——(2006) *Rainbow Bridge*, London: Gollancz.
——(2009) *Spirit: or the princess of Bois Dormant*, London: Gollancz.
Vint, S. (2007) *Bodies of Tomorrow: technology, subjectivity, science fiction*, Toronto: University of Toronto Press.

SHERRYL VINT

[THOMAS] NIGEL KNEALE (1922–2006)

British television, radio, and film scriptwriter.

Best known for his groundbreaking television sf, particularly the *Quatermass* serials, Nigel Kneale's *oeuvre* spans several genres. His most distinctive scripts hybridize sf and Gothic horror. Kneale wrote 20 original television programs, one original film screenplay, and over 30 short stories, as well as radio plays, adaptations for screen, and screenplays and prose texts based on his own television work. Although concerned with the horrific consequences of twentieth-century science, he suggests that culture, rather than technology, is to blame, and his extrapolations backward, as well as forward, in time contextualize technology in terms of long-standing beliefs and practices. Kneale also emphasizes the way phenomena are perceived. His sf unites mythology and scientific fabulation as forms and juxtaposes them as themes, stressing the imprudence of relying exclusively on either superstition or rationalism.

Kneale commenced his career in the 1940s, writing short fiction for magazines. A collection, *Tomato Cain* (1949), won both Somerset Maugham and Atlantic awards. While none of these stories are sf, some eloquently describe collisions between folklore and science. "The Tarroo-Ushtey," for instance, explores the way anxieties about modernity are articulated in the social imaginary. Nineteenth-century villagers on the Isle of Man are terrified by a noise from the sea. The local wise man says that it is the cry of a mythical beast, while a peddler states that it is a foghorn. The former's success in hoodwinking the villagers indicates that power is as much a matter of how machines are explained as how they are utilized. However, the utilization of technology is central to another short story, "Minuke," and a radio play, *You Must Listen* (1952), which both feature ghosts abusing telephone lines; a modern medium serves the same purpose as a spiritual medium. In *You Must Listen*, the voice haunting the line belongs to a jilted lover who committed suicide; for Kneale, a medium is only as good as the society whose messages it channels, yet electronic devices can also trigger the return of the socially repressed.

Kneale's interest in modern media was evident in his eagerness to read his stories on radio and his application, in 1951, to become a television producer. Eventually employed as a staff-writer for BBC television, he adapted Stanley Young's sf play *Mystery Story* (1952) and Charles Irving's *Number Three* (1953); respectively, these touch on dehumanization and nuclear power's apocalyptic potential, themes present in his first original sf, *The Quatermass Experiment* (1953). In this television serial, Carroon, an astronaut overcome in an atomic spaceship by an alien parasite, absorbs his fellow crew members. On Earth he mutates, absorbing any organisms he encounters. The plant-like monster, about to broadcast its seeds, occupies Westminster Abbey during a television broadcast about the abbey, which had appeared on television several weeks earlier during the transmission of Elizabeth II's coronation. The serial's finale therefore incorporates a setting with both a Gothic aura and televisual currency, and implicates the monarchy, Christianity, and television in the monster's threat to individuality. The scientist-hero's name, Quatermass, combines rationalist science (equation/mass) and Christian gatherings (mass). The serial links its Cold War theme – a man losing his autonomy in an age of totalitarian states, nuclear power, and space exploration – to historical encounters between the individual and ideology. However, much of the serial's horror comes from its scrutiny of Carroon's agonizing transformation, as scientists, reporters, foreign agents, detectives, and two of the astronauts' wives make their separate claims on him. His metamorphosis can be seen as a response to these irreconcilable social, professional, political, and personal demands.

The program was immensely successful, popularizing sf on television. It emulated – and was probably aided by – the success of John Wyndham's *The Day of the Triffids* (1951), which attracted a wider British readership to sf novels. Kneale and Wyndham helped fuel the monster sf that flourished during the 1950s. As in Wyndham's *The Kraken Wakes* (1953), little about Kneale's monsters is knowable. Quatermass infers that invaders come from a Saturnian moon in *Quatermass II* (1955) and Mars in *Quatermass and the Pit* (1958–59), but there is no proof for this. In *The Quatermass Experiment*, the alien embodies the disconcerting ineffability of space, signifying what lies beyond the limits of 1950s science. Quatermass's hubris is expressed in similar, albeit psychoanalytical, terms in *Quatermass II*, when his daughter confesses to nightmares about being alone in his rocket, amidst the darkness of space.

The first original British adult sf written for television, *The Quatermass Experiment* influenced much subsequent television sf, from *Doctor Who* (1963–) to *The X-Files* (1993–2002). It was also the first television drama to be adapted as a film (1955), and the first British television serial published in script form (1959), which allowed this live serial to achieve permanence and reach audiences abroad (it was through the script and film versions that US directors and screenwriters such as **Steven Spielberg**, John Carpenter, and Dan O'Bannon encountered Kneale's serials). While the strangeness and social consequences of media are often thematized in sf, *The Quatermass Experiment* was the first self-reflexive television sf, appearing when television was still, in a sense, a novum, and diagnosing the disturbing ease with which society allows television to channel evil. In 1954 the BBC aptly chose Kneale to adapt George Orwell's *Nineteen Eighty-Four* (1949), a story about social control through two-way "telescreens." In *Quatermass and the Pit*, a television cable brought in by news-hungry reporters reactivates a spaceship that triggers genocidal impulses. Kneale never approved of the film of his last sf script, *Halloween III: Season of the Witch* (Wallace 1982), but his anxieties about the capitalist exploitation of television become apparent when a company activates its killer-masks via television; this film extended the concerns about technocratic capitalism expressed in Kneale's "Speech by the Minister of Power, 1973" (1960), published in *Punch* magazine.

Kneale's awareness of television's subversive potential enabled him to write politically incisive sf. *Quatermass II*, about a top-secret synthetic food factory – actually a base for an (explicitly termed) "colonial organism" – conveys fears of cultural colonization: an old village is replaced by a new town, its community threatened by a brainwashed government's covert policies. Wartime anxieties also linger. The aliens' effective exploitation of wartime-style posters defamiliarizes Britain's own propaganda, so that Britain's response to Nazism seems equally immoral. The fact that the plot bears similarities to Ian Fleming's *Moonraker* (1955), in which a government-approved rocket base turns out to be run by Nazis, points to the theme's pertinence in the mid-1950s. Kneale's ironic mobilization of Otherness as a mirror-image of British propaganda, colonialism, and modernity becomes evident when Quatermass realizes that the alien base resembles his planned moon colony, while the explosion of his flawed spaceship makes him more an anti-hero, than a hero, of the atomic age.

The atomic age is implicitly thematized in *The Creature* (1955), later filmed as *The Abominable Snowman* (Guest 1957). Yeti-hunters realize they are pursuing an intelligent species, which may prevail after humanity has wiped itself out. This was Kneale's first juxtaposition of religion and rationalism. A scientist is contrasted with Buddhists, who share the Yetis' telepathic powers and live in peace with them. The Buddhists have a better understanding of the Yetis than the scientist, and the Yetis make better use of technology than humans. A cynical gunrunner says that his motive for the hunt is to satisfy the curiosity that radio and television have catalyzed. That media can also be utilized altruistically is made apparent when the Yetis use a radio to warn the scientist about a storm. Modernity is seen against a historical backdrop; characters discuss the technological sublime of modern media against the perennially sublime landscape of the Himalayas.

However, in Kneale's later sf history is implicated in, rather than contrasted with, modernity. *Quatermass and the Pit* reveals that aliens colonized human minds five million years ago, improving their intelligence but also instilling racism into them. In order to understand this returning repressed, Quatermass has to rely on superstition (the aliens are the devils of folklore), as well as rationalism. His phrase "We are the Martians" acknowledges that racism is inhuman and that "we" are racists, colonialists, and someone else's Other. Kneale probably never read *Childhood's End* (1953), but *Quatermass and the Pit* serves as a riposte to **Arthur C. Clarke**'s novel. In both, aliens resembling devils influence human evolution, but Kneale depicts colonialism as purely malevolent, and his aliens are far removed from Clarke's benign demigods. *The Road* (1963), about a cross-section of Enlightenment society witnessing a vision of future nuclear holocaust, implicates Enlightenment empiricism, epicurism, and colonialism in the historical "road" to atomic destruction. *The Crunch* (1964) is a less complex treatment of postcolonial themes: an ex-colony, Makang, holds Britain to ransom with a nuclear weapon. Only a Makangese man with superhuman physical endurance foils the detonation; Kneale hints that it takes superhuman restraint for an ex-colony not to seek justifiable revenge.

Most subversive was Kneale's *The Year of the Sex Olympics* (1968): a "high-drive" caste keeps the "low-drives" passive and the population down through television pornography, light entertainment, and an actuality show that resembles what we now call "reality television." In this dystopia, vocabulary is said to be "tension-free": for instance, the word "victorious" is no longer understood, while "vicarious" is seen as a keyword. Fiction and art have been repressed; the protagonist only learns how to tell a story when he has left society. The play's prescience matters less than what it implies about television of the 1960s: casually prurient documentaries and light entertainment seem harmless, but they easily become insidious tools for social control, particularly when they displace potently discursive forms. This play and *Wine of India* (1970), about a society in which people stay young for decades but are then contractually obliged to commit suicide, resemble Aldous Huxley's *Brave New World* (1932) in the way they deconstruct common utopian themes.

The Stone Tape (1972) and *Quatermass* (1979) combine reflexivity with history. In the former, scientists searching for a new audio medium analyze a haunting and realize that the building's stones are the medium they seek, the ghost a recording. While trying to control the medium, they wipe the "tape" and uncover a decayed recording, far more horrific for its lack of fidelity. Lack of sexual fidelity, at the same time, characterizes the group's misogynistic leader. Jill, his mistress, is upset by him and then killed by the decayed recording. His behavior is equated with hidden/repressed danger, but the greatest horror is the indecipherable image and sound of time, represented by the decayed recording. For Kneale, who was so concerned with historicizing futurology, nothing could be more disturbing than a past which can no longer be fully deciphered. *Quatermass* analyzes social decay, representing ancient sites as signals planted by aliens that harvest adolescents. It suggests that social collapse is rooted in history, but its conflation of hippies and punks as "planet people" lacks the precision of Kneale's earlier social critiques. However, when the serial satirizes television, it is just as incisive as Kneale's previous work.

Kneale's last television sf was *Kinvig* (1981), a poorly written sitcom, which is nonetheless interesting as an attempt to explore sf's permeation of the social imaginary. Despite often being dismissive of the genre when interviewed, Kneale was ever conscious of sf's social significance; in *The Quatermass Experiment*, a detective realizes he has to start reading sf in order to "catch up on fact."

See also: **Gerry Anderson, The Doctor, Gene Roddenberry, and J. Michael Straczynski**

Bibliography

Broughton, M. (forthcoming) *Nigel Kneale*, Manchester: Manchester University Press.

Chapman, J. (2006) "*Quatermass* and the Origins of British Television Sf," in J. Cook and P. Wright (eds.) *British Science Fiction Television*, London: I.B. Tauris.

Jacobs, J. (2000) *The Intimate Screen: early British television drama*, Oxford: Oxford University Press.

Johnson, C. (2005) *Telefantasy*, London: BFI.

Murray, A. (2006) *Into the Unknown: the fantastic life of Nigel Kneale*, London: Headpress.

Rolinson, D. and Devlin, K. (2008) "'A New Wilderness': memory and language in the television science fiction of Nigel Kneale," *Science Fiction Film and Television*, 1(1): 45–65.

MARK BROUGHTON

STANLEY KUBRICK (1928–99)

US filmmaker, cinematographer, screenwriter, film editor, and photographer, based for much of his career in Britain.

After working as a photographer for *Look* magazine and as a documentary filmmaker, Stanley Kubrick began directing feature films with the self-funded war film *Fear and Desire* (1953) and *Killer's Kiss* (1955), about a washed-up boxer involved with petty criminals. His first professional feature, the heist movie *The Killing* (1956), brought him to the attention of Hollywood, where he directed the anti-war

Paths of Glory (1957), starring Kirk Douglas, who then brought Kubrick in to replace Anthony Mann as director of *Spartacus* (1960). The experience of working on such a major picture left Kubrick unhappy with Hollywood. When he moved to the UK to film *Lolita* (1962), his relocation became permanent. He spent the next decade making three sf films: *Dr Strangelove or: How I Learned to Stop Worrying and Love the Bomb* (1964), *2001: A Space Odyssey* (1968), and *A Clockwork Orange* (1971). Kubrick's long pre-production process, and several abandoned projects, meant he would direct only four more films: *Barry Lyndon* (1975), which recounts the picaresque rise and fall of an eighteenth-century adventurer; *The Shining* (1980), about a haunted hotel, madness, and patriarchal violence; the Vietnam war movie *Full Metal Jacket* (1987); and the oddly muted erotic thriller *Eyes Wide Shut* (1999). In 1982 Kubrick optioned Brian Aldiss's "Supertoys Last All Summer Long" (1969), which was in development for 18 years, with story input from Ian Watson (and, uncredited, **Arthur C. Clarke** and Bob Shaw), while waiting for necessary advances in special effects technologies. On Kubrick's death, the project became **Steven Spielberg**'s *A.I.: Artificial Intelligence* (2001).

If *Dr Strangelove* had been faithfully adapted from Peter George's straight-faced thriller *Two Hours to Doom* (1958), it would have been just another in the cycle of well-crafted liberal melodramas about nuclear war which included *On the Beach* (Kramer 1959), *Fail-Safe* (Lumet 1964), and *The Bedford Incident* (Harris 1965). However, while writing the script, Kubrick began to find the rhetoric of nuclear deterrence and the strategies for waging and surviving nuclear war increasingly absurd, pushing the film toward black comedy. Paranoid General Jack D. Ripper orders nuclear bombers under his command to strike Soviet targets, hoping to force President Merkin Muffley into launching a full-scale attack before the USSR can retaliate. Over the protests of General Buck Turgidson (modeled on General Curtis LeMay), Muffley instead liaises with Premier Kissoff to bring down the planes if they cannot be recalled. The USSR, however, has a Doomsday Device: an automated system that will wipe out life on Earth and make the planet uninhabitable for a century if a single atomic bomb explodes on Soviet soil. A lone bomber, the *Leper's Colony*, commanded by Major "King" Kong, evades all attempts to stop it. As nuclear annihilation looms, Muffley's scientific advisor, Dr Strangelove (based on Americanized Nazi rocket scientist Wernher von Braun, the RAND corporation's Herman Kahn, and Rotwang, the mad scientist from **Fritz Lang**'s *Metropolis* (1927)), argues that they need to establish shelters in deep mineshafts, with ten sexually stimulating women to every man, so as to breed a massive population capable of defeating any surviving Soviets in the postapocalyptic world.

Kubrick's satire has four main thrusts. The first concerns modes of thinking rendered inappropriate by the nuclear age: the *Leper's Colony* enters Soviet airspace to the Civil War tune "When Johnny Comes Marching Home" (1863); climactic nuclear war is accompanied by Vera Lynn's recording of Second World War morale-booster "We'll Meet Again" (1939). The second focuses on strategic planning's tendency to normalize the incomprehensible and insupportable: Turgidson urges an all-out attack because calculations suggest that it would produce an acceptable loss of only 20 million, rather than 150 million, Americans. The third is concerned with our subordination to arbitrary systems. Procedures which dictate future actions are set in place even though they cannot anticipate every possible circumstance: when the damaged *Leper Colony* abandons its mission in favor of a target of opportunity, the bomber cannot be located. Kubrick's use of sets with ceilings and of wide-angle lenses, which extend the depth of field and horizontal plane of action, leaving figures isolated in immense surroundings, accentuates this sense of entrapment within systems. The fourth identifies the infantile phallic sexuality of the arms race: the celebrated opening sequence, spoofing the techno-eroticism of flag-wavers like *Strategic Air Command* (Mann 1955), depicts a B-52's mid-air refueling as a seductive dance between planes, to the tune of "Try a Little Tenderness" (1932), and as an act of penetration; the War Room staff quickly seize upon the sexual opportunities presented by Strangelove's mineshaft proposal; Ripper launches his attack because he can feel the communist conspiracy to fluoridate water sapping his purity of essence. These and other psychosexual revelations trouble the supposed rationality of nuclear strategy – just as punning character names and outrageous performances push against surface realism, and as the transitions from formal compositions to *verité*-style camerawork disrupt the sense of a single dominant aesthetic.

One draft of *Strangelove*'s screenplay depicted aliens trying to reconstruct the events that led to the Earth's destruction. Retained in Peter George's novelization, this framing device resonates with the final act of *A.I.* and with Kubrick's next film, *2001*. Inspired by several of Arthur C. Clarke's short stories, especially "The Sentinel" (1951), it was initially conceptualized as a Hollywood historical epic – a space-age version of *How the West Was Won* (Ford, Hathaway, Marshall, Thorpe 1962). Kubrick developed the script over several years with Clarke, beginning with a coauthored draft of a novel that could be used to raise funding and upon which the screenplay – and ultimately Clarke's own novel – could then be based. Unlike Clarke, who despite transcendentalist impulses typically explains everything in his fiction, Kubrick, who generally favored voice-over narration, removed all such exposition late in production, rendering his film all the more challenging and elusive.

A mysterious black monolith appears on a prehistoric African plain and apparently teaches prehuman apes to use bones as tools. Four million years later humans unearth a similar monolith on the moon. When sunlight strikes its surface, it beams a powerful radio signal toward Jupiter. Eighteen months later, the *Discovery* is en route to the gas giant when its infallible computer, HAL 9000, suffers a psychological breakdown and murders all but one of the crew. Venturing out toward a giant monolith orbiting Jupiter, astronaut Dave Bowman falls into a tunnel of lights, races over alien landscapes, and eventually – it seems – dies and is reborn as hyper-evolved posthuman Starchild, who returns to Earth.

Kubrick's future is equally an extrapolation from and a satire on 1960s corporate America, its banal inhumanity emphasized by the stilted conversations of depthless characters, many of whose exchanges are constrained by political agendas, checklists, and other predetermined procedures. The remorseless blandness of this futurologically scrupulous world is further demonstrated by Kubrick's muted eroticization of technologies, here a commentary on the gestation and birth of posthumanity rather than an opportunity for tittering. His wide-angle cinematography makes the various immaculate built environments even more unhomely: characters pass through such spaces, as emphasized by the astronauts' endless jogging around the *Discovery*, rather than inhabit them, and human characters never exchange conventional shot/reverse-shot sequences. Despite this element of critique, *2001*'s countercultural status has long been attributed instead to the trippy-ness of the psychedelic "Stargate" sequence.

2001's significance for the development of sf lies in its formal and technical achievements. Few, if any, prior sf films exhibited its artistic ambition. For example, when Kubrick matched images of docking spacecraft to Johann Strauss II's *Blue Danube Waltz* (1867), he returned film to the possibilities that opened up with the coming of sound before its relationship with the image became merely explicatory. Kubrick sections the soundtrack so that extra-diegetic music never accompanies dialogue scenes, leaving the audience bereft of normative emotional cues. This sense of being adrift in front of ambiguous images is captured in the film itself when a screen in Bowman's space-pod, tracking Poole's drifting corpse, imposes a three-dimensional Cartesian grid over space which we have repeatedly been shown has no fixed vertical or horizontal planes.

Half of the shots in *2001* are effects shots. They cost over half the budget and involved the development or invention of new techniques and equipment. Indeed, Kubrick's greatest influence on the genre was, arguably, to fuel the desire to produce a spectacular cinema of attractions. This can be seen in the career of Douglas Trumbull. A key member of *2001*'s effects team, he became one of the most influential figures in special effects, working on *The Andromeda Strain* (Wise 1971), *Close Encounters of the Third Kind* (Spielberg 1977), *Star Trek: The Motion Picture* (Wise 1979), and *Blade Runner* (Scott 1982), as well as directing *Silent Running* (1972) and *Brainstorm* (1983). Since the 1980s he has concentrated on developing exhibition technologies and theme park rides. It is also evident in the shortcomings of the films which attempt to ape *2001*'s aspirations, such as *The Black Hole* (Nelson 1979), *Star Trek: The Motion Picture*, *Contact* (Zemeckis 1997), and *Mission to Mars* (De Palma 2000). Often visually stunning, they are every bit as banal as the future *2001* depicts.

A Clockwork Orange, adapted from Anthony Burgess's 1962 novel about juvenile delinquency, original sin, and free-will, begins with a slow zoom out from the protagonist's eye and down the entire length of the Korova Milk Bar. This might lead one to expect another measured and stately film. But if *2001* abandoned *Strangelove*'s ribaldry to emphasize oppressive orderliness, *A Clockwork Orange* instead delights in bawdiness, vulgarity, and violence. Alex beats up tramps and rapes women for fun, but when he alienates his gang, they abandon him to the police. In exchange for his freedom, he volunteers for behavioral conditioning, which renders him incapable of stomaching violence. It also destroys his ability to listen to his beloved Beethoven's Ninth Symphony (1824). Former victims use this music to force Alex to attempt suicide, causing a political scandal. Alex's brainwashing is reversed in exchange for his endorsement of the government.

Kubrick's exuberant, disorienting handheld camera symbolizes the chaotic energy of the amoral, self-knowing but unashamed Alex, who himself represents for the state all that which must be suppressed. Like Alex in his over-the-top dress sense and performance of violence, Kubrick refuses restraint, peopling his film with stereotypes and grotesques, music-hall and sitcom humor, and a childish fixation on sexual organs, especially breasts. He joyously exhibits the filmmaking craft: a montage sequence that makes a row of porcelain Jesuses seem to dance; the gleefully artificial back-projection and fast-motion threesome; the tendency to present scenes rather than create more conventionalized spaces and character interactions; the excessive pop-art *mise-en-scène*; the badly done and utterly inappropriate images (religious and prehistoric epics, vampire films, orgiastic excesses) Alex envisions when he hears Beethoven or reads the Bible. While sf films such as *Wild in the Streets* (Shear 1968) celebrated the hopefulness of the counterculture, and *Privilege* (Watkins 1967) critiqued its complicity with structures of power, *A Clockwork Orange*'s irreverence and self-conscious poor taste sounded a warning of the backlash to come.

Although Kubrick made only three sf films, they are all among the most highly regarded in the genre. Probably only Andrei Tarkovsky, the rather more meditative director of *Solaris* (1972), *Stalker* (1979), and *The Sacrifice* (1986), equals or exceeds this achievement.

See also: **Arthur C. Clarke, David Cronenberg, Fritz Lang, George Lucas, Oshii Mamoru, and Steven Spielberg**

Bibliography

Agel, J. (1970) *The Making of Kubrick's 2001*, New York: New American Library.

Baxter, J. (1997) *Stanley Kubrick: a biography*, New York: Carroll & Graf.

Chion, M. (2001) *Kubrick's Cinema Odyssey*, trans. C. Gorbman, London: BFI.

Clarke, A.C. (1972) *The Lost Worlds of 2001*, New York: New American Library.

Freedman, C. (1996) "Kubrick's *2001* and the Possibility of a Science-Fiction Cinema," *Science Fiction Studies*, 25(2): 300–17.

Kolker, R. (ed.) (2006) *Stanley Kubrick's 2001: A Space Odyssey: new essays*, Oxford: Oxford University Press.

McDougal, S.Y. (ed.) (2003) *Stanley Kubrick's A Clockwork Orange*, Cambridge: Cambridge University Press.

Naremore, J. (2007) *On Kubrick*, London: BFI.

Schwam, S. (2000) *The Making of 2001: A Space Odyssey*, New York: The Modern Library.

MARK BOULD

FRITZ LANG (1890–1976)

Austrian filmmaker, active in Germany, France, and the US.

Born in Vienna to middle-class parents, Fritz Lang studied engineering, art and painting, and claimed to have traveled widely in Europe,

Africa, and Asia before joining the Austrian army at the outbreak of the First World War. Recovering from injuries and shell-shock, he began to write for the movies. He directed 16 films in Weimar Germany, several of them co-written and novelized by his wife, Thea von Harbou. After the Nazi Party, which von Harbou had joined, suppressed *The Testament of Dr Mabuse* (1933), Lang emigrated to France, where he made the posthumous fantasy *Liliom* (1934), and then to the US, where he directed 23 films, including westerns, thrillers, melodramas, and such quintessential *films noirs* as *Scarlet Street* (1945) and *The Big Heat* (1953). In 1958 he returned to Germany to direct a two-part remake of *The Indian Tomb* (1921), which he had adapted with von Harbou from her novel, and *The 1000 Eyes of Dr Mabuse* (1960). Nearly blind, he returned to the US but never directed another film.

Throughout his career Lang was obsessed with the fabric of capitalist modernity, developing a pulp-Expressionist critique of industrialization. The central icon of his films is the clock, signaling the rationalization of time and the economic domination of individual subjectivity. Although many would argue that Lang directed only two sf films, *Metropolis* (1927) and *Woman in the Moon* (1929), this narrow understanding of his work arises from a retrospective imposition of rigid genre categories onto complex texts and situations. Lang's Weimar films exemplify the popular- and mass-cultural loam out of which specific culture industries, such as US pulp publishers, extracted and niche-marketed particular generic constellations, including sf. For example, *Spiders, Part 1: The Golden Lake* (1919) follows Kay Hoog, millionaire sportsman and gentleman adventurer, as he battles a global criminal organization. The film is replete with gunfights, sieges, rope-ladder descents, parachute jumps; last minute escapes over rooftops, on horseback, by balloon, and down subterranean waterfalls; secret entrances, giant idols, Inca ruins, and a valley from which no white man has ever returned; abduction, bondage, human sacrifice; and a beautiful native princess who falls in love with the hero and is murdered when he spurns the advances of a beautiful enemy. While Hoog anticipates such sf adventurers as Doc Savage, overtly science-fictional elements are scarce – a closed circuit surveillance system; whatever anthropological veneer assistance from Hamburg's Ethnological Museum could lend its exotic sets and costumes – but this rich stew of colonial adventure is intimately tied to the emergence of sf (see Rieder 2008). Moreover, a shot in which multiple superimpositions reveal the international scope of the criminals' communications web hints at an emergent global – and postimperial – consciousness. *Spiders, Part 2: The Diamond Ship* (1920) added to the mix a tiger-guarded Chinese city hidden beneath San Francisco, domino-masked thieves in evening dress, Pinkertons, pirate treasure, Indian clairvoyants, hypnotic-telepathic experiments, and a yellow peril narrative.

In 1922 Lang adapted Norbert Jacques's 1921 newspaper serial as the two-part *Dr Mabuse: The Gambler* (1922), which was heavily influenced by Louis Feuillade's movie serials (e.g., *Fantômas* (1913–14), *Les Vampires* (1915), *Judex* (1916)). Eschewing the utopian aspects of Jacques's novel (in which Mabuse intends to leave decadent Europe and establish a pure, autocratic state in South America), Lang concentrates on making the criminal genius a focal point for the destructive forces of social dysfunction in contemporary Germany. Mabuse orchestrates complex schemes to manipulate the stock market, and uses his hypnotic powers to drive parasitic aristocrats to suicide. His many disguises capture the anonymity of the metropolis, the dissolution of traditional social hierarchies, and the fluidity of modern identity. Eventually driven mad, Mabuse is haunted both by his victims and by his machines, which transmute into demonic creatures. In *The Testament of Dr Mabuse*, Professor Baum uses Mabuse's notebooks to organize a massive criminal conspiracy and, possessed by Mabuse's ghost, turns to a campaign of terror, ordering the destruction of the harvest, the poisoning of water supplies, and attacks on railways, gasometers, chemical plants, banks, and the currency system. The apocalyptic hysteria driving Baum/Mabuse results from the domination of reason, symbolized by the ubiquitous machinery of the modern world. In the opening sequence, for example, nothing can be heard but the pounding of machines, and throughout the film the voice of Baum/Mabuse is relayed by radio and other means of mechanical reproduction so as to perform a kind of long-range hypnosis.

In his depiction of modern urban identity, Lang preferred abstractionism to the naturalism of his contemporaries working in the "street film" genre – which brought him almost inevitably to the utopian tradition. His monumentalist dystopian epic *Metropolis* is justly renowned for the complex effects work with which it envisioned a future city of towering skyscrapers, aerial roadways, and personal airplanes; for its choreographing of thousands of extras; and for the beautiful deco design of its robot. Recalling Claude Farrère's anti-labor novel *Useless Hands* (1920) as much as **H.G. Wells**'s socialistic *The Time Machine* (1895) or *When the Sleeper Wakes* (1899), it depicts a world divided between the pampered bourgeoisie and the indistinguishable proletarian masses who live in a subterranean enclave beneath the machines which sustain their city. Freder, the son of Joh Fredersen (the city's architect and autocratic manager), falls in love with the saintly Maria, who preaches patience to workers devastated by their exhausting, enfeebling labor: a savior will come, she promises, a heart to mediate between the head and the hands. Fredersen persuades mad scientist Rotwang to give his robot creation Maria's physical appearance and to send her among the workers as an agent provocateur so as to justify his use of violence against them. By night, robot-Maria's appearances at the Yoshiwara club whip the bourgeoisie into an erotic frenzy; by day, she incites the workers to anarchic violence against the machines. Cataclysm overwhelms the city before Freder finally steps forward to mediate between these economic classes.

Metropolis has often been derided for the absurdity of its plot – exacerbated by the loss, until 2008, of nearly a quarter of the film (one scene is still missing) – and for its ludicrous solution to the class antagonism at the heart of capitalism, despite being "the one for which we have generally settled: negotiation between exploiter and exploited classes (often represented by individuals rather than [economic] classes), undertaken by proxies who ultimately function as part of the apparatus for maintaining existing economic processes" (Bould 2005: 31–32). Lang's primary concern, however, is not so much narrative as the creation of an abstract total world – a closed cybernetic system, presided over by Fredersen – and a total filmic system of movement, shape, and texture, presided over by himself. Within this, a curious but informative parallel can be found between the inability of Fredersen's totalitarianism completely to control his system and the film's excesses – its millennial and sexual hysteria – which escape Lang's formal control. It is almost as if in addition to anticipating the development of cybernetics in the postwar period (in its exploration of the cybernetic imagination, Thomas Pynchon's *Gravity's Rainbow* (1973) repeatedly alludes to *Metropolis*), Lang intuitively, accidentally, provided an exemplar of chaos theory.

Spies (1928) reworks Mabuse's Berlin through *Metropolis*'s logic of abstraction. From the center of a web of information and telecommunications technologies, in a secret multi-level headquarters, Haghi – banker, genius (and the very model of a James Bond villain) – commands a global criminal network. Lang strips such thriller elements of specific content (we never learn what various stolen papers and subverted international treaties are about, or the purpose of Haghi's machinations) so as to foreground processes and significations, thus emphasizing three things: Haghi's split-second command

and control of information and resources; the ubiquity of copies and duplicates in the age of mechanical reproduction; and the surpassing of the nation-state by global corporations in the information age. (Lang's cybernetic imagination is even more strikingly captured in *M* (1931) in a five-minute montage of police combing city streets, open spaces, and wooded land in an ever-widening dragnet, and of forensic crime-scene investigations, interrogations, roustings, and identity checks, as the whole city is brought under surveillance and centralized control.) *Spies* also stages a rail crash – the iconic experience of the shock of modernity (see Schivelbusch 1986) – in which the camera viewpoint becomes that of the train engine as it ploughs into the back of another train (*Metropolis* twice matches the viewpoint to that of an explosion).

Despite being the most successful film in Germany in 1929, the year in which sound cinema became widespread, the silent *Woman in the Moon* has fared less well than *Metropolis* in popular and critical accounts. After 30 years of neglect and penury, Professor Manfeldt, ridiculed for his belief in the possibility of space travel (and that the mountains of the moon are rich in gold), finds himself at the center of a plot by ruthless international financiers – dubbed "five brains and a check book" – who steal his research. They wish to prevent any lunar expedition not under their command so that they can control and manipulate the gold supply to their advantage. The ensuing story features a magnificently staged rocket launch (Hermann Oberth and Willy Ley were scientific advisors), a rather archaic love triangle, and shenanigans familiar from older lunar narratives and colonial adventures. This mix, which looks rather peculiar nowadays, clearly resonated with Weimar audiences. On the one hand, there is the utopianism evident in the film's yearning for a return to paradise, a cooperative spirit, and a technological future; on the other, a strong sense of the growing irrelevance of the nation-state in the emerging capitalist world-market. In contrast to Mabuse and Haghi, this film's villains are not characterized as criminals but as businessmen who must sometimes commit crimes because of the demands of the economic system they personify.

Lang did not direct an sf film in the US, but many of his American films (such as *Fury* (1936), *You Only Live Once* (1937), *You and Me* (1938), *Western Union* (1941), *The Woman in the Window* (1944), *House by the River* (1950), *While the City Sleeps* (1956), *Beyond a Reasonable Doubt* (1956)) were concerned with the spread and socio-cultural impact of communications and media technologies, and with the bureaucratic-cybernetic management of everyday life. Lang's final film, *The 1000 Eyes of Dr Mabuse*, involves a series of mysterious crimes which seem to be connected to the long-dead Dr Mabuse and which center on the Hotel Luxor, originally built by the Nazis in order to spy on politicians and diplomats. A diabolical mastermind, posing both as a mystic and Mabuse, uses the hotel's updated surveillance equipment to gain control of an American industrialist's nuclear power plant and rocket production facilities, and thus precipitate global chaos from which he can profit. The irrationalism of capitalism is further emphasized by a modern businessman who depends upon astrological charts rather than actuarial tables to conduct his business, and the continuities drawn between Nazism and international insurance companies. Although relatively unknown, it is a fitting culmination to Lang's sf career.

See also: **Karel Čapek, David Cronenberg, Stanley Kubrick, Geroge Lucas, Oshii Mamoru, Steven Spielberg, and H.G. Wells**

Bibliography

Bould, M. (2005) *Film Noir: from Berlin to Sin City*, London: Wallflower.
Elsaesser, T. (2000) *Metropolis*, London: BFI.
Grant, B.K. (2003) *Fritz Lang: interviews*, Jackson: University Press of Mississippi.
Gunning, T. (2000) *The Films of Fritz Lang: allegories of vision and modernity*, London: BFI.
Luppa, I. (2009) "'Madonna in Moon Rocket with Breeches': Weimar sf film criticism during the stabilisation period," in M. Bould and C. Miéville (eds.) *Red Planets: Marxism and science fiction*, London: Pluto.
McGilligan, P. (1997) *Fritz Lang: the nature of the beast*, London: Faber and Faber.
Minden, M. and Bachmann, H. (eds.) (2000) *Fritz Lang's Metropolis: cinematic visions of technology and fear*, Rochester, NY: Camden House.
Rieder, J. (2008) *Colonialism and the Emergence of Science Fiction*, Middletown, CT: Wesleyan University Press.
Schivelbusch, W. (1986) *The Railway Journey: the industrialization of time and space in the nineteenth century*, Berkeley: University of California Press.
Telotte, J.P. (1999) *A Distant Technology: science fiction film and the machine age*, Hanover, CT: Wesleyan University Press.

MARK BOULD

URSULA K[ROEBER] LE GUIN (1929–)

US writer, critic, and essayist.

Ursula K. Le Guin's significant *oeuvre* includes novels, short stories, poetry, criticism, edited collections, translations, and children's books.

In addition to a prolific output, Le Guin's importance is ensured by the celebrated place of her fiction in the culture of sf. As a feminist writer, she has influenced and inspired several generations of sf readers, writers, and critics, male and female, and is credited with being influential in showing that sf has literary merit. She has won numerous awards, including five Hugos and five Nebulas, and has twice won the James Tiptree Jr Award, as well as being given the 1996 James Tiptree Jr Retrospective Award for *The Left Hand of Darkness* (1969).

This was the novel that first drew significant attention to Le Guin. Her fourth sf novel, it is set in the universe of the Ekumen, a loose collective based on trade in ideas and cultural knowledge rather than on conquest and colonization. Le Guin was to explore the consequences of the Ekumen's culture in much of her later work. The collection *Four Ways to Forgiveness* (1995) weaves together four encounters with Ekumen representatives; together these novellas, like *The Left Hand of Darkness*, are intense meditations on the nature of freedom and slavery (both literal and metaphorical), the problematics of gender and sexuality, the legacy of colonialism, and the difficulties of living in harmony with others – whether people, animals, or the land itself.

The Ekumen also allows Le Guin to interweave related and sometimes recurring characters, stories, and technological devices, such as the ansible, a form of instantaneous communication invented in *The Dispossessed: an ambiguous utopia* (1974). The character Old Music is a minor figure in "Forgiveness Day" (1994) but also the protagonist of "Old Music and the Slave Women" (1999). Such repetitions are not mere decorative flourishes or simplistic returns, but rather an important part of Le Guin's habit of revisiting and revising her fictional universes (see Attebery 2002). Through these returns, Le Guin expounds the importance of valuing process (often over results), a concept literalized in the short story sequence in *A Fisherman of the Inland Sea* (1994), beginning with "The Shobies' Story" (1990), that suggests teleportation might be as much a function of narrative imagination as of technological breakthrough: the travelers have to tell themselves the right story in order to arrive at their destination.

One of the effects of valorizing process is that a work is, in a sense, never finished. One of Le Guin's strengths is her willingness to engage with readers' responses to her work, a tendency illustrated by *The Left Hand of Darkness*. The novel tells the story of Terran Genly Ai, who is sent as an envoy from the Ekumen to the planet Gethen. Leaving the rest of the Ekumenical delegation in deep-sleep orbiting the planet, Genly descends alone. He believes initially this custom is because one person cannot represent a threat of conquest or colonization; later he decides that he was sent alone because his solitude forcibly immerses him in Gethenian culture, so he learns in ways he would not had he the support of a like-minded and, in Gethen's case, like-bodied group. Gethenians, alone amongst the sentient humanity of the Ekumen, have no permanent biological sex; rather, they cycle on a random monthly basis between male and female, sexed only when in the "kemmer" part of the cycle.

The novel is, as Le Guin herself has argued, a story of love and betrayal. Caught up in the politics of the Kingdom of Karhide, Genly flees to the neighboring state of Orgoreyn, only to be imprisoned as a Karhidish spy. When Genly is broken out of prison by Estraven, the Gethenian protagonist, the two flee together across the Ice, enduring many physical trials and learning to love each other. However, when Estraven enters kemmer and becomes transiently female, they choose not to express that love physically. The story ends when Genly is returned to Karhide and is able to summon his colleagues to the surface.

Given the importance of sexual biology to the novel, it is no surprise that much criticism has cohered around the question of whether the Gethenians are truly hermaphroditic (as their biology and culture indicate). Critics and readers disagree over whether to understand the Gethenians as all "really" men (since Le Guin tells most of the story from Genly's perspective, using the third person male pronoun for them) or "really" women (since they experience their sexual embodiment cyclically in ways that resemble women's menstrual cycles and can give birth to, as well as father, children). After a wave of approbation shortly after the novel was first published, complaints (often identified as feminist) surfaced. These critics judged harshly Le Guin's decision to use male pronouns, her unwillingness to allow Genly and Estraven to have sex, and the apparent negativity of any references to the feminine.

Le Guin responded to these criticisms in "Is Gender Necessary?" (1976), allowing that she might have been more clever in inventing the Gethenians, but continuing to defend her choices: the pronoun "he" is supposedly both male-specific and gender neutral in English. Later in "Is Gender Necessary? Redux" (1987), Le Guin admits her defensiveness and revises her opinion on the likelihood that male pronouns can encompass women and hermaphrodites, as well as noting that she had unnecessarily locked the Gethenians into heterosexuality. Her most recent return to Gethen – and latest imagining of an alternative embodiment of gender and sexuality – is the story "Coming of Age in Karhide" (1995), which tells of a young Gethenian's first kemmering, avoiding the pronoun problem by a combination of first-person perspective and repeated use of names and descriptors for characters outside the kemmer-house; inside, as the characters begin to experience a particular physical embodiment of sex, gendered pronouns come into use. While this is not necessarily unproblematic – after all, to what extent can a few hours' experience of having male or female genitalia render one either masculine/male or feminine/female? – it is more evidence of the ways in which Le Guin continues to change her fictive universes.

Certainly the most influential of Le Guin's sf novels – at one point a *Science Fiction Studies* survey of university and college syllabi revealed that it was the one book almost every sf course had in common – *The Left Hand of Darkness* has been immensely germinal for people writing from a feminist perspective or looking for ways to question discourses of gender and sexuality. Its influence on later sf is equally pervasive: one might include within its dialogic legacy **Gwyneth Jones**'s *Aleutian* trilogy (1991–97), Eleanor Arnason's *A Woman of the Iron People* (1991), Candas Jane Dorsey's *A Paradigm of Earth* (2001), Hiromi Goto's *The Kappa Child* (2002), and a host of others. *The Left Hand of Darkness* fundamentally altered the terrain in which First Contact stories are imagined, bringing to bear both postcolonial and feminist critiques of the idea of men rushing off to conquer the universe and exploit or enslave its resources and sentient beings.

Much of Le Guin's work can be considered postcolonial, not in the sense of existing after colonialism but rather because it critiques the conditions and consequences of colonialism, most self-evidently in *The Word for World Is Forest* (1972), but also in *The Dispossessed*, *Always Coming Home* (1985), *Four Ways to Forgiveness*, and *The Telling* (2000). In *The Word for World Is Forest*, she creates a situation in which human colonizers are destroying the forests of the planet Athshe for lumber to ship back to a deforested Earth, while also enslaving and abusing the Athsheans, who are treated as less than human. The nonviolent Athsheans, whose traditions are loosely drawn from Australian aboriginal culture, are inspired to fight back by Selver, who dreams the new thing: violence in response to violence. Only the intervention of the Ekumen's representatives, who enforce their rule against enslaving other intelligent species, saves the planet and species from destruction – but, of course, the experiences of colonization and Selver's dream have forever changed the Athsheans. Although Le Guin herself has dismissed the book as heavy-handed in its message – a response to ecological disasters and American involvement in Vietnam – it remains a potent critique of colonialism.

Le Guin's own background gave her a unique set of experiences and knowledges on which to base her superb world-creation skills. Her father, Alfred L. Kroeber, was an anthropologist who studied Californian First Nations, while her mother, Theodora Kroeber, wrote *Ishi in Two Worlds* (1961), a biography of a Yani Indian supposed to be the last of his tribe. The study of other cultures and the validation of alternative lifestyles clearly influenced Le Guin. She is also an important writer of fantasy, and the world creation of her *Earthsea* series – which begins with *A Wizard of Earthsea* (1968), is revisited and reimagined several times, and ends with *The Other Wind* (2001) – exhibits the same attention to detail, belief in the importance of naming, and imaginative power as her more science-fictional worlds. Le Guin's world creation goes beyond merely critiquing colonialist, sexist, racist, and homophobic outcomes: she also imagines future possibilities. Thus Le Guin's work includes a strong utopian strain, most clearly expressed in *The Dispossessed*, set on the moon Anarres of the planet Urras. The Anarresti are an anarchistic community made up of people who have fled the various capitalistic and totalitarian regimes of Urras; their lives are shaped both by the physical difficulties of their new world and by the rather larger emotional, intellectual, and practical difficulties of maintaining the anarchistic utopian impulse.

Focused on Shevek, a young Anarresti who grows up to be the most important physicist of his time and to create a workable merger of two dominant theories of time, *The Dispossessed* imagines a utopia of process, never complete. Indeed, Shevek comes to understand that utopia is not about achieving perfection but about the quest for an egalitarian, communal society – a quest whose value lies in working for the goals of equality, liberty, and communalism, rather than in achieving them. No matter how much the Anarresti are educated to eschew greed and accumulation of material goods, to value the well-being of others, and to esteem sharing of knowledge over self-promotion, there are always some who cannot or will not accommodate themselves to this way of life. Shevek concludes simply that one has to keep on trying.

Like *Always Coming Home* – a future California in which a "return" to native ways of life has taken place – *The Dispossessed* is concerned with what it means to live an ethical life, a motif also prevalent in many short stories, particularly "The Ones Who Walk Away from Omelas" (1973). This story takes up the philosopher William James's observation that if the perfect life could be bought at the cost of the torment of one single, lonely soul, it would still be too high a price.

Omelas is this world and the story is about those who cannot bear to pay that price – or, rather, to have it paid for them. Giving up power and material well-being is a constant theme in Le Guin's work, including her recent series for adolescents which starts with *Gifts* (2004).

More academic work has been written about Le Guin than about any other sf writer, including **H.G. Wells** and **Mary Shelley**. Indubitably one of the greatest sf writers of our contemporary period, Le Guin's place in the sf firmament seems assured.

See also: **Isaac Asimov, Greg Bear, Alfred Bester, Leigh Brackett, Octavia Butler, Samuel R. Delany, Philip K. Dick, William Gibson, Donna J. Haraway, Robert A. Heinlein, Frank Herbert, Nalo Hopkinson, L. Ron Hubbard, Gwyneth Jones, C.L. Moore, Kim Stanley Robinson, Joanna Russ, Mary Shelley, Neal Stephenson, Darko Suvin, Sheri S. Tepper, James Tiptree Jr, H.G. Wells, and Gene Wolfe**

Bibliography

Attebery, B. (2002) *Decoding Gender in Science Fiction*, New York: Routledge.

Bernardo, S.M. and Murphy, G.J. (eds.) (2006) *Ursula K. Le Guin: a critical companion*, Westport, CT: Greenwood.

Cadden, M. (2003) *Ursula K. Le Guin beyond Genre: fiction for children and adults*, New York: Routledge.

Cummins, E. (1993) *Understanding Ursula K. Le Guin*, Columbia: University of South Carolina Press.

Lefanu, S. (1988) *In the Chinks of the World Machine: feminism and science fiction*, London: The Women's Press.

Le Guin, U.K. (1979) "Is Gender Necessary?" [1976], in S. Wood (ed.) *The Language of the Night*, New York: Perigee.

——(1989) "Is Gender Necessary? Redux" [1987], in *Dancing at the Edge of the World: thoughts on words, women, places*, New York: Harper & Row.

WENDY GAY PEARSON

STAN[LEY MARTIN] LEE [BORN STANLEY MARTIN LIEBER](1922–)

US comics author, editor, and publisher.

Though active from the 1940s, Stan Lee built his reputation on his work as writer/editor of Marvel Comics in the 1960s. Collaborating primarily with the equally influential artist Jack Kirby (1917–94), Lee created some of comics' most recognizable characters and, by establishing their coexistence in the "Marvel Universe," revolutionized the concept of comics in America.

Beginning with *The Fantastic Four* (1961–), a group of superheroes with powers based on the four elements, Lee, Kirby, and the "bullpen" of Marvel creators offered a cavalcade of innovative superhero series: the Jekyll and Hyde-like *Incredible Hulk* (1962–); *The Mighty Thor* (1962–), a reincarnated Scandinavian god; the techno-knight-in-armor *Iron Man* (1962–); *The Amazing Spider-Man* (1963–); the mutant beings known as the *X-Men* (1963–); the blind acrobatic vigilante *Daredevil* (1964–), and others. Marvel's principal innovations were the qualities of irreverent irony and quirky realism in the superheroes, combining the traditional hero and his anti-heroic alter ego in order to form the "hero with problems." This literary characterization was most evident in the Fantastic Four's Thing, a quarrelsome, tormented stone creature with a Brooklyn accent and a self-deprecating sense of humor; in Lee and Steve Ditko's Spider-Man, a neurotic teenager endowed with the abilities and proportionate strength of a spider; and in threatening, yet ambivalent villains such as Magneto and Galactus. Another innovation was the use of modern scientific paradigms in the origins of the Marvel heroes: rather than being magical or vaguely otherworldly, their powers most often originated from radioactivity, tying them explicitly to atomic age, post-Sputnik sf.

Taking advantage of his position as writer/editor, Lee listed the (previously unacknowledged) creators of each story on the opening page, in a manner similar to film credits, exaggerating the merits of each and every story and creator with hyperbole: Kirby was nicknamed "The King" of comics; Lee was known as "The Man." Blended with elements from classical epics (grand heroes, cosmic scale, gods, pompous narrative flourishes), these humorous touches immediately created an adventurous, yet flippant mood. Similarly, the stories removed themselves from high seriousness and acquired a liberating air of levity. By writing in a semi-parodic mode, Lee nodded to standard literary conventions while indulging in high fantasy. Though realistic characterizations became Marvel's trademark, Lee never let them take precedence over a fantastical story or a successful pun, thus often subverting Marvel's doctrine of "believable," internally logical, and consistent fantasy writing. Many of his characters' names were alliterative (Peter Parker, Reed Richards, Matt Murdock, Scott Summers, Bruce Banner), as were most of his stories' titles, and while he struggled to make characters like Spider-Man talk approximately like 1960s teens, the language of characters like Thor or the Silver Surfer was extremely – often absurdly – poetical.

Lee's authorial persona, with frequent asides and information for the reader, encouraged the creation of a fan base of all ages and contradicted established conventions. Captions were frequently irrelevant to plot and imagery, and often lampooned the weaknesses of the genre and the expository quality of comics writing. A typical example was a scene (in *The Avengers* no. 27) where a villain raged against the heroes that outwitted him, shouting "they're escaping!" while Lee added a captioned footnote reading "Another bit of inspired dialogue by sleepy Stan!" Moreover, readers were encouraged to correspond with him, even to suggest potential storylines. He thus emulated a narrative style much like that of oral storytellers, shaping stories according to the criticisms and reactions of the audience. This creative power given to the reader was rather illusory, yet led to many fans acquiring enough confidence to later become professional creators themselves.

In order to lighten his workload, Lee instigated the "Marvel Method," a more production line-like creative process where the artist – most often Kirby – drew the story not from a full script, but from a slender plot that he and Lee concocted together. The artist had a free hand in crafting the tale, while Lee wrote captions and dialogue over the completed story and could thus edit the work and add his humorous, subversive touches quite comfortably.

Working within the confines of a monthly schedule, on issues ranging from 18 to 24 pages, Lee and Kirby highlighted the unique traits of comics storytelling, such as the exteriorization of interiority. Everything was communicated externally: character, emotions, and events were all depicted through action, in iconic fashion. Characters' appearances were consistently altered to portray emotion, even in cases where they wore helmets or masks, while objects and people were trailed by "motion lines," a dynamic narrative tool which substituted the cinematic movement that comics lacked. Since words introduce time by representing sound, the Lee–Kirby panels, in which characters spoke verbose paragraphs of text in the same moment it took them to throw a punch, seemed to contradict linear time. This temporal simultaneity created a nonlinear reading experience, equally distanced from our usual real-life perceptions and the linear conditioning of most narrative media. In reading Marvel Comics, readers seemed to perceive time spatially, in an sf fashion, for time and space appeared one and the same. Kirby's vibrant art and visionary concepts melded with Lee's witty characterizations, which infused the laconic dryness of pulp dialogue with florid, oblique humor. The results were bombastic epics, long-running plots, and subplots that overlapped and interlinked within each series over periods extending even to two years (a break from the comic-book tradition of single-issue tales).

These innovations, appealing both to children and to a teenage and college readership that appreciated Marvel's self-parody, sowed the seeds for the "Marvel Universe": a world replete with the irony in situating super-powered characters against a background that purportedly represented a "real" environment. This, in Marvel's case, was usually the city of New York, filled with vociferous citizens who witnessed and commented on the superheroes among them with a mixture of disbelief and nonchalance. Since the 1940s New York-dwelling creators of comics had depicted the city – or an approximate facsimile like Metropolis or Gotham City – in their work. This convenient setting, while requiring no extra research, grounded the extraordinary imagery against a backdrop of recognizable reality, thus making it more exciting and immediate. Lee and Kirby's approach to the Marvel Comics elevated this conceit to the next stage, transforming New York into a "real" place to house wry fictions, a landscape of urban signs, and, simultaneously, a permanently clean slate on which unlimited designs could be inscribed.

The convention that superheroes could meet (in stories known as team-ups or crossovers) dated back to pulp magazines and 1940s comics. But Marvel Comics made the most of their crossovers through a tighter sense of continuity: Lee promoted meetings between heroes as collectors' items, essential to readers who followed the ongoing story of a series. Instead of limiting each hero to his own magazine, the Marvel creators gradually created an all-enveloping background story for their comics. At any time, the Fantastic Four might meet Captain America, or Spider-Man might team up with the X-Men, in stories with connections to each character's past and repercussions for their future. One such meeting could even result in the creation of a super-team, as happened in 1963, when the Hulk, Iron Man, Thor, Ant Man, and the Wasp formed the Avengers.

Lee and Kirby's Universe wove together standard superhero/villain battles with soap-opera subplots, hilarious interludes, interlocking "epics," and a burgeoning pantheon of quasi-mythological figures that included Greek and Norse gods (often boldly recast, the underworld god Pluto, for example, posing as a shady Hollywood producer), Shakespearean pastiches (such as the Falstaffian swashbuckler Volstagg), and contemporary archetypes (such as the Silver Surfer, an initially villainous herald of the planet-devouring Galactus who bargained his freedom for the Earth's survival and evolved into a rebellious countercultural icon, representing the freewheeling surfer mentality).

The Marvel Universe acquired scope by appropriating such mythical archetypes, but also through assimilating existing heroic icons and genres. When Joe Simon and Jack Kirby's Captain America – conveniently a copyrighted trademark of 1940s Marvel Comics – joined the Avengers in 1964, Lee and Kirby did not revamp him but portrayed him as a 1940s anachronism thrown into the 1960s, without purpose or understanding of the new world, mirroring the confusion of an older American mindset in the context and morality of the 1960s. *Nick Fury, Agent of S.H.I.E.L.D.* (1965), a hard-boiled variation on James Bond, made use of the then-fashionable spy genre's conventions (gadgets, hidden headquarters, villainous secret armies), which were incorporated into other titles, thanks to the interactive nature of the Marvel Universe. Even Marvel titles that bore no thematic relation to the superhero genre were tied into the Marvel Universe: Fury was a veteran of *Sgt. Fury and His Howling Commandos* (1963), a tongue-in-cheek Second World War comic.

Mythology, fictional genres, parody, and comedic realism gave the Marvel Universe unparalleled scope. The heroes appearing and working together often came from different historical time periods and levels of fantasy, even different worlds. For these characters to meet in one world, or in New York, creators constantly invented interdimensional catastrophes that brought forth heroes from different planets, eras, and cultures. In other cases, characters such as immortal gods just continued to exist into the present. Divorced from their original contexts, such characters still maintained their iconic identities and traits. Full-fledged dragons plagued both Iron Man and Thor, when these two diametrically opposed heroes (representing science and myth) appeared together in *The Avengers*. Gradually, the Marvel Universe appropriated the worlds of Robert E. Howard (*Conan the Barbarian* (1970–)), Bram Stoker (*Tomb of Dracula* (1972–79)), and Stanley Kubrick (*2001: a space odyssey* (1976–77)), and characters from these series crossed into the mainline Marvel Universe. Such narrative audacities brought incompatible genres together in a completely nonlinear manner.

The Marvel Universe was thus composed of multiple cultural surfaces, all equally "authentic" to the readers. Within its vast confines, "magic" and "science" were coexisting and interchangeable. This often ended with a reestablishment of "realism." An apt example is the coexistence of various theological pantheons, which makes little sense in a fictional world but essentially reflects the coexistence of multiple, conflicting religions in our "real" world. By abandoning linear consistency, the Marvel Universe achieved a greater continuity, a perspective of constant intertextuality. This continuity, as practiced in comic books today, is more complex than anything to which the audiences of other media have become accustomed, and resembles more the encyclopedic practices of the Gnostics. The Gnostics crafted memory palaces; after Lee and Kirby, comic-book creators stock their worlds with names, rituals, sigils, and talismanic images, creating backstory information for vast fictional intertextual universes, imaginative spaces tied to specific publishing companies. (In a fitting coincidence, Marvel is also known as "the House of Ideas.")

Astonishingly, Lee and Kirby's influence remains largely unacknowledged. Lee, who eventually moved to publisher status and the supervision of Marvel movie adaptations, is perceived as a huckstering promoter of puerile fictions (by high culture aesthetes), a grey eminence (by fans and filmmakers, as he makes cameo appearances in most Marvel movies), and a figurehead of the comics industry (by the general public – a "Stan Lee Presents" rubric appeared in the company's publications until 2001). Kirby remains unknown, a godhead strictly for fans. Yet their narrative and metatextual inventions (at one point they even established a Marvel Comics publishing group in their world's New York, where comic-book stories were concocted in plotting sessions with the heroes themselves) gradually enabled comics to move from standard heroics to sophisticated techniques of addressing the conventions of the superhero genre and heroic fiction in general. Marvel Comics are partly responsible for the grandiosity of cinematic blockbusters, the breakneck action of video games, and the scope of modern sf and role-playing franchises. The legacy of The King and The Man endures.

See also: **Alfred Bester, Samuel R. Delany, The Doctor, Alan Moore, Oshii Mamoru, and J. Michael Straczynski**

Bibliography

Mondello, S. (1978) "Spider-Man: superhero in the liberal tradition," in J. Nachbar, D. Weiser, and J.L. Wright (eds.) *Popular Culture Reader*, Bowling Green, OH: Bowling Green University Press.

Oehlert, M. (1995) "From Captain America to Wolverine: cyborgs in comic books, alternative images of cybernetic heroes and villains," in C.H. Gray (ed.) *The Cyborg Handbook*, New York: Routledge.

Palumbo, D. (1981) "Comics as Literature: plot structure, foreshadowing, and irony in the Marvel Comics' *Avengers* 'cosmic epic'," *Extrapolation*, 22 (4): 309–24.

——(1999) "Science Fiction in Comic Books: science fiction colonizes a fantasy medium," in C.W. Sullivan III (ed.) *Young Adult Science Fiction*, Westport, CT: Greenwood Press.

ABRAHAM KAWA

STANISŁAW LEM (1921–2006)

Polish writer and critic.

Stanisław Lem was the most prominent continental European science-fiction writer after the Second World War, and his work – translated into over 40 languages – is widely admired for its originality of vision, philosophical sophistication, and inventive language. Often considered the writer who explored the literary and philosophical qualities of the genre to the furthest degree, he refused to treat it as formulaic commercial entertainment or, as in the Soviet bloc, a vehicle for political moralizing.

Lem wrote in a great variety of forms and styles: adventure novels, realistic stories, satirical fables, metafictions, quasi-fictional essays, and treatises on the role of technology in human culture. In all, Lem was concerned with a single theme: the inexorable collision between human consciousness's inherent inability to know itself and its ingrained need to do so. This paradox has wildly comic consequences in the humorous *The Star Diaries* (1954–71), *The Robot Fables* (1972), and *The Cyberiad* (1965–67); in the serious novels and pessimistic semi-fictional essays Lem wrote at the end of his career, it often leads to catastrophe.

Lem's early work came out of the stifling intellectual climate of Poland immediately following the Second World War. Trained in medicine, Lem began his career as a redactor of contemporary Western articles on science for a scientific journal. In this role he was introduced to cybernetics, which was demonized at the time in the Soviet sphere as a "bourgeois science." Lem was profoundly affected by cybernetics' radical redescription of reality in informational terms. By breaking down barriers between science, politics, and philosophy, and undermining the notion of a sovereign human subject, cybernetic systems theory provided a scientific language that grounded Lem's profoundly ironic vision of the human condition.

Born and raised in then-Polish Lvov, where he participated in underground resistance to the German occupation, he moved to the university city of Kraków in 1946. For most of his adult life Lem remained in Poland, and did not travel west of Berlin or east of Moscow. Insulated from the commercial forces of Anglo-American sf, his writing owes little to pulp and romantic formulas, drawing instead on the Central and East European traditions of grotesque fantasy and the classical sf of **Jules Verne**, **H.G. Wells**, and **Olaf Stapledon**. He was for a generation the most popular and influential writer of sf in the Soviet bloc; yet Lem was profoundly anti-utopian. In his fiction, technology and ideology represent independent forces of domination which, when combined, produce absurd and disastrous results.

Lem's early novels were written in the socialist-realist mode, depicting visits of formulaic technoscientific protagonists to planets with failed technological utopian societies. Although Lem disavowed the uninspired *Magellan Nebula* (1955), his first published novel, *The Astronauts* (1951), introduces one of Lem's characteristic themes, the indecipherability of truly alien phenomena that might be encountered in space exploration – a motif completely at odds with the conventions of Soviet sf, which proscribed the depiction of nonhumanoid aliens. Lem developed this theme in his most famous novels. In *Eden* (1959), human astronauts explore a planet on which the difference between natural and artificial phenomena is unclear, and where rulers perform grotesque but obscure eugenic experiments on their population. In *Solaris* (1961), Lem's best-known novel, scientists encounter a planet that appears to be an intelligent entity, but which cannot be analyzed scientifically and does not communicate. The novel is widely considered one of the masterworks of sf for the rigor with which Lem develops the premise of human science encountering something truly alien, and hence irreducible to familiar categories. In *The Invincible* (1964), a planet is inhabited by the products of a technological evolutionary struggle, "cyberflies," tiny inert units that converge to make a group mind that the human astronauts can neither understand nor defeat. *His Master's Voice* (1967) – the original Polish title translates literally as *The Voice of the Lord* – is perhaps Lem's most fully realized novel. It tells of a neutrino information stream from space that might be a "biophilic" message from a distant supercivilization. Narrated by a misanthropic mathematician enlisted to work on a Manhattan-Project-like military team to decipher the "Letter from the Stars," the novel is a meditation on possibilities of hope for an utterly fallen and self-deluding human world. Lem returned to the theme of alien contact in his last novel, *Fiasco* (1986), a tragic adventure in which utopian human space explorers fly to a planetary civilization captive to a high-technological arms race that has become automatic. In their increasingly frustrated efforts to communicate with, and disarm, the war planet, the utopian mission succeeds only in annihilating it.

Lem's realistic sf novels constitute only a small part of his work. Early in his career he experimented with different narrative forms, often showing the influences of modernist European writing. *The Investigation* (1959) is a fantastic detective novel with little scientific content. Corpses come mysteriously back to life, and the detective-protagonist tries hypothesis after hypothesis to explain this, without success, ultimately calling into question his own sense of self. *Memoirs Found in a Bathtub* (1973) shows the overt influence of Franz Kafka. The protagonist tries to understand and escape from a labyrinthine building ostensibly linked to the US war machine, but more credibly an image of the communicational entropy of communist bureaucratic despotism. *Return from the Stars* (1961) depicts the confusion and anomie of a heroic astronaut returning to an Earth that has been transformed through a chemical process that stifles the human urge for violence, and with it risk-taking.

Most of Lem's work is in shorter forms: stories, grotesque sketches, and fantastic fairy tales. The stories of the *Pirx* cycle (1973) follow the career of Pirx from cadet to space pilot. As a hero, Pirx is resolutely unheroic, and the stories contain no fantastic elements. Lem based the form on the boys' adventure format popular in socialist culture, but used it to present unexpected challenges, such as the debilitating ennui of space travel and the importation of neuroses into the programs controlling spaceships. By far the most popular of Lem's fictions have been the wildly playful stories and fables associated with *The Star Diaries*, *The Robot Fables*, and *The Cyberiad*. *The Star Diaries*, written over several decades, are narrated by Ijon Tichy, a combination of Lemuel Gulliver and Baron von Munchhausen, a modest and earthy space traveler who introduces one planetary civilization after another. Each presents a political or philosophical problem, developed to absurd conclusions, in fantastically comic form. *The Robot Fables* consists of fairy tales, as told by robots, in a silicon-based world. *The Cyberiad* develops the form to its whimsical extreme. Parodying François Rabelais and the Kalevala, two giant "constructor" protagonists, who are robot-masters of cybernetics, have the power to create and consume anything they wish, which Lem makes the occasion for extravagant intellectual farce.

It is in these sketches and fables that Lem's debt to the European tradition of the grotesque is most evident. This narrative form was particularly favored by Central and East European writers for satire and fantasy throughout the modern period. The style emphasizes striking incongruities, especially between completely natural, prosaic discourse and incomprehensible events. Grotesque fantasies emphasize everyday experience and language that is exaggerated, but never so far as to evoke a higher, transcendental order of things. The great masters of fantastic fiction east of Berlin – Yevgeny Zamyatin, Mikhail Bulgakov, **Karel Čapek**, Kafka – all wrote within this tradition.

Lem's influence dominated sf of the Soviet sphere, where he was for decades the most popular writer in the genre, as he was also in Germany. His relationship with US sf was fraught, however. With détente between the West and the Soviet bloc, US sf became increasingly accessible to Lem. He wrote a series of essays excoriating it as commercial trash that betrayed its birthright as philosophical literature, exempting only **Philip K. Dick**, whom he called "a visionary among the charlatans" (Lem 1992: 49). Lem's strong opinions enraged many established US sf writers, who were inspired to strip Lem of honorary membership in the Science Fiction Writers of America. Even Dick, by then mentally ill according to some, professed to believe Lem was a Soviet agent. Although Lem was indifferent to these events, they became a *cause célèbre* among US writers. Despite his disavowals, Lem did engage with US pulp sf. The influence of Fredric Brown, **Isaac Asimov**, and Robert Sheckley is evident, if unacknowledged. He was more forthcoming in his acknowledgment of Dick: *The Futurological Congress* (1974) is a dizzying homage to Dick's patented style of shifting realities, in which Ijon Tichy is (perhaps) transported into a "cryptopsychemocratic" dystopia, where reality is a product of the specific drugs one takes.

In addition to his fiction, Lem also wrote a number of ambitious nonfiction treatises, inexplicably none of which has yet been translated into English. *Science Fiction and Futurology* (1970) is a loosely linked set of essays on the creative conditions of sf's possibility, ostensibly from a socio-cybernetic view of the genre as a system of cultural practices. It is here that Lem most clearly develops his criticism of futurology as extrapolation unable to foresee the transformation of values in the future, and asserts fiction's superior ability to represent that irony. *Summa Technologiae* (1964), which many commentators consider one of Lem's most important works, uses both scholarship and inventive language to imagine the effect of cyber-technology on the refashioning of the human species. Although written in isolation from ongoing research and development in computers, Lem was remarkably prescient about trends such as virtual reality, simulation, artificial intelligence, entanglement, and consciousness-uploads, which he named with characteristic inventiveness *fantomatics*, *imitology*, *intellectronics*, *teletaxia*, and *fantoplication*.

In 1971 Lem published *A Perfect Vacuum*, a prismatic collection of metafictions masquerading as reviews of imaginary books. Although not all have sf themes, many do, ranging from "Non Serviam," an account of artificial "personoids" coming to self-awareness in a computer mainframe, to "The New Cosmogony," which asserts that the anomalies and paradoxes of cosmology can be attributed to communication among cosmic super-entities. Until the end of his career Lem continued to develop the imaginary essay through the collection *Imaginary Magnitude* (1973–81), which includes a lengthy meditation by an "enlightened" computer on the verge of becoming a Singularity.

Lem's works are unusually cerebral for the genre of sf and are almost completely devoid of eroticism and romance. Consequently, few of his works have been adapted for popular media, such as film. His first novel was made into a socialist-realist-style East German film entitled *Silent Star* (Maetzig 1960) in the US. Two markedly different film versions of *Solaris* were produced, both deviating significantly from the novel's vision. The first, by the celebrated Russian director Andrei Tarkovsky (1972), is considered a classic in the genre, although it substitutes spiritual nostalgia for irony and skepticism. Steven Soderbergh's version (2002) supplies a happy romantic ending in place of the novel's profoundly ambivalent one.

Lem is widely considered to be the sf writer who was most successful in bridging the gap between the popular genre and literature. He remains one of the most popular and respected sf writers in Europe, Japan, and Russia. In the Anglo-American sphere, because of his uncompromising rejection of commercial formulas, Lem is sometimes considered more a writer of belles-lettres than of sf.

See also: **Karel Čapek, Samuel R. Delany, Philip K. Dick, Greg Egan, Donna J. Haraway, Olaf Stapledon, Darko Suvin, Jules Verne, and H.G. Wells**

Bibliography

Csicsery-Ronay Jr, I. (1985) "The Book Is the Alien: on certain and uncertain readings of Lem's *Solaris*," *Science Fiction Studies*, 12(1): 6–21.

——(1991) "Modeling the Chaosphere: Stanisław Lem's alien communications," in N.K. Hayles (ed.) *Chaos and Order: complex dynamics in literature and science*, Chicago: Chicago University Press.

Hayles, N.K. (1986) "Space for Writing: Stanisław Lem and the dialectic 'that guides my pen'," *Science Fiction Studies*, 13(3): 292–312.
Lem, S. (1992) "Philip K. Dick: a visionary among the charlatans," in R.D. Mullen, I. Csicsery-Ronay Jr, A. Evans, and V. Hollinger (eds.) *On Philip K. Dick: 40 articles from Science-Fiction Studies*, Terre Haute, IN: SF-TH.
Swirski, P. (ed.) (1997) *A Stanisław Lem Reader*, Evanston, IL: Northwestern University Press.
——(2006) *The Art and Science of Stanisław Lem*, Montréal: McGill University Press.

ISTVAN CSICSERY-RONAY JR

GEORGE [WALTON] LUCAS [JR] (1944–)

US filmmaker, and developer of THX sound and special effects technology.

As the director of *THX 1138* (1970), writer–director–producer of the *Star Wars* saga (1977–), and founder of special effects company Industrial Light and Magic (ILM), George Lucas's impact upon the genre has been significant. He is most famous for his space opera, which began with *Star Wars: Episode IV – A New Hope* (Lucas 1977) and has grown into a multiple episode, multiple platform sf franchise that includes: five further features, *Star Wars: Episode V – The Empire Strikes back* (Kershner 1980), *Star Wars: Episode VI – The Return of the Jedi* (Marquand 1983), *Star Wars: Episode I – The Phantom Menace* (Lucas 1999), *Star Wars: Episode II – Attack of the Clones* (Lucas 2002), and *Star Wars: Episode III – Revenge of the Sith* (Lucas 2005); two live-action television movies, *The Ewok Adventure* (Korty 1984) and *Ewoks: The Battle for Endor* (Wheat and Wheat 1985); four animated television series, *Ewoks* (1985–87), *Droids* (1985–86), *Star Wars: Clone Wars* (2003–5, 2008); and *Star Wars: The Clone Wars* (Filoni 2008); and numerous digital games. Beyond these canonical texts, the franchise has also produced a vast array of ancillary products and texts that expand and embed the *Star Wars* universe into the homes of its countless fans, including tie-in novels, graphic novels, guides to the films, blueprints for the spaceships and vehicles, behind-the-scenes publications, soundtracks, condensed story albums, action figures, board- and role-playing games, to name a small selection. The original trilogy was adapted and dramatized for radio, produced by the National Public Radio (*Star Wars* (1981), *The Empire Strikes Back* (1983) and *The Return of the Jedi* (1996)), and turned into the *Star Tours* ride at Disney theme parks. Lucas's corporate vision for his trilogy, in which the films act as a hook around which the merchandising industry is built, set the standard for the synergistic multimedia business that Hollywood has become. While this phenomenally successful saga is likely to be Lucas's primary contribution to popular culture, within sf cinema his legacy will extend much further.

Star Wars was in fact not Lucas's first foray into the genre. That came instead through *Electronic Labyrinth THX 1138 4EB* (1967), made while he was a student at the University of Southern California, and later remade as his first feature film *THX 1138*. The original film, based on the script *Breakaway* by Walter Murch and Matthew Robbins, is a highly stylized, intensely cinematic experiment in which the avant-garde meets sf to create a dystopian vision of the future. Telling the simple story of one man's attempted escape from a repressive, alienated underground society in which humans are designated by numbers, Lucas conveys his vision through the coldly clinical *mise-en-scène*, as 1138 runs through an endless series of empty corridors and deserted basements, captured through the film's surveillance-like cinematography. The sound accompanying these images is an asynchronous montage of disembodied and slightly mechanized voices tracking 1138's escape, conveying the horrors of a dehumanized society through aesthetics rather than plot. The feature film continues to emphasize aesthetics over narrative, creating what Lucas describes as "cinema verité" sf. Largely shot in real locations and with extensive use of handheld camera, it draws upon the language of realism to present a decidedly familiar and yet unsettling future. The apartments, factories, corridors, and tunnels are clinical and mundane modernist spaces, while the seemingly boundary-less prison cell, with its white background that recedes into nothingness, is uncanny. Lucas creates a coherent vision of an alternate Orwellian society, with clear connections to our own, offering a commentary on the increasingly technologically dependent, commercially driven, and emotionally alienated society developing around him.

THX could not be further in style and narrative from Lucas's next sf feature, *Star Wars*. *THX* draws upon the visual style and narrative ambiguity of the avant-garde, whereas *Star Wars* is influenced by Saturday serials like *Flash Gordon* (Stephani 1936) and *King of the Rocket Men* (Brannon 1949); *THX* is slow paced and abstract, while *Star Wars* is kinetic and plot-driven; *THX* is dystopian but *Star Wars* echoes utopianism with its underdog narrative of the rag-tag Rebel Alliance standing up to the all-powerful Galactic Empire. This promise is seemingly achieved at the end of *The Return of the Jedi* (Special Edition 1997) with the montage of celebrations around the galaxy when the Empire is finally destroyed, which leave no room for doubt – unlike the more ambiguous and iconic ending of *THX*, when the title character emerges from the underground world to stand in a barren landscape as a blazing sun sets on the horizon, triumphant in escape but facing an uncertain future. Because the phenomenal success of *Star Wars* led to a dramatic change in subsequent cinematic sf, Lucas has often been criticized for sparking a transition from personal, independent, and experimental filmmaking to more commercial and youth-oriented blockbusters. The differences between *THX* and *Star Wars* do seem to reflect the changing face of cinema and sf in this period, but the two films have much in common as well. Both are intensely personal projects, each set within a society ruled by an oppressive governmental force. Both chronicle attempts by individuals to defy the government by embracing individuality: 1138 finds freedom in love, while Luke Skywalker finds it in his friends and the Force.

Furthermore, while the first *Star Wars* trilogy builds toward a utopian conclusion, the second, which chronicles Anakin Skywalker's transformation from innocent child to twisted Darth Vader, is a darkly cynical tale of political and personal corruption. In these later films, Lucas shows the audience how the oppressive Empire is born, not with soldiers and military might but rather through fear, deceit, and emotional manipulation. While not as structurally complex as *THX*, the demands of the serialized narrative, compounded by the extension of the story through a range of alternate viewing platforms, do facilitate more complex readings of the saga. This complexity is enhanced by the decision to tell the story out of chronological order, a structure that consciously problematizes the series' presumed utopian vision.

Lucas's impact upon sf extends beyond the specifics of individual films to his vision for a new type of cinematic sf aesthetic. In making *Star Wars*, he wanted to move away from the grand spectacle of previous films, such as **Stanley Kubrick**'s *2001: A Space Odyssey* (1968), as well as from their forward-looking content, creating instead a seemingly old-fashioned adventure tale set "a long time ago in a galaxy far, far away" with a kinetic pace achieved by modeling the flying upon Second World War dogfight footage. To accomplish this he continuously pushed the boundaries of technological innovation. With each film the energy of the flying sequences – from the X-wing and TIE-fighter skirmishes in *Star Wars* to the Millennium Falcon maneuvering through an asteroid belt in *Empire Strikes Back* to the attack of the Rebel Alliance on the Death Star in *Return of the Jedi* –

increased exponentially, as did the sophistication of the special effects. This approach would influence the visual and narrative style of sf throughout the 1980s in films such as *The Black Hole* (Nelson 1979), *Battle beyond the Stars* (Murakami 1980), and *The Last Starfighter* (Castle 1984), all of which use cutting-edge technology to tell old-fashioned space adventures.

Of course Lucas's influence did not come exclusively from his aesthetic vision for *Star Wars* but also from the manner in which he achieved it. When he began, existing special effects practices could not create the visual effects Lucas had envisioned. His ambitious ideas for space battles involving dozens of ships required numerous individual effects to be captured by a moving camera and composited together, which was beyond the technology of the time. Rather than accept this limitation, Lucas set about making the impossible possible by bringing together a group of young special effects artists to form ILM. This company was initially devoted to developing innovative ways to create the effects that Lucas had conceived for his films. Their leading technique was the computerized motion control camera that allowed for the precise and repeatable camera movements required to create the fast-moving special effects. This development was the first of many that enabled ILM to make a substantial contribution to rethinking how special effects are conceived and achieved in contemporary cinema. Over the years Lucas and ILM have continued to pull together leading specialists in model work, creature design, animation, stop- and go-motion, miniatures, matte work, visual special effects, optical compositing, and digital imaging – all of which have become fundamental to contemporary expectations of sf cinema. It is through this vision for ILM that Lucas has had the most profound effect upon the genre. Since *Star Wars*, ILM has created the effects for some of the most recognizable and influential examples of sf cinema and regularly leads the way in the technological innovations required to bring these futuristic visions to the screen. ILM was the first to produce an entirely computer-generated sequence in *Star Trek II: The Wrath of Khan* (Meyer 1982) and a computer-generated entity in the form of the alien water tentacle in *The Abyss* (Cameron 1989). They built upon their digital capabilities to create the body transformations of the T-1000 in *Terminator 2: Judgment Day* (Cameron 1991), and they merged model work with computer-generated imagery to bring dinosaurs convincingly back to life in *Jurassic Park* (Spielberg 1993). Most significantly, ILM has brought to sf an increasingly seamless merger of special effect into the "real" diegetic world. While contemporary special effects are often described as fueled by spectacle, more often it is the ideal of realism that drives the effects artist.

In his own work, Lucas continues to use his cinematic vision to push the boundaries of technology. While *THX* is a masterwork in sound design and the first *Star Wars* trilogy created a new language for model work and optical special effects, the second trilogy has led the way in digital cinema. The hard edges and tactile approach to the X-wing fighter, Millennium Falcon, and Death Star models have been replaced by the sleek, glimmering, and reflective surfaces of the space ships and cityscapes created for the later films. Although considered annoying by many fans, Jar Jar Binks was the first major character to be entirely created through computer-generated imagery. Furthermore, Lucas continues to revisit the original trilogy, redesigning the special effects with contemporary technologies – introducing additional characters or backdrops, enhancing pre-existing effects, and potentially transforming the films into 3-D – and in so doing maintaining the series' status as an exemplar of the most up-to-date special effects. Finally, Lucas's commitment to digital technology extends beyond special effects to film production as a whole, with *Attack of the Clones* standing as the first Hollywood feature to be made without the use of film, captured instead on high-definition digital video. The science of Lucas's sf vision extends beyond the borders of the frame and into the means of making and exhibiting cinema itself.

See also: **Leigh Brackett, David Cronenberg, Stanley Kubrick, Fritz Lang, Oshii Mamoru, and Steven Spielberg**

Bibliography

Lancashire, A. (2000) "*The Phantom Menace*: repetition, variation, integration," *Film Criticism*, 24(3): 23–44.

Pollock, D. (1999) *Skywalking: the life and films of George Lucas*, New York: DaCapo Press.

Shay, D. (1996) "30 Minutes with the Godfather of Digital Cinema," *Cinefex*, 65: 59–67.

Silvio, C. and Vinci, T.M. (eds.) (2007) *Culture, Identities, and Technology in the Star Wars Films: essays on the two trilogies*, Jefferson, NC: McFarland.

Smith, T.G. (1986) *Industrial Light and Magic: the art of special effects*, New York: Ballantine.

Vaz, M.C. and Duignan, P.R. (1996) *Industrial Light and Magic: into the digital realm*, London: Virgin.

STACEY ABBOTT

CHINA [TOM] MIÉVILLE (1972–)

British fiction author, literary critic, and political theorist.

China Miéville has received extensive acclaim, beginning with the International Horror Guild and Bram Stoker awards for his first novel, *King Rat* (1998); the **Arthur C. Clarke** Award for *Perdido Street Station* (2000) and *Iron Council* (2004); the British Fantasy Award for *The Scar* (2002); and numerous Hugo, Nebula, and World Fantasy nominations for his novels and short stories. Holder of an advanced degree in International Relations, Miéville has published a Marxist study of international law (2005) and a widely cited theoretical essay on fantasy (Miéville 2002a), but he is best known as a leading figure in the "New Weird" movement, which challenges the form, content, and function of both fantasy (by subverting Tolkienesque conventions and incorporating extensive ideological critique) and sf (by mixing elements of horror, fantasy, and sf, thus eschewing both realism and "hard sf"). Miéville's fiction may well exemplify an emerging wave of artistic innovation responding to the specific historical contradictions of life under capitalism in the *fin de siècle*, thus signaling a new era of cultural production that will supersede postmodernism (Burling 2009).

Miéville, a self-proclaimed "fantasy geek," has frequently asserted that he "never agreed with the idea that there's this rigid distinction between fantasy and science fiction and horror … they are part of the same tradition, which I generally call 'Weird Fiction'" (Miéville 2002b: 5). This fiction is characterized by "taking … impossibility and granting it its own terms and systemicity" (Gordon 2003b: 366). Thus new weird fiction is both "secular and political" rather than escapist and unengaged because, by surrendering to the impossible, "the fantastic will always-already be metaphorical but also [have] its own integrity" (Miéville 2005b: 50). The term is not delimiting or proscriptive but rather "a reaction against moralism and consolatory mythicism" (Miéville 2005b: 50), particularly as found in Tolkienesque fantasy. Challenging the Marxist contention of **Darko Suvin**, Carl Freedman, and others that sf is superior to fantasy, Miéville argues that both "share crucial qualities of cognitive seriousness" when written as internally plausible and rigorous (Miéville 2002a: 44).

Critical appraisal of Miéville's fiction has scarcely begun. Only a handful of scholarly articles have appeared, but *Extrapolation*'s 2009 special issue on Miéville constitutes the first major assessment and shapes the critical dialogue for the near future. Scholars, reviewers, and readers had already been impressed by the innovative and complex world-building in Miéville's debut novel *King Rat* (1998), which offers an energetic refunctioning of the Pied Piper of Hamelin fairy tale set under the streets of contemporary London. Miéville estranges the contemporary metropolis by offering a subaltern view emphasizing the "urban voodoo" (Miéville 1998: 99) inherent in postmodern capitalism. The novel establishes the recurring thematic importance of setting, especially urban locales, thereby emphasizing the "unfathomable heterogeneity and hybridity … [of] the modern capitalist metropolis" (Freedman 2003: 403).

With his second novel, *Perdido Street Station* (2000), Miéville fulfilled the imaginative potential suggested in *King Rat* by creating the world of Bas-Lag, which has even spawned a role-playing game. Mills (2002) has pointed out the influence of Mervyn Peake's Gormenghast on the depiction of the gothicized London-like city of New Crobuzon, while Gordon (2003b) has begun the task of assessing the novel's sprawling range of themes and characterizations, which take fantasy in an entirely new direction by combining and refiguring elements of sf, fantasy, and horror. The novel engages numerous issues, such as the relationship of capitalism to criminality, the charade of so-called democratic governments, the tyranny of police, the exploitation of labor and the poor by the wealthy elite, and the pressing concerns brought about by cultural and ethnic diversity. A stunning set of quasi-humanoid species populates New Crobuzon along with humans: the beetle-like khepri; the cactacae plant-folk; the aquatic vodyanoi; the flying wyrmen; the Remade; and more. The garuda, an eagle-like bird-people, are especially important in *Perdido*: they have created an egalitarian, communistic society in which genuine individuality is made possible and guaranteed only by a mutually respectful, collective social matrix. This thematic thrust directly challenges capitalist, liberal-humanist assumptions of individualism. While offering interlocking narrative lines unprecedented in previous fantasy fiction, such as the depiction of labor strikes and management retaliation, the corrupt relations of the city's police apparatus with Motley, a powerful and enigmatic crime lord, and a cooperative agreement between the Devil and the city's business leaders, the main thread concerns the threat posed by the slake-moths. These strange creatures "drink the … dreams" (Miéville 2000: 408) of the city's citizens, thus serving as a metaphor for the pacifying effects of ideological mystification. In sum, Miéville's New Crobuzon, like Charles Dickens's London, provides numerous possibilities for critiquing the social, economic, and legal dynamics of an industrialized urban economy.

The Scar (2002) expands upon the Bas-Lag universe via exotic settings and myriad species. The floating ocean city of Armada, a tour-de-force of metaphorical innovation, though populated by pirates and press-ganged criminals, refugees, ex-slaves, Remade, and other bizarre sentient species, confounds initial expectations by critiquing the capitalist dynamics which create, exploit, and perpetuate such subaltern classes. The city, though crassly mercantile, sharply contrasts with New Crobuzon by offering a haven where meaningful employment and social equality are possible for all citizens regardless of background. The novel revisits many of the species introduced in *Perdido Street Station* and introduces numerous additional ones, but perhaps the most important development is the emerging emphasis on the Remade as a metaphor for examining the inherent dignity and worth of those marginalized and dehumanized by the dynamics of capitalism.

The novel interweaves narrative lines which interrogate ontological and epistemological themes. The numerous episodes involving the five central characters cumulatively emphasize the dynamic, chaotic, and thus nearly unrepresentable welter of prior human activity and the potential for the future. Miéville's assertion, "I loathe Destiny" (Miéville 2002b: 5), is well confirmed by the novel's challenge to tidy, mystifying notions of the place and function of the individual in larger historical change. For example, the search for the "probability seam" known as the Scar functions as a metaphor implying the "infinity of outcomes" (Miéville 2002c: 435) inherent in social and political affairs, in opposition to reactionary assertions of destiny or providence.

Iron Council (2004), Miéville's most overtly political novel, is perhaps the first instance of fantasy fiction to portray in detail an attempted political revolution. Workers on a provincial railroad construction project are driven by their exploitative capitalist managers first to strike and eventually to seize control of the train and the construction resources. Calling themselves the Iron Council, this group eventually attempts to enter New Crobuzon in order to join forces with a second emerging urban revolutionary movement, which is extensively portrayed in its own right. As Freedman (2005) has convincingly argued, the novel explores the challenges to political revolution. The laying of plans by the urban revolutionaries, the spontaneity of the Iron Council's situation, the choosing of leaders, the importance of timing, the crucial matter of resources, and so forth, emphasize that determination is insufficient for success. The highly organized and well-funded capitalist military and legal apparatus is formidable and has all the advantages. The narrative extensively depicts the just cause and will of the downtrodden and exploited masses, especially the contrast between the frustrating efforts of well-meaning but overly theoretical urban intellectuals and the dynamic but insufficiently theorized efforts of the Remade and other disenfranchised railroad laborers of the Iron Council.

In a richly metaphorical finale of the caliber featured in *Perdido Street Station* and *The Scar*, the actant Judah invokes a time golem that suspends the inbound train just before it encounters the awaiting New Crobuzon military forces which are set to annihilate the Iron Council and prevent its entry into the city. The onrushing locomotive bearing the Iron Council is frozen in a perpetual present, rendered motionless, poised for arrival but never arriving, solidified as "an argument *in* time" (Miéville 2004: 541; emphasis in original). The Iron Council becomes, therefore, a monument, a symbol celebrating the inevitable revolution that can and will return when the time is right.

Miéville's short fiction, collected in *Looking for Jake* (2005), has received less critical attention. "The Tain," a novella first separately published as a chapbook in 2002 with an introduction by M. John Harrison (one of Miéville's main influences), has been described as having the effect of shattering preconceived perceptions such that "[you] may even change the way you look at yourself and the world around you" (DuMond 2003). This excellent assessment likewise applies to the collection as a whole in that it investigates the epistemological challenges and limits to understanding the contemporary world, as exemplified in stories such as "Details" (2002) and "Go between" (2005).

Un Lun Dun (2007) continues the project of subverting virtually every formulaic convention of fantasy, specifically the one-good-person-saves-the-world quest. The novel begins with the chosen one and her sidekick and the evil nemesis "the Smog," but as it continues the sidekick becomes more important than the hero and the traditional series of tasks to be accomplished is not properly completed. Perhaps most notable – as in *Perdido Street Station* – is the deliberate posing of the central conflict in nonmetaphysical terms; this story is decidedly *not* a tale of good versus evil, but rather one emphasizing the culpability of humanity for its own problems, in this case the environment.

Miéville's project of dismantling generic conventions promises to continue with his forthcoming work. *The City & The City* (2009) and *Kraken* (forthcoming in 2010) combine urban fantasy with, respectively, detective fiction and a quest narrative; and an sf novel is rumored to be forthcoming. Miéville must be understood as one of the most productive, socially conscious, and artistically innovative authors of speculative fiction (Burling 2006).

See also: **J.G. Ballard, Iain M. Banks, Arthur C. Clarke, Philip K. Dick, Nalo Hopkinson, Gwyneth Jones, Michael Moorcock, Alan Moore, Mary Shelley, Olaf Stapledon, and H.G. Wells**

Bibliography

Burling, W.J. (2006) "Wierd [*sic*] Science: the fantastic realism of China Miéville," *Political Affairs*, February: 32–35.

——(2009) "Periodizing the Postmodern: China Miéville's *Perdido Street Station* and the dynamics of radical fantasy," *Extrapolation*.

DuMond, L. (2003) "Review of *The Tain*," SF Site. Online. Available: <http://www.sfsite.com/04b/tt150.htm> (accessed 1 January 2009).

Freedman, C. (2003) "Toward a Marxist Urban Sublime: reading China Miéville's *King Rat*," *Extrapolation*, 44(4): 395–408.

——(2005) "To the Perdido Street Station: the representation of revolution in China Mieville's *Iron Council*," *Extrapolation*, 46(2): 235–48.

Gordon, J. (2003a) "Hybridity, Heterotopia, and Mateship in China Miéville's *Perdido Street Station*," *Science Fiction Studies*, 30(3): 456–76.

——(2003b) "Reveling in Genre: an interview with China Miéville," *Science Fiction Studies*, 30(3): 355–73.

Miéville, C. (1998) *King Rat*, New York: Tor.

——(2000) *Perdido Street Station*, New York: Del Rey.

——(2002a) "Editorial Introduction to Symposium on Marxism and Fantasy," *Historical Materialism: Research in Critical Marxist Theory*, 10(4): 39–49.

——(2002b) "Messing with Fantasy," *Locus*, 48(3): 4–5, 75–76.

——(2002c) *The Scar*, New York: Del Rey.

——(2004) *Iron Council*, New York: Del Rey.

——(2005a) *Between Equal Rights: a marxist theory of international law*, Netherlands: Brill Academic Publishers.

——(2005b) "New Weird," in J. Dann (ed.) *Nebula Awards Showcase 2005: the year's best science fiction and fantasy*, New York: ROC.

Mills, A. (2002) "Inspiration and Astonishment: Peake's influence on *Perdido Street Station*," *Peake Studies*, 7(4): 19–24.

WILLIAM J. BURLING

MICHAEL [JOHN] MOORCOCK (1939–)

British novelist, editor, and polemicist.

Michael Moorcock is best known as the author of popular works of fantasy such as the *Elric* saga; indeed, he is one of the most celebrated of contemporary fantasists, having received the British Fantasy Award five times. His sumptuous alternate-world romance *Gloriana, or The Unfulfill'd Queen* (1978) won the World Fantasy Award and the

John W. Campbell Memorial Award for best science-fiction novel of the year, a genre-straddling accomplishment that reflects not only the author's bountiful gifts but also his expansive, prodigal vision. Like earlier literary crossbreeds such as Fritz Leiber and Mervyn Peake – both acknowledged influences – Moorcock has produced a playful and erudite body of work that defies easy categories, eschewing clear distinctions between sf and fantasy in favor of the mutable dreamscapes of fabulation.

While his early career coincided with the assimilation of classic high fantasists such as J.R.R. Tolkien and C.S. Lewis into the genre, Moorcock has notably scorned this tradition, in *Wizardry and Wild Romance: a study of epic fantasy* (1987), as aesthetically impoverished and politically conservative. His own work, by contrast, draws on the more challenging and subversive experiments of the literary avant-garde, fusing these with the legacy of pulp sf; the result has been likened to a bizarre confluence of Edgar Rice Burroughs and William S. Burroughs. In his earliest work, the influence of the former predominated: as a teenager, Moorcock edited the fanzine *Tarzan Adventures*, for which he produced a number of overripe adventure stories (later gathered as *Sojan* (1977)). Their undeniable narrative vigor drew the attention of John Carnell, the premier professional sf editor in Britain during the 1950s and early 1960s, who invited Moorcock to contribute to *Science-Fantasy*. The outcome was an ongoing series featuring the world-weary Elric, albino warlock and emperor of the "Dragon Isle" Melniboné, which drew eclectically on a wide range of sources, from Robert E. Howard's lusty tales of Conan the Cimmerian to Clark Ashton Smith's languid visions of far-future Zothique. They were immediately and immensely popular, and the *Elric* saga now extends to almost a dozen novels and several spin-off properties, including comic-book adaptations, a role-playing game, and the 1975 album *Warrior on the Edge of Time* by the "space metal" band Hawkwind.

Much of Moorcock's other work throughout the 1960s and early 1970s came under the broad penumbra of sword-and-sorcery adventure, including the *History of the Runestaff* (1967–69), the *Erikosë* sequence (1970–87), and the *Chronicles of Corum* (1971–74), all multi-book series. He was incredibly prolific, and his work drew a ready audience not only among sf and fantasy fans but also from the youth counterculture, who found the dreamy decadence and brooding pop-occultism of his fiction peculiarly alluring. John Clute, one of the most perceptive critics of Moorcock's work, has chastised him for this crossover appeal, mocking the "weenybopper theosophies" that infest several of his 1960s novels, turning them into the equivalent of "Art Nouveau cartoons" and their author into something of a "purple sage" (Clute 1988: 89). Moorcock himself has admitted that much of this material was produced under punishing deadline pressures for frankly pot-boiling reasons, to raise funds for other projects, in particular *New Worlds* magazine, which he edited from 1964 to 1971. In fact, it was his work as a professional editor that established Moorcock as a significant figure within the field of sf specifically.

Founded in 1946 as a British counterweight to John W. Campbell's *Astounding*, *New Worlds* was the flagship magazine in the fleet of titles edited by Carnell, running hard sf and space opera by the likes of **Arthur C. Clarke**, John Brunner, Colin Kapp, and E.C. Tubb. Its sister publication, *Science-Fantasy*, was more eclectic and less scientifically oriented, and when Carnell stepped down in early 1964, offering the youthful Moorcock (whose vision and dedication he had come to admire) his choice of editorial posts, observers were surprised when he chose the harder-edged, more established, and more traditional *New Worlds*. Moorcock's decision was based less on the difference in content between the magazines than on the fact that the title *New Worlds* could be more broadly construed, connoting creative invention and ideational novelty. His goal was not simply to revamp an existing institution within the field but to strike out on fresh paths, bringing sf into productive conversation with the literary avant-garde and the contemporary arts. His vision was of a large-format, glossy publication, featuring cutting-edge design and ambitious fiction that fused the imaginative speculation of the best sf with the experimental impulses of surrealism, the collage novel, and the *nouveau roman*. While financial exigencies and the genre's innate conservatism forced him to adopt a more modest approach for the first few years, in both appearance and content, by 1967 he had accomplished most of his goals, and *New Worlds* had become a visually striking, conceptually dazzling, and historically groundbreaking publication.

From the very first, Moorcock's editorial persona was tart and pugnacious, as if spoiling for a fight with Old Guard readers. Columns and feature articles – especially by **J.G. Ballard**, who became *New Worlds*' resident propagandist as well as its most visionary writer – lambasted traditional sf as juvenile and reactionary, sang the praises of artistic outlaws like William S. Burroughs and Salvador Dalí, and ceaselessly exhorted the genre to grow up and face the sociopolitical realities of the 1960s. Ballard's championing of "inner space" became *New Worlds*' guiding principle, and under Moorcock's editorship the magazine eschewed interplanetary adventure in favor of delirious explorations of near-future mindscapes, hallucinatory critiques of contemporary mass media, and counterculturally inspired interrogations of technocractic society. The term "New Wave" began to be applied to this breed of fiction, and for several years in the mid-to-late 1960s it touched off a furious controversy that divided generations and transformed the genre. Younger writers in the US and Britain – Thomas M. Disch, Norman Spinrad, James Sallis, Langdon Jones – placed material in *New Worlds* that was unpublishable elsewhere because it was too aesthetically radical or politically militant, while several older talents – notably Brian W. Aldiss – joined the gaudy bandwagon, pushing themselves in startling new directions. A list of fiction published during Moorcock's tenure reads like a late 1960s roll of honor: Disch's *Camp Concentration* (1967), Pamela Zoline's "The Heat Death of the Universe" (1967), Aldiss's "Acid Head Wars" stories (1967–68), Spinrad's *Bug Jack Barron* (1967–68), **Samuel R. Delany**'s "Time Considered as a Helix of Semi-precious Stones" (1968), Ballard's *The Atrocity Exhibition* (1966–70). This period stands – along with the Golden Age of Campbell's *Astounding* (1939–45) and the early years of H.L. Gold's *Galaxy* (1950–55) – as one of the most brilliant and revolutionary in the history of magazine sf.

Unfortunately, despite financial assistance from the Arts Council, Moorcock was compelled to churn out a host of popular fantasies to pay the bills, and by the turn of the decade he was worn down by this nonstop hackwork and by the constant financial crises *New Worlds* suffered. In 1971 he passed the editorial reins to other hands as the magazine became a quarterly, then a semi-annual book series, and finally expired in 1976. Moorcock's major literary contribution to *New Worlds* – aside from his 1966 tale "Behold the Man," in which a skeptical time traveler replaces the historical Christ (which won a Nebula Award for best novella) – was a series of stories centering on polymathic libertine Jerry Cornelius, a cross between Bob Dylan and James Bond, who became something of a raffish mascot for the journal. *The Final Programme* (1965–66) and *A Cure for Cancer* (1969), the latter deploying playful collage techniques, were featured in the magazine, while later volumes in the series – *The English Assassin* (1972) and *The Condition of Muzak* (1977) – appeared as free-standing books. The series is notable not only as one of the most engaging and ingenious emanations of the British counterculture, at once celebrating and ironically critiquing its excesses, but also as the initial stage in an ongoing project that has seen Moorcock ambitiously weave his various fantasy heroes into a vast, intercommunicating network, an elaborate mosaic he has dubbed "the multiverse."

By contrast with the future histories of hard sf, Moorcock's multiverse scorns linearity and closure: his heroes slip through dubious time frames, exchange personalities, and blithely cross between genres, generating in the end not a cohesive schema but a ludic, mercurial masque. The most science-fictional of these recurring protagonists, aside from Cornelius, are Jherek Carnelian, volatile star of the *Dancers at the End of Time* sequence (1972–76), a far-future extravaganza of languorous swank and shifting sexuality, and Oswald Bastable, doughty stalwart of a series of inspired riffs on the classic scientific romance, beginning with *The Warlord of the Air* (1971). These works showcased Moorcock's skills as a whimsical pasticheur, effortlessly ventriloquizing and shrewdly renovating the Victorian-Edwardian progenitors of pulp sf; they have been seen as forerunners of the "steampunk" subgenre of the 1980s and 1990s. Above all, they showed what the author was capable of when freed from the pressures of potboiling and allowed to develop his own singular artistic vision.

While Moorcock continued to produce the occasional Elric fantasy to satisfy his avid fans, his work after the 1970s began to expand beyond the borders of genre, and he has been increasingly hailed – along with erstwhile New Wavers such as Ballard and Delany – as a major postmodern novelist. *Mother London* (1988), though it contains whiffs of ambiguous fantasy, is a complex mainstream novel, interweaving intensely imagined scenes of the 1940s Blitz with scathing satire of the enormities of 1980s Thatcherism. (Always ardently political, Moorcock fiercely opposed the rightward tilt of British politics; he issued a polemical pamphlet, *The Retreat from Liberty: the erosion of democracy in today's Britain*, in 1983.) Even more audaciously demanding, the *Colonel Pyat* tetralogy (1981–2006) – almost certainly Moorcock's finest accomplishment – began to appear in 1981 and has only recently been completed. The titles of the four books, read consecutively, render a sphinx-like judgment on the fate of the modern world: *Byzantium Endures* (1981), *The Laughter of Carthage* (1984), *Jerusalem Commands* (1992), *The Vengeance of Rome* (2006). Colonel Pyat (a.k.a. Maxim Arturovitch Pyatnitski), whose problematic life spans the twentieth century and who persistently – and rather improbably – comes into contact with an array of famous persons and events, narrates his experiences with a combination of bluster and apology, relish and regret. At once carefully researched historical novels and freewheeling absurdist parables, the books are potent meditations on the ethical-political paradoxes of modernity and bear serious comparison with similarly themed efforts by E.L. Doctorow and Thomas Pynchon.

In sum, Moorcock's work is a virtual microcosm of sf during the postwar period. Rooted in pulp, it moves through the experimental effervescence of 1960s' speculative fiction to the baroque, magisterial cynicism of postmodernism. Though his career serves as a funhouse mirror of the contemporary genre, reflecting back its glittering attainments and its flaws, Michael Moorcock remains, *sui generis*, always and absolutely himself.

See also: **J.G. Ballard, Iain M. Banks, Arthur C. Clarke, Samuel R. Delany, Philip K. Dick, Hugo Gernsback, Gwyneth Jones, China Miéville, Alan Moore, Mary Shelley, Olaf Stapledon, and H.G. Wells**

Bibliography

Baker, B. (2005) "Witness to the Ends of the World: colonialism, the scientific romance and Michael Moorcock's *Nomad of the Time Streams* trilogy," *Foundation*, 93: 40–48.

Clute, J. (1988) *Strokes: essays and reviews 1966–1986*, Seattle, WA: Serconia Press.

Delville, M. (1997) "Pop Meets the Avant Garde: music and muzak in Michael Moorcock's Jerry Cornelius stories," in M.A. Morrison (ed.) *Trajectories of the Fantastic: selected essays from the Fourteenth International Conference on the Fantastic in the Arts*, Westport, CT: Greenwood Press.

Glover, D. (1984) "Utopia and Fantasy in the Late 1960s: Burroughs, Moorcock, Tolkien," in C. Pawling (ed.) *Popular Fiction and Social Change*, New York: St Martin's.

Greenland, C. (1983) *The Entropy Exhibition: Michael Moorcock and the British "new wave" in science fiction*, London: Routledge and Kegan Paul.

Latham, R. (2006) "New Worlds and the New Wave in Fandom: fan culture and the reshaping of science fiction in the sixties," *Extrapolation*, 47(2): 296–315.

Moorcock, M. (1983) "Introduction," in M. Moorcock (ed.) *New Worlds: an anthology*, London: Flamingo.

Witcover, P. (1998) "The Purple Millennium: Michael Moorcock's *Dancers at the End of Time*," *New York Review of Science Fiction*, 11(4): 1, 8–11.

ROB LATHAM

ALAN MOORE (1953–)

English novelist, musician, and performance artist best known for his influential work in comics.

While almost all of Alan Moore's stories reveal an admitted tendency to "gravitate toward things that [have] an element of the fantastic in them" (Baker 2008: 19), his most celebrated work has been "concerned with the history of comics – subverting it, redefining it, challenging it, or often just celebrating it" (Parkin 2001: 9). Known as "the magus," and famous for his claim to worship the Roman snake-god Glycon, Moore has performed a kind of alchemy on several properties of comics, taking already-existing characters and archetypes and "transmuting base metal into gold" (Wolk 2007: 229). He began his career as a cartoonist, working under the pseudonyms Curt Vile and Jill de Ray (homophones of Kurt Weill and Gilles de Rais), but he has been most successful as an author. Although he has produced some entirely original work, such as *A Small Killing* (1991), the never-finished *Ballad of Halo Jones* (1984–86), and the never-finished *Big Numbers* (1990), "Almost everything else is Moore playing in someone else's sandbox" (Wolk 2007: 230): *Marvelman* (1954–63, 1982–93, from 1985 as *Miracleman*), *Swamp Thing* (1971–), and *Supreme* (1992–) existed when Moore took them over; *Watchmen* (September 1986–October 1987) was developed for Charleton Comics characters from the 1960s; *The League of Extraordinary Gentlemen* (1999–) and *Lost Girls* (1991–92, 2006) each appropriate literary characters; *From Hell* (1991–96) borrows heavily from Stephen Knight's *Jack the Ripper: the final solution* (1976); *V for Vendetta* (1982–88) finds inspiration in the historical Guy Fawkes; and the characters of *Promethea* (1999–2005), *D.R. and Quinch* (1983–85), and *The Bojeffries Saga* (1983–91) bear strong similarities to those of *Wonder Woman* (1941–), National Lampoon's *O.C. and Stiggs*, and *The Munsters* (1964–66).

Magic and formal structure are the most consistent elements in Moore's fiction. For him, magic is "a language with which to read the universe," used to uncover "the revelation that is in *everything*" (Babcock 2007: 129–30). Aside from magic-show performance pieces, however, Moore does not figure magic as an act of arcane invocation, but rather as an instance of creative invention: "There is something very magical at the heart of writing, and language, and storytelling" (Baker 2005: 10). The structuralist underpinnings of both language and magic support and organize Moore's narratives. He explains that: "In magic, you will have your grimoires, your big, dark book of magic secrets. Grimoires is simply a fancier French way of spelling 'grammar.' To cast a spell, as far as I understand it, is simply to spell" (Baker 2005: 10–11). Moore has his own grammar and has, on occasion, spelled out his formal approach, describing various techniques such as "the use of overlapping, or coincidental dialogue," or, as a variation on this, the "use of a synchronicity of image rather than of words, or even just a coincidental linkage of vague abstract ideas" (Moore 2003: 17). Moore repeatedly returns to this "'polyphonic' trick" in *Watchmen*, where "language or dialogue from one scene is attached to images from another, usually giving the words some kind of second meaning" (Wolk 2007: 242).

One favorite strategy is to impose a "basic elliptical structure, where elements at the beginning of the story mirror events which are to happen at the end, or where a particular phrase or a particular image will be used at the beginning and the end, acting as bookends to give the story that takes place in between a sense of neatness and structure" (Moore 2003: 15). *Batman: the killing joke* (March 1988) features this device, framing the story within Batman's entreaty to the Joker and the joke the villain tells in reply. Like the raindrop ripples that begin and end the story, these repeated monologues radiate outward in time and space, expanding in meaning and size. Here, as in many of Moore's stories, the interconnectedness of past and present is emphasized through visual echoes as the reader moves frame to frame, witnessing the tableaux of the past repeated in the present. Although he believes "experiment for experiment's sake is kind of self-indulgent" (Baker 2008: 27), Moore packs his famously detailed scripts with myriad elaborate structures, like the palindromic panel arrangement of the "Fearful Symmetry" chapter in *Watchmen*, or the buried sonnet sequence formed from dialogue in *Swamp Thing*. Despite having his own set of pet schemes, tropes, and moves, such as the "iambic gallop" (Wolk 2007: 235) for important passages, Moore consistently pushes new work into unfamiliar formal terrain. In *V for Vendetta*, he reluctantly abandoned thought balloons, author's voice captions, and sound effects, discovering that the "tone and quality of the story" changed, making everything "much more real and documentary" (Baker 2008: 27–28). In *From Hell*, Moore uses no captions whatsoever, relying on image and dialogue to lure the reader into "the still-warm corpse of history itself" (Alaniz 2003: 145). Eddie Campbell's black-and-white art emblematizes Jack the Ripper's moral worldview and, combined with the rigid, nine-panel format, allows for a clinical dissection of the page that mirrors the killer's dispassionate dissection of women's corpses (even the corpse of history itself).

Moore's early work includes scripts for *2000 AD* (1977–), *Doctor Who Magazine* (under various titles, 1979–), *Captain Britain* (1976–), and *Marvelman/Miracleman*. Like Robert Mayer's novel *Super-Folks* (1977), which Moore claims as an influence, or the later film *The Incredibles* (Bird 2004), Moore's *Marvelman* places superheroes in the real world, making Superman an "anachronism, and by 1986, would lead to a more realistic revamp of Superman himself" (Parkin 2001:

10). Moore eventually penned two fine *Superman* stories – "For the Man Who Has Everything" in *Superman Annual* no. 11 (1985) and "Whatever Happened to the Man of Tomorrow?" in *Superman* vol. 1, no. 423, and *Action Comics* no. 583 (September 1986) – but he broke into the American mainstream writing for DC's struggling *Swamp Thing*. Both this and his dystopian *V for Vendetta* were praised, but his most influential and critically acclaimed work is the Hugo Award-winning *Watchmen*, "arguably the magnum opus of superhero comic books" (Wright 2001: 271). Continuing *Marvelman*'s exploration of superheroes in the real world, *Watchmen* deconstructs and normalizes the concept of the superhero so that: "Far from representing a fantasy of power, the superhero in *Watchmen* has become just another facet of society, and is consequently debunked. Satire replaces explicit mythology" (Reynolds 1992: 108–09).

In Juvenal's *Satires*, the quotation "Quis custodiet ipsos Custodes?" (Who watches the watchmen?) refers to the problem of crafty wives, who will cheat even with the watchmen posted to guard them. By explicitly connecting the epigraph to the Tower Commission Report on the Iran-Contra Affair, *Watchmen* refigures Juvenal's question within the context of international Cold War politics. In *Watchmen*'s alternate history, the US has won the Vietnam War because, as one newscaster announces: "The Superman exists, and he's American." There are no "Watchmen," but there are costumed heroes called Minutemen and the son of a watchmaker who manipulates time and space (as does the reader, moving back and forth through the comic) after an experiment-gone-wrong transforms him into "Dr Manhattan," the only super-powered character in the graphic novel. Although this superman initially unbalances the US–Soviet arms race, he cannot allay the threat of nuclear annihilation. In fact, as his name implies, he exacerbates the problem. Semi-hidden doomsday clocks appear throughout, and the "grid of nine uniform panels on each page allows [the reader] to follow the fine-tuned passage of multiple stories moment by moment. Panels tick by like a metronome or a time-bomb, counting down to midnight. Several different stories interweave on the same page, setting up visual and verbal links and counterparts" (Gravett 2005: 82). There are no full-page panels until the catastrophic destruction of New York City in the final chapter. After the smaller, ticking panels, the effect is like an alarm going off. The "recurrent geometric motif" of the circular clock (Groensteen 2007: 155) continually returns in the circular, blood-stained smiley face, which, according to artist Dave Gibbons, became "a symbol for the whole series" (Salisbury 2000: 80).

The "formal rigor" of such gestures may occasionally come off as "airless and overdetermined" and *Watchmen* may be too "full of look-at-me-I'm-a-comic-book devices" (Wolk 2007: 238, 242), but Moore's postmodern, metatextual masterpiece altered the face of comics. On his "darker days," Moore believes that what readers and future artists took from his work was not "its urge to stretch the limits of the form and the medium," but rather "the violence, a certain kind of intellectual posture," that "seemed to condemn comics to a lot of very depressing and grim post-*Watchmen* comic books" (Doane 2007: 153). Much of Moore's later work attempts to reverse this trend: "*Supreme* was almost an act of atonement, as he lovingly recreated every last absurdity of the old-style Superman, and made them work for a modern audience," and *Tom Strong* (1999–) took the superhero "concept back to basics by invoking the pulp and legendary archetypes that inspired Superman" (Parkin 2001: 10).

After *Watchmen*, Moore left DC over disputes involving creator's rights and merchandising; disagreements would create similar breaks with Marvel and conflicts with the film industry. Although intermittently involved in mainstream comics, Moore's more recent work consists of largely atypical projects: the 600-page long *From Hell*, which chronicles the Jack the Ripper murders; the pornographic *Lost Girls*, which depicts the sexual adventures of now grown-up heroines from *Alice's Adventures in Wonderland* (1865), *Peter Pan, or the Boy Who Wouldn't Grow Up* (1904), and *The Wonderful Wizard of Oz* (1900); and *The League of Extraordinary Gentlemen*, which transforms Victorian pulp heroes such as Allan Quatermain, Captain Nemo, and the Invisible Man into Justice League-like heroes. *Promethea*, whose eponymous heroine is invoked through acts of imagination, represents the apotheosis of magic and formal structure. Issue number 12 consists of a 24-page long panel featuring the history of humanity mapped onto the twenty-two major arcana of a modified Tarot. "The Aeon," representing Judgment (Day), is Harpocrates, the Greek god of silence; he looks like Harpo Marx, dressed in an Ankh-covered robe, with a horn ("ankh ankh"). Each page has an anagram of Promethea's name ("Meet Harpo" accompanies this one), along with the information that, Phoenix-like, Aeon will rise from Aeon's ashes, and "Apocalypse, as 'World's End' seen / Need only revelation mean." Moore often points out the etymological affinities of apocalypse and revelation, suggesting that Promethea is "the Apocalypse. She is Revelation. It's what Apocalypse is. Apocalypse is Revelation … that ends the world" (Cooke and Khoury 2003: 33, my ellipsis). Moore ends many of his stories with apocalyptic revelations, but, as with Aeon and many of Moore's characters, the endings merely represent new beginnings. As Dr Manhattan tells Ozymandias in *Watchmen*: "Nothing ever ends, Adrian. Nothing ever ends."

See also: **Alfred Bester, Samuel R. Delany, Stan Lee, China Miéville, Oshii Mamoru, and J. Michael Straczynski**

Bibliography

Alaniz, J. (2003) "Into Her Dead Body: Moore & Campbell's *From Hell*," in smoky man and G.S. Millidge (eds.) *Alan Moore: portrait of an extraordinary gentleman*, Leigh-on-Sea, England: Abiogenesis Press.

Babcock, J. (2007) "Magic Is Afoot," in W. Christiansen (ed.) *Alan Moore's Yuggoth Cultures and Other Growths*, Rantoul, IL: Avatar.

Baker, B. (2005) *Alan Moore Spells It Out: on comics, creativity, magic, and much, much more*, China: Airwave.

——(2008) *Alan Moore on His Work and Career*, New York: Rosen.

Cooke, J.B. and Khoury, G. (2003) "Alan Moore and the Magic of Comics," *Comic Book Artist*, 25: 8–45.

Doane, D.A. (2007) "Alan Moore Interview", in W. Christiansen (ed.) *Alan Moore's Yuggoth Cultures and Other Growths*, Rantoul, IL: Avatar.

Gravett, P. (2005) *Graphic Novels: everything you need to know*, New York: Collins Design.

Groensteen, T. (2007) *The System of Comics*, Jackson: University Press of Mississippi.

Knight, S. (1976) *Jack the Ripper: the final solution*, New York: McKay.

Moore, A. (2003) *Alan Moore's Writing for Comics*, Urbana, IL: Avatar.

Parkin, L. (2001) *The Pocket Essential Alan Moore*, London: Pocket Essentials.

Reynolds, R. (1992) *Super Heroes: a modern mythology*, Jackson: University Press of Mississippi.

Salisbury, M. (ed.) (2000) *Artists on Comics Art*, London: Titan Books.

Wolk, D. (2007) *Reading Comics: how graphic novels work and what they mean*, Cambridge, MA: Da Capo Press.

Wright, B.W. (2001) *Comic Book Nation: the transformation of youth culture in America*, Baltimore, MD: Johns Hopkins University Press.

JIM CASEY

C[ATHERINE] L[UCILLE] MOORE (1911–87)

US Golden Age writer, and scriptwriter for film and television.

On her own and as half of one of sf's most successful writing teams, C.L. Moore played a major part in the genre's so-called Golden Age. A series of stories in *Weird Tales* and *Astounding* established her reputation for colorful prose, exotic settings, and emotional range and subtlety. She wrote prolifically through the 1930s and 1940s, although after her marriage to fellow writer Henry Kuttner in 1940 much of her work was written collaboratively with him and published under pseudonyms. In the 1950s Moore and Kuttner moved to California and began working on degrees in English and writing for Hollywood, which limited their time for fiction; after Kuttner's death in 1958, Moore concentrated on screenwriting. Her scripts for television series such as *Maverick* (1961), 77 *Sunset Strip* (1960, 1962), and the unconventional western *Sugarfoot* (1958–59) are available in the Warner Brothers collection at the University of Southern California but have not yet received critical attention.

Moore wrote one novel, *Doomsday Morning* (1957), but she is best known for half a dozen or so classic stories: her first publication, "Shambleau" (1933), which received renewed attention from feminist critics beginning with Susan Gubar (1980); "Black God's Kiss" (1934), which introduced a woman warrior named Jirel and more or less single-handedly invented the subgenre of Amazon fantasy; "The Bright Illusion" (1934), an interplanetary and interspecies romance; "Tryst in Time" (1936), in which two lovers are reborn until their paths finally meet; "The Children's Hour" (1944), which combines thwarted love and a unique version of the alien; and "No Woman Born" (1944), one of the first and still most memorable cyborg stories. This body of work would establish her as a major writer of the magazine era, but it represents just a fraction of her contribution, for it leaves out most of her collaborative work with Kuttner under 17 or so different pen names. Two of their bylines, Lawrence O'Donnell and Lewis Padgett, were staples of the anthologies of the 1940s and 1950s, such as Groff Conklin's *A Treasury of Science Fiction* (1948), which includes Padgett's "Mimsy Were the Borogoves" (1943) and O'Donnell's "Vintage Season" (1946), along with Moore's "No Woman Born." Padgett and O'Donnell even developed personas of their own: Padgett as the constructor of witty puzzles with an unexpected sting, and O'Donnell as a spinner of mysterious tales of longing and loss. Although it is generally accepted that Padgett was a bit more Kuttner and O'Donnell a bit more Moore, both were genuine collaborations. After they paired up, Moore, who was already working at the top of the sf field, quickly brought Kuttner up to her level. Moore later said: "Everything we wrote between 1940 and 1958, when Hank died, was a collaboration. Well, almost everything" (Gunn 1976: 189). Critics disagree on which stories constitute the "almost."

No one work fully represents Moore's contributions to sf, but a sampling of two stories published under her own name, two of

O'Donnell's, and one of Padgett's begins to suggest her range. "Shambleau," for instance, combines a twilit Martian setting, a classic tough-guy named Northwest Smith (a possible source for **Steven Spielberg** and **George Lucas**'s Indiana Jones), an alien femme fatale, and a kinky erotic charge. The story begins with an iconic scene of angry mob, endangered maiden, and rescuing hero, but the maiden is also a vampire of sorts, the hero transmutes into a willing victim, and the mob's violence is justified. Moore, then a bank clerk in Indianapolis, began writing the story halfway down a page of typing exercises: "In the middle of this exercise a line from a poem (by William Morris?) worked itself to the front and I discovered myself typing something about a 'red running figure'" (Moore 1975: 365). This figure, which she first imagined as a witch in a medieval village, is Shambleau, a name that designates both individual and species. This rescued "maiden" is actually an ancient and powerful being who uses her desirability to entrap victims whose energy she feeds on. A recurring set of images – brown skin, feline green eyes, writhing scarlet hair – conveys a sense of Shambleau as everything that is Other. She is the innocent stranger, the eroticized racial outsider, the dominatrix in red leather, and the source of both danger and forbidden pleasure. Her erotic charge is centered in her hair, which is first hidden by a turban and then revealed to be impossibly long and lush, enveloping, and animated like the snaky tresses of Medusa. Read from a masculine perspective, the story is one of erotic obsession, with the female body as a honeyed trap. Part of Moore's strength as a writer, though, is her ability to convey more than one message with the same images. A second reading sees Shambleau as an independent woman, a trader in illusion and pleasure, a tough gal getting by on her own in a hostile universe. Most subversively, Shambleau finds the whole situation, including Smith's conflicted response, highly entertaining. She is reminiscent of the laughing Medusa invoked by the feminist philosopher Hélène Cixous as an emblem of women's elusive and unconquerable selfhood.

This second reading of "Shambleau" is reinforced by other Moore stories in which powerful female figures attract men while remaining undefined by their passion. In "No Woman Born," a performer named Dierdre is maimed in a fire and her body replaced by a metal housing. Dierdre discovers, however, that her new mechanical body can do everything she used to do: sing, dance, flirt. Indeed it is immeasurably more powerful than any merely human body. As in the earlier story, the powerful, alien female is seen through male eyes, in this case those of her manager, John Harris; another masculine perspective is represented by the scientist Malzer who created the artificial body and transplanted Dierdre's brain into it. Both men are in love with Dierdre, or at least the character she has created. Both assume that they have control over her. As the story progresses, Dierdre demonstrates that she can fool audiences – including the two men – into accepting her as human and feminine. She, however, is still discovering what she has become. Different readings of this story emphasize its Frankenstein-like elements, with Dierdre as the Creature (Gubar 1980); its pioneering investigation of human–machine hybridity (Gunn 1976); its skeptical treatment of femininity as performance (Hollinger 1999); and its use of the superhuman theme to investigate gender coding (Attebery 2002).

"The Children's Hour" was published under the O'Donnell name but is generally considered to be Moore's work. Once again it presents a powerful feminine presence mediated through a masculine consciousness. The protagonist, Lessing, is an ordinary man leading an ordinary life until he is hypnotized and discovers a gap in his memories. The story unfolds as a mystery, with Lessing gradually filling the gap with recovered images, snatches of poetry, and finally a name: Clarissa. Like Shambleau and Dierdre, Clarissa is characterized partly through mythic and literary references. In this case, we are invited to construct an identity for the mysterious woman out of the myth of Danae in the golden shower, a speech from *Romeo and Juliet* (c. 1595), fairy tales about maidens in towers, the Longfellow poem (1860) from which the story's title is drawn, and several chunks of *Through the Looking Glass* (1871). If these do not all hold together as a single identity, so much the better, for Clarissa is not the simple girl she appears to be. Rather, the human Clarissa is one component of a multidimensional being, and her affair with Lessing merely one phase of her education. She is no longer – never really was – the Clarissa he knew, but rather what the narrative calls the Clarissa Pattern. Such a composite identity is potentially as powerful a metaphor for female empowerment in the face of masculine myths as the cyborg, as theorized by **Donna Haraway** and exemplified in Moore's fiction. If Dierdre is the perfect cyborg, Clarissa is the exemplar for a yet-unnamed counter-myth of feminine multiplicity.

Moore's work with Kuttner under the Lewis Padgett pseudonym usually concerns themes other than gender or emotional entanglement. It is probably not a coincidence that Padgett rhymes with *gadget*. Early Padgett stories carry on Kuttner's already-established interest in the curious contraption, both as a prop within the stories and as a model for storytelling. For instance, Padgett wrote a series of stories about an inventor named Gallegher, whose genius emerges only when he is drunk, leaving him the challenge of figuring out when sober (or hungover) exactly what the device was supposed to do. The gadget-like plot is exemplified by the many Padgett stories which involve paradoxes of time travel or solutions to impossible problems such as committing a perfect crime. One Padgett story, however, raises the level of the gadget yarn by incorporating it in a story of childhood perception and parental grief. The gadgets in "Mimsy Were the Borogoves" are futuristic educational toys accidentally sent back to the twentieth century. Similar toys were sent back to Alice Liddell in the nineteenth century; her descriptions inspire Charles Dodgson/Lewis Carroll to write his supposed nonsense stories and verses. As young Scott and Emma explore the toys, they become, as their parents finally realize, something other than human. With their new perceptions and clues from Carroll's "Jabberwocky" (1871) the children finally escape into the future or some other dimension, leaving their parents baffled and bereft.

It is a pity that Moore and Kuttner were never asked to adapt their own work for the screen. The movie *The Last Mimzy* (Shaye 2007) is a botch that hardly resembles "Mimsy Were the Borogoves." Lawrence O'Donnell's story "Vintage Season" is somewhat more recognizable in *Timescape* (Twohy 1992), also entitled *Grand Tour: Disaster in Time.* The latter story is most probably a full collaboration between Moore and Kuttner, for it combines both writers' frequent concerns in an elegantly written and powerful exploration of art, eros, time, and death. The premise is that tourists from the future visit various historical moments to savor their aesthetic impact. They seek out times of devastation, which oddly seem to occur just after particularly pleasant seasons. One such prime season is a perfect May sometime in the mid-twentieth century, when Oliver, the story's protagonist, rents rooms to three of these connoisseurs of disaster and falls in love with one, the languid and beautiful Kleph. They know, but he does not, that his house is a prime spot for watching the fall of a meteorite that will not only flatten the city but also bring a new plague, the Blue Death. When Oliver finds out what is going on, he begs them to intervene, only to discover that he and his time are not really real to them, even to the artist Cenbe, who is composing a multimedia symphony of catastrophes but has no sense of the human drama behind them. Oliver, dying of the plague, tries to leave a warning note, but it is burned along with his house in a vain attempt to stop the disease.

A perfect blend of Kuttner's logic, Moore's emotional depth, and their combined irony and stylistic sophistication, "Vintage Season" remains a touchstone of sf, and a good introduction to two (or four or 17) of the best writers of the era. Many other rich and strange Moore stories, both solo efforts and collaborations, remain to be rediscovered.

See also: **Isaac Asimov, Greg Bear, Alfred Bester, Leigh Brackett, Octavia Butler, Samuel R. Delany, Philip K. Dick, William Gibson, Robert A. Heinlein, Frank Herbert, Nalo Hopkinson, L. Ron Hubbard, Gwyneth Jones, Ursula K. Le Guin, George Lucas, Kim Stanley Robinson, Joanna Russ, Mary Shelley, Steven Spielberg, Neal Stephenson, Sheri S. Tepper, James Tiptree Jr, and Gene Wolfe**

Bibliography

Attebery, B. (2002) *Decoding Gender in Science Fiction*, New York and London: Routledge.

Gubar, S. (1980) "C.L. Moore and the Conventions of Women's SF," *Science Fiction Studies*, 7(1): 16–27.

Gunn, J. (1976) "Henry Kuttner, C.L. Moore, Lewis Padgett *et al.*," in T.D. Clareson (ed.) *Voices for the Future: essays on major science fiction writers*, vol. 1, Bowling Green, OH: Bowling Green Popular Press.

Hollinger, V. (1999) "(Re)reading Queerly: science fiction, feminism, and the defamiliarization of gender," *Science Fiction Studies*, 26(1): 23–40.

Moore, C.L. (1975) "Footnote to Shambleau … and Others," in L. del Rey (ed.) *The Best of C.L. Moore*, New York: Ballantine.

BRIAN ATTEBERY

OSHII MAMORU (1951–)

Japanese anime director and screenwriter.

Respected both in Japan and internationally, Oshii Mamoru (usually supported by screenwriter Itō Kazunori and composer Kawaii Kenji) creates cinema that, both in anime and live-action form, confounds and delights viewers. Audiences who expect formulaic tech noir fare are often puzzled and disappointed, but viewers interested in sf that is cerebral, challenging, and outstanding in its visual style find Oshii to be an ideal director. Less family-friendly than the work of Miyazaki Hayao, his main anime "rival" in terms of global recognition, Oshii's *oeuvre* invites viewers into unique worlds in which cyberpunk action and adventure mix with meditations on psychology and philosophy to create memorable visions of humanity at the beginning of the new millennium.

Influenced by American and British sf writers such as **Robert A. Heinlein** and **J.G. Ballard**, Oshii first became famous in the West for *Ghost in the Shell* (1995), a major inspiration for the Wachowski brothers' *Matrix* trilogy (1999–2003). Oshii has been compared with American and British live-action directors, such as David Lynch, in his interest in the surreal and the macabre, and some of Oshii's most famous films, notably *Ghost in the Shell*, clearly channel Ridley Scott's cyberpunk classic *Blade Runner* (1982). But Oshii's sophisticated visual style, employing both hand-drawn and computer-generated animation with an extraordinarily rich color palette, plus his probing psychological characterizations, make his films utterly distinctive viewing experiences.

Although at ease in the international world of contemporary sf, Oshii also shows definite traces of his Japanese background. Most obvious of these is his fascination with the links among species and even inanimate objects, and his explicit insistence that an anthropomorphic approach to the world is too narrow. Oshii's more holistic approach echoes the indigenous Japanese religion of Shinto, in which virtually anything – from animals to rocks to waterfalls – could be endowed with the *kami* (sacred) spirit. This vision is most beautifully realized in what some critics believe to be his masterpiece, *Ghost in the Shell 2: Innocence* (2004), in which cyborgs, humans, dogs, androids, and dolls all seem to possess an eerie connection with each other. Oshii is also comfortable exploring the boundary between dream and reality, an element that leads back to Buddhism and classical Japanese literature.

But Oshii can also be compared with certain modern masters of Japanese literature, most notably the Nobel Prize winner Kawabata Yasunari. Kawabata and Oshii are both poets of loneliness – many of their works show characters searching for connection and love against the background of a strange and seemingly uncaring universe. Consequently, despite the many action-packed moments of explosions, armored attacks, futuristic technology, and thrilling fight scenes, Oshii's most memorable visions show a main character alone in an indifferent world.

Perhaps the most breathtaking expression of this world view, and an example of Oshii's unique psychological and visual style, is a tour de force sequence in *Ghost in the Shell*. A film about a cyborg assassin who longs for spiritual transcendence and emotional connection, despite, or perhaps because of, her superb abilities as a killing machine, it questions the relation between human and machine and offers a cautious vision of technological transcendence. In this two-minute-long sequence, the cyborg, Kusanagi Motoko, rides a boat down a canal through the detritus and jumble of New Port City, a postmodern urban amalgamation of old and new, squalid and sophisticated, and natural and artificial. Rain begins to fall, emphasizing the vulnerability of Kusanagi's isolated figure and the isolation of the hurrying figures in the city around her. Through the exquisitely animated rain, we see Kusanagi gazing at the urban landscape only to find Doppelgängers of herself – a woman eating alone in a restaurant, armless black manikins outlined against the eerie brightness of elegant department store windows. Throughout the scene music resounds, set to the lyrics of a Shinto liturgy in which the gods are urged to come down to mingle with mortals. Such a slow, wordless scene would be inconceivable in most Western sf, and it is not strictly necessary to the film's narrative development. But the sequence lyrically sets the stage for Kusanagi's later decision to abandon her corporeal body and meld with a cyber-entity known as the Puppet Master. The Puppet Master itself is a creation that has links to both Buddhism and Shinto, as puppets or dolls and their animistic nature are an important aspect of Japanese tradition, while the cyberworld in which it dwells suggests the Buddhist notion of transcendence.

Oshii's awareness of the fragility of human connection may also be influenced by his personal experience. Born in Tokyo in 1951, Oshii often went to the movies with his private-detective father, who would even take him out of school to enjoy the guilty pleasure of watching films at odd times. It is perhaps no coincidence that in his 1987 experimental film *Twilight Q2: Labyrinth Objects File 538* one of the three characters is a detective. Although this may be an homage to his father, there is also a sense in Oshii's work overall of the director as a rather chilly observer, gazing at people's lives like a detective watching over a suspect, hoping to find some deeper meaning in the subject's life. Although he found work as an animator in his twenties, Oshii also played with the notion of going to a seminary, and an interest in and knowledge of Christianity plays a strong part in many of his films.

Alongside *Twilight*, Oshii also made the experimental art film *Angel's Egg* (1985), a stunningly drawn, almost wordless piece apparently inspired by his loss of faith in Christianity. Both of these are personal and challenging films, little viewed beyond his most fanatical admirers, but they already show Oshii's trademark dreamlike atmosphere. Oshii's first real commercial successes began with his helming some of the television (1981–86) and movie (1983, 1984) versions of the manga series *Urusei yatsura*, written by popular manga artist Takahashi Rumiko.

While Takahashi's antic zaniness may seem an odd fit with Oshii's cerebral melancholy, one of these films, *Urusei Yatsura Beautiful Dreamer* (1984), may be safely considered to be one of Oshii's early masterpieces. Already in *Beautiful Dreamer* we see one of his abiding preoccupations – his fascination with what he sees as the highly permeable boundary between reality and the virtual (or, in this case, reality and the dream). Set in the carnivalesque world of a high school festival, the film mixes Japanese folklore, postapocalyptic visions, and teenage romance to create an eerie but affecting work that forces the viewer to continually question his or her perception of the "real" by offering variations on the theme of dreaming.

In his next successes, the *Patlabor* series (1988) and the films *Patlabor 1: The Movie* (1989) and *Patlabor: The Movie 2* (1993), Oshii continued to demonstrate his ability to take conventional genres and add his own personal, and in this case political, elements to the mix. While the *Patlabor* works belong to the enormous and popular *mecha* genre of giant robotic machines that empower their human operators, Oshii's vision of *mecha* is far more challenging and ambitious than the usual action-adventure fare. Oshii was a young man during the antigovernment struggles of the 1960s, and a fascination with power and its abuses remains strongly visible in much of his work. Both *Patlabor* films involve terrorist plots led by enigmatic powerful men with dreams of a new political order based on the purgative forces of destruction. Their plans are challenged by a government squadron known as SV2 who use special "Labors" (gigantic robotic machines) to confront them. While both films end with the terrorists vanquished, the allure of violence and terrorism is effectively presented, in particular in the second *Patlabor* film, where one of the female members of SV2 is romantically linked with the terrorist.

Oshii's use of heroines involved in a complex dynamic with a powerful outside force reached its apogee in his masterpiece *Ghost in the Shell.* Although the movie is based on the popular manga by Shirow Masamune, Oshii molded the material to create his own unique vision. The film is a tour de force of explosive violence mixed with elegiac melancholy that, through its tormented cyborg heroine Kusanagi, raises the question of humanity's place in an increasingly posthuman, technologized world. Oshii continues this exploration in the sequel, *Ghost in the Shell 2: Innocence*, one of the most visually stunning animated films ever produced. A noir thriller revolving around the mystery of why a group of sexualized androids have started killing their masters, the film features Kusanagi's former partner Batou as the officer assigned to the case. Like Kusanagi, Batou is a cyborg searching for connection and meaning, be it through his love of his pet basset hound or his yearning for the now disembodied Kusanagi, who appears at the end of the film in the role of his "guardian angel."

The film involves several spectacular CGI sequences, one of which took an entire year to animate. In the film's most intriguing CGI sequence, Batou finds that the brain of his current partner, Togusa, has been "cyberhacked," causing Togusa and the audience to experience the same scene several times but with significant variations. Oshii had already explored this notion of the permeability of reality and its uneasy relationship to the virtual in *Beautiful Dreamer*, the first *Ghost in the Shell*, and in his live-action film *Avalon* (2001), but the sophisticated animation in *Innocence* makes this sequence particularly disturbing and memorable. *Innocence* ends disturbingly as well, with a vision of androids, dolls, animals, and humans in a complex circle of life in the twenty-first century.

Not all of Oshii's directed works achieve an exquisite balance of visual beauty, mind-bending ideas, and fascinating characterizations. His live-action works, such as *The Red Spectacles* (1987), *Talking Head* (1992), *Amazing Lives of the Fast Food Grifters* (2006), and perhaps even the critically praised *Avalon*, have never found much of a following, either inside or outside Japan. On the other hand, his screenplay for the animated film *The Wolf Brigade* (Okiura 2006) is a brilliant alternate history of a Japan occupied by Nazi forces, which includes scenes of brutal violence mixed with eerie evocations of Western folklore, particularly the tale of Little Red Riding Hood. Similarly, Oshii's involvement with *Blood the Last Vampire* (Kitakubo 2000) – a macabre fantasy with political overtones set at an American military school in Japan – is widely credited for giving the film its emotional and visual richness.

Oshii's *Sky Crawlers* (2008) is based on a series of novels and continues the director's fascination with the virtual and the real, in this case in the form of a "game" of life and death that is played out across the skies of a future Earth. Giant corporations have substituted war games for real wars and choose strangely affectless young people to pilot the airships. Frozen in adolescence, the young pilots still seek for meaning against the forces of capitalism and history. More subdued than *Innocence*, *Sky Crawlers* still conveys Oshii's trademark strengths – transcendently aesthetic imagery, enigmatic but intriguing characters, and complex metaphysical questions that will continue to occupy the viewer's mind once he or she leaves the theater. An original, imaginative, and immensely talented director,

Oshii has helped shape not only sf film but also our notions of the future itself.

See also: **Alfred Bester, David Cronenberg, Samuel R. Delany, William Gibson, Donna J. Haraway, Stanley Kubrick, Fritz Lang, Stan Lee, George Lucas, Steven Spielberg, and J. Michael Straczynski**

Bibliography

Cavallaro, D. (2006) *The Cinema of Mamoru Oshii: fantasy, technology and politics*, London: McFarland.

Napier, S. (2005) *Anime: from Akira to Howl's Moving Castle*, New York: Palgrave.

Ruh, B. (2004) *Stray Dog of Anime: the films of Mamoru Oshii*, New York: Palgrave.

SUSAN NAPIER

KIM STANLEY ROBINSON (1952–)

US novelist, short-story writer, and critic.

Kim Stanley Robinson is the winner of many major awards for his fiction, among them the 1983 World Fantasy Award for "Black Air," the 1986 Nebula for "The Blind Geometer," the 1991 John W. Campbell Award for *Pacific Edge*, the 1993 Nebula for *Red Mars*, the 1994 Hugo for *Green Mars*, and the 1997 Hugo for *Blue Mars*. Robinson's *Mars* trilogy (1993–96) is one of the most celebrated and widely discussed works of science fiction to have appeared since 1990, and a significant body of commentary on the entire range of his fiction continues to accumulate (see Burling 2009). Robinson's place in the terrain of late twentieth- and early twenty-first-century sf has sometimes been said to indicate a resurgence of hard sf because he eschews the noir stylistics and virtual realities of the cyberpunk movement, and just as studiously avoids any hint of magic or the supernatural or any of the melding of sf and fantasy elements characteristic of contemporary Gothic or "weird" fiction. But to categorize his work as a return to mid-twentieth-century hard sf hardly does justice to the intellectual vigor with which Robinson combines his broad-ranging engagement of contemporary science with steadfast realism, strong political commitments to utopian thinking and environmentalism, sophisticated elaborations of social and critical theory, and stunning renditions of natural landscapes.

In his major fiction Robinson has stuck closely to an extrapolative near-future realism that in several interviews he has aligned with the historical novel. Thus the *Mars* trilogy – *Red Mars* (1993), *Green Mars* (1994), and *Blue Mars* (1996) – works out the possibility of colonizing Mars in densely realistic detail; each of the *Three Californias* – *The Wild Shore* (1984), *The Gold Coast* (1988), and *Pacific Edge* (1990) – explores a pointedly different twenty-first-century setting's effects upon a pointedly similar cast of characters; *Antarctica* (1997) and the *Science in the Capital* trilogy – *Forty Signs of Rain* (2004), *Fifty Degrees Below* (2005), and *Sixty Days and Counting* (2007) – are "day after tomorrow" stories (as Robinson has called them) that depict realistically drawn characters coping with extreme, but possible, environmental conditions; and *The Years of Rice and Salt* (2002) is a massive alternate history spanning eight centuries and based on the premise of increasing the Black Death's fatality rate in Europe to 100 per cent. All of these pieces could be considered thought-experiments meditating upon the complex tensions between individual freedom and sociohistorical determination characteristic of the historical novel; even the supernatural visions of the protagonist of "Black Air" (1983), while they recall those of Coleridge's Ancient Mariner (1798), can be explained realistically as fevered hallucinations produced in him by the combination of the boy's cultural milieu, his dire circumstances, and malnutrition. The play between the grand sweep of history and intimate individual experience pervades all of Robinson's major projects.

Robinson's realist orientation is complicated and enriched by what might seem to be an anti-realist politics, his equally strong commitment to utopian thinking. But it would be more accurate to say that his work maintains a tension between reflecting on the nightmare of history and dreaming of a better world. A self-described member of the anti-capitalist left, Robinson has consistently projected the disastrous consequences of hypertrophied present-day capitalism – as in the suffocatingly overdeveloped Orange County of *The Gold Coast*, the rapaciousness of the "metanational" corporations in the *Mars* volumes, or the blithe irresponsibility of a barely fictional Bush-like president and his administration in *Science in the Capital* – and has also invented happier and healthier postcapitalist futures – in the communal, ecologically responsible, radically democratic society of *Pacific Edge*, in the eco-economics and grass-roots revolutionary organizations that eventually prevail on Mars, in the co-op takeover of Antarctica's service contracts in *Antarctica*, and in the tying together of environmental activism and economic justice by Phil Chase and his administration in *Science in the Capital*. Robinson's utopian futures are not depicted in the guided-tour mode of the earlier utopian tradition, but rather, like **Ursula K. Le Guin**'s *The Dispossessed: an ambiguous utopia* (1974) or **Samuel R. Delany**'s *Triton: an ambiguous heterotopia* (1976), immerse their readers in the day-to-day reality of a future that gradually unfolds itself in the background, in the style of the great early twentieth-century dystopias of Yevgeny Zamyatin or George Orwell. Robinson has insisted in interviews that he wants to move the notion of utopia away from elaborating static models of the perfected society to thinking about the process of working toward a more just and sustainable social order. This attention to process and to the texture of everyday life is largely responsible for the daunting length of the *Mars* and *Science in the Capital* trilogies, which, as Robinson has insisted, are not really trilogies but rather very long novels published in three volumes. But even in *Pacific Edge*, the shorter utopian installment of the *Three Californias*, individual tragedy balances and enriches the texture of the utopian society.

Robinson's commitment to complexity and realism in combination with utopian ambitions has challenged some critics to produce an accurate specification of the distinctive generic quality of his fiction. *The Gold Coast*, for example, has been examined as a paradigmatic example of the critical dystopia, a dystopian novel that includes utopian elements, as opposed to the nightmarish foreclosure of hope in a novel such as Orwell's *Nineteen Eighty-Four* (1949; see Moylan 2000); and *Science in the Capital* has already inspired the new generic terms utopian black comedy and proleptic realism (Luckhurst 2009). Without question the strongest note in critical responses to Robinson's utopianism, however, has been the critics' recognition of his syncretism and polyphony. Robinson's utopian societies are never univocal, speaking with a single voice. He consistently emphasizes the negotiation of ongoing, intractable difference rather than the establishment of equanimity. The *Mars* narrative, in particular, stages an immensely protracted and rich debate among a wide range of political, economic, and social ideas, as it spans two centuries' worth of plot, details the lives and points of view of dozens of major characters, and magnificently renders the geographical setting of an entire planet in the process of its transformation from the red, lifeless Mars of reality to the ocean-covered blue Mars of the postrevolutionary future.

Part of the richness of Robinson's fiction comes from his ability to integrate nonfiction genres into his novels. If the landscape passages on Mars are triumphant imaginative realizations of the data accumulated by recent scientific research and mapping of Mars (see Morton

2002), the equally impressive landscapes of Antarctica read more like travel writing based on Robinson's own experience (he visited Antarctica in 1995 as a grantee of the National Science Foundation's Antarctic Artists and Writers' Program) as well as on earlier travelers' accounts of the continent (several of which are summarized and argued over by characters in the novel). A good deal of the critical energy of *The Gold Coast* is generated by the history of Orange County being written by its protagonist. Digressions on political economy abound throughout Robinson's fiction, from the formulation of eco-economics in the Mars books to Charlie Quibler's spectacular tirade against the World Bank in *Science in the Capital.* Robinson's background as a Ph.D. in English and an accomplished literary critic (his dissertation was published as *The Novels of Philip K. Dick* (1984)) comes through in the psychologist Michel's use of structuralist semantics (*à la* Robinson's mentor Fredric Jameson) in *Red Mars*, or in the meditations of the character X on his reading of philosophy and critical theory in *Antarctica.* Robinson's novels thus add a dialogic interaction of genres to the density of their realism and the scope and complexity of plot, setting, and character.

The most important of these nonfictional genres in Robinson's sf is science itself. Robinson has said that the vocation of the sf writer is to bring the facts of science into conversation with the values explored in fiction. At the core of much of Robinson's fiction, therefore, one finds his remarkably lucid renditions of contemporary science and his speculative extrapolations of near-future science. The range of science writing that appears in his fiction is truly impressive. Mathematics, geometry, particle physics, geology, meteorology, paleoanthropology, sociobiology, bio-informatics, and ecology, among others, figure prominently, especially in his staging of the debates over terraforming in the *Mars* trilogy and the discussions of climate change in *Antarctica* and *Science in the Capital.* Of equal interest in all of these novels, as well as in *The Years of Rice and Salt*, is Robinson's dramatization of the institutional economics and politics of science. Indeed, as Jameson has argued in his reading of the *Mars* trilogy, all of the science in Robinson's fiction is ultimately an expression of his utopian belief in humanity's ability to rationally master its own history. Not only scientists but also, in an important sense, science itself figures as the protagonist of both the *Mars* and *Science in the Capital* trilogies, but only when and if science is able to extricate itself from the demands of what Robinson calls the updated feudalism of the capitalist social order.

An overall assessment of Robinson's stature in the history of sf would no doubt be premature, although Burling (2009) brings the critical reception of Robinson's work to a new height. For the moment, the *Mars* trilogy unquestionably stands as the centerpiece of Robinson's career. In addition to its solid commercial success in the US, it is one of the bestselling sf works ever in Europe. The honors bestowed upon it by Robinson's fellow writers and sf fans in the form of Nebula and Hugo awards have been matched by the attention it has garnered from literary critics, as more than half of all the critical commentary devoted to Robinson's work focuses on it. In addition, the *Mars* narrative stands at the end of a long and rich tradition of fiction about the neighbor planet that puts his achievement into conversation with some of the most popular, influential, and distinguished work in the genre – including, for example, **H.G. Wells**'s *The War of the Worlds* (1898), Edgar Rice Burroughs's "Under the Moons of Mars" (1912, as *A Princess of Mars* (1917)), Alexander Bogdanov's *Red Star* (1908), Stanley Weinbaum's "A Martian Odyssey" (1934), and Ray Bradbury's *The Martian Chronicles* (1950). Nonetheless there is a substantial and growing body of commentary on the rest of his work, especially the *Three Californias*, which, unlike the *Mars* narrative or *Science in the Capital*, constitute a true, conceptually organized, and formally coherent trilogy. *The Years of Rice and Salt* and the short story "The Lucky Strike" (1984) establish Robinson as a major practitioner of the alternate history. Among the works not discussed in this article, Robinson's subtle experiment in deconstructing the construction of historical narrative in his early novel *Icehenge* (1984) is certain to draw more critical attention than it has so far. Finally, *Antarctica* and *Science in the Capital* represent a discreet episode in Robinson's career that is sure to spark a great deal more discussion in the coming years.

See also: **Isaac Asimov, Greg Bear, Alfred Bester, Leigh Brackett, Octavia Butler, Samuel R. Delany, Philip K. Dick, William Gibson, Robert A. Heinlein, Frank Herbert, L. Ron Hubbard, Ursula K. Le Guin, C.L. Moore, Joanna Russ, Neal Stephenson, Sheri S. Tepper, James Tiptree Jr, and Gene Wolfe**

Bibliography

Burling, W.J. (ed.) (2009) *Kim Stanley Robinson Maps the Unimaginable: critical essays*, Jefferson, NC: McFarland.

Foote, B. (1994) "A Conversation with Kim Stanley Robinson," *Science Fiction Studies*, 21(1): 35–50.

Jameson, F. (2000) "If I Find One Good City, I Will Spare the Man: realism and utopia in Kim Stanley Robinson's Mars trilogy," in P. Parrinder (ed.)

Learning from Other Worlds: estrangement, cognition and the politics of science fiction and utopia, Liverpool: Liverpool University Press.

Luckhurst, R. (2009) "The Politics of the Network: Kim Stanley Robinson's *Science in the Capital* trilogy," in W.J. Burling (ed.) *Kim Stanley Robinson Maps the Unimaginable: critical essays*, Jefferson, NC: McFarland.

Morton, O. (2002) *Mapping Mars: science, imagination, and the birth of a world*, New York: Picador.

Moylan, T. (2000) *Scraps of the Untainted Sky: science fiction, utopia, dystopia*, Boulder, CO: Westview.

Szeman, I. and Whiteman, M. (2004) "An Interview with Kim Stanley Robinson," *Science Fiction Studies*, 31(2): 177–88.

JOHN RIEDER

[EUGENE WESLEY] "GENE" RODDENBERRY (1921–91)

US screenwriter and producer, and creator of the television series *Star Trek* (1966–69).

Although eventually canceled for low ratings, *Star Trek* generated highly successful movies, spin-off television series, books, comic books, animated adventures, collectible items, fan fiction, and academic scholarship. Many *Star Trek*-inspired phrases and characters have entered the lexicon, including "Beam me up, Scotty" and "Klingon." There is even a Klingon dictionary and a Klingon Language Institute. Roddenberry's importance as the creator of *Star Trek* has been recognized in invited appearances at NASA and the Air and Space Museum, among other national institutions, a star on Hollywood Walk of Fame, and posthumous admission to the Science Fiction Hall of Fame. Dozens of nonfiction books analyze the importance of *Star Trek* to science, religion, politics, race, fans, feminism, and more.

A decorated Second World War veteran and former Los Angeles police officer, Roddenberry drew on his innate optimism about human nature and the future to develop *Star Trek*, which mirrors his personal beliefs and philosophy. Roddenberry's vision of outward exploration captivated millions, while his nickname, "Great Bird of the Galaxy," evoked a grandiose, almost mythological presence. Roddenberry's dedication to an anti-religious humanism that was inclusive and wide-ranging has its most famous manifestation in the original *Star Trek*'s opening voice-over: "Space … the Final Frontier. These are the voyages of the starship *Enterprise*. Its five-year mission: to explore strange new worlds, to seek out new life and new civilizations, to boldly go where no man has gone before." While the series did not always live up to its lofty aspirations, its fundamental premise – that humans can and could find a way to unite and explore space – was a welcome and appealing worldview.

Roddenberry created, wrote, and produced the original series; while his participation in the subsequent *Star Trek* films was not as all-encompassing and dominating, he was crucial to the maintenance of the *Star Trek* legacy in the decade between the original series and the first feature film, *Star Trek: The Motion Picture* (1979). A featured speaker at college campuses and fan conventions, Roddenberry fueled fans' passions for the show and provided his audiences with the hope that there would be other versions. *Star Trek: The Motion Picture*, a financial success, has been followed by ten other feature films to date, the most recent being *Star Trek* (Abrams 2009).

In 1987 the second *Star Trek* television series, conceived and controlled by Roddenberry, began a long and successful run. *Star Trek: The Next Generation* (1987–94) broke all records for syndicated series, and was followed by three other series: *Star Trek: Deep Space Nine* (1993–99), *Star Trek: Voyager* (1995–2001), and *Enterprise* (2001–5). The *Star Trek* brand was considered powerful enough to flourish outside of network television, as a direct-to-syndication series, and to lead a new television network, UPN. Although Roddenberry sold *Star Trek* to the network as "*Wagon Train* [a successful western television series] to the stars," the series actually did far more than repeat the premise of a quest narrative. In several episodes, *Star Trek* promoted racial and ethnic tolerance, using the tropes of sf trenchantly to comment on current-day events. In episodes like "Arena" (1967) and "Let That Be Your Last Battlefield" (1969), the original series used aliens to show the importance of tolerance and the stupidity of ethnocentrism and racism. In "Arena," based on a Fredric Brown short story, Captain Kirk must battle the captain of an alien ship to the death: omnipotent aliens have decreed that both species are violent and that only one will be permitted to live. The aliens have attacked a human outpost, and Kirk at first determines that they must be destroyed. Kirk defeats the alien captain but refuses to kill him, demonstrating the importance of accepting and understanding cultural difference. In "Let That Be Your Last Battlefield," two alien groups discovered by the *Enterprise* crew are locked in a self-destructive battle: one group consists of half-black, half-white humanoids; the other group is a mirror image, colored half-white, half-black. The aliens see their differences as fundamental and are locked in a futile and endless struggle. The crew comments on the ridiculous racism in these aliens' attitudes, and the destructive power of racism is demonstrated when they discover the home planet of these warring groups has been destroyed. Not only the plots but also the casting of the crew in the original series showed Roddenberry's determination to represent the future as more progressive than America in the 1960s.

The original *Star Trek* boasted a diverse crew. Roddenberry's initial pilot cast Majel Barrett (soon to become his second wife) as the second-in-command on the starship *Enterprise*. But according to Roddenberry, NBC Studio executives believed that this casting provided too prominent a role for a woman, and a new pilot was written in which Barrett assumed the more gender-subordinate role of Nurse Chapel. Roddenberry's vision of a Federation, postcapitalist and postnationalist, was reflected in the bridge crew, which, though captained by a white man, Kirk, had a half-Vulcan, Mr Spock, as second-in-command; Uhura, an African-American woman, in charge of communications; an Asian-American helmsman, Sulu; and Russian-descendant Chekov as navigator. The Chief Medical Officer was Leonard McCoy, a white man, as was the Chief Engineer, Montgomery Scott. While the three lead roles and command positions remained white men, Roddenberry's vision remained radical for its time.

Star Trek was notable also for the first television interracial kiss, between Kirk and Uhura. Although the kiss was involuntary (an alien made them do it), "Plato's Stepchildren" (1968) nevertheless created enough of a stir that this episode did not air on certain US television stations. In her autobiography, actor Nichelle Nicholls (Uhura) reports that *Star Trek* was considered important by the civil rights activist Dr Martin Luther King Jr. Unhappy with her limited role in the series, Nicholls had decided to quit *Star Trek* and changed her mind only after Dr King called and asked her to continue. He saw her as a positive African-American presence on television. The significance of her character was also borne out by Whoopi Goldberg, who requested a continuing role on the next series, *Star Trek: The Next Generation*, because Lieutenant Uhura had been so inspirational to her.

Star Trek: The Next Generation featured not only Goldberg as the wise and powerful alien Guinan, who frequently advised the captain (and ran the ship's bar, Ten Forward), but also other women in key roles, including Tasha Yar as Chief of Security, Dr Beverly Crusher as the Chief Medical Officer, and Deanna Troi as the Ship's Counselor. This shift in women's power and influence aboard the *Enterprise* was reflected in a significant change in the famous voice-over, from "to boldly go where no man has gone before" to "to boldly go where no *one* has gone before." While illness kept Roddenberry from a leadership role in the second season of the new series, he had by then defined a worldview that would continue to shape future *Star Trek* texts.

Star Trek influenced generations of sf writers and fans, and provided one of the first mainstream sf texts to have a strong, enduring, and indelible impact on Western culture. While Roddenberry's unwillingness to recognize writers' contributions to the *Star Trek* universe is well documented, he nevertheless helped create bridges between sf writers – such as Harlan Ellison, Robert Bloch, and Theodore Sturgeon – and television, providing them with another medium for their writing. In Roddenberry's relentless promotion of the *Star Trek oeuvre*, he demonstrated the power and importance of fans. First, he used them to save the original series from cancellation (for one additional year), and, second, he demonstrated to US entertainment corporations that providing fans with additional versions of texts they loved could be highly profitable.

In addition to his work as producer of *Star Trek* television series and films, Roddenberry also wrote the novelization of *Star Trek: The Motion Picture*, a bestselling book that was one of more than 500 *Star Trek* novels published, some of which were written by acclaimed sf writers such as Vonda McIntyre, Theodore Sturgeon, Susan Schwartz, **Greg Bear**, Barbara Hambly, and Pamela Sargent. Roddenberry was active in reviewing *Star Trek* manuscripts submitted to Pocket Books; he had the power to reject manuscripts, and he fought hard for the maintenance of consistency in the *Star Trek* universe.

Roddenberry's insistence on *Star Trek*'s coherence, and his presentation of himself as its author, also helped promote academic scholarship's embracing of the text. There are numerous scholarly books on *Star Trek*, on topics ranging from fan culture (Joseph-Witham 1996), to race (Bernadi 1998), and gender (Roberts 1999). *Star Trek*'s tremendous popularity spawned a complex discourse about sf and television, and encouraged university courses to discuss the show, which in turn opened the door for many other popular culture texts to receive scholarly attention.

Roddenberry also developed other sf pilots and one non-sf feature film (*Pretty Maids All in a Row* (Vadim 1971)), but none of these has had the impact of *Star Trek*. He made five television pilots after the original *Star Trek* was canceled. After his death in 1991, his estate authorized two long-running sf television series: *Earth: Final Conflict* (1997–2002) and *Andromeda* (2000–2005), both based on pilots Roddenberry had developed decades earlier.

This posthumous work suggests the extensive range of Roddenberry's influence not only on sf but also on American culture generally. In addition to other acknowledgments of his influence, it is worth noting that the first US space shuttle constructed by NASA for test flights (completed September 1976, flown February to November 1977) bore the name of *Enterprise*, the *Star Trek* ship's name, and that its naming ceremony was attended by Roddenberry and members of the cast of *Star Trek*. Roddenberry's persistent and relentless promotion of *Star Trek* made it a worldwide, recognizable text and, in so doing, helped make sf mainstream.

See also: **Gerry Anderson, Greg Bear, The Doctor, Nigel Kneale, and J. Michael Straczynski**

Bibliography

Alexander, D. (1994) *Star Trek Creator: the authorized biography of Gene Roddenberry*, New York: ROC.

Barad, J.A. (2000) *The Ethics of Star Trek*, New York: HarperCollins.

Bernadi, D. (1998) *Star Trek and History: race-ing towards a white future*, New Brunswick, NJ: Rutgers University Press.

Broderick, J.F. (2006) *The Literary Galaxy of Star Trek: an analysis of the references and themes in the television series and films*, Jefferson, NC: McFarland.

Chaires, R.H. (2003) *Star Trek Visions of Law and Justice*, Dallas, TX: Adios Press.

Engel, J. (1994) *Gene Roddenberry: the myth and the man behind Star Trek*, New York: Hyperion.

Fern, Y. (1994) *Gene Roddenberry: the last conversation*, Berkeley: University of California Press.

Hanley, R. (1997) *The Metaphysics of Star Trek*, New York: Basic Books.

Joseph-Witham, H.R. (1996) *Star Trek Fans and Costume Art*, Jackson: University Press of Mississippi.

Nichols, N. (1994) *Beyond Uhura: Star Trek and other memories*, New York: Putnam.

Roberts, R. (1999) *Sexual Generations: Star Trek: The Next Generation and gender*, Urbana: University of Illinois Press.

Sackett, S. (2002) *Inside Trek: my secret life with Star Trek creator Gene Roddenberry*, Tulsa, OK: Hawk Publishing.

ROBIN ROBERTS

JOANNA RUSS (1937–)

US writer, critic, and feminist.

The author of eight novels, two collections of short stories (with many uncollected), and five volumes of criticism and feminist social commentary, Russ remains perhaps best known – especially outside sf – for *The Female Man* (1975), a book taken up by feminists around the world.

If allowed only one word to describe the most salient feature of Russ's *oeuvre*, that word would be "wit," in the fullest, historical, sense of the term. A savage intelligence and a subtle understanding of the smallest nuances of mood and emotion make for narratives of innuendo, implication, and often jarring lacunae; yet these narratives also argue the most pertinent politics of the personal within carefully constructed sf possibilities.

Indeed, although Russ argues that "science fiction, like much medieval literature, is *didactic*" (Russ 1995: 5) and "addresses itself to the mind, not the eye" (Russ 1995: 9), her own work presents a much more complex aesthetic. From the very beginning, it exemplifies **Samuel R. Delany**'s comment that "[p]ut in opposition to 'style,' there is no such thing as 'content'" (Delany 1977: 33). Russ is simply one of the finest stylists in modern American literature, whose work just happens to occur in sf and fantasy. Yet, as Farah Mendlesohn argues: "In her writing, fiction and non-fiction, Russ makes clear that she would choose the rupture, the apparent ugliness of anger and rebellion over the poisonous beauty" (Mendlesohn 2009: 5).

Russ quickly became one of the finest writers and critics of sf, bringing her intelligence and clarity to bear on that perennial problem, its definition. Indeed, in "Speculations: the subjunctivity of science fiction" (1973), she supplements Delany's important distinctions among naturalistic fiction, sf, and fantasy in terms of each one's relation to the real world. However, she expands his commentary, suggesting that the reader has a lot to do with how each genre is perceived:

> In science fiction the relation between the "secondary universe" of fiction and the actual universe is both implicit and intermittently more or less perceivable. It consists not of what is on the page but in the relation between that and the reader's knowledge of actuality. It is always shifting.
>
> (Russ 1995: 21)

Russ's sense of sf as a fluctuating mode serves her very well in her own writing, where she plays with such shifts as well as across genre boundaries within a single narrative. Her wit and intelligence lead to a refusal ever to accept simple or singular answers, or even questions. This explains why even her most famous and apparently most straightforwardly feminist novel, *The Female Man*, uses each of its four space/time continuums not merely to interact with but also to interrogate the other three as well as the reader's. In the most complete and subtle critical appreciation of Russ's work, Jeanne Cortiel utilizes

Julia Kristeva's "three 'generations' in twentieth century feminism" (Cortiel 1999: 7) to identify "three major concerns which run through and structure Russ's fiction: (1) woman's agency, (2) female sexuality, and (3) the indeterminacy of both of these categories" (Cortiel 1999: 9). What relates Cortiel's critique to Russ's own critical theorizing is her demonstration of how Russ's fiction tends, from the beginning, to shift among categories, possibly foregrounding one but, through the play of indeterminacy, disrupting the expectations such categories set up.

From the very beginning, Russ took up genre (and gender) expectations and subverted and supplemented them. Her second story in the *Magazine of Fantasy and Science Fiction*, "My Dear Emily" (1962), an important sign of things to come, perfectly demonstrates her approach. It both undermines and adds a new kind of *frisson* to the traditional vampire story, while also just touching on the woman-to-woman relationships that will dominate her later fiction. Russ's reputation really began to grow with what became known as the Alyx stories, a series of sword-and-sorcery tales that cheerfully overturned almost all the expectations of the genre as its tough little thief finds ways to beat the man in one sticky situation after another. Alyx is such an intriguing figure that Russ carried her into her first sf novel, *Picnic on Paradise* (1968), a move prepared for in "The Barbarian" (1968), in which Alyx defeats a foolish mage whose workshop reveals that he is merely an abuser of a future technology somehow thrust back in time or across a multiverse divide. Although Alyx serves as a mentor to a younger woman in "The Adventuress" (1967; also published as "Bluestocking" (1976)), she is a singular figure and – despite a somewhat erotic motif in her relationship with the younger Edarra – represented as heterosexual. As an empowered individual, she manages to sneak past the patriarchal mores of her world, but she does not represent any kind of feminist rebellion against them.

This remains true of her actions in *Picnic on Paradise*, where the Trans-Temporal Military Authority transports her into the twenty-fourth century and sends her to guide a group of tourists across a snowy planet during a commercial war. Marxist theory plays a more important part than does feminism in these early works. *Picnic on Paradise* remains a striking novel: an amazingly complex and stylish narrative that offers a sharp satiric vision of a consumerist future, while providing moments of distilled emotional depth. Alyx, her history of battles and survival written on her body, stands out against the picnickers' technologically supplemented bodies. As she shepherds them across a natural landscape they have never had to face, things go wrong: she loses the one man she comes to love, kills another, and perhaps offers some kind of knowledge of life to the one younger woman. Alyx also decides to create a Trans-Temp more like her. The final Alyx story, "The Second Inquisition" (1970), reveals how problematic that might be. Set in the mid-1920s, and narrated by the younger woman possibly mentored by a strange woman from the future fighting her fellow Trans-Temp agents, it suggests a greater connection between women than the earlier Alyx stories, and thus sets the stage for Russ's later fiction.

Despite Russ's later feeling that she failed in her representation of homosexuality in *And Chaos Died* (1970), the novel is another tour de force, especially in the way the writing mimes the almost psychedelic aspects of extrasensory powers. It is also another savagely funny excoriation of consumer culture. With perhaps her most famous story, the Nebula-Award-winning "When It Changed" (1972), Russ shifted from Marxist to feminist theory as the basis of her fictional critique. Yet the most interesting thing about Whileaway, the all-female utopian world, is the way it signs gender roles as cultural performance. In *The Female Man*, Whileaway is a possible future that will not be superseded by the appearance of "men," as in the story, but it is also just a hope, in one of many possible parallel universes. The four Js of the novel – Whileaway's Janet; cyborg-assassin Jael, super-spy in the war between Manlanders and Womanlanders; meek Jeannine, sad spinster in a world without the Second World War where the Depression continues in 1969; and witty Joanna, implied (and real) author, who becomes a Female Man in the book's world – interact in a variety of ways once Janet appears in Joanna's world, disrupting, if only slightly, its cultural assumptions. Anger and resistance drive the narrative, especially with the assassinations of men in Jael's world. *The Female Man* plays across a bewildering cornucopia of genres and styles, asking only that its readers dance as fast as it does. Although some of its figures might appear to represent essentialist feminism, their interaction disturbs such a reading, and allows all three aspects of Russ's vision full play. It is the first of her novels to fully engage with lesbian sexuality and politics.

We Who Are About to ... (magazine serialization 1976, book form 1977) subverts one of sf's oldest conventions, the space liner crashed on a "virgin" planet. This is perhaps Russ's most stringent novel, articulating through its wise, witty, highly civilized, and unforgiving narrator the slow development of "the single natural death, five murders, and two suicides which comprise the actual plot" (Delany 1996: 148). Critics have recognized that Russ also takes on such hard sf tales as Tom Godwin's "The Cold Equations" (1954), but with a complexity missing from them that makes her narrative hum. That the murders must necessarily be of those men who insist on trying to set up a traditional patriarchal colony, in which the women have to bear as many children as possible, especially for the alpha male, signals how Russ's expanding material and feminist politics play across the narrative. A disembodied figure, the narrator is, as Tess Williams argues, "the only one who can truly understand the possibility and non-negotiability of a 'new world'" (Williams 2009: 332).

What Cortiel refers to as "Sappho and the Erotics of the Generation Gap" (Cortiel 1999: 174), along with a sadder and more profound comprehension of patriarchal authority, energize *The Two of Them* (1978). The binary narrative represents its protagonist's escape from conformity into the adventurous life of an Intergalactic Trans-Temporal Authority operative, supported by her male mentor/lover, and her insistence, during an operation on a faux-Muslim world, on rescuing a young girl who would be destroyed for attempting to be a poet (a male-only occupation). Although Irene assumes she has agency, she discovers that even the best of men, having only her interests at heart, will try to control her when her actions seem to go against "his" rules. The novel lacks both the anger and the utopian desire of *The Female Man*; in the end, after killing her mentor, Irene and young Zubeydeh become a single mother and child in contemporary America, struggling, but on their chosen terms. Irene's relationship to her protégé is erotic but only in an educational manner, as mentor to student, yet the novel reiterates core feminist values, insisting that only a woman-to-woman relationship can offer any possibilities for the two of them. Interestingly, the narrative demonstrates that Irene, who has many names, has also many subjectivities, thus undermining any gender essentialism.

Russ's later work definitely enters the field of indeterminacy, especially as regards the representation of gender theory and politics in general. The fix-up *Extra(ordinary) People* (1984) demonstrates a complexity of structure and style hard to match in the field, not least in the Nebula-Award-winning "Souls" (1982). In all five stories, presented as a study project for some future child, gender has become merely an instrument to be played upon, and the range of roles within supposed gender conventions nearly infinite. The stories range over time and place, from medieval northern Europe through a nineteenth-century voyage to North America to strange futures, but each one represents the act of narration (oral or written) as central to the meanings imagined within it. *Extra(ordinary) People* represents the apex of

Russ's achievement, a complex intellectual and emotional rendering of body and soul in fictional worlds of strangely hopeful possibility.

Joanna Russ has written some of the finest prose not just in sf but in late twentieth-century fiction as a whole. Her stories, novels, and criticism set a standard few other writers can match. Genre- and gender-bending, Russ's fiction remains as powerful today as when it first appeared. To read her work is to engage with a brilliant mind, a subtle emotional intelligence, a superb stylist, and a complexly political provocateur, whose writing exhilarates the reader lucky enough to encounter it.

See also: **Isaac Asimov, Greg Bear, Alfred Bester, Leigh Brackett, Octavia Butler, Samuel R. Delany, Philip K. Dick, William Gibson, Donna J. Haraway, Robert A. Heinlein, Frank Herbert, Nalo Hopkinson, L. Ron Hubbard, Gwyneth Jones, Ursula K. Le Guin, C. L. Moore, Kim Stanley Robinson, Mary Shelley, Sheri S. Tepper, James Tiptree Jr, and Gene Wolfe**

Bibliography

Cortiel, J. (1999) *Demand My Writing: Joanna Russ/feminism/science fiction*, Liverpool: Liverpool University Press.

Delany, S.R. (1977) *The Jewel-Hinged Jaw: notes on the language of science fiction*, Elizabethtown, NY: Dragon Press.

——(1996) *Longer Views: extended essays*, Hanover, NH: Wesleyan University Press.

Mendlesohn, F. (ed.) (2009) *On Joanna Russ*, Hanover, NH: Wesleyan University Press.

Russ, J. (1995) *To Write Like a Woman: essays in feminism and science fiction*, Bloomington: Indiana University Press.

Williams, T. (2009) "Castaway: carnival and sociobiological satire in *We Who Are About to …* ," in F. Mendlesohn (ed.) *On Joanna Russ*, Hanover, NH: Wesleyan University Press.

DOUGLAS BARBOUR

MARY [WOLLSTONECRAFT GODWIN] SHELLEY (1797–1851)

British novelist, travel writer, biographer, and editor of Percy Bysshe Shelley's poetry.

Mary Shelley was the daughter of two of the most prominent British eighteenth-century freethinkers and philosophers: Mary Wollstonecraft and William Godwin. Wollstonecraft – who died shortly after her daughter's birth – was the author of *Vindication of the Rights of Women* (1792), a key work in feminist thought; Godwin was a radical political philosopher and novelist. From 1814 Shelley was in love and traveling around Europe with the Romantic poet Percy Bysshe Shelley – only marrying him in 1816. After spending the summer of 1816 in the company of Percy, Lord Byron, his physician John Polidori, and others, she conceived of and wrote her first novel, *Frankenstein, or the modern Prometheus* (1818; a much-revised second edition appeared in 1831).

The novel's core story is probably well known enough not to need extensive summary. Scientist Victor Frankenstein constructs and animates an eight-foot-tall artificial man, but, obscurely horrified by what he has done, abandons his creation and temporarily loses his memory. The creature (who is never named) comes into the world a mental *tabula rasa* to be written upon by experience – as it transpires, mostly the experience of others' hostility toward his hideous appearance. He learns not only to speak but also, improbably enough, to read and write by unnoticed eavesdropping on a peasant family. Thereafter he becomes murderous, a consequence not only of others' hostility but also of reading John Milton's *Paradise Lost* (1667) and identifying with the outcast Satan. Lonely, he seeks out his maker, demanding that Frankenstein create a monstrous bride. Frankenstein agrees and makes a second creature, but, belatedly alarmed at the implication of his two creations breeding and populating the world with monsters, he tears it to pieces. In revenge, the creature kills Frankenstein's own wife. Frankenstein then pursues his creation to the Arctic wastes, where he dies. The novel ends with the creature still alive, but promising to kill himself. Summarized so baldly, this perhaps seems a little clumsily plotted (Shelley was 19 when she wrote it), and the novel itself does sometimes lapse into a rather gnashing crudeness. But it also possesses remarkable imaginative power, not least in the embodiment, in both heart-wracked scientist and appalling monster, of two enduringly iconic archetypes of the genre.

The opinion that sf starts with Mary Shelley's novel has had several adherents but is most closely associated with British sf author and critic Brian Aldiss. For Aldiss, *Frankenstein* encapsulates "the modern theme, touching not only on science but man's dual nature, whose inherited ape curiosity has brought him both success and misery" (Aldiss 1973: 26). Aldiss also wrote his own oblique fictional treatment of the same story, *Frankenstein Unbound* (1974), in which a modern man is propelled by "timeslips" back to the Romantic era, where he meets not only Mary Shelley but also Frankenstein and his creature – the latter proving an eloquent commentator upon man's capacity for creation and the radical instability it engenders.

Whether or not it spawned an entire genre, *Frankenstein* certainly exerted considerable influence upon nineteenth- and twentieth-century culture. Several critics (see in particular Baldick 1987) have traced the energetic afterlife of Shelley's monster, via Carlyle, Dickens, and Marx, into the twentieth century in cinematic, televisual cartoon, and general cultural form: James Whale's movie *Frankenstein* (1931) has been perhaps the most celebrated, or at least the best known, of these adaptations, although it – like almost all adaptations – simplifies and distorts the lineaments of Shelley's tale.

For example, one feature of the novel rarely included in adaptations is its epistolary frame: the book's primary narrator, Robert Walton, is a restless English gentleman who commands a ship bound for polar realms in order to "accomplish some great purpose" for which his soul yearns (Shelley 1992: 17). It is inside the Arctic Circle that he meets the scientist Victor Frankenstein, who, near death, tells his own story, a narrative embedded within Walton's. The monster's lengthy first-person narration is subsequently reported by Frankenstein, creating a satisfying "Russian doll" textual effect. Apart from anything else, this formal structure makes it plain that the book is in a key sense self-reflexive: it is as much about the making of *stories* as it is about the making of monsters.

There is also an important obliqueness, or unclarity, about key aspects of Shelley's novel that adaptations often elide. Frankenstein is deliberately uncommunicative about how he was able to "infuse a spark of being into the lifeless thing" (Shelley 1992: 38). This "spark" is not specifically identified with electricity in the first (1818) version of the novel, and reads instead as a general metaphor for vitality. The 1831 edition includes a preface in which Shelley suggests ways in which this conceptual gap might be filled in ("perhaps a corpse would be re-animated; galvanism had given token of such things: perhaps the component parts of a creature might be manufactured" (Shelley 1992: 8) without elaborating. Whale's 1931 film makes clear that the creature is reanimated with electricity, and replaces what is in Shelley's novel an understated and even dour creation scene with a climactic electrical storm in which a monster – not "manufactured" like a robot but assembled, zombie-like, from dead body parts – is brought to juddering life.

In part, this speaks to the way the novel straddles pre-scientific and scientific discourses, marking the border at which modern science comes to cultural dominance. Frankenstein, in order to address his epistemological ambitions ("the world was to me a secret, which I desired to divine" (Shelley 1992: 38)), turns first of all to the magical writing of Renaissance alchemists Paracelsus and Cornelius Agrippa. University encourages him to abandon these figures in favor of post-Newtonian science: "Chemistry," he is told, "is that branch of natural philosophy in which the greatest improvements have been and may be made" (Shelley 1992: 41). The book mediates precisely the quasi-magical idiom we nowadays think of as fantasy (or horror) and the idiom of a recognizably modern conception of science. It is in this sense, perhaps, rather than in its Gothicism, that *Frankenstein* can be described as the first sf novel.

This mediation brings out one crucial aspect of the novel. Magic and necromancy have tended to be represented negatively in Western culture, as un-Christian and dangerous. Science, on the other hand, partakes of Enlightenment discourses of progress and social amelioration. Shelley's novel applies the moral schema of the first to the practice of the second, emphasizing the *consequences* of scientific activity rather than its genesis. This explains her vagueness about the scientific specifics of the creature's making. Frankenstein's work in fact entails a form of transcendental symbolic exchange. Bringing the creature from death to life leads directly, in the novel, to various key characters being thrust *from* life *to* death. This in turn establishes what amounts to an ethical cipher, one very often present in subsequent sf: that scientific or technological novelty inaugurated with the best of intentions entails unintended consequences, usually catastrophic. The great many sf texts that delineate evil flowing from intended scientific or rational good can claim descent from *Frankenstein*.

Though famous for *Frankenstein*, Shelley produced many other fictional and nonfictional works. She wrote historical romances based on actual figures – *Valperga* (1823) is set in the fourteenth century and *Perkin Warbeck* (1830) concerns the famous sixteenth-century pretender to the throne. She also wrote fictionalized autobiographies: *Mathilda* (written 1820 though not published until 1959) based on work by her mother, and *Lodore* (1835) and *Falkner* (1837), which are essentially retellings of Shelley's own life and acquaintances. It is as an example of this sort of writing, strange as it might seem, that Shelley's *The Last Man* (1826) is best considered. Although some critics regard this future-set novel as straightforwardly science-fictional, it is in fact as concerned with its fictional portrayals of Byron and Percy Shelley as with its apocalyptic narrative of plague ravaging a twenty-first-century world that, apart from the institution of Republican government, seems very little changed from the 1820s. Much of the novel depicts the interactions of Lord Raymond (a cipher for Byron), the Earl of Windsor (Percy Shelley), and the last man, Lionel Verney, a cross-gender version of Shelley herself. Plague functions as a metaphor for the corruption of this interpersonal (or political) connectivity, and one reason it works less well today as fiction than does *Frankenstein* is that this nexus of particular celebrity means less to us.

Certainly Shelley's contemporary appeal as a writer depended in large part upon her intimate association with these figures. A couplet by Leigh Hunt positions her, rather condescendingly, as wholly defined by her parents, her husband, and her monster: "And Shelley, four-famed – for her parents, her lord / And the poor lone impossible monster abhorred" ("Blue Stocking Revels" (1837); quoted in Grylls 1938: 211). Nor is this perspective entirely impertinent: *Frankenstein* is, among other things, a novel about being part of a family, about the generation of life and the toll taken by familial pressures. American critics Sandra Gilbert and Susan Gubar read Shelley as "this orphaned literary heiress" for whom "highly charged connections between femaleness and literariness must have been established early," particularly "in relation to the controversial figure of her dead mother" (Gilbert and Gubar 1979: 222). In what proved an influential early feminist reading of the novel, this biographical provenance informed Gilbert and Gubar's account of *Frankenstein* as a female appropriation of previously masculine myths of authorship and creation.

Since the 1970s, *Frankenstein* has been the subject of many perceptive feminist readings, far too many to cover here. Indeed, according to Diane Long Hoeveler, this novel "has figured more importantly in the development of feminist literary theory than perhaps any other novel, with the possible exception of Charlotte Brontë's *Jane Eyre*" (Hoeveler 2003: 45). The powerfully imaginative ways the novel deconstructs traditional understandings of "masculinity" and "femininity" (its potent new myth of the man who gives "birth" to life, and its effective critique of masculinist structures of society, science, and literature) speak both to the great changes in conceptions of femaleness that were starting to gain momentum in Shelley's day, and also to the potential of nonrealist modes of art such as sf to apprehend those changes. Debra Benita Shaw's feminist study describes sf as a whole as *The Frankenstein Inheritance* (Shaw 2000).

This success has its own limitations. To an extent Shelley's own career has been overwritten by the impact of *Frankenstein*. It could be argued that the novel has been, in effect, hijacked by its heritage; we tend to read it nowadays *as an sf novel* (which is to say, in ways conditioned by the habits of reading twentieth-century sf) rather than reading it as it was originally read and reviewed, as a novel of philosophical speculation – as, in other words, a novel in the tradition of Voltaire's *Candide* (1759), Mary Wollstonecraft's *Mary* (1788), or Godwin's *Caleb Williams* (1794). To read the book this way is to concentrate upon the first section as a meditation on the proper boundaries of human knowledge, and to read the creature's first-person narrative as a bold attempt to dramatize John Locke's theory of mind.

See also: **J.G. Ballard, Iain M. Banks, Leigh Brackett, Octavia Butler, Karel Čapek, Arthur C. Clarke, The Doctor, Nalo Hopkinson, Gwyneth Jones, Fritz Lang, Ursula K. Le Guin, China Miéville, Michael Moorcock, C.L. Moore, Joanna Russ, Olaf Stapledon, Sheri S. Tepper, James Tiptree Jr, Jules Verne, and H.G. Wells**

Bibliography

Aldiss, B. (1973) *Billion Year Spree: the history of science fiction*, Garden City, NY: Doubleday.

Baldick, C. (1987) *In Frankenstein's Shadow: myth, monstrosity and nineteenth-century writing*, Oxford: Clarendon.

Gilbert, S.M. and Gubar, S. (1979) *The Madwoman in the Attic*, New Haven, CT: Yale University Press.

Grylls, R.G. (1938) *Mary Shelley: a biography*, Oxford: Oxford University Press.

Hoeveler, D.L. (2003) "Frankenstein, Feminism and Literary Theory," in E.M. Schor (ed.) *The Cambridge Companion to Mary Shelley*, Cambridge: Cambridge University Press.

Shaw, D.B. (2000) *Women, Science and Fiction: the Frankenstein inheritance*, London: Palgrave.

Shelley, M. (1992) *Frankenstein, or the modern Prometheus*, ed. M. Hindle [1818], London: Penguin.

ADAM ROBERTS

STEVEN [ALLAN] SPIELBERG (1947–)

US director, producer, executive producer, and studio executive.

Following an apprenticeship at Universal TV, which included directing one segment of the pilot for Rod Serling's *Night Gallery* (1970–73), a Philip Wylie-scripted episode of *The Name of the Game* (1968–71) called "LA 2017" (1971) about a postapocalyptic corporate-run dystopia, and three television movies, Steven Spielberg began making cinematic features with *Sugarland Express* (1974) and *Jaws* (1975). The latter is often credited with creating the summer blockbuster, thus transforming Hollywood promotion, distribution, and exhibition strategies, and blamed for the death of the more experimental "Hollywood Renaissance," typically dated from 1968 until *Jaws*. Spielberg has directed 22 further films: half a dozen of them are in the top 25 all-time box-office successes, five are on the American Film Institute's 100 best films list, and eight are sf. His more than 100 producer/executive producer credits since 1978 include many sf or fantasy projects. He has worked in television drama (e.g., *Amazing Stories* (1985–87), *SeaQuest DSV* (1993–96), *Taken* (2002)), animation, documentary, and video games. In 1994 he co-founded Dreamworks SKG, Hollywood's first new studio in 70 years. Arguably the most influential figure in contemporary cinema, he has – along with friend and occasional collaborator **George Lucas** – also been charged with the infantilization of mainstream American film.

Premiering six months after Lucas's *Star Wars: Episode IV – A New Hope* (1977), *Close Encounters of the Third Kind* (1977) confirmed the box-office potential of sf for Hollywood at the end of a financially turbulent decade. Moreover, its narrative seems to model the transformation of American filmmaking it exemplifies. Beginning with Roy Neary and his family, it represents the cluttered, ramshackle lower middle-class lives of the post-counterculture baby boomers in a serio-comic tone, simultaneously recalling and distancing itself from the Hollywood Renaissance's attempts at social realism, even as its studied shot compositions signal a tight control over any improvisation. This sense of presentation, rather than exploration or interrogation, develops into the spectacular shots of ufological wonders with which the film concludes. The second part of the film is essentially a road movie, as Neary abandons his family and makes his way to Devil's Tower to rendezvous with the alien mother ship. A typical Spielberg child-man protagonist, he is caught between the adult world he inhabits and his deep yearning for childhood, magic, and wonder. His flight from responsibility is rewarded: while cast and audience alike stare, dazzled, at out-of-this-world technologies and overwhelming patterns of light, Neary gets to leave the world – and his suburban discontents – behind. In psychoanalytic terms, Neary is disturbed by his wife, who is both sexual *and* maternal, and finds a safe haven in the regressive return to the maternal breast or womb of the mother ship. The film thus demonstrates a utopian yearning it is incapable of coherently articulating and about which it is ultimately ambivalent.

The opprobrium *Close Encounters* attracted from many sf critics and fans – perhaps because it achieved a "sensawunda" with consummate technical skill but through images and discourses of ufology, long anathema to the sf community – was matched by that which greeted *E.T.: The Extra-Terrestrial* (1982), in which a cute, stranded alien befriends a boy, who aids its return home. Directly after a conversation concerning his absent father, Elliott first encounters E.T. Shot side-on to the backyard, this wish-fulfillment fantasy is staged as if Elliott is sitting in a cinema, with the alien emerging from a doorway as if from a screen. Initially, E.T. imitates Elliott, but the childlike alien is also one of the film's father-figures. The government is portrayed as a threatening father – through Keys, who leads the hunt for the alien, and his team of environment-suited home invaders, who make over the domestic space into a sterile, technological one – and science, especially militarized/bureaucratized science, is seen as a threat to wonder. But once Keys speaks for himself, revealing his own sense of wonder, it turns out that there might be a good father in charge after all.

Ultimately, *E.T.* succeeds in unveiling the extent to which the sf imagination is not driven by science or rationality, but by unconscious psychic mechanisms – that the alien is a screen onto which we project anxieties and desires. Furthermore, when Elliott uses his toys to educate E.T., Spielberg challenges another of the sf community's sacred cows, demonstrating not only that sf is culturally ubiquitous rather than a specialist literary taste, but also, through the prominence afforded a *Buck Rogers* comic strip, that this has always been the case.

Despite production credits on *The Twilight Zone: The Movie* (Landis, Spielberg, Dante, Miller 1983), the *Back to the Future* trilogy (Zemeckis 1985–90), *Innerspace* (Dante 1987), **batteries not included* (Robbins 1987), and *Arachnophobia* (Marshall 1990), Spielberg did not direct sf again for over a decade. *Jurassic Park* (1993), based on Michael Crichton's 1990 novel about a theme park stocked with genetically engineered dinosaurs, showcased Spielberg's ongoing commitment to cutting-edge technologies (here, computer-generated imagery) and his customary technical skill (long, fluid takes; composition in depth with multiple planes of action; and inventive choices, such as tracking an upward-tilted camera under a fence so as to move the action from one side to the other). These elements, though, are accompanied by a growing sense of predictability. Although the film dabbles with chaos theory, evoking the sensitive dependence on initial conditions within complex systems, it is clear, once its narrative parameters are established, what will go wrong and how things will be resolved. This sense of overwhelming familiarity – which is also part of Spielberg's appeal – extends to reiterations of his colonial imagination (although his depiction of people of color is less obviously racist than in the *Indiana Jones* films (1981–2008)), narrow vision of gender (the female scientist must be a botanist and yearn for marriage and children; her male partner must be educated into becoming – and wanting to become – a father, thus finding true fulfillment), and obsession with the centrality of parent–child (especially father–son) relationships. Like all of his work, *Jurassic Park* is replete with allusions to other films – allusions which never seem to construct a critical relationship between texts but merely offer the pleasure of recognition. This self-reflexivity without self-reflection extends to the *mise-en-scène*: the theme park's restaurant/gift-shop area is self-consciously filled with Jurassic Park merchandising, just as real-world stores would become packed with *Jurassic Park* merchandising. Such amusing if shallow ironies continue in the sequel, *The Lost World: Jurassic Park* (1997), in which an environmentally friendly, genial capitalist patriarch (allied with a spunky kid, an independent woman, and a child-man growing up to become a father) fights mendacious, profit-focused, corporate capitalists over the surviving dinosaurs.

A.I.: Artificial Intelligence (2001), adapted from Brian Aldiss's "Super-Toys Last All Summer Long" (1969) with input from Ian Watson (and, uncredited, Bob Shaw and **Arthur C. Clarke**), was in development by **Stanley Kubrick** throughout the 1980s and 1990s. After his death, the project passed on to Spielberg. Many saw this tale of a robot boy, David, programmed to love his owner as a cloyingly sentimental paean to mother–son relationships. However, it continually undercuts the narrative through scenes of genuinely creepy Oedipal intensity.

In his more recent films, Spielberg's child-men are not so much encouraged to grow up as to become blandly middle class. The home into which David is adopted is pristine. Monica, his "mommy," lives a life without options: her only social role and connections are as her husband's wife, and she is unable either to raise or to grieve for her terminally ill son, who is in suspended animation awaiting a cure. As her relationship with David develops, one begins to sense the relentless and oppressive nature of demands for unconditional love (even if she does not). An aura of obsession and desperation engulfs the nuclear family, and David's insistence on his individual subjectivity suggests that all such claims might be nothing more than childish tantrums. Spielberg's films are often deeply contradictory, but, by repeatedly staging apparently happy endings while underscoring the extent to which they are illusory, *A.I.* comes close to transforming those contradictions into genuine ambiguities.

Minority Report (2002), adapted from **Philip K. Dick**'s "The Minority Report" (1956), is similarly obsessed with issues of control. John Anderton, accused by the Pre-Crime Unit he heads of a murder he has not yet committed, goes on the run to prove his innocence. In doing so, this boy-man, stalled by guilt feelings over the abduction-murder of his son, uncovers a conspiracy, undermines the whole Pre-Crime system, and oversees the death of his corrupt father-figure. Anderton is thus saved from guilt and grief, and he is able to return to his middle-class life, tidying up his apartment and reuniting with (and impregnating) his estranged wife. In an impressive opening sequence, complex screen technologies enable Anderton to manipulate and orchestrate precognitive image fragments and other data so as to locate and prevent an imminent murder. The fearful future can thus be brought under control, removed from the uncertainties of history, and turned into a textualized present that can be shuffled, reshuffled, and contained. This sequence suggests Spielberg's growing self-awareness of his compulsive Oedipal repetitions, as does the inordinately neat "happy ending" which ties up all the loose ends (but which could all be a fantasy going on in Anderton's head after he is put into suspended animation as punishment for murders he did not commit).

War of the Worlds (2005), adapted from **H.G. Wells**'s 1898 novel, is set in a distinctly post-9/11 world. Blue-collar Ray Ferrier flees the alien invasion with his estranged children, trying to reach his middle-class ex-wife and her family. Escalating disaster pursues him: in early scenes a V8 engine on which he is working sits on his kitchen table; later, after a terrifying night hiding in his ex-wife's basement, he finds the engine of a crashed passenger jet in the front room. The alien invasion is lent an irreal spectrality by the saturated, glowing cinematography of Janusz Kaminski (Spielberg's preferred Director of Photography since *Schindler's List* (1993)) and by the design of the CGI. The sequence in which Ray emerges from a farmhouse basement into a dark and blood-saturated world captures something of Wells's Gothicism, while the film's proliferating contradictions, which have been criticized at length, arguably capture the overheated imagination of the so-called War on Terror.

Indiana Jones and the Kingdom of the Crystal Skull (2008), Spielberg's most recent sf film, was a global box-office hit, unremarkable except for the degree and extent of its familiarity. Harrison Ford returned as the protagonist who secured Spielberg's popularity in the 1980s, along with the racism and sexism for which the franchise has always been criticized (indigenous peoples are aggressive subhumans; women should become wives and mothers rather than aspire to knowledge). A succession of set-pieces, it exemplifies what in some ways has been most influential about Spielberg's work on the textual level: that is, a reorganization of the relationships among character, narrative, and spectacle, subordinating everything to the last. Moreover, by adding the Roswell incident and aliens from another dimension to the franchise's generic patchwork, Spielberg emphasizes once more that sf is not a pristine genre, separate from others, but part of a vast cultural imaginary upon which we all can draw.

See also: **J.G. Ballard, David Cronenberg, Philip K. Dick, Stanley Kubrick, Fritz Lang, George Lucas, and Oshii Mamoru**

Bibliography

Balides, C. (2000) "Jurassic Post-Fordism: tall tales of economics in the theme park," *Screen*, 41(2): 139–60.

Buckland, W. (1999) "Between Science Fact and Science Fiction: Spielberg's digital dinosaurs, possible worlds, and the new aesthetic realism," *Screen*, 40 (2): 177–92.

Gordon, A.M. (2008) *Empire of Dreams: the science fiction and fantasy films of Steven Spielberg*, Lanham, MD: Rowman & Littlefield.

Jess-Cooke, C. (2006) "Virtualizing the Real: sequelization and secondary memory in Steven Spielberg's *Artificial Intelligence: A.I.*," *Screen*, 47(3): 347–65.

McBride, J. (1997) *Steven Spielberg: a biography*, New York: Simon & Schuster.

Morris, N. (2007) *The Cinema of Steven Spielberg: empire of light*, London: Wallflower.

Sobchack, V. (1986) "Child/Father/Alien: patriarchal crisis and generic exchange," *Camera Obscura*, 15: 7–34.

——(2008) "Love Machines: boy toys, toy boys and the oxymorons of *A.I.: Artificial Intelligence*," *Science Fiction Film and Television*, 1(1): 1–13.

MARK BOULD

[WILLIAM] OLAF STAPLEDON (1886–1950)

British writer, philosopher, and social activist.

Olaf Stapledon's novels, especially *Last and First Men* (1930) and *Star Maker* (1937), are widely cited as influences by **Arthur C. Clarke**, Brian Aldiss, and Doris Lessing. Through these, and later writers such as Gregory Benford and Stephen Baxter, Stapledon's sense of epic grandeur and ethical conflict have influenced several generations of sf authors.

Born into a Liverpool shipping family, Stapledon was educated at Abbotsholme School and Balliol College, Oxford, before working in the Port Said office of the family business. A pacifist, he served during the First World War in the Ambulance Unit of the Society of Friends, experience he drew upon in *Last Men in London* (1932). He went on to become a social reformer and lecturer for the Workers' Educational Association and, extramurally, for the University of Liverpool, where he gained a Ph.D. in Philosophy in 1925. During the 1930s, influenced by the ideas of **H.G. Wells**, he campaigned for disarmament and World Government.

Last and First Men is an ambitious future-history of the human race, rising and falling through 18 separate species to end up upon Neptune, threatened with destruction by the expansion of the sun, and disseminating spores into the universe in the hope of eventual survival upon some hospitable world. The novel's opening – via the voice of a member of the 18th species of humanity telepathically influencing the mind of an obscure English academic – makes clear that this is no utopia, hardly even a novel, but "myth creation": an exploration of the spiritual and pragmatic poles of thought and the conflict between materialist science and transcendent religion, exemplified by Jesus and Socrates. It contains little dialogue and fewer named individuals. Humanity and the cosmos are the main "characters," and the rather chilly tone of its grandeur is perhaps the reason why Stapledon is not as widely read as he should be.

The novel is strongly influenced by Wells and biologist J.B.S. Haldane, whose visions of a future humanity colonizing Venus in his essay "The Last Judgement" (1927) were, like Wells's Martian invaders in *The War of the Worlds* (1898), adopted and expanded. Stapledon wrote to Wells, following the publication of *Last and First Men*, that he had read comparatively few scientific romances, although he told an interviewer in 1937 that he had read Wells, **Jules Verne** and Edgar Rice Burroughs. Wells responded enthusiastically to Stapledon – who acknowledged his debt to Wells's political writing – and Wells produced his own massive future-history in *The Shape of Things to Come* (1933).

Last and First Men posits that we are merely the first species of humanity, our history ended by nuclear war. The Second Men and their successors are weakened after a series of invasion attempts by semi-gaseous and telepathic Martians. Stapledon neatly revisits the moral territory of Wells's *The War of the Worlds* (1898), suggesting that the Martians, however alien, have their own right to survival. This dilemma recurs when the Fifth Men, threatened by the fall of the moon, escape to Venus and set about terraforming it and physically transforming themselves while exterminating the native species.

Stapledon's immediate future is perhaps interesting mainly as an example of how political "predictions" are rapidly overtaken by events (in this case the rise of Hitlerian fascism during the 1930s), although his twenty-first century has some fascinating forebodings of globalization and rivalry between the USA and China. The major interest of *Last and First Men* is in Stapledon's epic command of carefully charted timescales, conceived on an evolutionary scale. For example, the sojourn of the Fifth Men and their successors on Venus lasts longer than humanity's entire career on Earth. By the fourth timechart, we, the First Men, have been rendered invisible between the Rise of the Mammals and the Second Men.

Finally, the Eighteenth or Last Men reclaim the past through telepathic contact with previous civilizations, but this becomes endangered by Neptune's own imminent destruction. In the sequel, *Last Men in London*, Stapledon attaches this vision to a narrower compass, focusing on his future-narrator's relationship to the consciousness of his "host," Paul, who grows up in the early years of the twentieth century. Here, Stapledon's Wellsian concern with political and sexual reform comes to the fore, but the novel's fusion of cosmic and individual perspectives makes it one of his more difficult works.

Star Maker returns to the unalloyed cosmic perspective. Upon Caldy Hill on the Wirral (overlooking the house where Stapledon and his family lived), the narrator's vision of the universe evolving toward what might be called godhood evokes Wells's "Under the Knife" (1896) and W.H. Hodgson's *The House on the Borderland* (1908), but presents us with such purely sf concepts as the Dyson sphere (rings of artificial worlds circling a central star which physicist Freeman Dyson attributed to his reading of *Star Maker*) and the "sex radio" (stimulating brain centers with broadcast transmissions of sexual congress). Patrick A. McCarthy calls the book "no ordinary novel but a cosmic poem" (McCarthy 2004: 26), which he likens to Dante's *Divine Comedy* (c. 1307–21) in its cosmological and metaphysical speculations. Stapledon's vision of a universe full of life-forms striving to understand their place in the cosmic dance, and the series of alternative or parallel universes dependent upon altogether *other* physical laws, makes this Stapledon's masterpiece.

Odd John (1935), with its tragic mutant superman, and *Sirius: a fantasy of love and discord* (1944), about a dog with enhanced intelligence, are lesser only by comparison. *Odd John* explores the "superman" in the tradition of J.D. Beresford's *The Hampdenshire Wonder* (1911) and, of course, the Nietzschean "Übermensch." *Last Men in London* contains a section in which what we would now call mutants, with superhuman mental powers, seem to prefigure superior forms of humanity. In *Odd John*, Stapledon explored this speculation – which by then was becoming tainted with fascist racial ideologies – more fully. Protagonist John Wainwright is described by an admiring and subservient narrator sometimes addressed as "Fido." John's amorality, sexual predation, and contempt for the normal human race make for a difficult read. While we feel for his loneliness as he searches for his peers, the bleak Darwinian rivalry between "superior race" and John's "inferiors" (that is to say, *us*), which John Wyndham was to articulate in *The Midwich Cuckoos* (1957), presents us with a sinister moral dilemma. John and his fellow "supernormals" attempt to establish a utopian community on a remote island; an alliance of the Great Powers moves against them, to be met with collective suicide.

Sirius explores similar issues by imagining a dog gifted with a superhuman mind, raised by a scientist, Trelone, with his daughter Plaxy. The suggestion of sexual relations between Sirius and Plaxy worried critics and readers, even though cuts were made to the original text. The narrator Robert bears a similar relationship to Sirius as "Fido" did to "Odd John," and the sexual rivalry between them for Plaxy's affections adds tension to the novel. The end is somber and bleak; Sirius is the only one of his kind. While Trelone has created other "superdogs," even the most intelligent of them are far below Sirius's capacities, and the conflict within the dog between his "evolved" abilities and his canine nature is poignant.

Since **Mary Shelley**'s *Frankenstein, or the modern Prometheus* (1818) and Wells's *The Island of Doctor Moreau* (1896), the sf novel has asked what it is to be human by speculating about "created" or "artificial" humanity. Within this tradition, *Sirius* foregrounds Stapledon's political and ethical concerns. Although Stapledon seemed to see himself as a philosopher rather than a novelist, these latter two books are both closer to the conventional "novel" form and more focused upon questions of morality and meaning. Looking backward to the "Superman" novels, *Odd John* and *Sirius*, we may argue that they were specifically concerned with a question at the heart of Wells's uneasy treatment of eugenics, which was confidently if appallingly answered by Hitler's Germany: if a species, race, or group *really was* superior to another, is it justified in replacing its inferiors, by force, if necessary? Or, to put it in a way which was personal to Stapledon as a communist sympathizer and supporter of the 1917 Russian Revolution, if a revolutionary party *really was* the vanguard of a new and better order, could the mistakes and crimes committed in its journey to that order be justified? At the heart of these questions, of course, is the difficulty in proving "*really was*."

Stapledon's work is also driven by two other, broader questions: first, the nature of the relationship between individuals and the Darwinian sweep of evolution, and, second, the struggle against dismissing the suffering of individuals in the ideological embrace of the cosmic whole. Speaking as if from the viewpoint of the universal mind at the end of this process, Stapledon asks if it matters: can we write off the suffering of individuals if the final result is going to be a glorious "enhanced lucidity of the cosmical spirit itself?" (Stapledon 1937b: 324). The forthcoming struggle against a fascism which would destroy many of the values Stapledon thought had to be defended led him to wonder: "How to do this, yet preserve the mind's integrity, never to let the struggle destroy in one's own heart what one tried to serve in the world, the spirit's integrity" (Stapledon 1937b: 33).

The "mutant" stories tackle the question from a more "personal" angle: the position of the individual in the face of a society which had its own right to exist, but which was inferior to the "evolved" individual. This Darwinian dilemma is intrinsic to much British sf of the 1950s, not just Wyndham's *The Midwich Cuckoos* but also Clarke's *Childhood's End* (1953) and Theodore Sturgeon's *More Than Human* (1953). Stapledon, however, was more overtly political than Wyndham, Clarke, or Sturgeon, and the strength of his fiction lies in the way it harnesses a powerful imagination with social and political engagement. He influenced his successors through his use of the future as a location for vast and engaging possibilities rather than as a political or philosophical thinker. Of later writers of sf, it is perhaps Lessing rather than Stapledon's more "obvious" disciples who, in her *Canopus in Argos* sequence, most fully engaged with the way he brought morality, religion, and ethics, as well as scientific speculation, into his fiction.

While later fiction such as *Darkness and the Light* (1942), *Old Man in New World* (1944), *Death into Life* (1946), and especially *The Flames: a fantasy* (1947) – which speculates about life in the interior of stars like the sun – is of interest, Stapledon's masterpieces remain *Last and First Men*, *Star Maker*, *Odd John*, and *Sirius*. Here, he manages to encapsulate "local" anxieties about the tensions between collective and individual ethics which engaged the minds of so many artists of the 1930s and 1940s, while foregrounding the broader position of humanity in a cosmos which we barely understand. His position as a "mentor" for sf writers like Clarke, Aldiss, and Lessing is understood in scholarship. However, it may be argued that his depiction of the countercurrents of 1930s hopes and fears about the future has been overlooked among the difficulties of form and content which casual readers may find in his works.

See also: **J.G. Ballard, Iain M. Banks, Karel Čapek, Arthur C. Clarke, Gwyneth Jones, Stanisław Lem, China Miéville, Michael Moorcock, Alan Moore, Mary Shelley, and H.G. Wells**

Bibliography

Crossley, R. (1994) *Olaf Stapledon: speaking for the future*, Liverpool: Liverpool University Press.

Fiedler, L.A. (1983) *Olaf Stapledon: a man divided*, Oxford: Oxford University Press.

Haldane, J.B.S. (1927) "The Last Judgment," in *Possible Worlds and other essays*, London: Chatto & Windus.

Huntington, J. (1982) "Remembrance of Things to Come: narrative technique in *Last and First Men*," *Science Fiction Studies*, 9(3): 257–64.

Lem, S. (1986) "On Stapledon's *Last and First Men*," *Science Fiction Studies*, 13 (3): 272–91.

McCarthy, P.A. (1984) "*Last and First Men* as Miltonic Epic," *Science Fiction Studies*, 11(3): 244–53.

——(2004) "The Genesis of Star Maker," *Science Fiction Studies*, 31(1): 25–42.

McCarthy, P.A., Elkins, C. and Greenberg, M.H. (1989) *The Legacy of Olaf Stapledon*, Westport, CT: Greenwood Press.

Stapledon, O. (1937a) "Interview," *Scientifiction*, June: 8–10.

——(1937b) *Star Maker*, London: Methuen.

ANDY SAWYER

NEAL [TOWN] STEPHENSON (1959–)

US author.

Neal Stephenson published 11 novels between 1984 and 2008, most of which are explicitly sf or contain sf elements. His awards include the *Locus* Award for *Cryptonomicon* (1999) and the **Arthur C. Clarke** Award for *Quicksilver* (2003). With the exception of a short nonfiction book, *In the Beginning … Was the Command Line* (1998), Stephenson has published three distinct kinds of fiction: thrillers, sf, and historical slipstream.

None of the four thrillers – *The Big U* (1984) and *Zodiac* (1988) and the coauthored *Interface* (1994) and *The Cobweb* (1996) – significantly helped Stephenson's reputation. Each contains elements of sf, and the last three fit comfortably into the technothriller model, mass-market books driven by technological innovations amid intrigue, conspiracy, and tense action. In the earlier titles, Stephenson was searching for his voice, while the latter two, co-written with his historian uncle, George Jewsbury, and published under the pseudonym Stephen Bury (and later reissued as collaborations between Stephenson and Jewsbury's own pseudonym, J. Frederick George), were designed to be bestsellers that might fund the writing of the more difficult, literary novels he anticipated would not support a young writer's family. But between them, Stephenson produced his breakout success in the post-cyberpunk satire *Snow Crash* (1992), which attracted large audiences and precipitated an enormous critical and popular response, as did *The Diamond Age: or, a young lady's illustrated primer* (1995). Stephenson's reputation in sf rests primarily on these two novels.

Both show the imprint of 1980s cyberpunk and in some sense offer a corrective revision, understanding technology in far more optimistic and witty terms. Both also reveal an acute interest in intellectual history and innovations in information technologies, motifs that characterize everything Stephenson has done. Both seemingly support the posthuman transformation of *Homo sapiens sapiens*. *Snow Crash* opens with a wildly comic portrait of a near-future America reduced to burbclaves and franchulates – an atomized, Balkanized culture without any coherent core, except perhaps unconstrained selfishness, from the trivial (to cheat a pizza company from the 30-minute delivery guarantee) to the profound (to hack the brainstem and program all humanity to slavish obedience). One hero is Hiro Protagonist, an unemployed hacker; the other is Y.T. (who reappears in a minor role in *The Diamond Age* as Miss Matheson), an urban courier. Their opponent, who desires "a perfect monopoly" over *ideas*, is the "Lord of Bandwidth" (Stephenson 1992: 106) L. Bob Rife, a billionaire media mogul seeking the mythic speech of ancient Sumeria to reprogram the informational elites, that 10 per cent of humanity who cannot be seduced and subjected by the more common opiates of religion and popular entertainment. Hiro and Y.T. enter into an unlikely coalition with the Mafia and others to combat and finally defeat Rife's neurolinguistic virus.

A sort of *future steampunk* – a historically hybrid sf that blends nineteenth-century cultural contexts and cutting edge, future nanotechnologies – *The Diamond Age* begins with a parody of a cyberpunk character, executed some 30 pages into the novel, a bit of amusing metacommentary to note that Stephenson has cast off the specifically cyberpunk sensibility of *Snow Crash* with substantially greater maturity of both purpose and prose. But like *Snow Crash*, *The Diamond Age* features one of the central tropes of classic sf, the engineer paradigm. In *Snow Crash*, it is the computer hackers and their technological artifacts, such as the Babel/Infocalypse virus or the gargoyle Lagos's stack, the library of collated information, that position our heroes to fight back. In *The Diamond Age*, our worthy hacker is John Percival Hackworth, who designs the book's "primer" and who quests for the Alchemist capable of creating nanotech's Holy Grail, called The Seed. Set about 100 years into our future, *The Diamond Age* traces an alternative trajectory to *Snow Crash*: the burbclaves have become more serious, more stable Phyles, cultural and economic globally distributed tribes that have metastasized after the collapse of the nation-state; the antagonistic franchulates have become more coherent, robust multinational corporations.

At the request of an Equity Lord, Hackworth creates the "primer" for the technological, rather than ideological, interpellation of human subjectivity (Vint 2007: 143). But the Lord desires an almost eschatological end – since he thinks culture, even Neo-Victorian culture, generally produces mindless conformity and so constructs vapid iterations of the same, a stagnation that leads only toward çollapse, he wants a technological means to inculcate subversive individuality based solidly in a rigorous education in learning-how-to-learn (which comes primarily through logic, mathematics, and the information technologies associated with figures such as Alan Turing). The person most affected by this technology is Nell, transformed from under-class childhood origins into a heroic princess whose fundamental function, it transpires, is to save a lost mother and restore a traditional cultural balance best represented by the nuclear family and the classical virtues of *brilliance*, *joy*, and *bloom* – all developed and disciplined by the rational faculties in a combination of Enlightenment rationality and Victorian civility. We might say that Stephenson's novels remain more interested in heuristics than anything else; indeed, the major books are all, as *The Diamond Age*'s "primer" is subtitled, a "Propaedeutic Enchiridion" – *handbooks* that provide a *preface to teaching* (Stephenson 1995: 184).

Both of these books have been widely praised but also attacked. N. Katherine Hayles (1999, 2005a, 2005b), Sherryl Vint, and others have written persuasively about the sophistication of Stephenson's engagement with information technology and conceptions of posthuman subjectivity. On the other hand, **Gwyneth Jones** (1999) and Jan Berends (1997) have argued they include disturbingly racialized caricatures, and in some respects their politics, even when wrapped in the rhetoric of *subversion*, appear quiescent or nostalgic proponents of the present status quo. Stephenson's own vaguely libertarian politics, which distrust groups of all sorts and see worth only in individual integrity, personal honor, and loyalty, seem, especially in the context of the Culture Wars of the 1990s, equally progressive and reactionary.

Following *The Diamond Age*, Stephenson produced *Cryptonomicon*, to which his *Baroque* cycle – *Quicksilver, The Confusion* (2004), and *The System of the World* (2004) – is a pseudo-prequel. Together, these tomes comprise 3,552 densely interwoven pages weighing in at almost two million words, and thereby rendering any short summary utterly inadequate. Set at the end of the seventeenth century on the cusp of the Enlightenment, the *Baroque* cycle traces an oblique sequence of events linking scores of characters. Many are familiar figures from history (John Wilkins, Isaac Newton, Gottfried Leibniz), while others are inventions, such as Daniel Waterhouse, a distant ancestor of Randy Waterhouse, the main character of *Cryptonomicon* (set some 300 years later). Many readers resist calling these novels sf. But Stephenson thinks demarcating and defending generic borders less interesting than understanding sf as a subjunctive mode of possibility (see **Delany** (1977)): "There *is* a particular science fiction approach to the world, and it has nothing to do with the future" (Stephenson 1999: 6). Instead, the sf "approach" is "an awareness that things could have been different, that this is one of many possible worlds, that if you came to this world from some other planet, this would be a science fiction world" (Stephenson 1999: 6). This position understands sf as *speculative* rather than *science* fiction.

One way to conceptualize the *Baroque* cycle is as a kind of *slipstream*. A term initially coined by Bruce Sterling to denote when mainstream writers appropriate sf tropes, images, and themes, slipstream is used here in its loosest sense as designating any non-sf literature that contains many science-fictional elements – in short, a liminal genre in between mainstream and sf. In this sense, the *Baroque* cycle constitutes *historical* slipstream. Such an observation might also clarify an essential fact about Stephenson's *oeuvre*: he writes in the form once called the *novel of ideas*, which he then hangs on the devices and conceits of speculative fiction. While the novels do contain set-pieces of swashbuckling adventure or vigorous, occasionally violent action, Stephenson focuses on the descriptive analyses of ideas and traces their evolution and consequences: the history of science, metaphysics, information technology, money within market economies, and the transformation of the public and social spheres. He then luxuriates in those ideas and events, drawing them out at great length to build the extensive landscape of a fully realized alternative world.

As Paul Witcover quipped, Stephenson's encyclopedic erudition provides "porno for polymaths" (Witcover 2008: 25).

Some readers find both the great length and obsessive-compulsive focus taxing. However, not only does such a style recall much that is characteristic of the literature of ideas, but it also offers remarkable parallels with the postmodern project of writers such as Thomas Pynchon and David Foster Wallace: obsessive, intellectually ambitious, recursive, ironic, and at times exhausting. In discussing the phenomenon of why sf films such as *Star Wars: Episode III – Revenge of the Sith* (Lucas 2005) have been so popular despite their open superficiality, insistent use of the hoariest cliché, and aggressive evasion of inventiveness, Stephenson sheds some light on his own approach: "Modern English has given us two terms we need to explain" why people will pay good money for something incomprehensible or infantile: "'geeking out' and 'vegging out.' To geek out on something means to immerse yourself in its details to an extent that is distinctly abnormal – and to have a good time doing it. To veg out, by contrast, means to enter a passive state and allow sounds and images to wash over you without troubling yourself too much about what it means" (Stephenson 2005: A27). Such mindless sci-fi entertainments "consist of pure un-cut veg-out material, steeped in day-care-center ambience" (Stephenson 2005: A27). By implication, Stephenson sees his own work as "geeking out" and designed for a certain kind of ideal geek: a philosophical engineer with a sense of history and awe about future wonders, one especially interested in how alternative worlds can be built up and fleshed out in painstakingly minute, devilish detail – someone who refuses to be coddled by inane pap and prefers to be challenged by ideas, old or new.

In a return to a far more conventional kind of sf, *Anathem* (2008) extends and clarifies the arc of Stephenson's career, demonstrating that, even when writing within a venerable pulp genre such as space opera, he is primarily a philosophical novelist, one sharply at odds with what he once called the contemporary Cult of Brevity, a critique comically captured at the very beginning of the novel when one character remarks: "I suffer from attention surplus disorder" (Stephenson 2008: 5). As Stephenson says in the introduction to review copies of *Anathem*, his book (and by implication all of his writing) offers "a fictional framework for exploring ideas that have sprung from the minds of great thinkers of Earth's past and present" (quoted in Witcover 2008: 25). As a novelist of ideas, Stephenson privileges the *abnormal immersion* in the details of intellectual history and the future consequences of scientific innovation.

See also: **Isaac Asimov, J.G. Ballard, Greg Bear, Alfred Bester, Leigh Brackett, Octavia Butler, Samuel R. Delany, Philip K. Dick, Greg Egan, William Gibson, Robert A. Heinlein, Frank Herbert, L. Ron Hubbard, Ursula K. Le Guin, C.L. Moore, Kim Stanley Robinson, Joanna Russ, Mary Shelley, Sheri S. Tepper, James Tiptree Jr, and Gene Wolfe**

Bibliography

Berends, J.B. (1997) "The Politics of Neal Stephenson's *The Diamond Age*," *New York Review of Science Fiction*, 9(8): 15–18.

Delany, S.R. (1977) *The Jewel-Hinged Jaw: notes on the language of science fiction*, Elizabethtown, NY: Dragon Press.

Hayles, N.K. (1999) *How We Became Posthuman: virtual bodies in cybernetics, literature and informatics*, Chicago: University of Chicago Press.

——(2005a) "Is Utopia Obsolete? Imploding boundaries in Neal Stephenson's *The Diamond Age*," in W.K. Yuen, G. Westfahl, and A. Kit-Sze Chan (eds.) *World Weavers: globalization, science fiction, and the cybernetic revolution*, Hong Kong: Hong Kong University Press.

——(2005b) *My Mother Was a Computer: digital subjects and literary texts*, Chicago: University of Chicago Press.

Jones, G. (1999) *Deconstructing the Starships: science, fiction and reality*, Liverpool: Liverpool University Press.

Porush, D. (1996) "Hacking the Brainstem: postmodern metaphysics and Stephenson's *Snow Crash*," in R. Markley (ed.) *Virtual Realities and Their Discontents*, Baltimore, MD: Johns Hopkins University Press.

Stephenson, N. (1992) *Snow Crash*, New York: Bantam Spectra.

——(1995) *The Diamond Age*, New York: Bantam Spectra.

——(1999) "Cryptomancer," *Locus*, 43(2): 6, 76–78.

——(2005) "Turn on, Tune in, Veg out," *New York Times*, 17 June: A27.

——(2008) *Anathem*, New York: William Morrow.

Sterling, B. (1989) "Slipstream," *SF Eye*, 5: 77–80.

Vint, S. (2007) *Bodies of Tomorrow: technology, subjectivity, science fiction*, Toronto: University of Toronto Press.

Witcover, P. (2008) "*Locus* Looks at Books," *Locus*, 61(3): 23–25.

NEIL EASTERBROOK

J[OSEPH] MICHAEL STRACZYNSKI (1954–)

US television writer-producer working in the sf, horror, and crime genres.

J. Michael Straczynski is also the author of radio dramas, comic books, three novels (*Demon Night* (1988), *Othersyde* (1990), *Tribuations* (2000)), a number of short stories (many of them collected in *Straczynski Unplugged* (2004)), and *The Complete Book of Scriptwriting* (1996). His sf coheres around recurrent themes of opposition to corrupt authority, the distinction between duty and responsibility, the psychological role of faith, and the need to resist manipulation. This is most apparent in his key contribution to sf, the influential television series *Babylon 5* (1993–98).

Following a brief career as a journalist, Straczynski moved into television in 1983, scriptwriting episodes for children's animated series including *He-Man and the Masters of the Universe* (1983–85) and *The Real Ghostbusters* (1986–91). After developing a reputation for resigning when he felt stories were being compromised, he moved on to live action with *Murder She Wrote* (1984–96), *The New Twilight Zone* (1985–89) and *Jake and the Fatman* (1987–92). During his work on *Twilight Zone*, he originated *Babylon 5* (*B5*), an ambitious, politically charged space opera. Informed partly by Straczynski's childhood affection for literary sf's "sense of wonder" and by a growing dissatisfaction with American television's simplistic and escapist treatment of the genre, *B5*'s planned serial narrative marked a break with episodic sf television conventions. It also drew self-reflexively on the fantastic, particularly J.R.R. Tolkien's *The Lord of the Rings* (1954–55), and literary sf, especially the fiction of **Alfred Bester**, H.P. Lovecraft and **Isaac Asimov**. It owed an equal debt to British television's *The Prisoner* (1967–68) and *Blakes* 7 (1978–81). As such, it constituted a megatext as metafictively embedded in its genre as *Doctor Who* (1963–).

Straczynski spent five years looking for a network willing to support his project. His concept for a five-season epic which could be produced on a budget *and* be "quality" television was deemed impossible by almost every network he approached (Straczynski 1995: 8). Simultaneously, the networks felt that the lack of self-contained episodes would alienate new audiences, resulting in a niche market show of limited appeal. In reality, Straczynski was exploiting the continuous serial format common to soap operas; the developing storyline, with its multiple narrative threads and multilayered themes, would allow for character transformation and story development rarely seen in sf television. Two innovations with budgetary implications persuaded Warner Brothers to commission the show: the decision to locate the action on a space station at the hub of galactic events and the extensive use of CGI for special effects. Without the need for costly weekly sets and model work, the series' ambitious narrative could be realized within a restricted and restrictive television budget.

Straczynski's input was pervasive. Credited as *B5*'s creator and executive producer, he also wrote the show's pilot – "The Gathering" (1993) – 91 of the 110 episodes (including an uninterrupted 59-episode run) and six related television films: *In the Beginning* (1998), *Thirdspace* (1998),

River of Souls (1998), *Babylon 5: A Call to Arms* (1999), *The Legend of the Rangers* (2002), and *Babylon 5: The Lost Tales* (2007). Straczynski exercised creative control over all areas of production, including casting, costume, set design, visual effects, prosthetics, music, and editing, reflecting his recognition of, and determination to satisfy, the intelligence of a perceived "literate" sf audience. Accordingly, he constructed *B5* as a more complex entity, narratively, conceptually, and politically, than many of its precursors.

Structurally, *B5*'s extended narrative trajectory documents the "Dawn of the Third Age of Mankind," the maturation of the universe's "younger races" – humans, Narn, and Minbari – and the final war between two manipulative older races, the Vorlons and the Shadows. The scale of this war and the labyrinthine plotting undertaken by the older races contributed significantly to the series' defining sense of wonder. In terms of its visual style, *B5* employs sublime imagery throughout, especially in its representation of the Shadows and the Vorlons. The Shadows are black, spider-like denizens of an abyssal city who, cloaked and invisible for much of the series, operate secretly and subversively. In contrast, the enigmatic Vorlons appear as beautiful, luminous angelic forms. Clearly, such imagery, which maps directly onto conventional representations of good and evil, invites a simplistic binary interpretation of the two races. Straczynski subverts the viewers' preconceptions by subsequently revealing such assumptions as flawed. In Season Four, the Vorlons are exposed as restrictive parental figures requiring order and obedience from the younger races. In contrast, the Shadows are agents of social Darwinism, inciting chaos and conflict to exert evolutionary pressure. Both races are authoritarian and their defeat constitutes part of Straczynski's rejection of totalitarianism and the Orwellian pursuit of power for its own sake.

Refuting influential symbolism was one strategy by which Straczynski ensured *B5* was consistently unpredictable. He also regularly overturned audience expectations and avoided convenient resolutions. For example, in "Confessions and Lamentations" (1995) the protagonists' actions prove ineffective and result in the death of an entire alien species. Such bleak outcomes marked a decisive break with previous American sf television, particularly the often trite denouements of the *Star Trek* franchises. The universe was a capricious place, Straczynski suggested, and in so doing he brought a new sense of realism to sf television. The social, political, and emotional maturation of the young races in *B5* emblematized a formal maturation, in effect a decisive step in sf television's incorporation of adult themes and situations. As Straczynski notes:

> We've pioneered a new form of television storytelling. We've raised the bar in terms of what people should expect from a science fiction series. We've made the point that you don't need to lumber an sf series with cute kids and even cuter robots, you don't need to make the show camp, don't need to treat the audience like children, and you don't need to avoid real science.
> (Straczynski 1995: 17).

Rather than adopting a politically conservative, utopian perspective on the future, Straczynski depicted a more conflicted vision of the evolution of humankind. Its serial structure prevented complex political events from requiring convenient solutions. Political corruption, the conflict between loyalty and duty, the psychological and emotional consequences of war, personal crises, and the implications of advanced technology were all dramatized extensively and convincingly across the narrative arc. Nevertheless, Straczynski's conviction that an individual can effect positive change provides a core of optimism to *B5* which can seem naive. This naiveté is qualified, however, by his recognition that individuals can, equally, initiate catastrophic events with far-reaching implications.

To assist in developing the trajectories of his heroic and tragic figures, Straczynski drew on the structuring device of the Campbellian monomyth. These individual "heroic cycles" were microcosmically related to the macrocosmic cycle charted across the series, which emblematized the conclusion of humanity's metaphorical childhood. This reflection of universal change in human transformation informs *B5*'s spiritual and mythic sensibility. Indeed, Straczynski intended *B5* to provide new myths through the medium of television. He achieved this by drawing on the traditional structures of the monomyth, whilst stylistically deploying Jungian symbolism and archetype. As a result, *B5* resonates with the "collective unconscious" of traditional mythic narratives. Straczynski recontextualized these mythological structures and their attendant symbolism to "point to the past but [speak] in the voice of future history; … [providing] a sense of continuity and destiny" (Straczynski 1995: 9). *B5* was an interrogation, reinterpretation, and reinvention of the myths that underpin society and which are slowly being eroded or lost. *B5*'s dramatization of various religious practices, and its avowed commitment to fostering a sense of mystery transcending the physical universe, indicated Straczynski's affirmation of the importance of the spiritual for sentient life. Negotiating his own atheism, he advocated the role of faith in psychological well-being over any religion's claim to represent a transcendental truth.

The scope, depth, and intricacy of *B5* earned Straczynski a number of awards, including two Hugos (for "The Coming of the Shadows" (1995) and "Severed Dreams" (1996)), two Emmys (for "The Gathering" and "Parliament of Dreams" (1994)), and the Ray Bradbury Award for Dramatic Screenwriting. When *B5* won the 1996 Universe Reader's Choice Award for Best Special Effects in a Genre TV Series, Straczynski's reliance on CGI was endorsed. His embracing of new technology was further reflected in his use of the burgeoning internet for interacting with fans, with whom he engaged at an unprecedented level, employing the internet to build communities and networks in a manner analogous to the sf pulp magazine's letters pages. Hence, with *B5* Straczynski looks both forward and back, textually, narratively, and generically. His Janus-faced perspective faltered, however, with *Crusade* (1999), a sequel series to *Babylon 5: A Call to Arms*, in which the Drahk, allies of the banished Shadows, infect Earth with a nano-plague that will kill all life within five years. Drawing retrogressively on *Star Trek*'s narrative structure, *Crusade* follows the crew of the *Excalibur* as they search for a cure. Centered on a ship with a largely human crew, *Crusade* lacked the cultural and political richness, epic sensibility, and mythic tone that provided *B5* with its originality. The series was canceled after thirteen episodes following Straczynski's creative differences with Turner Network Television.

Maintaining an interest in plague-related narratives after the cancellation of *Crusade*, Straczynski produced *Jeremiah* (2002–4), a television adaptation of the Belgian comic by Hermann Huppen. Set 15 years after a plague has killed everyone over the age of puberty, *Jeremiah* is postapocalyptic sf reminiscent of the BBC's *Survivors* (1975–77). In its explorations of the relationships between sons and their literal and metaphorical fathers, it readdressed Straczynski's preoccupation with maturity and authority less symbolically than *B5*. Although he penned only 19 of its 35 episodes, Straczynski's signature enigmatic prophecies, labyrinthine storytelling, narrative foreshadowing, and occasionally portentous scripting inform the plot.

Following a difficult relationship with MGM, Straczynski left *Jeremiah* before a third season was commissioned to concentrate on comic-book writing. In 1999 he scripted *Rising Stars* for Top Cow/Image Comics, before developing his own imprint, Joe's Comics, for which he wrote *Midnight Nation* and *Delicate Creatures*. In 2000 he was commissioned by Marvel to write *The Amazing Spider-Man*, *Supreme Power*, and *Fantastic Four*, and since that time he has produced a number of graphic novels. In February 2008 he announced that he would no longer be working exclusively for Marvel, but would also contribute to DC and Image titles. His comic-writing career did not mark a complete withdrawal from screen sf, however. He has continued to produce telefilms set in the *B5* universe and, more recently, has established his own production company, And the Horse You Rode in on Productions, through which he intends to produce more sf films.

Straczynski is a notable figure in sf not only for his innovation, literary awareness, and the diversity of his projects, but also for his capacity to work successfully in varied media. His primary contribution to the genre, however, is *Babylon 5*, a seminal text that reshaped American and associated television space opera. Its influence can be seen in the evolving story arcs of *Star Trek: Deep Space 9* (1993–99), *Farscape* (1999–2004), and, most notably, *Battlestar Galactica* (2003–), which demonstrates a comparable preoccupation with conflicts between loyalty and responsibility, myth, and spirituality. Given the inertia of much American sf television, this was a considerable achievement.

See also: **Gerry Anderson, Alfred Bester, Samuel R. Delany, The Doctor, Nigel Kneale, Stan Lee, Alan Moore, and Oshii Mamoru**

Bibliography

Bassom, D. (1996) *Creating Babylon 5*, London: Boxtree.

James, E. and Mendlesohn, F. (eds.) (1998) *The Parliament of Dreams: conferring on Babylon 5*, Reading: Science Fiction Foundation.

Killick, J. (1997) *Babylon 5 Season by Season, Numbers 1–5*, London: Boxtree.

Lane, A. (1997) *The Babylon File*, London: Virgin.

Plume, K. (2000) "Interview with J. Michael Straczynski," IGN.com, 5 September. Online. Available: <http://uk.movies.ign.com/articles/035/035904p1.html> (accessed 1 December 2008).

Straczynski, J.M. (1995) "The Profession of Science Fiction, 48: approaching Babylon," *Foundation*, 64: 5–19.

——(1998) *The Coming of the Shadows*, London: Boxtree.

JENNIFER WOODWARD

DARKO [RONALD] SUVIN (1930–)

Theorist, editor, and poet.

In his role as a founding editor of *Science-Fiction Studies* (later published as *Science Fiction Studies*) and as a major scholarly voice in his own right, Darko Suvin has played a central role in the establishment of sf as a legitimate and significant field of scholarly inquiry. Suvin received his Ph.D. from and first taught at Zagreb University in the former Yugoslavia. After running afoul of some political currents at the university, Suvin emigrated to North America, ultimately settling in 1968 at McGill University in Montreal, where he was Professor of English and Comparative Literature until his retirement in 1999. In 1979 he was named the tenth recipient of the Science Fiction Research Association's Pilgrim Award to honor his lifetime contributions to sf scholarship.

Suvin, along with R.D. Mullen, founded *Science-Fiction Studies* in 1973, at a moment when academic literary studies was becoming increasingly receptive – in response in part to the vibrancy of the New Left and in part to the innovations of a burgeoning critical theory (both movements that also deeply influenced Suvin's thought) – to scholarly work in the area of what was then referred to as "paraliterature" (popular and genre fiction including sf, fantasy, mystery, horror, romance, and comics). From his earliest work, Suvin refused the marginalization of sf implied by this characterization, not only locating the genre within a long literary tradition of popular transgressive fictions that stretched back to the work of Lucian of Samosata, Thomas More, and François Rabelais, but also consistently maintaining that the finest contemporary sf is among the best of all literature produced in the present. "The stakes" at play in science fiction, Suvin would later argue in an essay on paraliterature, "thus, are the highest imaginable … the education of *Homo sapiens* for earthly salvation" (Suvin 1988: 20). Here we see the combination of artistic, philosophical, and political commitment characteristic of all of Suvin's writing, as well as a deep advocacy of the radical transformative and utopian potential located within the best examples of the genre. Indeed, utopian fiction is itself, Suvin argues, both "one of the roots" of modern sf and in the present "the sociopolitical subgenre of SF, it is social-science-fiction or SF restricted to the field of sociopolitical relationships or to sociopolitical constructs understood as crucial for the destiny of people" (Suvin 1988: 38; see also Suvin 1979: Ch. 3).

Science Fiction Studies rapidly became the most significant academic journal in the fledgling field, bringing a new sophistication and scholarly rigor to the study of the genre, and providing a venue for scholars whose work and debates would play an important role in future scholarship. A partial list of those published in its pages under Suvin's editorship includes prominent academics such as Peter Fitting, John Huntington, Fredric Jameson, and Tom Moylan, as well as such major sf writers as **Stanisław Lem**, **Samuel R. Delany**, **Ursula K. Le Guin**, and **Joanna Russ**. At the same time, in his own writing and in his work as an editor Suvin helped to introduce an anglophone audience to a rich global sf tradition, particularly from the Soviet Union and Eastern Europe, as in *Other Worlds, Other Seas: science-fiction stories from socialist countries* (1970).

Suvin's first published scholarly essays on sf appeared in the mid-1950s, and in English at the end of the 1960s, including his ground-breaking "On the Poetics of the Science Fiction Genre" in the important 1972 issue of *College English* (see Moylan 2000: 42–45). Many of Suvin's early sf essays were brought together in his landmark book *Metamorphoses of Science Fiction: on the poetics and history of a literary genre* (1979). It is in these writings that Suvin develops his deeply influential definition of sf "as the *literature of cognitive estrangement*" (Suvin 1979: 4, original italics). Suvin further elaborates his definition in the following way: "*SF is, then, a literary genre whose necessary and sufficient conditions are the presence and interaction of estrangement and cognition, and whose main formal device is an imaginative framework alternative to the author's empirical environment*" (Suvin 1979: 7–8, original italics). And finally, he adds: "*SF is distinguished by the narrative dominance or hegemony of a fictional 'novum' (novelty, innovation) validated by cognitive logic*" (Suvin 1979: 63, original italics).

The force of this definition is twofold. On the one hand, Suvin's emphasis on "cognition" – the outlook that "sees the norms of any age, including emphatically its own, as unique, changeable, and therefore subject to a *cognitive* view … not only a reflecting *of* but also *on* reality" (Suvin 1979: 7, 10) – suggests the connection of modern sf to nineteenth-century literary realism, and hence its distance from other traditional and modern forms such as myth, folk (fairy) tales, and fantasy. While on this ground, Suvin draws a marked distinction in his earlier works between sf and modern fantasy; he has modified his stance in some of his most recent writings, arguing for example: "If all estranged genres aspire to be read as parables, then each Fantasy text also has a tenor and cannot be simply dismissed because of its vehicle" (Suvin 2000: 211; for further elaborations on the distinctiveness of modern fantasy, see Suvin (2006) and Jameson (2005: 57–71)).

This final statement points toward what Suvin argues sf shares with other fantastic genres: they are all fictions that engage in the operation of estrangement. In some ways this insight stands as Suvin's most significant contribution to sf studies. He takes the notion of *ostranenie* from the literary critics of the early twentieth-century Russian Formalist school, most prominently Viktor Shklovsky, and the further elaborations upon it offered by the Marxist playwright and thinker Bertolt Brecht. (One of Suvin's other major contributions to modern literary studies is to be found in his voluminous writings on Brecht.) Through his emphasis on the genre's estranging labors – its ability to view its present moment through a critical, distancing eye – Suvin undercuts the commonplace assumption that sf represents a species of futurology, developing prognostications of technical or social developments to come. This insight is further developed in Jameson's discussions of sf (Jameson 2005; for further analysis of the influence of Suvin's theoretical work, see Moylan (2000) and Parrinder (2000)).

Moreover, Suvin's definition illuminates a deep kinship between sf and the larger cultural and literary experiments and innovations of late nineteenth- and early twentieth-century modernism, something also suggested by his deployment of the Marxist philosopher of utopia Ernst Bloch's equally modernist concept of the "novum": "a totalizing phenomenon or relationship deviating from the author's and implied reader's norm of reality" (Suvin 1979: 64; also see Moylan 2000: 45–46). Suvin argues that sf comes into its own as a genre with the work of **H.G. Wells**: "He endowed later SF with a basically materialist look back at human life and a rebelliousness against its entropic closure. For such reasons, all subsequent significant SF can be said to have sprung from Wells's *Time Machine*" (Suvin 1979: 221). (Suvin has also written extensively about the institutional and ideological context for this emergence in *Victorian Science Fiction in the UK: the discourses of knowledge and power* (1983).) This makes the original narrative technology (*technē*) of sf as deeply modernist as film, the two developments converging early on in Georges Méliès' experimental film *A Trip to the Moon* (1902), which was derived in part from Wells's work. Moreover, the genre contains within its later history two distinct modernist phases (see Wegner 2009 and Wegner forthcoming). Not coincidently, the majority of Suvin's writings on sf focus on these two periods: the first high modernist moment of the 1920s and early 1930s, which includes the work of authors such as Yevgeny Zamyatin, **Karel Čapek**, and **Olaf Stapledon**; and a second modernism, beginning in the late 1950s and extending through the 1970s, the moment of the so-called New Wave (the moment too of the consolidation of the academic field of sf studies), marked by a new formal and thematic experimentation and a tremendous diversification of both the genre's authorship and audience, and which encompasses authors such as **Philip K. Dick**, Lem, Cordwainer Smith, Arkady and Boris Strugatsky, Delany, Johanna and Günter Braun, Russ, and, most significantly for Suvin, Le Guin (see Suvin 1988). The conclusion of this second modernist period is signaled by the emergence in the early 1980s and subsequent immense popularity of cyberpunk, a development of which Suvin has written critically, arguing that, despite its contributions to a widening of contemporary sf to include "the new vocabulary of lyricized information interfaces," it has broken with the utopianism of a previous generation of sf by too readily conceding to the central Thatcher/ Reagan-era tenet that the global neoliberal order is "inevitable and unchangeable" (Suvin 1991: 359, 357).

More recently, Suvin has written about a potential "end" of sf, as its niche in the publishing market diminishes and the barriers between the genre and fantasy further erode. He argues that sf "appeals to social groups with confidence that something can at present be done about a collective, historical future – if only as dire warnings" (Suvin 2000: 238). On the contrary, "Fantasy's appeal is to uncertain social classes or fractions who have been cast adrift and lost that confidence" – and it is the latter outlook that increasingly predominates in the public that has historically made up the two genres' readerships (Suvin 2004: 4). If there is a future for sf, Suvin argues, it lies with what he calls a radical "Le Guin to K.S. Robinson line" that has inherited "a commitment for the use of warm reason to at least illuminate why people live so badly together, and perhaps to think about radical changes in the way they live … either the adventure of SF will become integrally critical, or it will eventually be outflanked by Fantasy and fail as a mass genre" (Suvin 2004: 5).

Suvin's major English-language work on sf has been collected in four volumes: *Metamorphoses of Science Fiction*; *Victorian Science Fiction in the UK*; *Positions and Presuppositions in Science Fiction* (1988); and *Defined by a Hollow: essays on utopia, science fiction, and political epistemology – a Darko Suvin reader* (forthcoming). This last work also includes a rich sample of Suvin's poetry and some of his prose essays. Suvin has also co-edited two volumes of essays collected from the first five years of *Science Fiction Studies* (published in 1976 and 1978), and the collections *H.G. Wells and Modern Science Fiction* (1977) and *US Science Fiction and War/Militarism* (2005).

See also: **Jean Baudrillard, Karel Čapek, Samuel R. Delany, Philip K. Dick, Donna J. Haraway, Ursula K. Le Guin, Stanisław Lem, Kim Stanley Robinson, Joanna Russ, Olaf Stapledon, H.G. Wells**

Bibliography

Jameson, F. (2005) *Archaeologies of the Future: the desire called utopia and other science fictions*, London: Verso.

Moylan, T. (2000) *Scraps of the Untainted Sky: science fiction, utopia, dystopia*, Boulder, CO: Westview.
Parrinder, P. (ed.) (2000) *Learning from Other Worlds: estrangement, cognition and the politics of science fiction and utopia*, Liverpool: Liverpool University Press.
Spiegel, S. (2008) "Things Made Strange: on the concept of 'estrangement' in science fiction theory," *Science Fiction Studies*, 35(3): 369–85.
Suvin, D. (1979) *Metamorphoses of Science Fiction: On the Poetics and History of a Literary Genre*, New Haven, CT: Yale University Press.
——(1988) *Positions and Presuppositions in Science Fiction*, Kent, OH: Kent State University Press.
——(1991) "On Gibson and Cyberpunk SF," in L. McCaffery (ed.) *Storming the Reality Studio*, Durham, NC and London: Duke University Press.
——(2000) "Considering the Sense of 'Fantasy' or 'Fantastic Fiction': an effusion," *Extrapolation*, 41(3): 209–47.
——(2004) "The Final Chapter?: on reading Brian Stableford – part two," *SFRA Review*, 267: 2–6.
——(2006) "On U.K. Le Guin's 'Second Earthsea Trilogy' and Its Cognitions: a commentary," *Extrapolation*, 47(3): 488–504.
Wegner, P.E. (2009) "Ken MacLeod's Permanent Revolution: utopian possible worlds, history, and the *Augenblick* in the 'Fall Revolution'," in M. Bould and C. Miéville (eds.) *Red Planets: Marxism and science fiction*, London: Pluto Press.
——(forthcoming) "Jameson's Modernism; or, the Desire Called Utopia," *Diacritics – A Review of Contemporary Criticism.*

PHILLIP E. WEGNER

SHERI S[TEWART] TEPPER (1929–)

Prolific US author and former Planned Parenthood executive.

Sherri S. Tepper came to sf as a second career; until she was 53 she had published only poetry. Her early works for young adults (the *True Game* trilogy of trilogies (1983–86) and the *Marianne* trilogy (1985–89)) have the character of fantasy, although the *True Game* series has a sf premise. Later fantasies include *Beauty* (1991; winner of the 1992 *Locus* Award), a reworking of classic fairy tales with a grim contemporary twist. She has written horror and mysteries under pseudonyms (B.J. Oliphant; A.J. Orde; E.E. Horlak). Tepper has continued to include elements of fairy tale, folklore, horror, and the supernatural in a number of acclaimed and much loved sf novels.

The Awakeners (1987; initially published as *Northshore* (1987) and *Southshore* (1987)) attracted critical attention and announced some of the themes – planetary romance, gender roles, environmental issues, commensal species, the evils of fundamentalist religion – to which she has remained faithful. *After Long Silence* (1987) (later published in the UK as *The Enigma Score* (1989)) is another very attractive genre tale, notable for its marvelously strange imagined landscapes, but her reputation was established with *The Gate to Women's Country* (1988).

Set on the northwestern seaboard of the US, some centuries after a global nuclear war, the novel describes a refuge society where arts, crafts, and scientific knowledge are preserved in walled enclaves of women and children. The majority of men and all male adolescents live in stark garrisons outside. Female prostitution exists, but the only sanctioned sexual relations are at "carnival," a brief period when the warriors are welcomed into the streets. Ostensibly the women are the weak partners in this arrangement, obliged to support the garrisons with their labor and skills, and to hand over all male children to their "warrior fathers." The reality – suggested by oblique hints but concealed until the last pages – is very different. Flashing backward and forward in time, we follow the fortunes of Stavia, daughter of a prominent citizen of Women's Country, as she pursues an illicit friendship with Chernon, a duplicitous, and finally irredeemable, young warrior. Their relationship (the girl deceiving herself, helpless in the throes of sexual attraction, the boy motivated by cold self-interest from the start) mirrors the secret truth. Chernon believes, until the end, that all the power is on his side, but he is wrong. The warriors of Women's Country believe that they dominate the women, and that they are the fathers of their "warrior sons." In fact – as Stavia discovers when initiated into the Ruling Council (the "Damned Few") – both the couplings of carnival and all nonsanctioned sexual transactions are barren. Women approved for breeding by the "Damned Few" are artificially inseminated, without their knowledge or consent, with the sperm of specially chosen "servitors", men with kindly, civilized traits. Meanwhile "wars" between the garrisons are engineered, and controlled to ensure that the most aggressive and vicious of the troops and officers are most likely to die. Scenes from a pseudo-Classical play called *Iphigenia at Ilium*, rehearsed at intervals throughout the novel, point to the moral. A situation that looks like a Greek tragedy for the unlucky women who have survived men's wars is really a black and mordant comedy. The proud warriors are being systematically culled, and selectively bred, out of existence.

Despite a negative position on both male and female homosexuality, and Tepper's insistence on the right of a "wise" elite to control reproductive rights, *Gate* swiftly joined the canon of feminist sf. It shares many motifs with other feminist works: postcatastrophe scarcity conditions; effortful utopia (for feminists, *utopia* always means *hard work*); regenerative female-ordered governance; the vital project of eliminating organized violence from human society; even the psychic powers that some servitor (civilized) males are developing. Tepper's version is unusual in presenting young characters of both sexes as appetite-driven and self-destructive, and in characterizing the fate of the warrior breed as a tragic, guilty secret. Her evenhandedness may account for the book's wide appeal, but it is deceptive. Tepper's views on the problem of gender are draconian, and can be merciless.

The Gate to Women's Country, with its narrow scope and single focus, is anomalous in Tepper's work. In *Grass* (1989), the artistic space in which she conducts her vivid experiments made its first developed appearance. On overcrowded Earth, a patriarchal religion called "Sanctity," closely modeled on the Mormon Church, rules with an iron fist. Abortion is condemned, contraception forbidden; the brutalized excess population gets shipped out for slave labor on prison planets. Marjorie Westriding, former Olympic dressage and puissance medalist, wronged wife, and troubled Old Catholic, struggles to do good in the teeming slums, aware that she is merely salving her own guilt. Meanwhile, an apocalyptic plague is spreading through the settled worlds: highly infectious, hideous in its effects, and invariably fatal, except on the planet called Grass. When Marjorie's diplomat husband, Rigo Yrarier, is posted to Grass, on a mission to find out anything he can about the rumored cure, the family (all accomplished riders) soon discover that their briefing was seriously flawed. The "bons," the aristocratic elite among the human settlers, were supposed to be keen fox-hunters, riding to hounds Old English style. In reality, the Hunt on Grass is orgiastic torture, forced upon the enthralled human riders for the malign entertainment of native semi-sentients. In spite of all warnings, Marjorie's obnoxious husband and rebellious daughter fall under the dreadful spell. But the fearsome Hounds, the terrifying Mounts, and the "foxen" they pursue are bound together in an extraordinary puzzle, part ecological, part mystical, which Marjorie must unravel to save the settled worlds, and her own soul – with the help of the demon lover who brings ecstasy and enlightenment, a saintly, aged archaeologist, and the spiritual presence of the Arbai, a vanished Elder Race.

Widely recognized as a major classic, and undoubtedly Tepper's most splendid achievement, *Grass* is a crowded and spacious canvas in which many genres combine: a painful family saga; a scientific mystery; a creepily effective sf horror tale; and a close-fought, climactic battle between Good and Evil. Secondary histories, secondary characters, are delineated in lively detail, not forgetting El Dio Octavo, Marjorie's courageous, faithful steed (in Tepper's novels, animals are often significant characters). Above all, there is the planet itself, the haunted paradise, one of the loveliest of sf's imagined worlds:

> Grass! Ruby ridges, blood-coloured highlands, wine-shaded glades … Orange highlands burning against the sunsets. Apricot ranges glowing against the dawns. Seed plumes sparkling like sequined stars. Blossom heads like the fragile lace old women take out of trunks to show their grandchildren.
>
> (Tepper 1996: 7).

It is an intensely *feminine* brew, yet *Grass* also carries Tepper's most radical feminist message. Here there are no draconian solutions. Instead there is the "foxen," imago form of Grass's metamorphic dominant species. Like the chimera figure in the *Marianne* trilogy, he represents a potent, idealized image of what *the masculine* means in Tepper's worldview – part-beast, part-angel, part fellow-traveler; monstrous, irresistible, and indispensable complement. In her dealings with this majestic alien, Marjorie Westriding not only takes on the role of the investigative scientist-hero, she is also the type of humanity, encountering otherness. Thus, at the heart of Grass, we find the gender problem resolved through a classic sf diptych: on one hand the blundering, exciting, serendipitous struggle to understand a bizarre and deadly alien species, on the other childhood's end. Marjorie and her "foxen" lover complete each other. Having achieved union, they are ready to move on – through the technologically mediated transcendence of the Arbai Door – to a higher level of existence.

Grass was followed, in a loose trilogy, by *Raising the Stones* (1990) and *Sideshow* (1992). Marjorie reappears briefly in *Raising the Stones*, and again as an angelic troubleshooter in *Sideshow,* but the real link between the novels is the intervention of the Arbai, the vanished Elder Race. Such beings, who leave artifacts of fabulous power behind them, are a staple of sf. Here the "Arbai Device" (or "The Hobbs Land Gods") – a (meta)genetically engineered fungus with the power, when buried shallow with a suitable corpse, to render the belief system of a community concrete and effectual – is used to interrogate the phenomenon of religion. What if our gods were living beings, dependent on our worship? What if God's presence in the world made us good? What if evil creeds brought supernatural demons to life? In *Raising the Stones* the focus is on fathers and sons, the sons of human society in its original, matrilineal state who re-invent their absent fathers as gods, and found abusive belief systems on a myth of fatherhood. No match for *Grass*, this is still a serious work. The homely utopia of Hobbs Land lovingly evokes an ideal Deep West US, and Sam Girat, anti-hero, is Tepper's most effective human male character: sympathetic yet recalcitrant; hell-bent on ruining everyone's life, yet full of goodwill. *Sideshow*, a less successful novel, brings the story to its resolution, reprising the motif of Marjorie's personal ascension (through horrors to transcendence) on a hugely magnified scale, taking us to the apocalyptic End of Man.

Later novels explore the same themes, reworking variants on the same motifs, with unflagging invention, energy, and conviction. *Gibbon's Decline and Fall* (1996) tackles gender politics in a much richer form than *The Gate to Women's Country*, through the fortunes of a group of college roommates – one of whom, the mysterious Sophia, may be the Third Person of the Trinity (Holy Wisdom) incarnate. *Six Moon Dance* (1998) and *The Singer from the Sea* (1999) return to dark and intriguing planetary romance. Issues about population and commensal species take the foreground in *The Companions* (2003), in which the creed of "Firstism" (introduced in *Shadow's End* (1994)) has wiped out almost every living species on Earth, and homage is paid to Tepper's beloved dogs. What if we met sentients who perceived and communicated only through smell? In *The Margarets* (2007), balanced between sf and fairy tale, Earth's domestic cats get their turn, as whimsical, galactic foster-children.

Tepper has admitted, ruefully, that she sometimes wishes she could get herself a "polem-ectomy," because on occasions the polemic gets in the way of the literature. Her anger is a valid sf mode, and arguably justified by our present situation on the brink of environmental catastrophe, but her absolutes can be bewildering and can seem self-defeating. She presents the traditional gender roles as a nest of horrors yet believes they cannot be changed, and she insists that homosexuality is unnatural (though not blameworthy). Eugenics may be used to build utopia, and the masses need not be consulted. There is no escape from a horrific future, or from the terrible dance of the conjoined twins (a Tepper image of human sexual relations, later reprised as an image of the human condition: monster and angel, joined at the hip), except through Divine Intervention. Her popularity, despite the uncompromising harshness of her vision, may rest on the fact that readers are never asked to embrace revolutionary change, only to cheer for the good guys. But above and beyond her anger, and her conservatism, Tepper is "that unusual kind of writer, a *born* story-teller," with the added value of a sophisticated, rigorous, sf mind. "In the space of only a few years, she became one of sf's premier world-builders," says Peter Nicholls (Nicholls 1993: 1211–12). She will be read, and studied, for this natural talent and marvelous skill long after sf polemicism has turned to different targets.

See also: **Isaac Asimov, Greg Bear, Alfred Bester, Leigh Brackett, Octavia Butler, Samuel R. Delany, Philip K. Dick, William Gibson, Robert A. Heinlein, Frank Herbert, Nalo Hopkinson, L. Ron Hubbard, Gwyneth Jones, Ursula K. Le Guin, C.L. Moore, Mary Shelley, Neal Stephenson, James Tiptree Jr, and Gene Wolfe**

Bibliography

Beswick, N. (1997) "Ideology and Dogma in the 'Ferocious' Sf Novels of Sheri S. Tepper," *Foundation*, 71: 32–44.

Nicholls, P. (1993) "Sheri S. Tepper," in J. Clute and P. Nicholls (eds.) *The Encyclopedia of Science Fiction*, London: Orbit.

Reid, R.A. (2004) "'Momutes': momentary utopias in Tepper's trilogies," in M. Batter (ed.) *The Utopian Fantastic: selected essays from the Twentieth International Conference on the Fantastic in the Arts*, London: Praeger.

Tepper, S. (1996) *Grass* [1986], London: HarperCollins.

GWYNETH JONES

JAMES TIPTREE JR [BORN ALICE BRADLEY] (1915–87)

Pseudonym of US author and psychologist Alice Hastings Bradley Sheldon.

Author of two novels and more than 60 short stories – several of which she published under the second pseudonym Raccoona Sheldon – James Tiptree Jr received Hugo, Nebula, World Fantasy, and *Locus* awards for her groundbreaking work in new wave and feminist sf. In 1991 Pat Murphy and Karen Joy Fowler established the James Tiptree Jr Award in her honor for works of sf and fantasy that expand notions of sex and gender.

Tiptree's personal biography is every bit as remarkable as her literary legacy. She was born in Chicago to Herbert Bradley, a lawyer and naturalist, and Mary Hastings Bradley, well-known fiction and travel writer. She spent much of her childhood traveling Africa and

India with her parents before eloping with William Davey at the age of 19. The marriage lasted until 1941, during which time Tiptree explored careers in graphic art, painting, and art criticism. In 1942 Tiptree joined the army and worked in air intelligence, where she met her second husband, Huntington Sheldon. After the Second World War the couple briefly ran a chicken farm, before accepting work with the newly established CIA. Tiptree resigned from the CIA in 1955, returned to school, and received her Ph.D. in experimental psychology in 1967.

After deciding against a career in academia, Tiptree published her first sf story, "Birth of a Salesman," in 1968. This marked the debut of the Tiptree persona, which shared all of its creator's biography except her gender. In 1969 Tiptree earned her first Nebula nomination for "The Last Flight of Dr Ain," and by the early 1970s she was equally renowned for her hard-hitting stories about the future of sex and gender and her refusal to appear in public. This led some members of the sf community to speculate that Tiptree was really a woman. When Tiptree revealed her true identity in 1977, some authors and fans expressed resentment at being so thoroughly fooled; most, however, applauded her for calling into question their assumptions about the gendered nature of writing. Although some critics feel the impact of her writing diminished once the mystery of her gender was resolved, Tiptree continued to publish steadily, enjoying a final burst of creativity in the mid-1980s. Her life ended in 1987, when Tiptree shot to death her ailing husband and herself.

Like many authors, Tiptree used the stuff of her own life story as inspiration for her fiction. For example, the experience of the Second World War and Nazism led her to explore the danger of sacrificing people in the name of racial purity or similarly abstract political ideals. This concern informs Tiptree's earliest stories, such as "Parimutuel Planet" (1968, later reprinted as "Faithful to Thee, Terra, in Our Fashion"), which imagines that humans might destroy the Earth and themselves for the sake of a well-fought war, and "The Last Flight of Dr Ain," in which the eponymous protagonist engineers a disease to kill all higher primates so that the Earth can revert to a pristine state. Tiptree also drew upon her work as an experimental psychologist to make a similar point about the danger of sacrificing laboratory animals and other helpless creatures in the name of progress. This is particularly apparent in "And I Have Come upon This Place by Lost Ways" (1972) and "The Psychologist Who Wouldn't Do Awful Things to Rats" (1976), both of which feature protagonists on the verge of brilliant scientific careers who become disillusioned by the cruelty their professions entail. Whether they depict the demise of an individual career or the destruction of an entire race, Tiptree's stories are often meditations on the danger of alienation from oneself and one's world.

As the daughter of a suffragette, an avowed feminist in her own right, and a woman who pursued a variety of masculine careers in an era when it was unfashionable to do so, it is perhaps no surprise that the kind of alienation most endemic to Tiptree's work is that of women and men from one another. This kind of alienation is most often expressed as masculine violence against women. Such violence is central to two stories originally published under the Raccoona Sheldon byline: "Your Faces, O My Sisters! Your Faces Filled of Light!" (1976), in which a young woman who believes she lives in an all-female utopia is raped and murdered by men while other women stand by and do nothing, and "The Screwfly Solution" (1977), in which aliens secure the Earth for themselves by releasing a virus that converts men's sexual impulses into homicidal ones.

Sex and death are linked together throughout Tiptree's work. For example, "The Girl Who Was Plugged in" (1973) explores how the beauty myths propagated by commodity culture might cause men to unleash deadly hostility against women, while the women from the peaceful, all-female future of "Houston, Houston, Do You Read?" (1976) realize that they must kill three male astronauts from our present to prevent the men from reintroducing aggression into their world. As this last story suggests, Tiptree occasionally imagines that the direction of violence in the battle of the sexes might be reversed. Invoking the time-honored tendency in men's sf to treat women as alien others, Tiptree often displaces female violence toward men onto literal aliens, as in "The Mother Ship" (1968, reprinted as "Mama Come Home"), where human men experience rape and death at the hands of female space invaders. Similarly, in "Love Is the Plan, the Plan Is Death" (1973), a spider-like alien raises and then mates with his beloved, only to be eaten by her in the end.

Although Tiptree often treats the battle of the sexes as a literal struggle to the death, some of her stories imagine futures where things are different for women and men. The cloned women of "Houston, Houston" struggle heroically to create social conditions that will liberate their daughters from genetic predispositions toward certain patterns of behavior, and they are genuinely sorry that they must kill the one astronaut from our own time who would have been a gentle "beta male" but for his patriarchal upbringing. In a similar vein, the female protagonist of "The Women Men Don't See" (1973) dreams of a future where women are liberated from patriarchy and then attempts to secure that future for herself and her daughter by arranging to leave Earth with a group of aliens. Finally, "The Milk of Paradise" (1972) relates the tale of a human man who is irrevocably changed by his upbringing amongst an alien species. Although the humans who "rescue" Tiptree's protagonist look down upon these aliens as inferior creatures, it is the humans – with their casual cruelty to both aliens and one another – who come off poorly, and the reader cannot help but rejoice when the man is reunited with the visually repulsive but physically sensuous beings who raised him.

In many of Tiptree's stories, humanity's only hope is to embrace the alien and become posthuman. The women of "A Momentary Taste of Being" (1975) finally gain equality with men when humanity learns that it is actually the sperm of an alien race. And in *Up the Walls of the World* (1978), gender inequality disappears when representatives of the human and Tyrenni races exchange bodies, experience one another's very different cultural attitudes to gendered labor, and then finally reach a new state of mutual understanding by shedding their physical bonds and merging with an unsexed alien overmind. Significantly, Tiptree does not just uncritically celebrate this transition from human to posthuman. She also mourns what might be lost – such as humankind's accomplishments in "A Momentary Taste" and the joys of the body itself in *Up the Walls* – and reminds readers that this transition from one way of being in the world to another can be, quite literally, a form of death for those who experience it.

Tiptree's alienations are poignant for readers because her characters are so thoroughly human. Her stories often give voice to those who are marginalized in classic sf, including teenage girls ("The Girl Who Was Plugged in," "The Only Neat Thing to Do" (1985)), middle-aged women ("The Women Men Don't See," *Up the Walls of the World*), and beta males ("Her Smoke Rose up Forever" (1974), "Houston, Houston"). Tiptree also adds unexpected depth to classic sf character types, presenting readers with bug-eyed monsters who are motivated by love rather than hostility ("Love Is the Plan," "The Only Neat Thing"), scientists who are ordinary rather than brilliant or mad ("Her Smoke Rose up," "The Psychologist Who Wouldn't Do Awful Things," *Up the Walls*), and soldiers who suffer guilt for their seemingly heroic actions (*Brightness Falls from the Air* (1985), "Yanqui Doodle" (1987)). These characters are not cast as victims or saviors, villains or heroes, or saints or sinners. Instead, they acquire some or all of these traits over the course of the average Tiptree story, which is precisely what makes them so memorable and real.

Tiptree uses a variety of innovative writing techniques to make room for her diverse characters. For example, the stream of consciousness and first person perspectives of stories such as "Her Smoke Rose up" and "Houston, Houston" provide readers with an intimate understanding of the agonies and triumphs that Tiptree's beta males experience as they struggle with the scientific, social, and sexual norms of their worlds. Elsewhere, Tiptree uses radically juxtaposed points of view to create believable female characters. This is particularly evident in "The Women Men Don't See" and "The Screwfly Solution," where male narrators cast themselves as stereotypical heroes trying to save equally stereotyped helpless women from the dangers of the world around them. In each case, however, the women seize control of these narratives, demonstrating to readers (if not the male narrator himself) that they are competent subjects capable of saving themselves. Even when the actions they take end in death, Tiptree insists that these female characters, much like the beta males of her other stories, are more truly heroic than any conventionally brilliant scientist or brave starship captain because they take control of their lives even when they cannot hope to profit by doing so.

Finally, Tiptree gives voice to women and other marginalized people by rewriting traditional sf scenarios. Perhaps the most striking examples of this are *Up the Walls* and "Collision" (1986), both of which radically revise the classic alien-encounter story. While pioneering tales in the tradition typically granted narrative authority to a single human who was part of a like-minded group encountering a very different alien other, Tiptree uses multiple points of view to depict such encounters as taking place between heterogeneous groups struggling with surprisingly similar professional and personal issues. Elsewhere, Tiptree updates the female adventure story as it was first told by women sf writers of the early twentieth century. These writers made space for unconventional voices by folding the adventures of women and other marginalized people into letters and journals that were, over the course of the story proper, discovered and read by male narrators. Tiptree employs a similar technique in "The Only Neat Thing," which relates the heroic death of a teenage girl explorer through taped missives. In this case, however, two other women discover the tapes: a young communications officer and a middle-aged space station executive. And in *The Starry Rift* (1987), a collection that includes "The Only Neat Thing," Tiptree imagines an even more distant future in which the lost girl explorer's tapes are rediscovered by a group of offbeat aliens including an older beta male librarian and two young lovers. For Tiptree, then, the female adventurer is not an anomaly in an otherwise homogeneous masculine and human world, but part and parcel of an often difficult but always diverse future. And it is precisely through the creation of such futures that James Tiptree Jr has earned an enduring place in the sf canon.

See also: **Isaac Asimov, Greg Bear, Alfred Bester, Leigh Brackett, Octavia Butler, Samuel R. Delany, Philip K. Dick, William Gibson, Donna J. Haraway, Robert A. Heinlein, Frank Herbert, Nalo Hopkinson, L. Ron Hubbard, Gwyneth Jones, Ursula K. Le Guin, C.L. Moore, Joanna Russ, Mary Shelley, Neal Stephenson, Sheri S. Tepper, and Gene Wolfe**

Bibliography

Frisch, A.J. (1982) "Toward New Sexual Identities: James Tiptree, Jr," in T. Staicar (ed.) *The Feminine Eye: science fiction and the women who write it*, New York: Frederick Ungar.

Galef, D. (2001) "Tiptree and the Problem of the Other: postcolonialism versus sociobiology," *Science Fiction Studies*, 28(2): 201–22.

Heldreth, L.M. (1982) "'Love Is the Plan, the Plan Is Death': the feminism and fatalism of James Tiptree, Jr," *Extrapolation*, 23(1): 22–30.

Hollinger, V. (1989) "'The Most Grisly Truth': responses to the human condition in the works of James Tiptree, Jr," *Extrapolation*, 30(2): 117–32.

Phillips, J. (2006) *James Tiptree, Jr: the double life of Alice B. Sheldon*, New York: St Martin's Press.

Siegel, M. (1986) *James Tiptree Jr*, San Bernardino, CA: Borgo Press.

LISA YASZEK

JULES [GABRIEL] VERNE (1828–1905)

French novelist, short-story writer, and dramatist.

Often called the "Father of Science Fiction," Jules Verne invented and popularized an early brand of hard sf called the *extraordinary voyage*. His series of more than 60 novels combine the epic qualities of the imaginary voyage *à la* Lucian with a concern for scientific verisimilitude and didacticism *à la* Kepler. They feature adventure-filled quests to the ends of the Earth and beyond, where the heroes make use of scientific knowledge and the latest technology to explore "known and unknown worlds" (the subtitle for the series). Expertly marketed by his publisher Pierre-Jules Hetzel, Verne's novels became bestsellers in France and around the world. Today he is ranked as the third most-translated author of all time, according to UNESCO's *Index Translationum*.

Verne's life and works can be divided into four periods: 1828–62 (before Hetzel), 1863–86 (early novels), 1887–1905 (later novels), and 1905–19 (posthumous works). Born and raised in Nantes, Verne was sent by his father in 1848 to study law in Paris, but he fell in love with the theater, writing a number of plays and serving as the secretary of the Théâtre Lyrique in 1852. He also published articles on scientific topics and a few short stories, including "A Voyage in a Balloon" (1851) and "Master Zacharius" (1854). Verne's early writings display many of the narrative traits that will later characterize his extraordinary voyages: melodramatic plot twists, quick-witted dialogue, attention to historical detail, and a tone that oscillates between the Positivist and the Romantic.

In 1857, unable to make a living from his writing, Verne became a stockbroker at the Bourse de Paris. He spent his spare time at the Bibliothèque Nationale reading, collecting scientific news items and copying them onto note cards, and dreaming of a new kind of novel that would combine both science and fiction. In September 1862 Verne submitted to Hetzel a story about an exciting aerial trek across Africa in a high-tech balloon. Hetzel immediately accepted the novel for publication. Following the success of *Five Weeks in a Balloon* (1863), Hetzel then offered Verne a long-term contract for more novels of the same type. Verne quit his job at the Bourse, saying "My friends, I bid you adieu … I've just written a novel in a new style, truly my own. If it succeeds, it will be a gold mine" (Evans 1988: 21). And a gold mine it would prove to be, not only for Verne and his publisher but also for world literature, as Verne's extraordinary voyages would give birth to a new literary genre.

Verne's historic meeting with Hetzel began his most creative period, which would continue until the latter's death in 1886. Hetzel rejected his next novel, the futuristic/dystopian *Paris in the 20th Century*, but Verne went on to write *Journey to the Center of the Earth* (1864), a novel that would become one of his most popular. After deciphering a cryptogram, Professor Lidenbrock, accompanied by his reluctant nephew, Axel, and a resourceful guide named Hans, journey to an extinct volcano in Iceland, descend into the Earth, and discover a vast underground world. The sources for the story include then-popular "hollow Earth" theories as well as growing public interest in geology, paleontology, and the new ideas of Darwin. Narrated in the first person by the impressionable young Axel, the novel's discursive structure maintains a balance between Lidenbrock's detailed scientific exposés and his nephew's poetic *rêveries*. This delicate intertwining of fact with fantasy, mathematics with myth, and didacticism with daydreaming will constitute the narrative core of many of Verne's most successful extraordinary voyages.

Verne's 1865 *From the Earth to the Moon* and its sequel *Around the Moon* (1870) comprise the first "realistic" (scientifically plausible) manned lunar voyage in Western literature. Breaking with the long tradition of utopian imaginary voyages to the moon, Verne based his tale on modern astronomy and astrophysics. Many of Verne's technical extrapolations would prove true 100 years later during America's Apollo program. If Verne's principal error was to launch his "space-bullet" using a gigantic cannon, such a choice was a logical extension of the other major focus of these novels: humorous satire of Yankees and their post-Civil War weapons technology.

In 1866 Verne's first "polar quest" novel appeared, *The Adventures of Captain Hatteras*, which chronicles a danger-filled voyage to the North Pole and recalls Sir John Franklin's real-life Arctic expedition 20 years earlier. *The Children of Captain Grant* (1867) details an around-the-world search for a castaway (a recurrent topos in Verne's *oeuvre*). That same year Verne purchased his first yacht and, ensconced in the ship's cabin with its portable library, he soon completed a novel about oceanography that would be published as *Twenty Thousand Leagues under the Sea* (1869).

The sheer imaginative power of *Twenty Thousand Leagues*, the brooding and enigmatic genius of Nemo, and the "dream machine" character of the *Nautilus* itself (named after Fulton's experimental craft of 1797) have made it the most memorable of all Verne's extraordinary voyages. Verne originally wanted Nemo to be a Pole and his implacable hatred to be directed against the Russian czar (a direct reference to the bloody Russian suppression of Poland in 1863). But Hetzel was concerned about the possible political ramifications and the likelihood of the book being banned in Russia. Both author and publisher were adamant but eventually reached a compromise. It was decided that Nemo's identity and motives would remain intriguingly mysterious – at least until the novel's sequel, Verne's robinsonade *The Mysterious Island* (1874).

In 1872 Verne published his most commercially successful novel, *Around the World in 80 Days*. Among other sources for this circumnavigation novel was Edgar Allan Poe's "Three Sundays in a Week" (1850). On a wager, the imperturbable Englishman Phileas Fogg and his servant Passepartout set out to circle the globe in 80 days, experiencing along the way many adventures ranging from the rescue of an Indian princess to a shoot-out in the Old West. The surprise ending was rendered all the more effective in its initial published format, a suspense-filled weekly serial in the Parisian newspaper *Le Temps*. Published in volume, the novel quickly set new sales records both in France and abroad, and an extravagant stage adaptation of the work (written by Verne and Adolphe D'Ennery) proved extremely successful, with more than 2,000 performances between 1874 and 1900.

Verne published a curious novel in 1879 called *The Begum's Millions*, which, when viewed in retrospect, seems to foreshadow certain changes in the author's attitudes to science and human values after 1886. The only utopia/dystopia in Verne's fiction, it tells the story of two scientists – Dr Sarrasin of France and Herr Schultze of Germany – who receive a huge inheritance from a long-lost relative who was the widow (begum) of a rich Indian rajah. Each decides to build the city of his dreams: Sarrasin a modern utopia built on the principles of hygiene and Schultze a fortress-like factory to produce high-tech armaments. A kind of Nietzschean megalomaniac, Schultze is Verne's first truly evil scientist. Although his murderous schemes are defeated in the end by a providential *deus ex machina*, he expresses for the first time in Verne's *oeuvre* the idea that personal power generated by scientific knowledge can breed moral corruption.

Verne's novels from 1886 to 1905, although varied, often reflect this change of tone. They show a slow metamorphosis away from his earlier Saint-Simonian optimism toward an outlook that is more often pessimistic, cynical, and anti-progress. This contrast can especially be seen in those later novels that include characters from, and/or continue the plot from, earlier works, such as *Topsy-Turvy* (1889) and *Master of the World* (1904). These sequels invariably contain some form of *reversal* when compared to their prequels. In *Topsy-Turvy*, for example, Barbicane and the other ballistics engineers of Verne's moon novels, indifferent to the catastrophic environmental damage that would result, now seek to alter the angle of the Earth's axis in order to melt the polar ice cap and uncover vast mineral wealth. The once-heroic Robur of *Robur the Conqueror* (1886) becomes, in *Master of the World*, a demented psychopath who threatens global terrorism with his high-tech, Transformer-like vehicle called *The Terror*. In both novels, only the intervention of providence saves the day.

Many other post-1886 novels target social and environmental issues: the cruel oppression of the Québécois in *Family without a Name* (1889), the intolerable living conditions in orphanages in *Foundling Mick* (1893), the dire effects of colonial imperialism on Polynesian island cultures in *Propeller Island* (1895), the dangers of science used for military purposes in *Facing the Flag* (1896), the overhunting of whales in *The Ice Sphinx* (1897), and a Dreyfus-like case of judicial error in *The Kip Brothers* (1902), among others.

With a drawer full of nearly completed manuscripts in his desk, Verne died in March 1905; two years later a sculpture depicting the author rising from his tomb and engraved with the words "Towards immortality and eternal youth" was placed over his grave. In 1926 the American-based publisher **Hugo Gernsback** would use a representation of Verne's tomb as a logo for his first magazine of "scientifiction," *Amazing Stories*.

From 1905 to 1919 Verne's son, Michel, arranged for the publication of the remaining manuscripts: eight novels and several short stories. Since the late 1970s these posthumous works have been the topic of great controversy among Verne scholars. On close inspection, it was learned that Michel's hand in their composition was much greater than had been supposed. The debate about their authenticity continues to this day.

During the century since his death, Verne has become a cultural icon for sf, and the general public now remembers him as much for movies and theme-park rides as for his novels. From Georges Méliès' *A Trip to the Moon* (1902) to the more recent 3-D blockbuster *Journey to the Center of the Earth* (Brevig 2008), Verne is arguably "the best dead writer Hollywood has ever had" (*Time* 1960). Over 300 full-length movies and TV shows have adapted Verne's works, with versions derived from *Around the World in 80 Days* and *Twenty Thousand Leagues under the Sea* leading the way (Taves 2005: 1).

Jules Verne's reputation within the French literary establishment and among English-language scholars has evolved during the past few decades. In France, Verne's *oeuvre* appears to have finally shed its stigma as paraliterature. For some Anglo-American critics of sf, however, Verne's status as one of the originators of this genre seems to be increasingly eclipsed by that of **Mary Shelley** and/or Hugo Gernsback. Although sf can be viewed as the convergence of many different narrative traditions, it was Verne's extraordinary voyages that established the first successful "institutional 'landing point' and ideological model" (Angenot 1978: 64) for the genre. By the early twentieth century, before the term existed in its current sense, Jules Verne was synonymous with sf.

See also: **Samuel R. Delany, Hugo Gernsback, Stanisław Lem, Mary Shelley, Olaf Stapledon, Darko Suvin, and H.G. Wells**

Bibliography

Angenot, M. (1978) "Science Fiction in France before Verne," *Science Fiction Studies*, 5(1): 58–66.

Butcher, W. (2006) *Jules Verne: the definitive biography*, New York: Thunder's Mouth Press.

Evans, A.B. (1988) *Jules Verne Rediscovered: didacticism and the scientific novel*, Westport, CT: Greenwood Press.

——(2008) "Jules Verne in English: a bibliography of modern editions and scholarly studies," *Verniana*, 1: 9–22.

Har'El, Z. "Zvi Har'El's Jules Verne Collection." Online. Available: <http://jv.gilead.org.il/> (accessed 1 January 2009).

Lottman, H. (1996) *Jules Verne: an exploratory biography*, New York: St. Martin's Press.

Martin, A. (1990) *The Mask of the Prophet: the extraordinary fictions of Jules Verne*, Oxford: Clarendon Press.

Science Fiction Studies, 32(1) (2005), special Jules Verne Centenary issue.

Smyth, E.J. (ed.) (2000) *Jules Verne: narratives of modernity*, Liverpool: Liverpool University Press.

Taves, B. (2005) "Adapting Jules Verne's *Journey to the Center of the Earth*," *Extraordinary Voyages*, 12(1): 1–13.

Taves, B. and Michaluk Jr, S. (1996) *The Jules Verne Encyclopedia*, Lanham, MD: Scarecrow Press.

Time (1960) "The New Pictures," 15 February. Online. Available: <http://www.time.com/time/magazine/article/0,9171,871494–1,00.html > (accessed 1 January 2009).

Unwin, T. (2005) *Jules Verne: journeys in writing*, Liverpool: Liverpool University Press.

ARTHUR B. EVANS

H[ERBERT] G[EORGE] WELLS (1866–1946)

British novelist, essayist, and screenwriter.

If anyone can claim to be the founding father of modern sf it is H.G. Wells. He brought to the scientific romance a haunted, Gothic imagination reminiscent of **Mary Shelley** and Edgar Allan Poe, together with a gift for technological anticipation that outstripped **Jules Verne**'s. He invented such themes as time travel, interplanetary warfare, and the totalitarian future city, and his Martians in *The War of the Worlds* (1898) were the first of the "bug-eyed monsters" – sinister and biologically plausible aliens. Unsurpassed in the genre as a storyteller, he was also a pioneer of political sf, drawing on utopian speculation and philosophical satire. His later career was that of a prophet and sociologist for whom the future was, in his own phrase, "the shape of things to come" rather than a location for fantastic adventures.

The son of a shopkeeper, Wells left school at 13 and spent his early years as a draper's apprentice. He passed a number of examinations in science and, in 1884, entered the Normal School of Science, South Kensington, on a government scholarship. Here he took a year's course in biology under Charles Darwin's friend and ally T.H. Huxley, who influenced Wells profoundly. Wells's years at college were undistinguished, and he failed his finals in 1887. Nevertheless, within a few years he had become a science teacher in London, gained his B.S. degree, and published a much-reprinted biology textbook. Meanwhile he struggled to complete the time-travel story that had made its first appearance in the *Science Schools Journal* as "The Chronic Argonauts" (1887–88).

In 1893–94, forced by ill health to retire from teaching, Wells began writing the short stories that became *The Stolen Bacillus* (1895). He quickly developed the trademark style that was to make his name synonymous with scientific romance. Starting from a recognizable setting, such as a scientific laboratory, astronomical observatory, or engineering workshop, the narrative suddenly and unexpectedly shifted into the unknown. The resulting uncanny events are recounted deadpan in the style of a newspaper report or scientific paper, a deliberate reaction against the hysterical emotionalism of the earlier Gothic. Yet Wells's stories of hallucination and the paranormal were no less terrifying for being placed within a supposedly skeptical, rationalistic context.

Many of his most famous stories – "The Remarkable Case of Davidson's Eyes" (1895), *The Invisible Man* (1897), "The Country of the Blind" (1904) – center on a visual aberration, where the protagonist can see what is invisible to others. The discovery of other worlds frequently involves optical instruments, such as the telescope trained on Mars at the beginning of *The War of the Worlds* or the microscopes that figure in several other stories. Nurtured on the evolutionism of Huxley and Darwin, Wells brooded on the *fin-de-siècle* themes of biological degeneration, environmental adaptation, and species extinction. These forebodings are vividly present in his first major works, *The Time Machine* (1895) and *The Island of Doctor Moreau* (1896).

In the former, the Time Traveller fast-forwards through thirty million years and returns to describe what he has seen to his astonished dinner guests. In the year 802,701 he struggles to survive in a landscape of ruins inhabited by two posthuman species, the ineffectual but friendly Eloi and their creepy subterranean masters, the Morlocks. The species are a satirical reflection of the class divisions of the nineteenth century, with the Morlocks descended from the industrial proletariat and preying on the degenerate remnants of the former capitalist class. The Time Traveller journeys on into the remote future to witness life regressing back into the sea under the influence of solar cooling, a prediction ratified by Lord Kelvin's Second Law of Thermodynamics. *The Time Machine*'s sobering vision of human destiny leads to a distinctly stoical conclusion – "If that is so, it remains for us to live as though it were not so" (Wells 2005: 91) – but universal degeneration takes a more anguished form in *The Island of Doctor Moreau*, where a demonic vivisectionist and plastic surgeon turns wild animals into semi-human creatures in his remote Pacific island laboratory. Not only do the grotesquely remodeled Beast Folk revert to their original state, but the human beings on Moreau's island descend into bestiality as well. Wells combines a gripping adventure tale with a haunting meditation on the Huxleyan theme that humanity is descended from apes, not angels.

If the redeeming feature of our species, according to the evolutionists, is our capacity for spiritual awareness and scientific knowledge, even this is questioned in Wells's early writings. Moreau ruthlessly perverts the aims of science, while the Time Traveller's revelations would point toward mass despair and race suicide if taken seriously. The imminent extinction of human beings seems a very real possibility in *The War of the Worlds*, but this novel (initially serialized in the mass-market *Pearson's Magazine*) has a much more bracing outcome than its predecessors. Faced with a campaign of extermination by the unremittingly hostile Martian invaders, humanity is on the receiving end of treatment it usually reserves for pests and vermin.

Terrestrial infantry and artillery are powerless against the Martians' Heat-Ray, a device which seemed wholly fantastic until the invention of laser weapons. London, evacuated by its terrified inhabitants, is dominated by the giant tripods with which the octopus-like invaders bestride the Earth. Nevertheless, there is a dramatic reversal as, following impeccable biological logic, Wells contrives that the Martians are finally defeated, though not by human agency. The novel's conclusion hints at continuing deadly competition between Earth and Mars as they struggle for eventual galactic supremacy. At the same time, the Martian defeat gives a new urgency to the ideals of a world state and global unification, ideals which became almost synonymous with Wells's later career. In novels such as *The World Set Free* (1914) and *The Shape of Things to Come* (1933), he dropped the theme of alien invasion while retaining the pattern of a devastating future world war followed by a concerted attempt at world reconstruction: a kind of benign apocalypse.

Wells's early cycle of sf novels was concluded by two fascinating but flawed works, *When the Sleeper Wakes* (1899) – revised as *The Sleeper Awakes* (1910) – and *The First Men in the Moon* (1901). *The Sleeper* uses a "Rip van Winkle" device to portray a future capitalist megalopolis in the grip of merciless tyranny. When Graham the Sleeper is wakened in the twenty-first century, he becomes the figurehead of a popular rebellion, making this the first of Wells's explicitly political fictions. The teeming future city with its skyscrapers, moving roadways, and mini-aerodromes soon became a standard sf prop, even though Wells himself rapidly abandoned it as technological prophecy, pointing instead to the forces leading to suburbanization and population dispersal. *The First Men in the Moon* is a largely comic series of adventures ending in grotesque satire. Bedford and Cavor, an opportunist and an unworldly scientist, get to the moon in a spaceship powered by anti-gravity, only to find themselves taken prisoner by sinister aliens. Bedford escapes, while his companion, entranced by the Selenites and their antlike society, manages to transmit his observations back to Earth. His messages, culminating in an interview with the Grand Lunar, are strongly Swiftian in their satirical manner but at variance with Bedford's comparatively light-hearted narrative. For all its brilliance, *The First Men in the Moon* lacks the imaginative unity of *The Time Machine* and *The War of the Worlds*.

As the new century began, Wells emerged as a prophet of social reorganization in *Anticipations* (1901), while his sf anticipated new kinds of military hardware. The aerial dogfights of *The Sleeper* were succeeded by tank warfare in "The Land Ironclads" (1904) and atomic bombs in *The World Set Free*. The theme of benign apocalypse reappeared in *The Food of the Gods* (1904), in which two scientists develop a miraculous baby food, resulting in a race of young giants who prepare to take over the world. (The food also escapes from the laboratory to produce giant rats and killer wasps.) Another story of miraculous transmutation to what is effectively a posthuman state is *In the Days of the Comet* (1906), in which green vapors from a comet passing close to the Earth bring about an end to belligerence and the construction of a socialist world-state.

Two other books from this period have had a lasting impact. *A Modern Utopia* (1905), set on a planet in a remote galaxy with a population genetically identical to that of Earth, is Wells's only formal utopia, a mixture of imaginative narrative and sociopolitical commentary incorporating a deliberate synthesis of previous utopian thought from Plato to William Morris. It is "modern" both in its narrative self-consciousness and in its conception of utopia as an evolving, not a perfected, society. Three years later Wells published *The War in the Air* (1908), in which an ordinary, undistinguished, and confused young man, Bert Smallways, becomes a stowaway on the German Kaiser's fleet of giant airships setting out to bomb New York. Smallways's misadventures in a world thrown into chaos prefigure those of numerous other sf innocents down to Arthur Dent in Douglas Adams's *The Hitch-Hiker's Guide to the Galaxy* (1978).

After *The World Set Free*, sf was thrust aside as the First World War brought carnage on a scale that few except Wells could claim to have foreseen. As the cataclysm unfolded, he redoubled his efforts to campaign for a peace settlement capable of guaranteeing global stability. The League of Nations and, later, the United Nations owe something to Wellsian propaganda. His later sf includes *Men Like Gods* (1923), a utopian romance set on a parallel planet, and *Mr Blettsworthy on Rampole Island* (1927), where picaresque adventure is mixed with psychiatric case history in another grim warning about human belligerence. The one late Wellsian work to exert a lasting influence in the sf field was *Things to Come* (Menzies 1936), the film adaptation of his future-history novel *The Shape of Things to Come.* Wells wrote the script and exerted control over many aspects of the production, clashing frequently with the dynamic Hungarian impresario Alexander Korda. There were memorable performances by Ralph Richardson as the barbaric future warlord and Raymond Massey as the gaunt, hooded Wellsian superman representing the "Air Dictatorship." Beginning with a chilling anticipation of the 1940 London Blitz, *Things to Come* had little box office appeal, although it remains a benchmark in epic sf cinema. Wells's enduring popularity as a writer has been reflected in numerous other cinema, radio, and television adaptations, while films such as *Sleeper* (Allen 1973), *Time after Time* (Meyer 1979), and *Independence Day* (Emmerich 1996) bear an unmistakably Wellsian stamp.

The most famous Wells adaptation was Orson Welles's 1938 broadcast of *The War of the Worlds* for CBS radio, which caused widespread panic with its all-too-realistic news bulletins reporting a Martian attack on New Jersey. Crowds gathered in the streets, farmers armed with shotguns roamed the New Jersey countryside looking for Martians, and the Governor of Pennsylvania offered to send troops. The next day's newspapers spoke of a wave of mass hysteria among the program's six million listeners. Probably no other work of sf in any medium has had such a devastating impact. Wells's best writings are not just superb entertainment; they remain uncomfortably prescient.

See also: **J.G. Ballard, Iain M. Banks, Arthur C. Clarke, The Doctor, Hugo Gernsback, Gwyneth Jones, China Miéville, Michael Moorcock, Alan Moore, Mary Shelley, Steven Spielberg, Olaf Stapledon, Darko Suvin, and Jules Verne**

Bibliography

Holmsten, B. and Lubertozzi, A. (eds.) (2001) *The Complete War of the Worlds: Mars' invasion of Earth from H.G. Wells to Orson Welles*, Naperville, IL: Sourcebooks.

Huntington, J. (1982) *The Logic of Fantasy: H.G. Wells and science fiction*, New York: Columbia University Press.

McConnell, F.D. (1981) *The Science Fiction of H.G. Wells*, New York: Oxford University Press.

Parrinder, P. (1995) *Shadows of the Future: H.G. Wells, science fiction and prophecy*, Liverpool: Liverpool University Press.

Wagar, W.W. (2004) *H.G. Wells: traversing time*, Middletown, CT: Wesleyan University Pres.

Wells, H.G. (2005) *The Time Machine*, ed. P. Parrinder, London: Penguin.

PATRICK PARRINDER

GENE [RODMAN] WOLFE (1931–)

US writer.

Gene Wolfe has won or been nominated all the major awards for sf literature, including both the Hugo and Nebula, has been inducted into the Science Fiction Hall of Fame, and is widely considered one of the finest practitioners of sf. Nonetheless, he is not as widely known within or outside the field as his accomplishments would suggest, because his work is challenging: highly allusive, metaphorical, symbolic, and ambiguous. Knowledge of mythology, ancient history, geography, Gnosticism, and medieval allegory, among other topics, prove helpful for gaining a full understanding of Wolfe's writing.

Best known for his interconnected *Solar* cycle – *The Book of the New Sun* (1980–83), *The Book of the Long Sun* (1993–96), *The Book of the Short Sun* (1999–2001) – Wolfe is also a master of the novella, both linked novellas such as *The Fifth Head of Cerberus* (collected 1972) and *The Wolfe Archipelago* (collected 1983), and stand-alone novellas such as "Tracking Song" (1975), "Seven American Nights"

(1978), "The Last Thrilling Wonder Story" (1982), and "Memorare" (2007). He also produced a fine body of short stories. Some of his works might be described more accurately as fantasy or horror, although he himself has little concern for genre rules. Among his most important non-sf works are the *Latro* series (*Soldier of the Mist* (1986), *Soldier of Arete* (1989), *Soldier of Sidon* (2006)), and *The Wizard Knight* series (*The Wizard* (2004), *The Knight* (2004)). Recurring motifs include isolated people, particularly children, alien or inverted myths, confrontation between different sentient species, ghosts, and journeys; his themes include loneliness and isolation, memory, identity, haunting, and spirituality. In part because of these themes, especially his explorations of Roman Catholicism and haunting, and in part because of his use of arcane vocabulary and bodies of information, his sf often has the feel of fantasy.

The Fifth Head of Cerberus established Wolfe's reputation in sf and shows his recurring motifs and themes with great power. It consists of three novellas: the title story, "A Story, by John V. Marsch," and "V. R.T.". The first describes the coming of age of a cloned scion of a stagnant dynasty in a decaying city on a colonized planet; the second reconstructs a myth of shape-shifting native twins of the less-populated sister planet; and the last consists of a jumble of documents about and by the anthropologist who appeared in the first story and constructed the myth in the second one, but is now imprisoned and possibly insane. All three stories are ambiguous, with unreliable narrators and no clear division between dreaming and waking states. They are linked by common metaphors for erosion of identity – clones, twins, shape-shifting – and the unreliability of memory – drugs, cultural interference, insanity. These moody, puzzling, Borgesian, and stylish novellas set Wolfe apart from the more naturalist tradition of sf writing.

The Book of the New Sun, comprising *The Shadow of the Torturer* (1980), *The Claw of the Conciliator* (1981), *The Sword of the Lictor* (1981), and *The Citadel of the Autarch* (1983), with an associated novel, *The Urth of the New Sun* (1987), adds a complex Gnostic vision into its epic story of a summer in the life of a young man, Severian. Written in the form of his memoir recorded ten years later, it describes his rise from an apprentice torturer, to Autarch of a vast South American land, to savior who will renew the world's dying sun. This tetralogy is Wolfe's masterpiece. Its baroque style, with complex sentences, a vast and esoteric vocabulary (although even the strangest words are in the *OED*), a huge cast of characters, embedded stories, and a maze-like structure, is perfectly controlled and highly effective. These elements, as well as repeated images of gigantism, gates, caves, roses, cannibalism, suns, light and shadow, and more, contribute to its symbolic richness. Central motifs of life, death, and rebirth, as well as the Christ-like figure of Severian, strongly associate the series with Christianity, and Wolfe instructs the reader that everything has three meanings: its practical meaning, the reflection of the world about it, and "the transubstantial meaning" (Wolfe 1980: 272), a triplex allegory very close to the medieval quadruplex mode. The Christian story of death and rebirth is supplemented by themes related to memory, personal identity, and personal responsibility. Despite similarities to C.S. Lewis and the other Inklings, and the archaic language and low technology of many of the societies depicted, it is also a work of sf. Severian's torture guild is housed in an abandoned spaceship hull, and aliens, genetic manipulation, space travel, and time travel are important parts of the labyrinthine plot and contribute symbolically to the books' meaning. Thus, in *The Book of the New Sun*, Wolfe has created a science fantasy that combines the tone of the fantastic with the speculations of sf to demonstrate compatibility between science and spirituality.

The Book of the Long Sun both resonates with *The Book of the New Sun* and works as a separate series. It takes place in the same far future, but on the *Whorl*, a huge generation ship at the end of its journey, waiting to settle twin planets that will be the setting of Wolfe's third series. Its protagonist, Patera Silk, is another young man rising from obscurity, this time a parish priest who makes animal sacrifices and becomes a ruler and then, again, a savior. He is a less severe man than Severian, more modest and lacking Severian's eidetic memory; he is not the narrator, and the style is less baroque, dominated by dialogue and fight scenes rather than metaphors. As in the earlier series, Silk is a faithful servant of the true god, here called the Outsider, in contrast to the false pantheon that hides the identities of uploaded personalities in the ship's mainframe. As in *The Book of the New Sun*, the series is really one very long, seamless novel that takes place over a surprisingly short time. Rather than the maze-like labyrinths of the earlier series, here it is the rush of events in the course of just a few weeks, involving a huge number of people, that may confound the reader and remind her that Wolfe should be read multiple times. Peter Wright (2003) contends that the difficulty in comprehending these books stems from Wolfe's desire to thwart the reader, but it seems more likely that it is the result of the complexity of his vision and his skill in shaping his narrative to reflect that complexity; multiple readings bring greater understanding and expose more layers of meaning.

The Book of the Short Sun – On Blue's Waters (1999), *In Green's Jungles* (2000), *Return to the Whorl* (2001) – completes the vast cycle of connected works that began with *The Book of the New Sun*. Like each of the other series, this is essentially one novel in multiple volumes. It is haunted by similar themes, many of the same characters, similarly ambiguous narration, and a Gnostic vision of a universe in which individuals are infused with a personal revelation of the divine that is expressed simultaneously through myth and science. Again, there is a quest: Horn (the narrator of the second series), having left the *Whorl* to settle on the planet Blue, now seeks to return there to find his spiritual hero, Silk, and bring him back to save Blue. Horn seems to die and be transformed, coming to incorporate (literally) Silk and perhaps Severian, and his narration is infected not only by these transformations but also by the revelation at the end of the final volume that the story has been supplemented by Horn's descendants. By the end of *Return to the Whorl*, it becomes apparent that the three series form a continuum of psychological and spiritual development: Severian comes of age, Patera Silk finds his true vocation, and Horn matures into a father-figure.

Over the course of these series, Wolfe's style has become increasingly spare, more reliant on dialogue and action, its metaphors more covert. This has not simplified his vision, although it has made the surfaces more easily appreciated. It is instructive to compare a passage from the beginning of the first series with one from the beginning of the last. Near the beginning of *The Shadow of the Torturer*, Severian indicates how he will tell his story and what it will mean:

> Just as all that appears imperishable tends toward its own destruction, those moments that at the time seem the most fleeting recreate themselves – not only in my memory (which in the final accounting loses nothing) but in the throbbing of my heart and the prickling of my hair, making themselves new just as our Commonwealth reconstitutes itself each morning in the shrill tones of its own clarions.
>
> (Wolfe 1980: 10)

Here are the elevated vocabulary ("imperishable," "clarions"), metaphorical language ("Just as … "), baroque sentence structures (parentheses, dashes, periodicity, parallelisms), overt philosophy (fleeting life and transformation), and sharp sensory description ("throbbing," "prickling") that account for the lushness of Wolfe's earlier work. In contrast, consider a short passage from the beginning of *On Blue's*

Waters, in which Horn declares his intentions: "It is facts I need – facts I starve for. To Green with fancies!" (Wolfe 1999: 17). Here Horn is terse, declarative, unpoetic, forceful, and practical, and such is the tenor of the entire series. Of course, the facts for which Horn starves are as elusive and allusive as they are in *The Shadow of the Torturer*, but the vehicle conveying the story has changed.

Since the completion of this long cycle, more of Wolfe's energy has turned to non-sf – work closer to fantasy, horror, and ghost stories – although still published within the genre category. That said, *Pirate Freedom* (2007) employs time travel, and his novella "Memorare," published in a special issue of the *Magazine of Fantasy and Science Fiction* (April 2007) honoring Wolfe, describes a cemetery in space. *Pirate Freedom* is both a ripping yarn, as one would expect of a pirate tale, full of sword fights and battles at sea, and, in the tradition of the best saint's lives, a bloody and scandalous version of the quest for God and faith. "Memorare" describes a documentary director down on his luck as he puts together a video on memorials in space. As in *Pirate Freedom,* description is minimal: action, suspense, and dialogue dominate, and there is none of the lushness of Wolfe's pre-2000 fiction. On its surface, the story functions as a meta-narrative about the clash between commerce and truth, entertainment and art. Nevertheless, its central speculation about a memorial that seduces visitors with visions corresponding to their desires invites consideration of neo-Platonic philosophy, and its title, referring to the Roman Catholic prayer to the Virgin Mary repeated in the body of the story, enriches this neo-Platonic interpretation. The characters and we must lift a veil to find the truth of these stories, a demand consistently made of Wolfe's readers. Each work demonstrates the skill with which Wolfe constructs every detail – plot, character, image, word choice – to contribute to the complex overall effect and meaning. Such density can be demanding and exhausting, but it is always rewarding.

See also: **Isaac Asimov, Greg Bear, Alfred Bester, Leigh Brackett, Octavia Butler, Samuel R. Delany, Philip K. Dick, William Gibson, Robert A. Heinlein, Frank Herbert, L. Ron Hubbard, Ursula K. Le Guin, China Miéville, C.L. Moore, Kim Stanley Robinson, Joanna Russ, Neal Stephenson, Sheri S. Tepper, and James Tiptree Jr**

Bibliography

Andre-Driussi, M. (1994) *Lexicon Urthus: a dictionary for the Urth cycle*, Albany, CA: Sirius Fiction.

Borski, R. (2004) *Solar Labyrinth: exploring Gene Wolfe's Book of the New Sun*, New York: iUniverse.
Gordon, J.L. (1986) *Gene Wolfe*, Mercer Island, WA: Starmont.
Wolfe, G. (1980) *The Shadow of the Torturer*, New York: Simon and Schuster.
——(1999) *On Blue's Waters*, New York: Tor.
Wright, P. (2003) *Attending Daedalus: Gene Wolfe, artifice and the reader*, Liverpool: Liverpool University Press.
——(ed.) (2007) *Shadows of the New Sun: Wolfe on writing/writers on Wolfe*, Liverpool: Liverpool University Press.

JOAN GORDON

INDEX

Main sections for fifty key figures are **bolded**; titles of prose fiction cross reference to their author, other media listed by both title and director, plus by other key producers as appropriate.

Related titles from Routledge

Fifty Key American Films

Edited by John White and Sabine Haenni

Fifty Key American Films explores and contextualises some of the most important films ever made in the United States. With case studies from the early years of cinema right up to the present day, this comprehensive Key Guide provides accessible analyses from a range of theoretical perspectives.

This chronologically ordered volume includes coverage of:

- *Citizen Kane*
- *Casablanca*
- *Psycho*
- *Taxi Driver*
- *Blade Runner*
- *Pulp Fiction*

As well as a raft of well-known examples from the big screen, the careers of America's best known talent, such as Lynch, Scorsese, Coppola and Scott, are defined and discussed. This book is essential reading for students of film, and will be of interest to anyone seeking to explore the legacy and impact of American cinema.

ISBN13 978-0-415-77296-9 (hbk)
ISBN13 978-0-415-77297-6 (pbk)
ISBN13 978-0-203-89113-1 (ebk)